Modern Scholarship on European History

HENRY A. TURNER, JR.
Editor

EUROPEAN
DIPLOMACY
BETWEEN
TWO WARS

EUROPEAN DIPLOMACY BETWEEN TWO WARS, 1919-1939

Edited with an Introduction by
HANS W. GATZKE

CHICAGO
Quadrangle Books
1972

Library of Congress Catalog Card Number: 71-158826

SBN Cloth 8129-0198-3   SBN Paper 8129-6168-4

CONTENTS

EUROPEAN
DIPLOMACY
BETWEEN
TWO WARS

Introduction

M ORE THAN twenty-five years have passed since the end of the Second World War, and still there is no comprehensive study of the origins of that war comparable to the several major works on the origins of World War I. One reason why the causes of the second war have not aroused the same interest is that the issue of responsibility for that war is so much more clear-cut. While controversy over the origins of the war of 1914 continues,[1] no historian thus far has convincingly challenged the generally accepted view that it was Adolf Hitler who plunged Europe into war in 1939.[2] This is not to deny that the coming of "Hitler's War" was facilitated by faulty Western diplomacy, and that "peaceful" German expansion prior to 1939 was made easier by Western permissiveness and fear of war. But compared with Hitler's acts of commission, his opponents' acts of omission bear at best a secondary share of responsibility.[3]

The picture is not quite so clear when we shift our attention from the immediate to the long-range causes of World War II. In many respects the second war was an outgrowth and continuation of the first. The term "twenty years' armistice," while trite, is nonetheless true. But while there have been many books on the crises of the thirties, there have been few on the less dramatic diplomacy of the twenties. There are several major works on the Munich Conference of 1938, for instance, while there are still no comparable treatments of the equally important Locarno Conference of 1925. What has been written on European diplomacy before 1933, moreover, must now be rewritten in the light of fresh documentation that has become available in recent years.

That documentation is plentiful indeed. Except in France and the Soviet Union, the diplomatic (and, in some instances, military and naval) archives of all the major powers are now open to scholars. In addition, all nations, including Russia and France (though the latter only for the years since 1932) are in the process of publishing more or less extensive selections from their archival holdings. If we supplement this mass of official material with the memoirs and personal papers of the men who made foreign policy, and if we round out these sources with information found in parliamentary debates and in the press, the amount of source material becomes staggering enough to be almost discouraging. Before any general study of the inter-war period can be made, much monographic spadework needs to be done.

The years between the wars naturally divide themselves into chrono-logical subdivisions: the "war after the war," culminating in the Ruhr crisis of 1923; the "era of good will," symbolized by Locarno; the "Great Depression," a watershed between the two wars; the years after 1933, when Germany seemed merely bent on further revision of Versailles; and, finally, "the road to war," when Hitler's quest for *Lebensraum* became clear for all to see. Such division of a brief time span into still shorter segments, however, must not distract us from the long-range trends that mark off the whole period from what had gone before and what came after.

Before 1914, Europe had been the world's nerve center, and European diplomacy had affected people's lives everywhere. A generation later, Europe had clearly lost its pre-eminence. The decline of European influ-ence, we now realize, had begun before World War I and was merely hastened by that war.[4] This fact, however, was not realized by the men who made peace in 1919. Had the United States continued its wartime involvement in European affairs, and had Russia then attained its present power, "the political collapse of Europe" would have become evident earlier and subsequent developments would have been different. As it turned out, the diplomacy of the twenties and thirties remained centered upon Europe, artificially so, with the no-longer-great powers trying to play their traditional roles and asserting an influence they no longer possessed. In the past, European diplomacy and the European balance of power had been the determining factors in world affairs. In the future, Europe would become only one of several factors. The period between the wars was thus the last phase of predominantly Europe-centered diplomacy.

Left to themselves, the statesmen of Europe tried, as best they knew, to repair the damages caused by history's most terrible war. First of all, they faced political problems stemming from territorial and political change. Despite (or because of) the peacemakers' efforts to apply the principle of self-determination and make political and ethnic boundaries coincide, the map of Europe after the war showed far more serious ten-sion spots than before. Demands for territorial revision were the most constant source of international unrest between the wars, not only on the part of the vanquished but also on the part of a "have-not" nation such as Italy, who felt she had not gotten all she deserved, and on the part of the Soviet Union, who had been deprived of large areas without being consulted.

Added to these political problems were a great many economic ones. These grew out of the war, but they were aggravated by other causes—territorial changes, unequal resources, population pressures, rising tariffs, and the general effect of extra-European economic competition upon a continent which hitherto had enjoyed uncontested economic supremacy. The most chronic headache of the diplomats of the 1920's was the reparations problem. There was hardly an international conference that did not have to deal with it. The tangle of reparations and inter-Allied debts was never resolved; it was merely swept away by the tide of the Great Depression. The inability of economists to understand and cope with the deeper causes of Europe's economic malaise did much to heighten the latent political tension of the inter-war years.

Another troublesome issue was military security. Here the main problem was a vengeful Germany, bent on undoing the "injustices" of Versailles. Germany, to be sure, had been drastically disarmed. But she was suspected of evading her disarmament restrictions; and, besides, her superior manpower and industry left her a potential menace. The peacemakers at Paris had hoped that German disarmament would eventually be followed by general disarmament. In this they had popular backing, especially in countries that had experienced war on their own soil. But Allied pacifism found little echo in Germany, where a proud people believed that its armies had not been defeated at the front but had been "stabbed in the back" by traitorous politicians at home. Signs of continued German militarism merely bolstered French fears and reluctance to disarm. By the time the Disarmament Conference assembled in 1932, the shadow of Hitler was already upon Germany, and talk of disarmament soon gave way to preparations for war.

The problems outlined thus far—political, economic, and military—while differing in detail from those which statesmen had faced in the past, still were not entirely new. The same did not hold for an ideological threat to the peace which had arisen during the First World War—communism. Before 1914, another ideology—nationalism, especially in such extreme manifestations as Pan-Germanism or Pan-Slavism—had at times interfered with international relations. Communism was different. Internationalist in aims and appeal, it threatened to subvert the social and economic order everywhere. Communism's victory in Russia made her the spearhead of world revolution and put the Soviet Union under permanent suspicion. The fact that early attempts to spread revolution, especially in Germany, had failed, did not allay Western fears. In opposition to communism and largely as a result of communist propaganda, its antithesis, capitalism, gradually changed from an economic doctrine into a comprehensive counter-ideology. As Western charges of a "communist conspiracy" were met by Soviet counter-charges of a "capitalist conspiracy," a crusading element entered into international affairs that had not been there before.

Anti-communism in time became a common ingredient of a number of rightist movements, collectively referred to as fascism. Compared with communism, fascism did not become a potent force in international relations until the 1930's. In some ways it was merely a continuation of traditional nationalism. In its stress on a nation's "historic mission" to rule over "inferior" peoples, fascism posed a potential threat to peace and the status quo. This threat became real with Hitler's brand of fascism, National Socialism. Initially, National Socialism was seen as merely a more aggressive brand of Pan-Germanism. The ultimate implications of Hitler's racist claims of Germanic superiority only became clear on the eve of World War II. Until then, the dangers of fascism were overshadowed by its claims to be the most effective bulwark against communism.

Europe's statesmen during the inter-war years could hardly be expected to find solutions to problems we ourselves are still wrestling with. The peacemakers of 1919 did realize that the "Great War" had been a major turning point. The victory of democracy, so they were told by President Wilson, must also be reflected in international affairs. The "new diplomacy," born in war, was to be free from the evils of the "old diplomacy." It was to be open rather than secret, and it was to achieve security by collective action under the auspices of the League of Nations, rather than by traditional alliances.

Some signs of a new style of diplomacy did appear between the wars. Some diplomatic negotiations were now carried on in the open. Whether this was an improvement, however, is open to doubt, because with outside involvement came outside pressure. Not that publicity was universal. Except for international conferences and the proceedings at the League of Nations, most diplomatic discussions were still held behind closed doors. At the same time, with parliaments and the press asserting their influence on policy-making, the role of the professional diplomat declined.[5] Increasingly the meddling of high-ranking amateurs interfered with the orderly conduct of diplomacy by experts. In authoritarian regimes—Mussolini's Italy, Hitler's Germany, and Stalin's Russia—it was the chief of state who often singlehandedly determined foreign policy, using the apparatus but rarely the expertise of his foreign service. As war approached and hurriedly summoned summit meetings replaced carefully prepared conferences, even the heads of democratic states ignored their professional advisers.

The main innovation and instrument of the "new diplomacy" was to be the League of Nations. Wished upon Europe by the United States, the League at the start was deprived of its most promising feature, American participation. A body that had been envisaged as global thus remained essentially European. Among European statesmen, however, the League had few wholehearted supporters. The fact that there was no general agreement on the League's purpose further limited its effectiveness. France saw the League primarily as a means of maintaining the status quo. Germany, on the other hand, once she was admitted to Geneva in 1926, hoped to use the League as an agency for the revision of her grievances. Great Britain welcomed the League as an organization for collective security and peaceful change, so long as collective security did not entail automatic obligations and peaceful change did not affect vital British interests. Measured against the expectations of its early sponsors, the League's record was one of almost total failure.

The central problem of European diplomacy between the wars, surpassing all others in importance and persistence, was the problem of Germany. The failure to integrate that dynamic country into a viable European concert before the war had not been resolved by Germany's defeat. Despite the draconic peace of Versailles, Germany remained a major power and as such a threat to the peace. Only a permanent alliance among the victors might have contained that threat; but such an alliance presupposed a degree of Allied unity that no longer existed.

As far as Germany was concerned, revision of the Versailles *Diktat* was the overriding aim of virtually all Germans, regardless of class or party. Deeply divided as they might be on domestic issues, in the realm of foreign policy they presented a far more solid front than either the French or the British. Where the Germans differed was merely on how best to achieve the revision of Versailles—by proving, through "fulfillment," the injustice and inefficacy of the treaty; or by obstructing its implementation. Given her military weakness, Germany had no choice but to follow the first course. In time it netted her a whole string of adjustments, concessions, and revisions. Yet the leading advocate of Germany's "fulfillment" policy, Gustav Stresemann, had to pursue his policy under constant attacks from Germany's noisy nationalists, who scorned his gains as insufficient. Once Germany regained military strength under Hitler, grudging fulfillment gave way to peremptory demands, and Allied resistance turned into fearful compliance.

Looking back at the twenties and thirties, one is tempted to ask if the rise of Hitler and the subsequent war could not have been avoided if the concessions made to Hitler under threat had been made freely to the moderate democratic regimes that preceded him. This is a plausible question, if one assumes that a powerful democratic Germany would have been satisfied in the long run with anything short of complete restoration of the status quo of 1914, supplemented by the German portions of the former Austro-Hungarian Empire. In this connection we do well to remember that this program was exactly what those moderate Germans who gave their lives opposing Hitler were still demanding during World War II, despite all that had gone before.[6] Viewed in this perspective, one cannot help wondering if any peaceful solution to the "German problem"—that is, how to give this energetic people the place it felt it deserved, without at the same time awarding it hegemony over Europe —would have been possible, even if there had been no Hitler.

The country most deeply worried by Germany's demands for revision of the peace settlement was France. Not only had she, together with Belgium, suffered most heavily from the war, but she had never forgotten the earlier German invasion of 1870–1871. Just as France had recovered from her defeat then, so Germany would surely recover from her defeat now. The fact that less than forty million Frenchmen were facing close to seventy million Germans made France's situation more precarious still. It was natural, therefore, that the German preoccupation with revision should be matched by French obsession with security. That obsession has come in for much criticism, but it was not unjustified. Having given up at the peace conference their designs on the left bank of the Rhine in return for a promise of joint American-British protection against Germany, the French rightly felt cheated when the Anglo-Saxon powers reneged on their promise. This left only demilitarization and temporary Allied occupation of the Rhineland as protection against possible German invasion. The Locarno agreements of 1925, while hailed as an earnest of Germany's peaceful intentions in the West, were hardly a substitute for a military alliance. France's former ally Russia, furthermore, disabled by revolution and generally ostracized, was neither willing nor geographically able to mount guard on Germany's eastern frontier. If anything, as a revisionist power and fellow outcast, she shared Germany's demand for the re-partition of Eastern Europe. France hoped to fill the void left by Russia through closer relations and alliances with the Eastern succession states. But these small countries, divided by rival interests and caught between Germany and Russia, were as much a threat to the peace as a source of support in war. As for France's neighbor Italy, she had in the past been a doubtful ally at best, and now was nurturing her own set of revisionist grievances, some of which threatened French interests in the Mediterranean.

Looking at the whole picture as it appeared to the French, their stubborn insistence on whatever possible guarantees for their security the peace settlement provided certainly becomes understandable. Any concessions to Germany, be they territorial, economic, or military, were seen as affecting French security. What to the rest of the world might appear as minor changes, to France were erosions of her security. The more so since any concession, far from satisfying the Germans, only made them ask for more. With German militancy feeding French resistance, and French resistance in turn feeding German militancy, Franco-German relations were caught in a vicious circle from which there seemed no escape, except through intervention by some third force.

That third force could only be the Anglo-Saxon powers. As has been pointed out already, America's role in European affairs after 1919 was negligible, especially compared with her involvement after 1945. We cannot here explore the causes of America's return to isolation. Its extent may have loomed larger because of the hopes which American participation in war and peacemaking had aroused. On issues involving American interests—inter-governmental debts, naval disarmament, and collective security—the United States did play an active and often constructive role. But such sporadic participation merely makes us more aware of the many lost opportunities, when the influence of the New World might truly have served "to redress the balance of the Old."

Great Britain, too, tried to maintain the freedom from continental entanglements that she thought she had enjoyed before 1914. Her ideal then had been one of "splendid isolation," to be *of* Europe but not *in* Europe, to be not part of a continental balance of power but to hold the decisive tie-breaking voice in such a balance. For a variety of reasons, Britain did not share France's preoccupation with European security. Relations with her empire and the Commonwealth tended to inhibit continental involvement. Britain's security worries were global and naval, rather than European and military. The fact that the airplane posed a major threat to the British Isles dawned on her only in the 1930's. In 1934, Prime Minister Stanley Baldwin was ready to concede that Britain's frontier was on the Rhine. As for the remainder of Europe, however, Great Britain did not share France's concerns, especially over the status quo in the East. On the contrary, she made her disinterestedness in that area quite clear.

Great Britain also differed from France in her attitude toward Germany. Anglo-German naval rivalry, so important before 1914, was a thing of the past. German economic competition, once thought a major cause of friction, had long been recognized as insignificant compared to the advantages of mutual trade. Thus while France, for reasons of security, tried to keep Germany economically weak, Britain, for reasons of prosperity, wanted her to become strong again. On this and numerous other issues, French insistence on fulfillment of Versailles contrasted with British readiness to compromise. How far these different attitudes were determined by national interests and how much they were due to differences in national character and tradition, is difficult to say.[7] For whatever reasons, the British throughout the inter-war period were certainly far more inclined toward appeasing Germany than were the French.

With Germany, Italy, and the Soviet Union potential threats to the peace, and the United States clearly on the sidelines, European stability depended on close collaboration between Great Britain and France. Yet relations between the wartime allies, already strained by differences at the peace conference, continued to cool and came near the breaking point over the Ruhr crisis in 1923. Britain, it seemed, had no more desire to see France become the dominant power on the continent than she had wished to see Germany. Only when the French relented in their rigid and repressive policy toward Germany did the situation gradually improve. The Dawes Plan of 1924 seemed to hold out hope for the eventual solution of the reparations problem; the Locarno agreements of 1925 relieved tensions in the West; Germany's entry into the League in 1926 signaled her return to fully equal status; and the adherence of virtually all nations, including Russia and the United States, to the Pact of Paris (the Kellogg-Briand Pact) in 1928 promised an end to war.

None of these hopeful developments, however, did away with the underlying threat to stability posed by German revisionism; they merely ensured that future changes were to be by peaceful means. Germany's unwillingness at Locarno to recognize the status quo in the East as she had done in the West clearly showed which direction she intended her revisionism to take. France's efforts in 1925, and again in the early thirties, to contain Germany by means of an "Eastern Locarno," not only ran into German opposition but found little support from Great Britain. The British did not share France's view that revision of the status quo in Germany's favor anywhere would ultimately lead to revision everywhere. Locarno was as far as Britain was ready to commit herself. While under its terms she had to help either France or Germany, depending on who violated the agreement, there can be little doubt that the British were psychologically more prepared to aid the French than the Germans. But meanwhile the multilateral nature of Locarno inhibited any bilateral Franco-British security arrangements against an emergency such as arose in 1936, when Germany reoccupied the Rhineland. The consequences of that event showed how right France had been in considering Europe's status quo indivisible. With Germany rearming and with the Rhineland no longer serving as a protective *glacis,* France was no longer in a position to come to the immediate aid of the small nations of Eastern Europe. Henceforth she had to content herself with following Britain's lead in seeking accommodations with Hitler, if need be at the expense of those same nations. French search for security through containment had given way to British search for security through appeasement.

The last act in France's efforts to stop Hitler by encirclement had been the mutual assistance pact she concluded with the Soviet Union in 1935. Had such rapprochement come earlier, and had it been more wholehearted, Germany might well have been kept in her place. But Russia, through much of the inter-war period, remained an outcast, isolated from the mainstream of European diplomacy. Communism was the main reason, but there were others, notably Soviet refusal to honor Russia's prewar and wartime foreign debts. Meanwhile the Russians had their own grievances, chiefly stemming from Allied intervention against the revolution at its birth. Despite mutual antagonisms and suspicions, however, there was one area in which collaboration between Russia and the West held out great promise. As an underdeveloped country of great economic potential, the Soviet Union seemed a fertile field for foreign trade and investment. The exchange of raw materials for machinery, in turn, would prove invaluable to Soviet industrialization. Both the Allies and Germany tried to avail themselves of the economic opportunities which the Soviet Union offered. In this contest, Germany came out slightly ahead, though she never achieved what she hoped for. Differences between capitalist and communist ways of doing business were partly responsible. More fundamental was the universal fear and distrust of communism, kept alive by the conspiratorial activities of the Comintern, the Soviet-controlled agency for propagandizing world communism. Comintern interference in the domestic affairs of other nations, together with Soviet recalcitrance in her foreign dealings, were seen as signs that, despite Russian denials, communism had not abandoned its world-revolutionary aims.

The Soviet Union thus never really played the role in European diplomacy between the wars to which her potential power entitled her. Some Western observers hoped that in time Russia would revert to capitalism; others feared or hailed the "communist experiment" as the wave of the future. Only when Hitler suddenly posed a more immediate threat to the peace did the Western powers draw closer to the Soviet Union. In 1934 the Soviets were finally admitted to the League of Nations; in 1935 they concluded mutual assistance pacts with France and Czechoslovakia; by 1939 they had emerged as the main advocates of containment against Germany. But the mutual suspicions of the past were never really overcome, just as the "community of fate" that linked Germany and the Soviet Union ever since the Treaty of Rapallo in 1922 had never been completely forgotten, even during the ideological war between Nazism and communism. The Hitler-Stalin pact of August 23, 1939, was first and foremost a ruthless deal, an exercise in *Realpolitik*. But as an alliance between the continent's most powerful revisionist countries, each distrusted by the West, the pact was not without historic roots.

In dealing with so crucial a subject as the diplomacy leading to the Second World War, one is tempted to look for missed opportunities. If Hitler was responsible for the immediate coming of the war, could not at least some of its long-range causes have been avoided? We have already expressed doubts concerning appeasement, even of a democratic Germany, as a long-range guarantee of peace. The alternative, containing Germany by superior force, not only called for close collaboration between Britain, France, and, it was hoped, the United States, but it also required that Russia side with the Western powers. As it turned out, it was Russia, rather than Britain, who enjoyed the privilege of choosing sides in 1939. Had a *modus vivendi* been found with Russia during the 1920's, more generous concessions could then have been made to a democratic Germany in the hope of appeasing or, if not, of containing her. It was thus not merely differences between France and Britain that helped prepare the ground for war, but also their failure to understand Russia's key position in European affairs and the role which both Russia and the United States were destined to play in maintaining Europe's "precarious balance."

To understand European diplomacy between the wars, therefore, the subject must be studied in the broadest possible sense. If this collection of articles focuses on a few key events, most of them involving Germany, such narrow scope has been dictated by limitations of space and a desire to give unity to what might otherwise have been an incoherent book. The criteria for selection were sound scholarship and use of fresh material. Wherever possible, preference was given to contributions that stress the interaction of domestic and foreign affairs. Diplomatic documents alone are merely the skeleton of diplomatic history. Lack of space also restricted the number of contributors. As the appended bibliography shows, the list of European diplomatic historians is impressive. Still, there remains much work to be done.

NOTES

1. The controversy has been kept alive by Fritz Fischer's *Germany's Aims in the First World War* (New York, 1967), and *Krieg der Illusionen: Die deutsche Politik von 1911 bis 1914* (Düsseldorf, 1969). Fischer puts the major blame for that war on Germany.

2. The most imaginative attempt at such a challenge is A. J. P. Taylor's *The Origins of the Second World War* (New York, 1961).

3. An excellent introduction to the literature on the diplomacy of the 1930's is D. C. Watt, "Appeasement: The Rise of a Revisionist School?", *Political Quarterly*, XXXVI (April 1965), 191–213. Professor Watt provides interesting alternatives to the traditional study of the origins of World War II.

4. The most discerning discussion of Europe's decline is Hajo Holborn's *The Political Collapse of Europe* (New York, 1951).

5. On the declining influence of the professional diplomat, see Gordon A. Craig and Felix Gilbert, eds., *The Diplomats, 1919–1939* (Princeton, 1953).

6. See the chapter by Hermann Graml on the foreign policy ideas of the German Resistance, in Hermann Graml, Hans Mommsen, Hans-Joachim Reichhardt, and Ernst Wolf, *The German Resistance to Hitler* (Berkeley, 1970).

7. Arnold Wolfers, *Britain and France Between Two Wars* (New York, 1940), pp. 212ff. Despite its early date, this remains the best book on Anglo-French relations in this period.

ARNO J. MAYER

The Problems of Peacemaking

At the beginning of our period, and casting its shadow upon the events of the next twenty years, stands the Peace Conference of 1919. Most of the standard histories of that event were written decades ago and are by now quite dated. Much new material has become available in recent years, calling for corrections and reassessment.

One such fresh view is provided in Arno Mayer's Politics and Diplomacy of Peacemaking *(New York, 1967), of which the present chapter forms the Prologue. The book addresses itself primarily to the influence which the threat of communism exerted on the diplomacy of peacemaking. But just as in his earlier book,* Wilson vs. Lenin: Political Origins of the New Diplomacy 1917–1918 *(New Haven, 1959), Professor Mayer places his subject in the widest historical and geographic context and throughout emphasizes the relationship of domestic to foreign policy. In substance, as in method, this is diplomatic history at its best. The author teaches history at Princeton. His chapter is republished with his kind permission, as well as that of the publishers, Alfred A. Knopf and George Weidenfeld & Nicolson, copyright © 1967 by Arno J. Mayer.*

FOR QUITE some time reasoning by historical analogy has been the stock in trade of modern statesmen and their advisers, particularly when confronted with big questions. In 1918–1919 the history of the Congress of Vienna was considered to be the most pertinent guide to the making of peace, and the history of the French Revolution, including Europe's reaction to it, the most pertinent guide to dealing with the Russian Revolution. Of course, each statesman's interpretation of these paradigms was marked by his own ideological preferences, national interest calculations, political exigencies, and personal tastes. But all alike searched the history of the Vienna Congress and the French Revolution for policies to be emulated, shunned, or applied in modified form. All participants both used and abused historical analogies precisely because then, as now, such analogies were vital aids in the analysis and discussion of the quagmire of contemporary history.

The peacemakers of 1814–1815 and 1918–1919 convened to settle the accounts of a multilateral, unlimited, and ideological conflict; to legalize a new territorial status quo; to agree on safeguards and sanctions against future transgressions by the major defeated enemy; and to explore ways of putting the peace and concert of Europe on more enduring foundations. In both Vienna and Paris each statesman pursued these overarching objectives while simultaneously striving to maximize the national interest of his own country.

These two sets of constantly jarring objectives were pursued within a framework of power politics. Conflicting national interests were accommodated through mutual compensations and concessions. In 1814–1815 as in 1918–1919 the major powers assumed responsibility for bringing and maintaining in balance the international system of sovereign states. They arrogated to themselves the right to settle all basic territorial, military, economic, and political issues before securing approval for their decisions from the plenary congress or conference. The secondary and minor powers were cast in the role of suitors, suppliants, or satellites. They promoted their interests primarily by deftly capitalizing on the jockeyings, rivalries, and needs of the big powers.

Not surprisingly, on the eve of the Paris Peace Conference Charles K. Webster urged the British Foreign Office to look for precedents to the negotiations that had concluded the Napoleonic Wars. At Vienna the assembled statesmen had upheld the cardinal distinction between major and minor powers; had adjusted borders according to the dictates of the balance of power; and had agreed on diplomatic procedures to be followed in the future.[1] Shortly after the Conference Webster also claimed that "however puny" the problems of 1814–1815 appeared next to those of 1918–1919, the Vienna settlement was the only one which in "scope and importance" could be compared to the Versailles settlement: "the boundaries of almost every state in Europe were remodelled; a barrier was erected against and reparations were inflicted upon the dominant military power; colonial territories were redistributed; new international organizations were erected; and even schemes for the perpetuation of world peace were considered."[2]

As a conventional diplomatic historian with a passion for the functional, procedural, and technical aspects of peacemaking, Webster tendered advice to a foreign office dominated by practitioners of the Old Diplomacy, most of whom were of gentlemanly background.[3] These and other factors predisposed him to stress the important but, in the last analysis, surface similarities between Vienna and Paris.

At the turn of the century Woodrow Wilson had joined the New Historians in their rebellion against this one-dimensional political and legal history. He was interested "not so much in what happened as in what underlay the happening; not so much in the tides as in the silent forces that lifted them." For him law and government were "regulative rather than generative," and he refused to be satisfied with legal and political history that got at "the surface only, not at the heart of affairs." [4]

In any case, given his progressive *Weltanschauung,* which was solidly rooted in this New History, Wilson was bound to probe into the direction in which a re-enactment of history was likely to take the world. Early in the deliberations he explicitly rejected the Congress of Vienna as a valid precedent. His reasons were that this Congress had presided over a vast restoration, both national and international, and had charted the Holy Alliance which sought to "extend the system of monarchical and arbitrary government in the world." Wilson passionately begged that "such would not be the purpose of the present conference." [5]

Ideologically and temperamentally the President would readily have reconciled himself to an enlightened restoration calculated to head off a White reaction. But a restoration had been difficult to launch and sustain after 1814–1815, at the end of a revolutionary cycle. How much more difficult to launch and sustain one in 1918–1919, at the beginning of such a cycle! In 1814–1815 the peacemakers were secure in having the support of powerful and influential political, social, economic, and administrative strata which craved domestic order and international stability; they could build on governmental organisms which had survived almost intact; and they needed concern themselves almost exclusively with territorial divisions.

The peacemakers at Paris were not nearly so well served. To begin with, in 1918–1919 the leaders and forces favoring moderate reconstruction at home and abroad were fatally buffeted by *enragés* of the Left as well as of the Right. This erosion of conservative liberalism had been well advanced by 1914; the war and revolution merely exacerbated it. Moreover, in Germany, throughout the Danubian basin, in the Balkans, and in Turkey governmental structures were shaky, in ruins, or embryonic. Also, though by no means least important, in both defeated and victor Europe questions of economic and social reconstruction and reform were generating intense political heat. Needless to say, these divisive and explosive domestic conditions were bound to affect the work of the Peace Conference, thereby complicating the assignment of the assembled statesmen far beyond what had faced their predecessors after Napoleon's fall.[6]

According to Ferrero, the Big Four were confronted with a Himalayan task.

> Everything was destroyed, commercial treaties and treaties of alliance, conventions between State and State relating to the most jealously guarded interests, the public and private law of every single State. The elite of the greater European nations, and more especially its youth who would have been called to govern in ten or fifteen years' time, were mown down. The Prussian, no less than the English and French, aristocracy were decimated. The same was true of the middle classes both in France and Germany. The better part of the Russian nation was dispersed or dead. Everywhere the balance of wealth was upset; vast fortunes were made without labour by ignorant, incapable, or cowardly persons, while the flower of the population was ruined or perished in the trenches. The national fortune even of the richest peoples, was heavily mortgaged in order to meet gigantic war obligations. It is by no means rash to estimate these burdens as amounting to more than half their total possessions. Finally, during the war there was revealed to all eyes the double soul—which wishes for power and at the same time for justice—of the State created by the French Revolution and by the nineteenth century. In this war all the most generous sentiments which make life dear to men were exalted; but at the same time the most terrible offensive weapons which the world has ever seen were brought into action. The States of Western Civilization finally dared to do what to previous ages would have seemed madness if not a crime, and that was, to arm the masses.

Ferrero went on to warn that the apprenticeship of the successor states, which would be arduous and tedious even under the most favorable of circumstances, would be doubly difficult in the "midst of a Europe devastated, bled white, convulsed, and impoverished by the war." [7] *The New Europe* refused to share this pessimism, even though it conceded that Central Europe was "as nearly a *tabula rasa* as a civilized continent could be." [8]

This awareness of the unparalleled scope and complexity of peacemaking in the wake of the world war and the world revolution was widespread. According to Villard of *The Nation,* the statesmen were charged not with simply closing a war but with fully recasting the inherited world order. Notwithstanding Wilson's ecumenical promise, at this juncture the world was "less safe for democracy than at any previous period in modern times . . . and the whole modern order of society was on trial for its life." [9] For the Paris correspondent of the *Philadelphia Ledger* the Conference had to balance and square "the accounts of a whole epoch, the deeds and misdeeds of an exhausted civilization." [10]

As early as May 1918 H. G. Wells, who in September 1914 had held out the promise of *The War That Will End War,* could "conceive no such Peace Congress as those that had settled up after other wars settling up after this War." There were no precedents to go by because this war had been "enormously bigger than any other war . . . and had struck deeper at the foundations of social and economic life." With commendable candor Wells confessed that he doubted that the Western intelligentsia and political class even began "to realize how much of the old system was dead today, how much had to be remade." [11] This doubt was confirmed once the Paris Conference began to flounder. Wells promptly joined thirty prominent Western intellectuals who compared themselves to those "gloomy prophets and the first apostles" who in experiencing the "agony of Babylonia and Imperial Rome" had cried out that the decomposition of these great powers "was due less to the choc of [external] invasion than to the weight of their own [internal] crimes." These modern brainworkers saw themselves as more "despairing and paralyzed" than the witnesses of past political cataclysms because the decadence confronting them was "more universal, more profound, and more incurable" than that of ancient Greece and Rome.[12]

These and similar expressions of the post-armistice *Weltschmerz, crise de conscience,* or failure of nerve serve to call attention to the deep and multivarious crisis that, starting in 1917, the Great War precipitated throughout the world: the Bolshevik Revolution in Russia, the nationalist rebellions throughout the Dual Monarchy, the November Revolution in Germany, the post-armistice neurasthenia in the Allied nations, the Kemalist revolution in Turkey, the rice riots in Japan, the May Fourth Movement in China, and Gandhi's first Swaraj campaign in India. In each of these countries an old order was being jostled by a new one; in some, revolution and counterrevolution were squaring off. It was with this crisis-torn world, particularly with a crisis-torn Europe, swirling about them, that the Big Four were expected to negotiate a lasting diplomatic settlement.

As of the mid-nineteenth century the inseparability of strain or defeat in war and reform or revolution became increasingly apparent. Russia's defeat in the Crimean War was followed by the reforms of the sixties; Austria's defeat at Sadowa led to the compromise of 1867; France's defeat in 1870–1871 brought first the fall of the Second Empire, then the Commune, and eventually the birth of the fragile Third Republic; China's defeat in the Sino-Japanese War stimulated an outburst of anti-imperialist nationalism and prepared the ground for the "Hundred Days" of 1898; Russia's defeat in the war with Japan contributed to the revolution of 1905, followed by the Octobrist reforms; and, finally, Russia's exhaustion in the Great War precipitated first the March uprising and then the November Revolution of 1917.

The Russian Revolution came as a timely reminder of the costs of military exhaustion and defeat under conditions of mounting political tensions. Otherwise both the Allies and the Central Powers might well have held out for unconditional surrender. Had it not been for the demonstration effect of the Bolshevik Revolution neither side would have considered the Wilsonian points as an acceptable basis for armistice negotiations. In the event the armistice was concluded just in time to limit the political consequences of military defeat in Central and East Central Europe to less than revolutionary proportions. But even with this eleventh-hour finish, the legacy of disruption and convulsion was far from negligible.

Granted, neither Germany nor Austria went Spartacist; and Hungary remained bolshevik for only 133 days. Even so, particularly since Allied policies contributed to this outcome, it would be wrong to dismiss the danger of revolution as having been at best a sham or at worst a conspiracy. Admittedly, the social and political carriers as well as the precipitants of unrest varied in composition and intensity from country to country, and from month to month. But the fact remains that there were grave disorders, rebellions, and strikes throughout defeated Europe, notably because politicians and labor leaders had ready-made organizational weapons with which to capitalize on political instability, unemployment, food shortages, and runaway prices.

In her diary Beatrice Webb raised a question that haunted Europe's political class, including the chief statesmen, throughout the Peace Conference: "Are we confronted with another Russia in Austria, possibly even in Germany—a Continent in rampant revolution . . . ?" [13] For General Smuts Europe was reduced to her "original atoms," with no hint of the "new political forms" within which these might be joined.[14] Curiously, it was the conservative liberal and legalistic David Hunter Miller who stressed, quite properly, that whereas the peacemakers of 1814–1815 only had to reconcile disputes "between well-known and established powers," those of 1918–1919 had to bring about "order out of chaos in practically all of Europe east of the Rhine, and north of the Danube, as well as restoration and a new life in various other parts of Europe and Asia." [15] Likewise, Walter Lippmann noted the absence of "stable government anywhere east of the Rhine," warning that no one knew "what Germany would be, nor Russia, nor the twenty-odd nationalities of Eastern Europe and New Asia." [16] With good reason Woodrow Wilson acknowledged the wisdom and necessity of postponing the Conference "until there were governments in Germany and Austria-Hungary which could enter into binding agreements." [17] While Smuts exuberantly proposed that the League be made the trustee of the politically untrained peoples "left behind by the decomposition of Russia, Austria, and Turkey," [18] Wilson and his advisers did their best to press the Allies into helping the "receiver" and successor governments of the defeated empires to consolidate themselves.

Of course, even without the force of the Soviet Russian example and the activities of local bolshevik parties, this chaos would have developed and caused concern. But as it was, the bolshevik regime, by its mere survival as well as through its flaming manifestoes, provided encouragement to all far-Left radicals and stirred especially Independent Socialists into greater militancy. In addition, Lenin offered food to the Ebert-Scheidemann government, sent the Radek mission to Berlin, charted the Third International in early March 1919, and built up the Red Army. Counterrevolutionaries in particular vastly exaggerated the scope and aggressive nature of these steps, thereby making the specter which was haunting Europe doubly terrifying.

Naturally not only the Big Four or Five but also the experts within each delegation differed among themselves in their estimates of the nature and seriousness of the revolutionary threat, and hence in their prescriptions for containing it. Moreover, as in 1792–1794, the coherence and unity of the counterrevolutionary crusade were undermined by rival national interests, uneven material capabilities, and shifting domestic pressures. Even so, in spite of these grave dissonances, the Paris Peace Conference made a host of decisions, all of which, in varying degrees, were designed to check bolshevism: the victors made territorial concessions to Poland, Rumania, and Czechoslovakia for helping to stem the revolutionary tide beyond their own borders; they gave military assistance and economic aid to these and other border lands as well as to the Whites for their armed assault on Soviet Russia and Hungary; they stepped up their direct military intervention in Russia; they rigorously enforced the blockade against bolshevik Russia and Hungary; they rushed economic assistance to Austria and the successor states to help stabilize their governments; and they drafted the charters of the International Labor Organization (ILO) and the League of Nations with a view to immunizing the nonbolshevik Left against the ideological bacillus of the Bolshevik Revolution.

Some of these measures constituted a defensive containment policy, a *cordon sanitaire* calculated to prevent the revolution from spreading beyond bolshevik-controlled areas; other measures were aimed at the outright overthrow of Lenin and Béla Kun. But all alike were decided, orchestrated, sanctioned, or condoned by the peacemakers in Paris. Furthermore, all alike—intentionally or unintentionally—contributed to sparing defeated Europe further revolutionary infections. During the pivotal year of 1918–1919, when defeated Europe was most vulnerable, the armed intervention, reinforced by the blockade, forced Lenin to exhaust his scarce military and economic resources in defensive operations. Outside Russia he was reduced to countering the massive material intervention by the Allies with ideological appeals.

At the time, the outcome of this first round in the international civil war of the twentieth century seemed to be very much in the balance. According to Ray Stannard Baker, "at all times, at every turn in the negotiations, there rose the specter of chaos, like a black cloud out of the east, threatening to overwhelm and swallow up the world. There was no Russia knocking at the gates of Vienna! At Vienna, apparently, the revolution was securely behind them; at Paris it was always with them." [19] At one time or another every delegation played on this fear of the bolshevik specter for its own purposes, thereby making the threat even more pervasive than it need have been.

The uses and abuses of this spuriously inflated bogy of bolshevism were as numerous then as they are today. With intermittent support from Lloyd George, President Wilson sought to convince Georges Clemenceau that Germany would succumb to Spartacism unless the Allies promptly lifted the blockade and proffered moderate peace terms. Back home, when Congress threatened to refuse his first major foreign aid bill, Wilson reluctantly but successfully frightened Capitol Hill with tales of the horrors of bolshevism sweeping over the entire European continent.

Naturally, the vulnerable "receiver" governments of Germany, Austria, and Hungary were the most boisterous advocates of this Wilson line, insisting that should their countries be swallowed up by bolshevism the advancing flood would not stop at the borders of the victor nations. Ironically, the German government itself diminished the blackmail value of Spartacism by repressing it sternly at home and by fighting bolshevism eagerly in the *Baltikum*. On the other hand, Count Michael Károlyi invited the bolsheviks into the Hungarian government in order to make his threats more credible. As for the Poles and the Rumanians, they received vast amounts of financial, economic, and military aid from the Allies for their assault on Soviet Russia and Soviet Hungary. Roman Dmowski and John Brătianu, supported by Ferdinand Foch and Winston Churchill, styled themselves as selfless champions of anti-bolshevism, all the time extorting exorbitant territorial annexations for their counter-revolutionary services. Even Eleutherios Venizelos, whom Harold Nicolson mysteriously paired with Lenin as "the only two great men in Europe," [20] was not above trading on the bolshevik scare; neither were Thomas Masaryk and Eduard Beneš.

In brief, at one time or another most delegations at the Paris Peace

Conference wielded the specter of bolshevism as a weapon and a threat. In each instance the assault on or containment of bolshevism was calculated to advance a government's foreign policy goals while at the same time fortifying its political position at home. *Contra communismo saepe; pro patria et politica semper.*

This twin assignment of stabilizing governments throughout defeated Europe and of containing if not destroying the Russian Revolution called for day-to-day consultations, decisions, and directives. Here, then, was one of the chief sources of that "vast quantity of executive work which was thrust upon the Conference of Paris and which found no parallel at Vienna." [21] Once the Paris Conference is placed in its historical context this executive work can no longer be deplored as a festering diversion from the real stuff of diplomacy, from negotiations of frontier adjustments, colonial redistributions, and reparations. In fact, this diversion, which vastly complicates diplomacy, may yet turn out to be the essence of peacemaking in an era of international civil war. It certainly deserves more than passing mention that the peacemakers of 1918–1919 manipulated blockades, wielded military and economic aid, and ordered counterrevolutionary military interventions. Properly to carry out this assignment of preventing Europe "from going to smash under [their] feet," they established the Supreme Economic Council, the Directory for Relief, the Blockade Committee, and the Supreme Council.[22]

The tight interlocking of international and domestic policies in both defeated and victor nations complicated the diplomacy of peacemaking still further.

Since in the defeated nations governments had to be formed before plenipotentiaries could be sent to the Paris Peace Conference, foreign policy platforms became decisive weapons in the struggle for political control. In November 1917 the bolsheviks had seized power in Russia primarily though not exclusively on a promise of immediate peace; and they were determined to maintain themselves in power without external aid until fellow revolutionary regimes could come to their rescue.

After the armistice, in Germany, Austria, Hungary, and the successor states, rival political parties, notably those which eventually formed or controlled the governments, claimed that they were best qualified to secure favorable terms from the Big Four. The essential corollary of this pledge was the insistence that successful performance in the peace negotiations was the passkey to domestic rehabilitation, reconstruction, and reform.

But whereas in Russia the bolsheviks had seized power from below, in Germany, Austria, and Hungary inveterate power elites invited the leaders of the nonrevolutionary forces of movement to act as receivers for bankrupt regimes. They pressed Friedrich Ebert, Friedrich Adler, and Károlyi into accepting these receiverships, not only because at home each was an ideal foil against revolutionary and anarchist excesses, but above all also because each was alone likely to inspire confidence in the Allies, notably in Wilson.

The promise and, in the case of Austria, the fulfillment of Allied goodwill and aid played a crucial role once these provisional govern-ments tried to transform their receiverships from above into popular mandates from below. The Social Democrats and their collaborators forewarned the electorates—and the Allies punctuated these warnings —that in case of chaos or revolution their countries could expect neither food, nor credits, nor favorable peace terms, with the result that there would be massive starvation, especially in the large cities. On the other hand, they promised that provided order was maintained and reformist republican regimes established, the victors, under pressure from Wilson and the Allied Left, would provide economic aid and grant moderate peace terms. By mid-January the triumph of the parties of the July Coalition in the campaign for the German Constituent Assembly best attested to the nature and successful application of this political formula. Within two months Károlyi's withdrawal in favor of Béla Kun, which was precipitated by the peremptory Vix Note, demonstrated the failure of the same formula in Hungary.

Just as the peacemakers could ill afford to ignore this interplay of national and international politics in the defeated countries, they could not ignore it in their own. In 1814–1815 the peace was negotiated "in elegant and ceremonious privacy . . . [by] a group of Aristocrats, life-trained as statesmen or diplomats," [23] who considered themselves responsible to crowned sovereigns and barely worried about partisan pressures. The situation was not so serene a century later, when seasoned party politicians of *petit bourgeois* background—two professors, a jour-nalist, a solicitor—gathered around the conference table. The Big Four were responsible to parliaments, and they never seriously considered insulating themselves from the political parties, pressure groups, mass media, and mass electorates, which were highly agitated over the peace question. To be sure, compared to Metternich, Castlereagh, and Talley-rand, the Big Four were "amateur" diplomats. It does not follow, how-ever, that because they aligned the methods and procedures of diplomacy with the prevailing requirements of party and mass politics they under-stood less about international affairs than their illustrious predecessors.

Churchill rightly emphasized that the peacemakers of 1918–1919 were orators, mass leaders, and men of action, "each of whom had to produce a triumph for himself and his Party and give satisfaction to national fears and passions well founded or not." But why go on and call them "embarrassed demagogues," as Churchill did? [24] Probably nostalgia for both cabinet diplomacy and status politics accounts for the still widely espoused defamation that these "plenipotentiaries were essentially politicians, old parliamentary hands, and therefore expedient-mongers whose highest qualifications for their own profession were draw-backs which unfitted them for their self-assumed [diplomatic] mission." [25]

Even during the prewar decades the growth of party, mass, and crisis politics had substantially eroded cabinet diplomacy, with politically based foreign policy actors superseding professional diplomats. By 1918–1919 this erosion of the methods, procedures, style, and personnel of the Old Diplomacy was completed. There was no going back, least of all at the opening of a revolutionary era with soaring class and party strife at home and abroad. And yet the very day the Conference was formally inaugurated the *Temps* called on the Central Powers not to allow party conflicts to disturb international relations; not to use foreign intervention "to upset the internal equilibrium of nations"; and not to bring into play party polemics in the peace deliberations. At the same time it inveighed against making partisan use of half-accurate information about these negotiations.[26] *Mirabile dictu.*

With the armistice the political truce burst wide open in the victor nations, the forces of order and reaction seizing the offensive. In the United States the congressional elections of November 1918 returned a Republican Senate, thereby undermining domestic support for Woodrow Wilson's moderate peace project; in England the coupon election of mid-December 1918 returned a grim House of Commons, resolved to hold Lloyd George to a Carthaginian course; in Italy, in late December, Leonida Bissolati, Italy's foremost Wilsonian, resigned from Orlando's cabinet. Heartened by these developments, on December 29 Clemenceau defiantly proclaimed his skepticism of the Wilsonian program, certain that the war-hardened Chamber of 1914 was determined to have a punitive settlement.

According to Nicolson this upsurge of vindictiveness was a spontaneous prolongation of wartime passions into the post-armistice period. Irrational hatreds swelled up and consumed "alert but ignorant electorates," which thereafter made it "impossible even for supermen to devise a peace of moderation and righteousness." [27] But was this outburst of revengeful jingoism all that spontaneous? And, if it was, did the governments and their supporters, which had known how to mobilize these hatreds, do anything to revaluate these mass sentiments?

There are numerous indications that the clamor for a punitive peace was stirred up as part of a vast political design. Except for the proto-fascist new Right, the leaders, parties, pressure groups, patriotic leagues, and newspapers that sparked this agitation also favored rigorously conservative or outright reactionary social and economic policies. In fact, the forces of order appear to have taken advantage of the intoxication of victory either to preserve or advance their class interests and status positions under an ideological cover which was a syncretism of jingoist nationalism, baleful anti-Wilsonianism, and rabid anti-bolshevism. Whoever was not a superpatriot was denounced as a fellow traveler of the bolsheviks and stood accused not only of disloyalty but also of advocating a sellout peace.

The revolutionary segments of the socialist and labor movements were not the primary targets of the jingoist *cum* anti-bolshevik campaign. Its aim was to rout and disconcert the very core of the forces of change, to do so now, preemptively, before the fast-growing Left had a chance to rally around Wilson and to make political gains from the high cost of living, rising taxes, and the strains of reconversion. In addition to championing a Wilsonian peace, this Left—this noncommunist Left—was battling for the forty-eight-hour week, collective bargaining, graduated income taxes, and social welfare measures.

Already in the prewar decade the Left and the Right in Britain, France, and Italy had faced each other with mounting bitterness over these same issues. Compared to then, of course, in 1918–1919 the economic and fiscal crisis was infinitely more acute; the membership and following of the labor movement were vastly greater; the Russian Revolution stood forth both as an invigorating and a frightening example; and the Right was able to claim credit for timely preparedness as well as victory. But notwithstanding these important permutations and mutations the continuities with the prewar situation were all too apparent. Specifically, in the struggle over labor, tax, and welfare issues, the extremists of the Right frightened conservatives into inflexibility by deliberately exaggerating the revolutionary posture and the foreign policy pacifism of the Left. In turn, this creeping inflexibility played into the hands of the radical Left, which charged the Right with domestic reaction and warmongering. By mid-1914 the moderate leaders of both camps were rapidly becoming hostages to their respective extremists, with the result that the politics of compromise and accommodation became increasingly deadlocked. Witness the threatened strike by the Triple Industrial Alliance and the Ulster crisis in Britain, the impasse over the three-year law in France, and Red Week in Italy.

The war merely sharpened this polarization of politics and labor-management relations, at the expense of the conservative-reformist center. Victory strengthened, hardened, and emboldened the refractory Right: the Russian Revolution had a similar impact on the militant Left. Both extremes left indelible marks on the politics and diplomacy of the victor powers in 1918–1919. Because the jingoist Right had champions or sympathizers in the legislatures, foreign offices, interior ministries, armed services, conservative parties, and editorial offices, its preemptive thrust was felt in a vast range of developments: in America, in the November elections, in congressional obstruction of a Wilsonian peace, in the Red

Scare, and in the drive for "normalcy"; in England, in the coupon election, in parliamentary opposition to the appeasement of Germany and Soviet Russia, and in the government's sham reconstruction program; in France, in the gestation of the *chambre bleu horizon,* in Clemenceau's intransigence toward Germany and Soviet Russia, in the resolute repression of strikes, and in parliament's obstinate refusal to approve nonregressive taxes; and in Italy, in Sidney Sonnino's domination of the peace delegation, in Gabriele d'Annunzio's expedition to Fiume, in the growth of the *Fasci de combattimento,* and in Orlando's failure to check inflation.

Except for frightening established governments and societies and serving as a pretext for the excesses of the *avant garde* of anti-bolshevism, the extreme Left had no leverage outside the labor movement. Its leaders, most of them nationally unknown, concentrated their organizational, propagandist, and conspiratorial activities on the rapidly expanding Socialist parties and trade unions, making special efforts to enlist the new recruits. They fed on each and every grievance, sparked local strikes, participated prominently in mass demonstrations, and worked their propaganda presses overtime. In 1918–1919 these zealots helped generate a mood of impatience among the rank and file, thereby goading their Majoritarian and Independent rivals into a greater sense of urgency about the labor cause. These political and syndicalist militants should not be denied their share of the credit for the enactment of the forty-eight-hour week by the Allied parliaments and for the labor movement's concerted and partially successful opposition to direct military intervention in Russia.

Without this impatience and activism on the Left, Woodrow Wilson's moderating influence would have been completely nullified. As it was, precisely because the moderate forces of movement were so decisively checked even before the start of the Conference, Wilson had only limited leverage. Moreover, he was hesitant to appeal to the Left for help for fear that the militants would seize the initiative for themselves. Wilson was condemned to labor in a political field, both national and international, in which measured reformism, so essential to the achievement of his diplomatic aims, was fatally emasculated.

Wilson's principles and aims, like all such pronunciamentos, were destined to be honored in the breach. The conditions that had prompted their formulation and acceptance in early 1918 had passed into history: there was no longer any need to restrain the Soviet government from signing a separate peace with the Central Powers; with the success of the revolution from above in Berlin the rebellion against the Kaiser and Erich Ludendorff no longer required encouragement; and after the armistice the Allied governments could dispense with the support of their own forces of movement. Above all, the Allied cabinets were much less prone to bend to the ideological and diplomatic wishes of the Wilson administration once victory had drastically reduced their dependence on American military and economic power. Besides, no programmatic guidelines had complicated the labors of the peacemakers of 1814–1815.

Even so, the President's Fourteen Points and subsequent pronouncements were not simply shunted aside. By making their two reservations with regard to the freedom of the seas and reparations the Allies conceded that Wilson's prescriptions had crystalized into a public touchstone for the coming peace negotiations; and the pre-armistice exchanges with Germany even endowed them with a measure of contractual force.[28]

But quite apart from any moral or legal obligation to Germany, until May 1919 the Allied governments could not afford to disavow Woodrow Wilson publicly. The President's ideology and America's economic bounty were expected to exercise a moderating influence on revolutionary conditions in defeated Europe and on the post-armistice neurasthenia in the victor nations. Without the still potent spell of Wilsonianism the swing toward Leninism within the Left might well have assumed considerable proportions. Especially the Independents, but also the Majoritarians, trusted in the President to block a punitive peace, thereby thwarting the offensive of the Allied Right, consolidating the reformist regimes in the defeated nations, and giving the lie to Lenin's charge that Wilsonianism was but an insidious bourgeois-capitalist smoke screen.

The frenzied enthusiasm that greeted the President upon his arrival in Europe was not without political and class overtones. While socialist, labor, and radical-bourgeois leaders and their followers wildly cheered him, their opponents berated them for apotheosizing Wilson for selfish, partisan purposes. On the eve of the Conference the Allied governments were sufficiently apprehensive about this united front of Wilson and the Left that they purposely obstructed contacts between them. On the other hand, the governments of the defeated nations continued to profess their faith in Wilson until well after they knew that his cause was lost. As for the governments of the successor states, they courted Wilson's favor in their bid for favorable frontiers and economic aid. In sum, throughout most of the Conference the President and his arsenal of spiritual and material resources were considered indispensable by each delegation as well as by the Berne International. Significantly, even Clemenceau was careful not to risk a break with Wilson; and notwithstanding his anti-Wilsonian tirades, Lenin was eager for the President to blunt the military edge of the counterrevolutionary intervention.

At the time of the Congress of Vienna Tsar Alexander I certainly did not play such a pivotal role as did Wilson. Quite apart from the fact that the League of Nations was to serve as an instrument for peaceful change in the international arena while the Holy Alliance was designed to freeze the new status quo at home and abroad, the Tsar had considerably less leverage than Wilson. Whereas Alexander was confined to cooperation with fellow sovereigns and to military means of intervention, Wilson could marshal popular support for the League and dispose of substantial economic and financial resources which were of critical importance to the exhausted nations of Europe.[29]

R. S. Baker quite rightly stressed that the use of the "economic weapon" to achieve diplomatic and political ends "was only in its crude beginnings at Paris," and that the world would get "a fuller taste of it in the future." [30] During the Conference all nations—large and small, old and new—brought their economic resources into play; and the Conference as a whole, supported by the neutrals, enforced a strict blockade against bolshevik Russia and Hungary.

But America's use of the economic weapon was particularly noteworthy. She had a vast reservoir of instantly available capital, food, and manufactures, and her delegation had a precocious understanding of economic power as an instrument of control in the international politics of this dawning era of civil war.

The armistice was not signed as yet when U.S. officials in Europe advised Washington that since America's "economic and financial support would be essential to the Allies in the post-war period" material pressures might be used to force an acceptable interpretation of "our own principles and policies." [31] Wilson himself chose Armistice Day solemnly to declare that it would be America's "fortunate duty to assist by example, by sober, friendly counsel and by *material aid* in the establishment of a just democracy throughout the world"; [32] and he may well have had the economic weapon in mind when he told his advisers, during the crossing to Europe, that the U.S. would fight for a new order "agreeably if we can, disagreeably if necessary." [33]

Colonel House shared the view of many U.S. officials and business leaders that the Allies were "vitally interested in what manner we propose to use our great strength" in finance, commerce, shipping, raw materials, and food.[34] As for D. H. Miller, he confidently predicted that Wilson's covenant would be accepted without any American concessions because "Europe was bankrupt financially and her Governments were bankrupt morally . . . [and] the mere hint of the withdrawal of America . . . would see the fall of every government in Europe without exception, and a revolution in every country of Europe with one possible exception." [35]

Members of the British delegation confirmed this diagnosis. According to Keynes, in early 1919 "Europe was in complete dependence on the food supplies of the United States; and financially she was even more absolutely at their mercy." In Nicolson's judgment this economic dependence made the Allies "entirely subservient to the dictates of Washington" and gave Wilson an "overwhelming force of compulsion." In retrospect, both Keynes and Nicolson recall that it never occurred to them that, "if need arose, Wilson would hesitate to use" America's economic and financial power, and both attribute this hesitancy to his having been a prophet instead of a man of power.[36]

In actual fact, the American delegation played a leading role in the formulation and implementation of diplomatically and politically intended economic policies toward Soviet Russia, bolshevik Hungary, the successor states, and the new regimes in Germany and Austria. But whereas Wilson readily used the economic weapon to strangle bolshevism, to support fledgling nations, and to stabilize the governments of the defeated nations, he hesitated to exert pressure on the Allies. This hesitation, however, was due to political considerations, both domestic and foreign, rather than to his prophetic disposition.

At home influential senators, the patriotic leagues, the jingoist press, and select interest groups mounted a campaign against the use of the economic weapon for a Wilsonian peace of the sort advocated by the European Left. To make matters worse, the three Allied premiers were well informed about this opposition and proposed to foster and harness it for their own purposes. By early December 1918 the London *Spectator* assured its readers that Wilson did not have the "least chance of getting any treaty ratified which was repugnant to the sentiments of the Republican party"; and that since the opinions of that party were "framed in unreserved support of Great Britain and France" the Allies could approach the Conference "with all confidence." [37] Within a month the Boston *Transcript* (independent Republican) hinted that since the Allied statesmen were familiar with the American opposition as well as with the American Constitution they might be "inclined to heed rather the view of the American majority than that of a President whose general policies had been discredited by the popular vote." [38] Meanwhile Senator Henry Cabot Lodge set out to encourage the Allied Carthaginians to join him in standing up to Wilson.[39]

As the *Springfield Republican* suggested, in order to "neutralize the influences working against him in his own country" the President would have "to rally sympathetic elements in Great Britain, France and Italy." [40] In fact, the Right on both sides of the Atlantic was apprehensive about the progressive *domestic* implications of a peace of reconciliation, just as the Left was nervous about the conservative domestic consequences of a vindictive settlement.

Radical publicists called attention to this political struggle "not between nations but between parties whose constituency transcended all national boundaries." For the purposes of peacemaking "the progressive wings of the American parties, British labor and liberals, French and Italian and Belgian liberals and socialists were one party; the Lodges and

Milners and Carsons and Clemenceaus and their following of imperialists and protectionists constituted the opposing party." [41] To be sure, radicals were blind to the broad popular support of the Right and crudely divided the political spectrum into two monolithic blocs. But except for these blind spots this characterization of the transnational political confrontation had considerable merit, not least because it acknowledged the inevitability of the politics of intervention. Frederick Jackson Turner quite rightly anticipated that the conservative forces of different nations were on the verge of cooperating internationally, in imitation of their socialist rivals. [42]

Theoretically the Right indignantly and violently objected to external intervention in the internal affairs of nations. In practice, however, it championed counterrevolutionary intervention in bolshevik countries and relied on informal transnational contacts elsewhere. Naturally Lenin and Karl Radek disdainfully rejected this principle of nonintervention in the internal affairs of other nations [43] and proceeded to devise organizational mechanisms with which to maximize the effectiveness of their predesigned interference abroad. Meanwhile, Wilson searched for political support for the material and ideological intervention for which he was so much better equipped than Lloyd George, Clemenceau, Orlando, and even Lenin.

As noted before, his supporters were in retreat in the United States as well as in Europe. In America *The New Republic, The Nation,* the League of Free Nations Society, the Committee of 48, segments of organized labor, and internationally minded businessmen and financiers were fighting a rear-guard battle against onrushing conservatives, super-patriots, and anti-communists. Simultaneously in the Allied nations the noncommunist Left and the radical bourgeoisie were in disarray. Perhaps this narrow political base at home and in the Allied countries accounts for Wilson's hesitancy to go over the heads of the Big Three. The hardening of opinion in his own country sensitized him to the hardening of opinion in London, Paris, and Rome. Moreover, quite apart from being careful not to encourage the revolutionary Left, Wilson was worried about weakening governments, including the Polish and Rumanian governments, that carried the brunt of the containment of and the intervention in Russia.

In sum, a frontal attack on the victory-hardened Allies, which socialists and radicals on both sides of the Atlantic urged upon the President, was not to be undertaken lightly. The task and responsibility would have been staggering, the risk immense—the more so for a statesman and politician sworn to reason rather than passion, to agreement by consent rather than coercion, to reform rather than revolution. The issue is hardly whether or not Wilson was sincere about his principles and aims; nor is the issue one of the quality of his strategic and tactical skills as diplomatist and politician. Even assuming Wilson scored exceptionally high on all these counts, a prior question must be considered: how pertinent and consequential was Wilson's reformist project in the crisis setting of 1918–1919?

Unlike Clemenceau, the President strained to understand this crisis in its world-historical context. Both he and Lloyd George consistently rejected the conspiratorial view of the Russian Revolution, which they saw as a variant of the French Revolution in scale, ecumenical appeal, and duration.

Wilson's concern was less with the importance of the revolution for Russia than for Europe and the world. He saw the example of the revolution, embellished by stirring manifestoes, acting upon crisis-torn societies which in the prewar years had been rife with discontent and agitated by revolutionary parties and ideologies. According to Isaiah Bowman, the President told his advisers on the S.S. *George Washington* that the poison of bolshevism was spreading because it was "a protest against the way in which the world had worked." [44] William Bullitt, who was present on this same occasion, recorded Wilson as saying that the only way he could "explain the susceptibility of the people of Europe to the poison of Bolshevism, was that their Governments had been run for wrong purposes." Wilson then added his prediction that unless the peace were made "on the highest principles of justice it would be swept away by the peoples of the world in less than a generation." In that event he intended "to run away and hide on the Island of Guam or somewhere else remote, for there would follow not mere conflict but cataclysm." [45] A bit later, when pleading with the Big Three for an accommodation with Lenin, he warned that "there was certainly a latent force behind Bolshevism which attracted as much sympathy as its more brutal aspects caused general disgust." Wilson attributed this sympathy to "a feeling of revolt throughout the world against large vested interests which influence the world both in the economic and in the political sphere." [46]

It was precisely because the Russian Revolution was "a menace to others" that Wilson was so reluctant to leave Russia to "settle her own affairs in her own way." [47] With the help and encouragement of his key advisers, notably of Herbert Hoover, Wilson spearheaded various Allied efforts to tame the Russian Revolution. In fact, these efforts came to be central to Wilson's overall peacemaking strategy.

Whereas the Entente governments tended to advocate either direct or indirect military intervention—with America providing most of the funds, the material, and the food supplies—the American delegation gave first priority to diplomatic, economic, and ideological intervention. Not that the Wilson administration backed out of or cut back the armed intervention started in mid-1918. Still, by comparison it was particularly intent on exploring those avenues that might obviate military measures partially or altogether. Of course this nonmartial approach suited Wilson's view of the dynamics of the Russian Revolution, his diplomatic style, and America's foreign policy capabilities.

Rather than denounce the Bolshevik Revolution as either a sinister conspiracy or a vile crime, Wilson saw it as the natural and fitting culmination of lingering popular dissatisfactions with the tsarist regime, catalyzed by the strains of war and enthusiasm for the seductive promises of the bolshevik ideology. Such dissatisfaction and ardor could not be conquered by force of arms, not least because a military onslaught threatened to restore the *ancien régime.* Clemenceau and, to a lesser extent, Lloyd George were not particularly bothered by the prospect of the Whites replacing Lenin, so that the irresolution of their intervention in the Russian civil war was not a function of political scruples but of overstrained resources and anti-interventionist pressures. Wilson, however, refused to close his eyes to the ideological and political aftergrowth of the destruction of the Soviet regime. The qualified recognition of Alexander Kolchak, which was delayed until late May 1919, mirrored his desperate but unrealistic and self-deceiving attempt to transform the unmistakably counterrevolutionary intervention into a crusade for the democratization of Russia. That even his worst fears were justified was amply demonstrated once the Allied-sponsored overthrow of Béla Kun was followed by a White terror and by anti-Semitic pogroms.

On the intellectual plane the President understood that revolution and counterrevolution inevitably incited and needed each other. In terms of policy, however, he simply could not admit the impossibility of a moderate middle course. Like it or not, America was one of the senior partners in a coalition resolved to contain or destroy the Bolshevik Revolution. To achieve this objective the Allies needed the military services of Finland, Poland, Rumania, and Germany, even at the price of allowing conservative and reactionary forces in these countries to benefit from this anti-bolshevik campaign.

It was to avoid paying this distasteful political price that the American delegates wanted to explore the use of nonmilitary methods of intervention. Their aim was to moderate and domesticate rather than destroy the revolutionary regime in Russia. In their judgment the ideological canons of bolshevism and the lust for power of the bolshevik leaders were not the primary moving force of the Soviet dictatorship. According to some American officials Lenin's iron rule at home and revolutionary agitation abroad were part of a *levée en masse* by a revolutionary government fighting for its life against internal insurgents and foreign invasion in a country bled white by war. Provided these mainsprings of revolutionary dictatorship were removed or reduced, the Soviet leaders could afford to relax their iron grip and agree to a united front of the Left for the reconstruction, modernization, and reform of Russia. The Allies could contribute to this relaxation of revolutionary discipline and terror not only by stopping their intervention and lifting the blockade but also by providing economic and technical assistance.

The Buckler-Litvinov conversations, the Prinkipo proposal, and the Bullitt mission were so many efforts in this direction. All alike were opposed and sabotaged by the entire French delegation, by key members of the American and British delegations, by anti-appeasement forces in the Allied parliaments, by all but one of the Russian *émigré* groups in Paris, by the Whites in Russia, and by the governments of most of the new states along Russia's western borders. Some were motivated by power-political considerations and others by age-old national hatreds, but all alike called forth and embodied counterrevolutionary economic, social, and political forces. There was no corresponding reservoir of support for moderation. Wilson knew this; and so did Lenin.

Chances for a negotiated accommodation were never very good. The Big Four, including Wilson, insisted on military conditions that were designed to favor the Whites and their borderland allies and sought to extract debilitating political concessions in exchange for lifting the blockade and providing food. In turn, Lenin was careful not to play any of his spare trumps, notably critical and advanced military positions and control of the railways. Whereas strictly territorial issues might have been compromised, mutual distrust stemming from irreconcilable political, economic, and social persuasions stood in the way of an overall settlement—at a time that both sides still hoped for total victory. Lenin was not about to trust Wilson, whom he righly suspected of being a prisoner—even if a reluctant prisoner—of the counterrevolution.

With the March-April crisis the Russian question once again became acute. The stand of the Right toward bolshevism both inside and outside Russia stiffened still further in the face of rising labor unrest in the Allied countries, renewed Spartacist outbreaks in Germany, the estab-lishment of a Soviet outpost in Bavaria, the triumph of Béla Kun in Hungary, and the explosive instability in Vienna. This rigidification was well under way when rumors of the Bullitt mission incited the die-hards to protest furiously against any dealings with Lenin and to urge stepped-up military measures.

Once again caught between the appeasers and the irreconcilables, Wilson abandoned a direct diplomatic approach in favor of an untried economic formula. The Nansen Plan for a commission of neutrals to feed Russia originated in the American delegation. At first, in order to broaden its ideological appeal, the letter drafted by Hoover for Fridtjof Nansen's signature was supposed to be countersigned by Karl Hjalmar Branting. But the leader of the Second International preferred to stay in the background. Under the Nansen scheme the Russian bolsheviks were asked to halt military operations "against our allies" on all fronts and to waive "political recognition or negotiation" in exchange for food and other essential supplies to be provided by a neutral relief agency. Obviously, the arrangements for the distribution in Russia of this "wholly non-political" relief would be decisive, primarily because their political implications were the crux of this proposal.

In fact, political rather than humanitarian purposes were at the heart of the Nansen Plan. This political design was forcefully sketched out by Hoover in a remarkable letter to President Wilson, dated March 28, 1919.[48]

In this letter Hoover brilliantly summarized the key tenets of the Wilsonian view of the bolshevik problem: Russian bolshevism was a condition to be cured rather than a conspiracy to be destroyed; there were considerable sources of bolshevik contagion outside Russia; the spiritual appeals of the bolshevik ideology were far from negligible; the reactionary consequences of a military crusade against bolshevism could not be ignored; and a military truce combined with economic aid was most likely to redirect the revolutionary currents into reformist channels in Russia.

But the letter also struck some novel chords. Above all, Hoover made an insidious comparison of the "foolishness" of bolshevik economic doctrines with the unequaled excellence of the American economic system. Moreover, he envisaged the possibility that doctrinally the bolsheviks were sworn to export their economic and political system, if need be even by force of arms. Without abandoning the view that the bolshevik system was primarily a product of historical conditions, Hoover now stressed the doctrinal sources of Soviet conduct.

As a result, while Hoover's policy recommendations dovetailed with Wilson's drive to give priority to nonmilitary intervention, they also embodied a new departure. Accordingly, Wilson was urged to couple his economic intervention with an ideological counteroffensive. Hoover wanted the President to issue a manifesto criticizing the doctrine, promise, and practice of bolshevism and setting forth the aims and methods of reformist and democratic capitalism. In other words, just as the recently completed crusade against the Central Powers had required and profited from the Fourteen Points, so this incipient crusade against the rival social-political system required an anti-bolshevik manifesto.

Even though Wilson successfully insisted on certain political assurances as a precondition for recognizing Kolchak, he never went on to issue a full-blown manifesto proclaiming the objectives of the Big Powers' participation in armed containment and intervention. Perhaps he never did so because he could at best be halfhearted about an operation whose carriers and objectives were too counterrevolutionary for his own liking. The words and principles of a Wilsonian pronounce-

ment would have been blatantly incompatible with the whole thrust of
the enterprise, thus making it that much easier for Lenin and his champions to expose the hypocrisy of the democratic-reformist ideology. A
declaration like that issued at Pillnitz against the French Revolution
would have been more appropriate, but Foch or Churchill, rather than
Wilson, would have had to formulate it.

It may well be that the democratization and moderation of the counterrevolutionary side in a civil war is a historical impossibility. In any case,
Wilson lacked the courage, the political support, and the diplomatic
leverage to force a credible effort for accommodation with Lenin; or,
failing this, to make the operation essentially *defensive*. The intervention
continued, with each participant's contribution determined by a variety
of factors—among them power capabilities, domestic political pressures,
national rivalries, and changing estimates of chances for the overthrow
of the bolshevik regime.

The military operations of this intervention impinged only occasionally
on the politics and diplomacy of peacemaking. On the other hand, precisely because peacemaking and the containment of bolshevism were so
tightly interlocked the one could never be separated from the other.
Once again it was Baker, the participant-historian of liberal persuasion,
who faced up to this dilemma.

> The effect of the Russian problem on the Paris Conference . . .
> was profound: Paris cannot be understood without Moscow. With-
> out ever being represented at Paris at all, the Bolsheviki and Bol-
> shevism were powerful elements at every turn. Russia played a more
> vital part at Paris than Prussia. For the Prussian idea had been
> utterly defeated, while the Russian idea was still rising in power.[49]

The revolution in Russia and the specter of revolution over liberated
and defeated Europe left its mark on the entire settlement. Still according to Baker, the President could not risk breaking up the Conference
because of "the need to hold the world steady, keep order and fight both
extremes—militarism on the one hand and Bolshevism on the other." [50]
This policy of caution benefited the counterrevolution more than it benefited the revolution. Wilson wound up giving his consent to a diplomatic
course that was decidedly right of center and not halfway between Foch
and Lenin, as Baker implied.

Thorstein Veblen was the first to note that the compact to reduce
Soviet Russia and contain bolshevism "was not written into the text of
the Treaty [but] may rather be said to have been the parchment upon
which that text was written." In his view this was the only objective that
the Big Four held in common. Veblen suggested, furthermore, that
Wilson's "apparent defeat . . . was not so much a defeat, but rather a
strategic alignment designed to compass what was indispensable, even

at some cost to his own prestige—the main consideration being the defeat of Bolshevism at any cost—so that a well-considered view of the President's share in the deliberations of the Conclave would credit him with insight, courage, facility, and tenacity of purpose. . . ." [51]

In order to appreciate the world-historical importance of the Paris Peace Conference, it is necessary to view it against the background of the extreme complexity of the international and domestic politics of 1918–1919. This complexity was due to the convergence of the end of the Great War with the start of the Bolshevik Revolution in Russia, the collapse of political authority in Eastern and Central Europe, the threat of revolution throughout defeated Europe, and the right-wing upsurge inside the victor nations. These unanticipated and unintended consequences of the war produced conditions of national and international disequilibrium that rendered this peacemaking task more extensive and more intricate than any previously on record. Moreover, the interplay of national and international politics reached unequaled intensity. As a result, more than ever before, peacemakers had to be politicians in addition to being diplomatists. Also, the opportunities, purposes, and instruments for intervention in the internal affairs of other states assumed unparalleled proportions.

The debates and decisions of the Conference cannot be studied, therefore, as if these new conditions had not existed. The analytic framework of conventional diplomatic history simply must be enlarged to accommodate the complexities of international relations in an age of mass and crisis politics, in an age of international civil war. Furthermore, its scope must be broadened in order to show the impact of the dialectic between revolution and counterrevolution on the national and international level upon the processes of diplomacy. Thirdly, diplomatic history must abandon its national or bilateral perspective in favor of a multilateral, comparative, and transnational approach.

In any event, only a comprehensive diplomatic history can explicate the politics and diplomacy of peacemaking after the Great War. Without slighting the customary personal jealousies, national rivalries, and security dilemmas at the Paris Conference table, it will then have in its purview the domestic politics in the participant nations, the specter of bolshevism, and the intervention in Russia. Moreover, this updated diplomatic history will note that while the Peace Conference was in session in Paris, the charter meeting of the Third International was held in Moscow, the precursors of German Nazism fought bolshevism through the Free Corps, Benito Mussolini scored his first fascist triumphs in Italy, and an awakening India provoked the British into the Amritsar massacre.

NOTES

1. Charles K. Webster, *The Congress of Vienna, 1814–1815* (London: G. Bell and Sons, 1945). Webster completed this handbook for the Historical Section of the Foreign Office in August 1918; it was first published in 1919. See also Pertinax: "L'Exemple du Congrès de Vienne," *Echo de Paris,* December 18, 1918.

2. Webster, "The Congress of Vienna 1814–15 and the Conference of Paris 1919: A Comparison of their Organization and Results," *The Historical Association Leaflet No. 56* (London, 1923), p. 2. See also Sir Ernest Satow, "Peacemaking Old and New," *The Cambridge Historical Journal,* I, No. 1 (1923), 23–60; and F. S. Marston, *The Peace Conference of 1919: Organization and Procedure* (London: Oxford, 1944), pp. 56–57.

3. See Rupert Wilkinson, *Gentlemanly Power: British Leadership and the Public School Tradition* (London: Oxford, 1964).

4. Woodrow Wilson, "The Variety and Unity of History," in Howard J. Rogers, ed., *Congress of Arts and Science: Universal Exposition, St. Louis, 1904* (Boston: Houghton Mifflin, 1906), II, 3–20.

5. *Papers Relating to the Foreign Relations of the United States: The Paris Peace Conference, 1919* (hereafter cited as *F.R., P.C., 1919*), III (January 28, 1919). 751, 753.

6. Pertinax, writing in *Echo de Paris,* November 16, 1918.

7. Guglielmo Ferrero, *Problems of Peace: From the Holy Alliance to the League of Nations* (New York: G. P. Putnam, 1919), pp. 260–262.

8. *The New Europe,* November 14, 1918, pp. 98–100.

9. Oswald Garrison Villard: "The Truth About the Peace Conference," *The Nation,* April 26, 1919, p. 647. This was Villard's first article after his return from Europe.

10. E. J. Dillon, *The Inside Story of the Peace Conference* (New York: Harper, 1920), p. 5. See also "The Scope of the Settlement," *The Nation,* November 23, 1918, p. 618.

11. H. G. Wells, *In the Fourth Year: Anticipations of a World Peace* (London: Chatto and Windus, 1918), p. 11.

12. See Henri Barbusse, *La Lueur dans l'abime: Ce que veut le Groupe Clarté* (Paris: Editions Clarté, 1920), pp. 5, 148.

13. Margaret I. Cole, ed., *Beatrice Webb's Diaries, 1912–1924* (London: Longmans, Green, 1952), pp. 133–134, entry of November 4, 1918.

14. Cited in David Hunter Miller, *My Diary at the Conference of Paris,* 21 vols. (privately printed; New York: Appeal Printing Company, 1924), III, 36.

15. Memorandum by Miller, dated November 21, 1918, cited in *F.R.,P.C.,1919,* I, 354–357.

16. Walter Lippmann, *The Political Scene: An Essay on the Victory of 1918* (New York: Holt, 1919), p. 31.

17. Wilson to Edward Mandell House, November 10, 1918, cited in *F.R.,P.C., 1919,* I, 128.

18. Cited in Miller, *Diary,* III, 36.

19. Ray Stannard Baker, *Woodrow Wilson and World Settlement,* 3 vols. (Garden City, N.Y.: Doubleday, Page, 1923), I, 102.

20. Harold Nicolson, *Peacemaking, 1919* (New York: Harcourt, Brace, 1939), p. 271.

21. Webster, "The Congress of Vienna 1814–15 and the Conference of Paris 1919," p. 6.

22. Baker, *World Settlement,* II, 365. Cf. André Tardieu, *La Paix* (Paris: Payot, 1921), pp. 118–19; Winston Churchill, *The Aftermath* (London: Macmillan,

1941), pp. 143–144; Nicolson, *Peacemaking,* pp. 117–18, 139; Paul Birdsall, *Versailles Twenty Years After* (New York: Reynal and Hitchcock, 1941), p. 57.

23. Churchill, *Aftermath,* p. 120. Cf. Satow, "Peacemaking Old and New," pp. 52–53.

24. Churchill, *Aftermath,* pp. 120–121.

25. Dillon, *Inside Story,* p. 99.

26. *Le Temps,* January 18, 1919.

27. Nicolson, *Peacemaking,* pp. 7, 63–65.

28. Webster, "The Congress of Vienna 1814–15 and the Conference of Paris 1919," pp. 8–9.

29. See Satow, "Peacemaking Old and New," p. 37, and H. W. V. Temperley, "Attempts at International Government in Europe: The Period of the Congress of Vienna (1814–25) and the Period Since the Treaty of Versailles (1919–22)," *Historical Association Leaflet No.* 56 (London, 1923), pp. 16–17.

30. Baker, *World Settlement,* II, 349.

31. George McFadden, representative of the War Trade Board in Europe, to Robert Lansing, November 9, 1918, cited in *F.R.,P.C.,1919,* II, 729–31.

32. Cited in *F.R.,P.C.,1919,* I, 1.

33. Cited in Charles Seymour, *The Intimate Papers of Colonel House,* 4 vols. (Boston: Houghton Mifflin, 1928), IV, 282.

34. House to Lansing, November 23, 1918, cited in *F.R.,P.C.,1919,* I, 170. See also Patrick Hurley to Wilson, December 12, 1918, cited in *F.R.,P.C.,1919,* II, 662.

35. Miller, *My Diary,* III, 259.

36. John Maynard Keynes, *The Economic Consequences of the Peace* (New York: Harcourt, Brace, 1920), pp. 38–39, and Nicolson, *Peacemaking,* pp. 41–42.

37. Cited in *The New Republic,* December 14, 1918, p. 176.

38. Cited in *The Literary Digest,* January 11, 1919, p. 10.

39. "I am sending you a copy of the speech which I made on Saturday [December 21, 1918, in Congress] which was intended chiefly for the benefit of the Allies." Lodge to Theodore Roosevelt, cited in Roger Burlingame and Alden Stevens, *Victory Without Peace* (New York: Harcourt, Brace, 1944), p. 204. See also Lodge's letter to Henry White on the eve of White's departure for Paris, cited in Allan Nevins, *Henry White* (New York: Harcourt, Brace, 1944), p. 172.

40. *Springfield Republican,* December 15, 1918; forwarded by Tumulty to Wilson, December 17, 1918, in Wilson Papers, VIII A:3.

41. *The New Republic,* December 21, 1918, p. 212. By March 21, 1919, in discussing the outburst of Republican opposition to Wilson, the *Daily News* (London) commented that "the lines of division today run not perpendicularly between nations, but horizontally through nations."

42. Frederick Jackson Turner, "International Political Parties in a Durable League of Nations" (November 1918), in Ray Stannard Baker Papers, Firestone Library, Princeton University.

43. "This principle of non-intervention was the principle which guided legitimist Europe after the Congress of Vienna, while in the struggle for liberation, international Communists all along advocated the energetic intervention in the affairs of the whole world." Karl Radek, *Ein offener Brief an Philipp Scheidemann* (*c.* November 20, 1918; w.p.), pp. 2–3.

44. Cited in Seymour, *Intimate Papers,* IV, 282.

45. Bullitt's diary notes on the S.S. *George Washington,* entry of December 9, 1918, in Bullitt Papers.

46. *F.R.,P.C.,1919,* III (January 16, 1919, a.m.), 583.

47. In late December Wilson told a British official that "Russia should be left to settle her own affairs in her own way so long as she did not become a menace to others." Notes on interview with Wilson by Frank Worthington, Deputy Chief

Censor, dated December 28, 1918, National Archives, Secret File, Document 811.001W/163.

48. The full text of this letter is in the House Papers, 10:37; excerpts are cited in Herbert Hoover, *The Ordeal of Woodrow Wilson* (New York: McGraw-Hill, 1958), pp. 117–119. (The original version of Mr. Mayer's article contains an extensive quotation from the Hoover letter, here omitted for reasons of space. EDITOR.)

49. Baker, *World Settlement*, II, 64.

50. *Ibid.*

51. See Veblen's review of Keynes, *The Economic Consequences of the Peace*, first published in the *Political Science Quarterly*, September 1920, and reprinted in Leon Ardzrooni, ed., *Thorstein Veblen: Essays in Our Changing Order* (New York: Viking, 1934), pp. 462–470.

HANS W. GATZKE

Russo-German Military Collaboration During the Weimar Republic

The Weimar Republic and the Soviet Union seemed predestined for close relations. Not only had Germany and Russia been traditionally friendly, World War I notwithstanding, but their fate in that war had created a "community of fate" between these two outcasts from the European family of nations. The agreement which they concluded at Rapallo in 1922 was thus suspected in the West of being an alliance, rather than merely a treaty of friendship. There were Germans who hoped that some day it might become such, and there were others who expected great economic advantages from it. But these hopes, kept alive by the Treaty of Berlin in 1926, were disappointed. The main obstacle to real friendship was communism. Only in the military sphere did the two achieve a degree of partnership. The fact that this partnership violated the terms of Versailles gave it a special significance.

The author of this chapter and editor of this volume is Professor of History at Yale. Among his books are Germany's Drive to the West: A Study of Germany's Western War Aims During the First World War *(Baltimore, 1950);* Stresemann and the Rearmament of Germany *(Baltimore, 1954); and* The Present in Perspective *(Chicago, 1965). This article first appeared in the* American Historical Review, LXIII, No. 3 *(April 1958), 565–597.*

Few chapters in the history of the Weimar Republic have aroused as much interest among publicists and historians as the secret relations between the Reichswehr and the Red Army.[1] Yet until recently, very little reliable information has been available on this important subject. Only since World War II has sufficient material become available to establish, beyond mere conjecture, the main facts of these Russo-German activities. The most important of these new sources are the papers of General Hans von Seeckt [2] and the reminiscences of some of the German officers who participated in these dealings.[3] These sources are not very extensive, and the hope that they may some day be supplemented by information from German Army records will probably prove vain, since most of the documents pertaining to Russo-German military relations were "regularly and systematically" destroyed.[4] Nor does it seem likely that the Russians will make any revelations about their own share in these top secret operations.

This paucity of evidence, however, has been somewhat relieved by the recent opening to research of most of the documents of the German Foreign Ministry for the Weimar period.[5] It may seem surprising that these documents should contain any information on so secret a subject, because it has been generally accepted that the *Auswärtiges Amt,* while aware of the Reichswehr's affairs, knew very little about their details.[6] But the materials we shall examine here will prove otherwise. Not only do they throw new light on the role of Germany's civilian authorities in these secret relations, but they also confirm, correct, and supplement what information we already have. It is not proposed here to retrace in detail the whole course of Russo-German military collaboration, but rather to integrate these new materials into the story as it has been known thus far.

We still know very little about the beginnings of this collaboration, and the new documents do not add very much to our knowledge.[7] The first contacts between the German military and the Soviets apparently took place during the second half of 1919 and are closely associated with the name of Karl Radek. As Russian delegate to the founding congress of the German Communist party, Radek had been arrested in connection with the Spartacus Rebellion in February 1919.[8] In a letter of March 11, 1919, addressed to the journalist Alfons Paquet, Radek expressed fear for his life and asked to be put in touch with Major von Schubert, formerly German military attaché in Russia and soon to be active in Russo-German military negotiations. "A military person," Radek added, "can be more helpful in these matters than anyone else." [9] It may have been due to Schubert's efforts that Radek, apparently in August 1919, was transferred to less restricted quarters and was permitted to receive visitors. It was during the discussions that Radek held in his "political salon" that the idea of Russo-German collaboration, economic and perhaps military, was first broached, but it was to be some time before these vague feelers grew into specific negotiations. General von Seeckt, despite undoubted interest in some arrangement with the Soviet Union, seems to have steered clear of any direct contact with the Russians until after the latter had been defeated by Poland in the summer of 1920.[10] At that time, in August 1920, the Russians used Seeckt's friend Enver Pasha to sound out the head of the Reichswehr about possible military collaboration. It may be assumed, however, that prior to that time contact had been established between the lower echelons of the two armies. This seems indicated from a letter by Baron von Maltzan (leading exponent in the *Ostabteilung* of the Foreign Ministry of a Russo-German *rapprochement*), in which he stated that Germany had established contact (*Tuchfühlung*) with the Soviet army during the Russo-Polish war.[11]

The first concrete negotiations concerning Russo-German military collaboration, according to present information, took place during 1921. We need not here review in detail the sketchy facts that have become known about these talks.[12] It is sufficient to say that by early 1921 a special section devoted to Russian affairs had been set up in the Reichswehr Ministry (the *Sondergruppe R*), and in the spring of that year conversations were begun between members of the Reichswehr (von Niedermayer, Tschunke, von Schubert, von Schleicher, Hasse, and occasionally von Seeckt) and Russian representatives (Kopp, Krassin, Karakhan, Radek, and others). The purpose of these negotiations was to reach some agreement by which Germany would provide financial and technical aid in building up Russia's armament industry (with possible concessions to German firms such as Junkers and Krupp) and obtain from Russia the necessary artillery ammunition that she was prohibited from manufacturing under the Treaty of Versailles.[13] The initial discussions, on the German side, were entirely under military direction, but the German chancellor, Joseph Wirth, was kept informed and gave his blessing, without, however, initiating his cabinet or President Ebert into these military secrets.[14] Baron von Maltzan tells of being consulted, some time before September 1921, by Wirth and two leading members of the Reichswehr, about these Russo-German negotiations. These developments, in Maltzan's opinion, were "clearly in the interest of Russo-German policy," but neither the Foreign Ministry nor the German representative in Moscow should become involved in their technical details. He did insist, however, that the Foreign Ministry be kept informed of the general trends in Russo-German military collaboration, "in order to coordinate these with possible developments (*Nuancierungen*) in our relations with Russia." When Germany's first *chargé d'affaires*, the economist Wiedenfeld, went to Moscow in September 1921, he was told by Maltzan that military negotiations were under way but that he was not to get involved in them. According to Maltzan, all future foreign ministers and ministers of finance were briefed about the Reichswehr's Russian operations by their predecessors and by the Reichswehr Ministry.[15]

Germany's negotiations with Russia, however, were not restricted to the military field. There were parallel talks on economic and political matters as well. The world received a startling revelation of how far the Russo-German *rapprochement* had gone when the two powers concluded the Treaty of Rapallo on April 16, 1922. Although it was ostensibly primarily an economic agreement, there could be no doubt about the treaty's political significance. Furthermore, almost from the start there were rumors that the agreement also contained secret military clauses.[16] A study of the German documents, however, does not bear out this suspicion.[17] There actually was a secret exchange of notes, but it dealt with economic matters.[18] On the other hand, there is evidence that the Germany military, in their simultaneous negotiations with Russia, were going far beyond what their government was ready to concede. According to Maltzan, Foreign Commissar Chicherin, on the eve of Rapallo, told Chancellor Wirth about "the promises which Herr N. [Niedermayer] had made in the name of the Chancellor to him, Chicherin." These proposals considerably exceeded the terms agreed on earlier between Wirth and the Reichswehr. "Wirth," Maltzan adds, "was extremely annoyed and in my presence corrected the statements which Herr N. had made to Chicherin." [19]

As this incident shows, the Reichswehr in 1922 was still pursuing a virtually independent course in its negotiations with Soviet authorities. According to Brockdorff-Rantzau, first German ambassador to Moscow after Rapallo, "the military authorities, until November 1922, proceeded on their own in Moscow and Niedermayer presented the Russians with fantastic plans which they at first took seriously, but which subsequently were recognized as impossible." [20] To correct this dualism in German policy and to supervise the Reichswehr's dealings with the Soviet Union became one of the foremost tasks of the new ambassador.

Count Brockdorff-Rantzau, one of the outstanding political talents of the Weimar Republic, was one of the most decisive influences in Russo-German relations during the twenties.[21] His attitude toward the Soviet Union had already undergone several changes since the end of the war. Prior to the Treaty of Versailles, the Count had opposed any one-sided German alignment with the West against Russia or with Russia against the West.[22] Under the impact of the harsh terms of Versailles, however, Rantzau had abandoned his opposition to any Russo-German *rapprochement*. While fully aware of the dangers of Bolshevism, he felt that these were less of an evil "than the consequences of the undignified helotism into which our vengeful and rapacious enemies have forced us for generations to come." [23] To initiate economic and political relations with the Russians, Brockdorff-Rantzau, in 1920 and again in 1921, had proposed to head a German mission to Moscow. Yet nothing came of his plan.[24] Throughout this period he was in close contact with Maltzan, who was preparing the ground for what ultimately bore fruit at Rapallo.[25] The Treaty of Rapallo, however, much as it reflected Brockdorff-Rantzau's own desire for a *rapprochement* with Russia, by no means met with his full approval. He felt that both the time and the method of the negotiations had been unfortunate.[26] Yet when he was offered the ambassadorship by President Ebert in May 1922, he admitted that the treaty might be a "turning point" in Germany's foreign policy, and under certain conditions he was ready to accept the appointment.[27]

It was during the summer of 1922, when confirmation of his appointment was still pending, that Brockdorff-Rantzau first became fully aware of the relations that had grown up between the Reichswehr and Russia. They were brought to his attention by Chancellor Wirth, and they immediately met with his opposition.[28] Much as he considered himself an "apostle of revenge" against the West, Rantzau opposed a military alliance with Russia as premature and dangerous, since it would lead to the isolation of Germany and her dependence upon the Soviet Union. The controversy that developed over this issue, especially between Rantzau and Seeckt, almost prevented the former's going to Moscow.[29] Only after he received the necessary assurances that no military agreements would be concluded with the Russians behind his back did Brockdorff-Rantzau accept his assignment. A formal reconciliation with Seeckt took place in January 1923, at which time, according to Rantzau, "agreement of our views on all important questions was established."[30]

But the army did not keep its promise of fully informing the ambassador about its dealings with the Russians. At the time Rantzau took over his post, the talks that had begun in 1921 had not as yet led to any firm agreement. In December 1922, therefore, the Russians asked that a leading member of the Reichswehr be entrusted with the negotiations,[31] and in February 1923 General Otto Hasse, chief of the *Truppenamt* (General Staff), headed a military mission to Moscow. Brockdorff-Rantzau was informed of Hasse's appointment but did not participate in the negotiations. "As far as I can see," he complained in a letter to Foreign Minister von Rosenberg, "the military are again conducting their arbitrary policy. You know what I want! In the final analysis I have the same aim as the military. But I do not want to have the direction of things taken out of my hands and to have my policy upset. Radek told me recently: 'The fault of the Germans is that they cannot wait.' The man is right. The few among us who can wait and who know what they want should restrain their premature ambitions."[32] Hasse, Rantzau added, had actually spoken of the "great war of liberation" which could be expected "in three to five years." If any of this leaks out, the Count concluded, "it may ruin the Reich." There was a good chance for such a leak, since Hasse had committed the blunder of writing an "extremely compromising" letter to the chief Russian negotiator, Rozengolts, which the Soviets might have used to blackmail Germany.[33]

The Hasse mission failed, partly because its leader was not the most adroit of negotiators, partly because Trotsky, who was commissar of war, became ill at the time.[34] To continue the negotiations, which Chicherin termed "decisive for the future relations of Russia to Germany,"[35] a second mission was sent in late April 1923, under Lieutenant Colonel Mentzel and Major Tschunke. "I told the leader, when he called on me," Rantzau wrote to Maltzan on April 28, 1923, "that I am the head of the house here, and that I wish to be kept regularly informed about the progress of negotiations."[36] Two weeks later, Rantzau wrote: "Morsbach [Mentzel] is doubtless of better caliber than the impossible Heller [Hasse] and has achieved certain results."[37] But soon again he complained that Mentzel had failed to tell him "about several important points" and had been much too hasty in his dealings with the Russians, offering them thirty-five million goldmarks without getting anything in return. This German eagerness, Rantzau felt, was unnecessary, since the Russians "need us more than we need them."[38]

This latter fact seemed borne out as the Russians kept urging that the tentative arrangement reached with Mentzel be made more definite.[39] In late June, the Reichswehr and the Foreign Ministry agreed among themselves "to continue and extend the existing business," that is, the military relations with Russia.[40] A few days later, Chancellor Cuno met with Minister of Finance Hermes, Minister of Reconstruction Albert, and Secretary of State Maltzan to discuss the financing of the Russian undertakings, about the importance of which there seemed to be general agreement.[41] To meet Russia's requests for some more definite understanding, Brockdorff-Rantzau now suggested that a Soviet delegate be invited to Berlin.[42] The Russians hesitated at first to accept the invitation, since they were not told what exactly was to be discussed at the meeting and since the Reichswehr tried to discourage their visit.[43] Finally, on July 22, 1923, Rozengolts (or Raschin)[44] arrived in Berlin, and a week later he met with Germany's top civilian officials.

Prior to this meeting, Brockdorff-Rantzau drew up a memorandum for Chancellor Cuno in which he stated his views on the military question. "The basic idea behind Chancellor Wirth's Russian policy," Rantzau wrote, "was sound. But its execution was muddled and therefore a failure." In a desire "not to burden the government with the responsibility for the negotiations," Wirth had not kept well enough informed about the Reichswehr's negotiations, thus permitting the latter to embark on schemes which were far more advantageous to Russia than to Germany. In the meantime, Brockdorff-Rantzau continued, the negotiations had taken on political significance and therefore should now be conducted by political rather than military authorities. For the future the Count proposed "not only to continue but to extend the existing collaboration, but only on certain military-technical and political conditions." There was to be a virtual German monopoly in those Russian armament firms that received German aid, so that no other power could invest in these works and no foreign nationals other than Germans could be employed in them. About political conditions, Brockdorff-Rantzau said: "There can be no question of a political or military alliance. But we should try to secure ourselves against the most dangerous eventuality, an attack by Poland." Since Poland would not dare launch such an attack without the aid of France, "such an arrangement would also indirectly protect us against a French attack." These conditions, Rantzau felt, could be obtained, "since in the first place Russia needs us for the reconstruction of her armaments industry, and needs us urgently, because she can find no other power for that purpose; and in the second place, since a successful attack by Poland against Germany, strengthening Poland, would be so dangerous to Russia that she will have a vital interest in preventing such a development." [45]

As this memorandum shows, Brockdorff-Rantzau was no longer opposed to Germany's military policy in Russia. As he had said earlier, his aims were actually the same as those of the Reichswehr. He merely differed in his methods. By being less eager, he felt, Germany could gain greater concessions from the Russians, not only militarily but politically. It was as an aid to his political plans that Brockdorff-Rantzau valued and supported the military ties being developed by the Reichswehr. But how did he envisage Germany's relations with Russia, if he did not want a military or political alliance? An earlier memorandum, written before he went to Moscow, gives the answer.[46] "The immediate aim of our policy," Rantzau had written in August 1922, "must be to get a Russian pledge to come to our aid in case of an Allied attack against Germany's frontiers." Such a pledge, the Count felt, was not a military alliance but a mere defensive agreement, which could be easily explained away in case its existence became known abroad. In return for such a concession, Germany would aid in the military and economic reconstruction of Russia. Yet "the promotion of Russia's military strength," Brockdorff-Rantzau concluded, "must only go so far as is necessary to keep Poland and the Little Entente in check and to aid a development toward the East (India)." [47]

These, then, were the aims of Brockdorff-Rantzau and of Chancellor Cuno in their negotiations with Rozengolts. The meeting with the Russians (Rozengolts, Krestinsky, and Ustinov) took place in utmost secrecy on July 30, 1923, at the apartment of Count Ernst Rantzau, Brockdorff-Rantzau's brother.[48] It lasted for almost three hours, and its tone was "informal and amicable." Cuno began by relating how, as director of the Hamburg-America Line, he had been one of the first to advocate close economic ties with the Soviet Union. He then stated the two conditions which Brockdorff-Rantzau had outlined in his memorandum the previous day—a special position for Germany in the development of Russia's military industry and some form of protection for Germany against attack, especially from Poland. Rozengolts criticized Germany for not doing enough on her own to prepare for such an attack,[49] but Cuno pointed out that Germany "had to avoid giving the impression of preparing for a war of revenge. The more inconspicuous the preparations were made, the more advantageous they were." He added "that more was being done to repel an enemy attack than was known even in initiated circles." Rozengolts on the whole seems to have reacted favorably to Cuno's proposals, and he promised a written reply from his government. A tentative plan covering the expansion of Russia's armament industry and the production of war material for Germany was subsequently agreed upon between the Reichswehr and Rozengolts. The negotiations were to be concluded by Brockdorff-Rantzau in Moscow.

The Count himself was thoroughly satisfied with the results of the meeting. The fact that the Russians had come to Berlin and had promised to make written counterproposals relieved Germany of the sole onus in case the negotiations should become known outside. Furthermore, the program for Russo-German military collaboration had now been combined with political conditions which, if they were not honored by the Russians, could serve as an excuse for withdrawing Germany's military aid.[50] The next step was to provide the necessary funds for the undertakings. The sum of thirty-five million goldmarks which Mentzel had promised the Russians was no longer considered adequate and was now raised to seventy-five million. It took a series of meetings between government officials, Reichswehr members, and industrialists before this increased amount was appropriated. At one point Brockdorff-Rantzau threatened that he would "refuse to accept responsibility for the political relations between Germany and Russia" if the money was not granted, whereupon the president of the Reichsbank, Havenstein, agreed to the additional amount, which seriously strained the resources of the Reich.[51]

By the time Brockdorff-Rantzau was ready to return to Moscow, therefore, chances for a far-reaching Russo-German agreement on military and political matters seemed promising indeed. But at this point, several things went wrong. On the eve of his departure, Rantzau paid a call on President Ebert and on Stresemann, the latter having recently succeeded Cuno as chancellor. Both men, it turned out, were deeply opposed to any kind of military deal with the Soviet Union and asked that any German collaboration with Russia be restricted entirely to economic matters.[52] In view of such new directives from his superiors, Brockdorff-Rantzau, upon his return to Moscow, did not seriously press the terms that had been discussed with Rozengolts. When Radek promised him an early Russian reply to Germany's proposals, the Count treated the whole matter as "academic." This sudden German coolness naturally irritated Radek. "You cannot expect," he exclaimed, "that for the measly millions you offer us, we shall undertake any one-sided political obligation. As for the monopoly you demand for German industry, we have not the slightest intention of granting it. On the contrary, we take everything military we need wherever we can find it. Thus we have bought airplanes from France and will also get some from England." [53] Rantzau's calculation that the Russians needed Germany more than Germany needed Russia thus seemed to be overly optimistic.

To confuse matters still further, the German military, despite instructions that future negotiations were to be carried on solely by Brockdorff-Rantzau, had resumed their direct talks with the Russians even before the Count's return. On August 22, a delegation consisting of "Direktor Eckhardt, Direktor Fritz Teichmann (Gesellschaft zur Förderung gewerblicher Unternehmungen G.m.b.H.), Direktor Freiherr von Hagen (Chemische Werke Stolzenberg, Hamburg), [and] Professor Egon Graf" arrived in Moscow.[54] Maltzan had warned the German *chargé d'affaires* to tell the delegation "not to enter into any binding agreements before the return of the ambassador," [55] but this, apparently, did not keep the military from pursuing their usual independent tactics.

By this time, the Reichswehr had established its own headquarters in Moscow, the *Zentrale Moskau* or *Z. Mo.*[56] There had already been a heated debate with Brockdorff-Rantzau over the appointment of a chief Reichswehr representative in Russia. The ambassador's choice was Major Fischer of the *Sondergruppe R,* whom he had known during the Versailles negotiations and whom he valued as experienced and tactful.[57] Instead, the Reichswehr insisted on either Tschunke or Niedermayer, neither of whom Rantzau liked.[58] Yet both Tschunke and Niedermayer appeared in Russia in the fall of 1923, and while Rantzau managed to get on with Tschunke, he was deeply suspicious of Niedermayer, whom he considered a "fantastic and unscrupulous adventurer." [59] The Reichswehr, however, by "retiring" Niedermayer and insisting that he had become "older and quieter" since his debut in Russia in 1921, was able to keep him in Moscow.[60] Yet it seems to have been Tschunke who at first functioned as the Reichswehr's chief representative in Russia. The ultimate head of the *Zentrale Moskau,* Colonel von der Lieth-Thomsen, was at this time still in Berlin, although he did visit Russia in October 1923 and March 1924 "to inspect, with Rozengolts' permission, Russia's air-force and aircraft industry." [61]

Because of Ebert's and Stresemann's opposition to any military dealings with Russia, and in order to stop the Reichswehr's independent negotiations, Brockdorff-Rantzau, in February 1924, suggested that Germany drastically curtail her Russian activities. "I urgently recommend," he wrote to Stresemann, who was now foreign minister, "not to spend a penny of German money for war materials in Russia, to limit all orders to a minimum and to use the credits granted by the Reich to support German industries in Russia, not for military purposes, but industries that indirectly serve rearmament and that, in case of need, can be transformed into war industries." A draft agreement, Rantzau added, which a certain "Herr Brown" was just then bringing from Berlin, seemed to fit the above requirements.[62] When Brown got to Moscow, he found that the military had already entered into such "careless and catastrophic" agreements and had so committed Germany, that, according to Brockdorff-Rantzau, "we cannot suddenly abandon this whole project without seriously endangering our political relations with Russia." There was some hope, Rantzau added, that the Reichswehr members might disagree among themselves over the Russian business and the "gentlemen of the *Fachministerium* might thus counteract and neutralize each other." [63]

The fact that there was disagreement not only between Reichswehr and Foreign Ministry but even within the Reichswehr itself came to light in a heart-to-heart talk between Brockdorff-Rantzau and Niedermayer. Like nothing else, it showed the confusion which reigned in Russo-German military relations. Niedermayer apparently had tried for some time to see the ambassador, in order to iron out some of their differences. Rantzau complained about Niedermayer's past blunders, including the "Neumann coals," [64] but Niedermayer insisted that everything he had done had been on instructions from his superiors, who then had left him in the lurch. "As a soldier his hands were tied, and there were many things he could not speak about." But now he was ready to act, if need be, against his superiors, "to keep the guilty from doing any more harm." According to Niedermayer "the agreements which thus far had been concluded were so catastrophic that in his opinion Herr von S. [Seeckt] would have to contact the foreign minister personally" to save the situation. The main fault, Niedermayer said, lay with Mentzel, Tschunke, and Eckhardt, and he added: "The sad part is that some gentlemen have acted from motives of personal ambition, and in an attempt to conclude treaties at all cost, have committed themselves to the Russians in the most irresponsible way." Rantzau, who recognized Niedermayer's good intentions in thus turning against his comrades and superiors, replied that he wanted to avoid a major showdown. The best solution, he said, would be to annul the agreements with Russia. Since for political reasons that could not be done, some way had to be found to change the existing military collaboration gradually into a primarily economic one.[65]

There is no evidence that Brockdorff-Rantzau's aim to deemphasize the Reichswehr's dealings with Russia had any success. It seems that the commitments which the army had already made were such that they could not be abandoned without harmful political repercussions. And as the Foreign Ministry under the direction of Stresemann and Secretary of State von Schubert (who had succeeded Maltzan) now gradually embarked on its *rapprochement* with the West, the military wire between Berlin and Moscow assumed new importance, especially to those who, like Brockdorff-Rantzau, advocated an eastern orientation of German foreign policy.[66]

How far exactly the military contacts between Germany and Russia had developed by this time is difficult to say. By the middle of 1924, the Gesellschaft zur Förderung gewerblicher Unternehmungen G.m.b.H., or Gefu, an organization established by the Reichswehr in Berlin to direct its military-industrial relations with Russia, and the Z. Mo. in Moscow certainly were going concerns, as were the Junkers, Stolzenberg, and Krupp concessions in various parts of Russia.[67] Prior to 1925, Russo-German military collaboration consisted almost exclusively of industrial production for military purposes, with Germany supplying financial and technical aid and in some cases establishing German firms on Russian soil. But this form of collaboration, it seems, had not been very successful. Beginning in 1924, therefore, Germany embarked on a new round of activities in the Soviet Union, concerned not so much with the production but with the testing of war materials and with the training of German military personnel in the use of weapons and equipment forbidden under the Treaty of Versailles.[68] Ultimately the Reichswehr operated three such experimental and training stations in Russia; Lipetsk (airplanes), Saratov (gas), and Kazan (tanks).[69] This innovation, however, did not mean that the military collaboration in the industrial field was abandoned. In early 1926 the *Gefu* was dissolved (apparently because it had never worked too well and had misused its funds for financial speculations in Holland),[70] and its activities were taken over by a new body, the *Wirtschaftskontor*, or *Wiko*.[71]

As for the relations between the Moscow embassy and the *Zentrale Moskau*, the talk between Brockdorff-Rantzau and Niedermayer seemed to have cleared the air; with the assignment of Colonel Thomsen to duty in Moscow (probably in May 1924), relations became quite cordial.[72] In a letter to Brockdorff-Rantzau in 1926, Thomsen speaks of the ambassador as "Germany's most important man" and blesses his own good fortune for having won Rantzau's confidence and for having been trained in "the school of his thoughts and decisions."[73] The improved relations between embassy and Z. Mo. manifested themselves in several ways. While in the past the communications between Z. Mo. and *Gefu* had been via the *Narkomindel* and Russian couriers[74] (since the Reichswehr was afraid that the Foreign Ministry would open and read its letters), the Reichswehr now used the courier and code services of the Moscow embassy, so that all routine communications between Z. Mo. and the Reichswehr Ministry became known to the embassy and the Foreign Ministry.[75] In addition, Rantzau now began taking a hand himself in Germany's military dealings with Russia. When there was danger, in April 1924, of Junkers abandoning its Russian subsidiary because neither the Reichswehr nor Russia was buying enough of its planes, Rantzau intervened and told Berlin that the liquidation of Junkers' Russian interests "must be avoided at all cost." [76] A few weeks later the ambassador brought the matter to Trotsky's personal attention, complaining that Russia appeared rather lukewarm in her military dealings with Germany.[77]

While the ambassador thus showed himself an able advocate of the Reichswehr's interests, direct contacts between Reichswehr and Red Army continued. In June 1924, Major Fischer, Captain Vogt, and Colonel Thomsen conferred with Rozengolts about sending ten German fliers to the Soviet Union.[78] In January 1925, Rozengolts visited Berlin to negotiate with General Hasse.[79] In July 1925, Secretary of State von Schubert informed Brockdorff-Rantzau that a delegation of German officers in mufti was planning to participate in the Red Army's maneuvers the following month and that in return several high-ranking Russian officers, camouflaged as "Bulgarians," were to visit the Reichswehr's fall maneuvers.[80] Rantzau was none too enthusiastic about these visits, since the news might leak out, especially since the Russians seemed less interested in secrecy than the Germans. Yet he also realized that the exchange might "help the political relations between the two countries." He added: "It would be utopian, however, to hope that this collaboration might have any effect upon the often mentioned 'common war aim' " (a reference to possible joint Russo-Germain action against Poland).[81] A subsequent report from the Reichswehr delegation itself told of the friendly reception it had found in Russia: "Greatest assistance in every respect, unhampered access to all installations and operations. Personal relations extremely polite. . . ." [82]

Even though relations between the embassy and the Zentrale Moskau had improved, they still were far from what they might have been. What was still more important, neither military nor civilian negotiators had thus far been able to derive any political benefits from Germany's military dealings with Russia. To be sure, the Russians, beginning in December, 1924, had dropped hints about a military alliance with Germany,[83] but Rantzau persisted in his opposition to anything so far-reaching. What he wanted was a political agreement that would serve as a counterweight to Germany's growing involvement with the West and at the same time might be used to put pressure on Poland. In January 1926, the ambassador once again criticized Germany's Russian policy. "The collaboration in military reconstruction," he wrote, "according to leading Russian government circles, constitutes the most important link between Germany and the Soviet Union. Yet in its present form this collaboration, unfortunately, has brought no *political* advantages worth mentioning to *us*. The reason is that the negotiations which the German military have conducted with Russia have been carried on without sufficient contact with Germany's leading political figures." He himself, Rantzau charged, "had *never* been reliably informed about the actual status of the negotiations" and thus could not obtain the political and economic advantages he hoped to get from Russia in return for military concessions. To clear up this area of conflict between Reichswehr and civilian authorities, Rantzau demanded that the Reichswehr be prevented from maintaining direct relations with Soviet politicians, that a single representative of the Reichswehr (Colonel von der Lieth-Thomsen) be appointed in Russia, who should be responsible to the ambassador, and that the ambassador be given exclusive control over German funds to be spent for military purposes in the Soviet Union. This last point was the only guarantee, Rantzau felt, that these funds would be used not merely for the military strengthening of Russia but to procure war materials for Germany.[84]

Brockdorff-Rantzau, however, did not get very far with his suggestions. At that moment Germany was actually on the verge of concluding a neutrality agreement with Russia; it was signed in Berlin on April 24, 1926.[85] While the final negotiations were still under way, a Russian mission, headed by Vice Commissar of War Unshlikht, visited Berlin.[86] At a luncheon given by Soviet ambassador Krestinsky and attended by Chancellor Luther, Stresemann, Schubert, Seeckt, and General Wetzell, Unshlikht told of vast Russian plans for the production of heavy artillery, poison gas, and precision instruments. For this, he said, Russia needed Germany's financial support and guarantees that Germany would buy a certain share of her military products. In return Germany might send officers to be trained at these new industrial centers. The German civilians, it seems, were quite stunned by these sudden overtures. The chancellor replied that Germany, of course, was ready to collaborate with Russia "in all projects of peace," but he did not comment any further or show any approval of Unshlikht's proposals. "The Russians," one of the participants commented afterward, "kept talking about armaments, while we kept talking about other things." This did not seem to faze Unshlikht. He had already discussed this matter with the Reichswehr, he said, and merely wanted the government's reaction. Seeckt remained silent throughout.[87]

Here, then, the Reichswehr had again embarked on a venture without consulting its civilian colleagues. What was the government to do? In the draft of a letter to Brockdorff-Rantzau, Secretary of the State Schubert discussed the pros and cons of the Unshlikht plan. Its advantages, both military and political, were obvious, since it would give Germany a hold over Russia that might be used to influence the latter's relations with France and Poland. Yet there were also important disadvantages. If such a venture became known, Schubert wrote, "we would lose all our political credit in the world." Germany's military dealings with Russia in the past "could be explained and excused on the basis of our political situation after Versailles. But an extension of our activities at this point, between Locarno and Geneva [i.e., Germany's entry into the League] would be judged a great deal more harshly." On balance, therefore, Schubert and Stresemann felt "that to pursue this project cannot be reconciled with the general lines of our policy." [88]

As this and earlier statements show, much of the government's attitude toward the Reichswehr's relations with Russia was determined by an ever-present fear that the rest of the world might find out about the clandestine dealings, leaving Germany isolated and entirely dependent upon the Soviet Union. The Reichswehr, on the other hand, seems to have been much less worried about such a possibility. In the summer of 1926, an exchange of political prisoners was being discussed between Germany and Russia, as a friendly gesture connected with the Treaty of Berlin.[89] At one point the negotiations threatened to break down over a certain Skoblevsky, a Soviet citizen, who had been convicted in Germany for plotting the assassination of several leading citizens, including General von Seeckt.[90] The Russians were very eager to secure the release of this top agent, but the Germans refused to free so dangerous a criminal. Brockdorff-Rantzau, in an urgent letter to Stresemann, pointed out that such refusal might have the most serious consequences. The Russians, he wrote, would probably act with "ruthless brutality," revealing to the world their military agreements with Germany. "I have emphasized more than once," he warned, "that we are in the hands of political blackmailers." [91] Most of the cabinet, under Rantzau's pressure, gradually came around to his views. Only Reichswehrminister Gessler, supported by Colonel von Schleicher and Major Fischer, opposed the freeing of Skoblevsky as endangering the security of the Reich. There was no reason to fear, Gessler insisted, that Russia would reveal any secrets; if there were, he would prefer to terminate Germany's military activities in Russia rather than free Skoblevsky! [92] The matter was finally settled as Rantzau had suggested, but Gessler remained adamant to the end, threatening even to resign.[93]

It was in connection with the Skoblevsky discussions that the Foreign Ministry tried to clarify how far exactly Germany's military relations with Russia were violating the terms of the Versailles Treaty. In the first place (its memorandum on the subject [94] stated), Germany supported, with money and personnel, "parts of Russia's armament industry and the firm of Junkers in Moscow," in order to import their products into Germany. This violated Article 170 of the Treaty. A similar partnership existed for the poison-gas works at Ivoshenko, which produced gas for import into Germany. This was in violation of Article 171. Furthermore, Germany had sent repeated military, naval, and air missions to the Soviet Union—Hasse, Mentzel, Fischer, Wilberg, Vogt, and Spindler. These violated Article 179 of the Treaty of Versailles. In addition, "with the knowledge and support of the German government, former officers, sometimes especially deactivated for this purpose, have been active as instructors with the Red air force." [95] Besides these clear violations, the Foreign Ministry memorandum mentioned other German activities in Russia, "which perhaps did not constitute a direct violation of the letter of Versailles," but which, "if they became known, might compromise the German government." In this category belonged Germany's participation in Russian military industries even if their products were not sent to Germany and the training of German personnel at Lipetsk and Kazan.

Germany's concern over possible detection of these illicit relations with the Soviet Union, however, was really unnecessary. The Western Powers had known for some time that there was more to Russo-German relations than met the eye, and French and Polish intelligence were remarkably well informed about these matters. [96] During the second half of 1926, moreover, a series of "revelations" occurred, ironically enough not in Russia but in Germany. Despite their sensational nature, these incidents left no mark upon Germany's relations with the West. There had been signs during the summer of 1926 that the Reichswehr was getting ready to move to Germany large quantities of the grenades that had been produced in Russia over the past years. [97] Both Brockdorff-Rantzau and Dirksen had warned the Reichswehr against so dangerous an operation at a time when Germany was about to enter the League of Nations, but they were told that all necessary precautions would be taken. [98] The Reichswehr, apparently, was not careful enough, because on December 3 and 6, 1926, the *Manchester Guardian,* in two articles, not only told all about the transport of ammunition from Leningrad to Stettin but also revealed many other aspects of Russo-German military collaboration. [99] What these articles failed to reveal was supplied in a sensational speech delivered by Socialist deputy Scheidemann before the Reichstag on December 16. [100] Here was the situation which Brockdorff-Rantzau and others had dreaded for years. As might be expected, both Germany and Russia were deeply worried about the possible consequences of these revelations. Special care was taken that the official declaration that the German government had to make on these matters neither admitted nor revealed too much. [101] According to Major Tschunke, the incident struck "a heavy blow" at Germany's military activities in Russia, necessitating a number of important changes.[102] From the evidence we now have, Tschunke's statement seems somewhat exaggerated; most of the changes that took place in Russo-German military dealings actually seem to have been contemplated before the revelations occurred.

On November 19, 1926, Brockdorff-Rantzau had a most enlightening discussion with Reichswehrminister Gessler about the problem of Russo-German military relations.[103] Gessler tried to present the whole matter as a purely political affair. Brockdorff-Rantzau pointed out that he had never really been thoroughly informed about the Reichswehr's dealings. Gessler then tried to make out as though nothing could really be proved against Germany, but Rantzau reminded him of Hasse's letter to Rozengolts. Gessler thereupon proposed simply to disavow Hasse, if anything leaked out. "In the past," he added, "we were unable to produce grenades in Germany and hence depended on production in Russia. But now we can make grenades in Germany and therefore we shall terminate things in Russia." But Brockdorff-Rantzau was still worried. "I myself," he said, "am in danger. If something leaks out, I shall either look like an ass or a scoundrel (als Esel oder als Schweinehund)." So what was there to do? Gessler wanted not to break with the Russians but merely to put matters on a basis "which does not compromise us." Rantzau: "But how shall the matter be continued? My idea is as follows: We will try to put matters more and more on an economic basis, i.e., we promise to support certain factories, but on condition that we supply materials which, in an emergency, can be used for war production." [104] Gessler agreed. "The situation," he repeated, "has changed now. On the basis of our new agreements with the entente we can now produce grenades ourselves." "But what shall I tell the Russians?" Rantzau asked. "Tell them," Gessler said, "that we do not want to break off relations. I don't want to break off things overnight but want to let them slowly peter out (versanden)." Rantzau: "I agree from the point of view of German-Russian policy. May I tell Chicherin that we have adopted a wholly new policy?" Gessler: "Yes. I will and can pursue the matter only if in future I remain in closest contact with you and the Foreign Ministry."

Shortly after Brockdorff-Rantzau and Gessler had thus agreed that there should be some changes in Germany's military relations with Russia, the December revelations further confirmed the need for such changes. A Foreign Ministry memorandum of December 24, 1926, stated that these revelations "had not done the harm to Germany's foreign policy in West and East which had at first been feared." But as there might be further Socialist indiscretions, this would be a good time, the memorandum added, "to reduce the mutual military relations to acceptable and useful proportions." To end these relations entirely, the memorandum said, was impossible (since it would have bad political effects), unnecessary (since some military relations were permissible and useful), and impractical (since the military might continue its contacts anyway behind the back of the Foreign Ministry). The memorandum therefore made a number of specific proposals for reducing Germany's military activities in Russia.[105] Most of these proposals were already being carried out. By early 1927, Germany, according to Major Fischer, had almost entirely withdrawn from the Junkers works in Russia; the poison-gas works and the import of Russian grenades had been discontinued; the flying- and tank-schools had been transformed into private enterprises; and the *Wiko* had been stricken from the commercial register and had disappeared.[106]

The exact extent of these changes was further clarified in a meeting between Secretary of State Schubert, Dirksen, General Wetzell, and Major Fischer on January 24, 1927. Schubert insisted on this occasion that he wanted to get a clear picture of the whole matter, since "it was no longer possible for the Foreign Ministry to follow its past practice of wanting to know as little as possible about these things, so as to be able to say that these matters were unknown to the Foreign Ministry." General Wetzell thereupon confirmed again that the Junkers, gas, and ammunition matters were all finished. The only German operations still functioning in the Soviet Union, he said, were the following: (1) the flying-school at Lipetsk, which was a private enterprise supported by German government funds, (2) the tank-school at Kazan, which was similarly organized (there were no active Reichswehr members employed in either, and the trainees were placed on inactive status), (3) some "scientific experiments with poison gas," in which Germany participated merely in an advisory capacity, and finally, (4) the yearly military missions to Russia's maneuvers. German activities under points 1 and 2, Wetzell admitted, were doubtless contrary to the peace treaty, but those under 3 and 4 he considered legal. It was absolutely necessary, Wetzell added, to gain some experience in aerial and tank warfare, since "these two weapons will play a decisive role in any future war." Schubert, on the other hand, wondered if "these military advantages were so decisive as to make up for the political risks which the continued operation of the tank- and flying-schools involved." But Wetzell assured him that the Russians were sufficiently interested in their collaboration with Germany to keep it secret. "If, on the other hand, Germany should break off her military relations, Russia might approach France or some other power," and Germany would lose all the political and military advantages she had derived from her military collaboration. These activities, Wetzell added, are "vital for our army," and he urgently requested continuing them. Secretary of State von Schubert reserved final judgment until after he had discussed the matter with Stresemann to see "whether the political risk which this involved for our policy in the West, the liberation of the Rhineland, and the restoration of Germany's full sovereignty, could be run." [107]

A few days later, Stresemann, at a meeting with General Heye (who had succeeded Seeckt as *Chef der Heeresleitung* the previous October), agreed to the continued operation of Kazan and Lipetsk, yet specified that no officers on active service should be sent to these schools during 1927.[108] At the same time, news from Moscow indicated that the Russians as well as Brockdorff-Rantzau were in favor of continuing the existing collaboration.[109] On February 26, 1927, a special cabinet meeting was called to discuss the Russo-German military question and to endorse the Stresemann-Heye agreement.[110] In May, a further meeting of Stresemann, Gessler, Heye, and Blomberg once again confirmed the policy that henceforth was to govern the Reichswehr's relations with Russia.[111]

The changes that were thus introduced into the Reichswehr's Russian operations after the various revelations of December 1926 were primarily tactical. According to Gustav Hilger, who was present in Moscow during all these years, Germany's military collaboration with Russia was actually intensified after 1926. "The Foreign Ministry," he writes, "capitulated to the generals with the greatest of pleasure. All concerned, from Stresemann on down, were resolved not only to continue as before with military co-operation, but to intensify it, though with the greatest caution." [112] This statement is perhaps a little too strong, since the Foreign Ministry continued to express its concern over possible further revelations of the Reichswehr's Russian ventures. Yet at the same time the collaboration in these ventures, not only of the Foreign Ministry but of other government agencies as well, was now more active than ever before. The Finance Ministry took a hand in facilitating the transport of war materials to Russia.[113] Stresemann even agreed to Germany's continued participation in experiments with poison gas.[114] The *Zentrale Moskau* (renamed *Heim Deutscher Angestellter Moskau* and since early 1928 under the direction of Niedermayer) continued its activities in close collaboration with the embassy.[115] The Foreign Ministry was kept informed on the number of Reichswehr members assigned each year to duty in Russia,[116] and other officers, in addition to those stationed in the Soviet Union, continued to go on temporary missions.[117]

One of the most important of these missions occurred in the fall of 1928, when General von Blomberg, chief of the *Truppenamt,* together with several other officers, observed the maneuvers of the Red Army. The visit, carefully conducted so that the officers avoided meeting the military attachés of other powers, was a great success. "Commissar of War Voroshilov," Blomberg reported, "had given orders to show us everything and to fulfill all our wishes. . . . The reception of the German officers everywhere was friendly, often cordial, and very hospitable."

Blomberg visited the three German establishments, Lipetsk, Kazan, and Saratov (or "Tomka," the experimental station for poison gas "in operation since the beginning of this summer"), and found all of them in the best condition. According to Blomberg, these operations were expected to reach their "full capacity" by 1929. "The great value [of these institutions] for our military preparations (*Rüstung*) is beyond a doubt. . . . [Russian] interest in them is considerable, even though the advantages from these installations predominantly favor the German side." Blomberg had long discussions with the Red Army's top leaders. Voroshilov immediately turned to the question of Poland and asked "if in case of a Polish attack the Red Army could count on Germany's help." This, Voroshilov said, "was a decisive question for the Soviet Union," and he added "that in case of a Polish attack upon Germany, Russia was ready to give any possible aid." Blomberg evaded a definite answer, saying that this was, after all, "a matter of high policy for which the political authorities were alone responsible." [118]

With Reichswehr and Foreign Ministry thus collaborating more closely than ever before, Brockdorff-Rantzau felt somewhat left out of the picture, a fact about which he complained in a letter to Stresemann in April 1928. It had been himself, after all, he wrote, who had played a leading role in these matters for the past five years and who had always considered Russo-German military relations "one of the most important bonds of our common policy." "If now, without my knowledge, an agreement is being concluded between your Excellency and the Reichswehrminister, according to which the secret agreements between Germany and Soviet Russia are not only to be continued but expanded, I consider this a danger which, in my opinion, cannot be overrated." [119] At the time Rantzau wrote this, Russo-German relations were at a particularly low ebb, due to a number of incidents, especially the famous "Shakhty trial" of German engineers. [120] Stresemann admitted that "after the unheard-of attitude of the Russians he would now be much cooler toward the Reichswehr Ministry" than he had been a little earlier. He also claimed that the Reichswehr as well as his own subordinates in the Foreign Ministy had told him that Germany's new military policy in Russia amounted to a decrease rather than an increase in military relations. At the same time he felt "that an immediate cessation [of these relations] was out of the question for political reasons." [121]

Brockdorff-Rantzau was quite right when he called the bond between the Reichswehr and Red Army one of the most important and steadying factors in Russo-German relations. Despite the relatively few individuals initiated into its secrets, changes in personnel do not seem to have had any decisive effect upon a policy that was so advantageous to both partners. In Russia, after Trotsky's fall, Voroshilov and Unshlikht carried on, as did Litvinov when Chicherin resigned in 1930. On the German side, Heye took over from Seeckt in 1926, Groener from Gessler in 1928, Dirksen from Brockdorff-Rantzau after the latter's death in 1928, and Curtius from Stresemann, who died in the fall of 1929. This does not mean that some individuals were not more deeply involved in these relations than others. Seeckt certainly was the most instrumental, and the fact that the role of the Foreign Ministry in these military dealings became more pronounced after 1926 was no doubt due to his dismissal. Curtius, as we shall see, was less involved than Stresemann, and Dirksen probably more so than Brockdorff-Rantzau. But the important point is that the Reichswehr's operations in Russia continued, regardless of who was in charge of German military or foreign policy.

The last chapter in Russo-German military relations on which the German Foreign Ministry documents shed any light began in the fall of 1928. It concerned the resumption of military-industrial collaboration, which had been deemphasized since 1926. The initiative in this case came from German business interests, but both Reichswehr and Foreign Ministry were sufficiently involved to give the negotiations at least a semi-official character. In October 1928, the firm of Krupp was approached by Soviet representatives with a request for aid in the production of high-grade steel and artillery. Before taking any action, Krupp asked the Reichswehr Ministry which, after consultation with the Foreign Ministry, told Krupp to go ahead. Negotiations took place in April 1929, and resulted in a preliminary agreement needing only final confirmation by Krupp to become binding. Krupp made it perfectly clear that nothing would be done without the Reichswehr's approval, especially as the agreement provided for Krupp to share a number of its production secrets with the Soviet Union.[122] Most of the agreement (except for the clauses providing Russia with steel) fell through when it was found to be in violation of the *Kriegsgerätegesetz* (the law regulating German arms production).[123] There is no record of what either the Foreign Ministry or the Reichswehr thought about the matter. Dirksen, who was now ambassador in Moscow, felt that this was "a case of useful collaboration," which he was inclined to favor, provided Germany's interests were sufficiently safeguarded.[124] A few months later, Dirksen reported that the Russians were trying to build up a war industry of their own, under the direction of "Herr Ulrich," that is, General Uborevich, as chief of ordnance. To achieve their purpose, they needed foreign aid, and this they hoped to get from Germany. The question of whether Germany should provide such aid, Dirksen said, was "of great political significance." It would certainly be a mistake, he warned, to consider the whole matter as merely an economic venture of concern only to German business. The Russians would always look upon it as a political matter, and it was "closely connected with our other operations here in the past. If we refuse to collaborate, our operations here will decline." [125]

To help in building up their war industry, the Russians had secured the services of a German consultant, "Herr Ludwig," better known as General Ludwig, former *Chef des Waffenamtes* of the Reichswehr. In January 1930, Ludwig told *Ministerialdirektor* Trautmann of the Foreign Ministry about the scope of Russia's military plans, which covered the production of everything from anti-aircraft guns to poison gas. There would be no military disadvantages for Germany from aiding the Russians, Ludwig pointed out. "The Russians," he said, "had remained practically on the level of 1914 in their military preparations" and had to start from scratch.[126] Ludwig's statements were supported by Major Behschnitt of the Reichswehr Ministry, who stressed that here was a welcome opportunity for Germany's armament industry to gain both money and experience. There was no danger that Germany might be compromised, since the Reichswehr was not in any way involved. If Germany did not help Russia, Behschnitt argued, some other power would.[127]

As these statements by Ludwig and Behschnitt show, the military were heartily in favor of aiding Russia in her contemplated armaments program. The Foreign Ministry, however, was less enthusiastic. Secretary of State Schubert was away at The Hague, and both Köpke (his deputy) and Trautmann (head of the *Ostabteilung*) reported to him. Trautmann was highly skeptical and advised against any attempt to take political advantage of Russia's request.[128] Köpke was somewhat more optimistic and had "no special reservations" about the matter, though he "did not feel too comfortable about it." [129] Schubert agreed with Trautmann and asked that a final decision be postponed until after his return from Holland.[130]

In the meantime, when Krupp had failed to ratify its agreement with the Russians, the latter had turned to another of the big German steel companies, Rheinmetall, as a possible sponsor of the new Soviet armaments program. The director of Rheinmetall, Eltze, in late January 1930, reported to the Foreign Ministry on the plans he had discussed with Soviet authorities. They were quite similar to those of Krupp. There was to be a "construction bureau" staffed by German engineers to plan the production of military equipment to be produced, with the aid of Rheinmetall and other German firms, mostly in neutral countries. Director Eltze was quite emphatic in his desire to do nothing that would run counter to the wishes of the Foreign Ministry and create political complications for Germany.[131] According to Trautmann, there might easily develop such complications; the activities proposed by Rheinmetall might become known outside Germany, and Germany might also put herself more and more in Russian hands and lose any freedom of action to follow a different course. Trautmann agreed that there were military advantages to the plan, "but the question is whether these advantages are worth the risk and whether it would not be better for us to remain quiet for several more years in the military field, since we shall have no opportunity of using these experiences in the foreseeable future. On the other hand it cannot be denied that the military advantages are predominantly on Russia's side. We will build for the Russians, i.e., the Bolsheviks, an armament industry at a time when they are trying to bring about a revolution with us." Trautmann, therefore, advised against Eltze's project of setting up a German "construction bureau" for Russia. As for supplying Russia with war materials from German establishments in neutral countries, he foresaw no complications.[132]

By early February 1930, Rheinmetall and the Soviet Union had reached a tentative agreement. Under its terms, the German firm promised to place at Russia's disposal six "constructions" (mostly artillery), of which four were already in use by the Reichswehr. These were to be produced in Russian factories with the aid of a German "construction bureau" and with German material assistance. The net profit from these operations was estimated at four million marks.[133] The question was: What position should the Foreign Ministry take? At a meeting of Schubert and his advisers, it was decided to ask Rheinmetall not to conclude the agreement. If this could not be done without causing serious political damage, then Eltze was to make it clear that he was acting entirely at his own risk without consent of the Foreign Ministry. "The idea of combining a political deal with this matter," Schubert wired Dirksen, "has been turned down because of a standing cabinet order against any further expansion of this kind of industrial activity in Russia." [134]

No sooner had this decision been communicated to Moscow than the Reichswehr, which prior to this time had not shown much interest in discussing the matter,[135] called the Foreign Ministry and asked that no negative decision be made without consulting the Reichswehr Ministry. On February 10, General Hammerstein, Heye's successor as chief of the army command, called on Schubert and explained that initially the Reichswehr had hoped to keep the whole matter on a purely business basis. The Russians, however, had made a political issue out of it, threatening that if the agreement failed, "the friendship between the Russian and German army could not be maintained . . . that the whole German-Russian relationship depended upon the conclusion of this agreement." Schubert, on the other hand, was afraid that some day Russia's guns might go off against Germany, either as a result of a direct Soviet attack or in the course of world revolution. Hammerstein considered a revolution unlikely as long as the Russians were "satiated," and he felt that the kind of project proposed by Rheinmetall would help to satiate them. As for a Russian attack, "that after all would be primarily against Poland, which would only be agreeable to us." Besides, Hammerstein said, Russia's military preparations had a decidedly defensive character. He warned against antagonizing Uborevich, who was extremely pro-German, and he begged Schubert to reconsider and perhaps amend his instructions to Moscow.[136]

On the day Schubert had his talk with Hammerstein, two letters from Dirksen, which echoed the Reichswehr's sentiments, arrived in Berlin. In a letter to Moltke, the ambassador warned against interfering in the negotiations between Rheinmetall and the Russians, since this might have "far-reaching consequences politically" and since the whole future of Russo-German military collaboration was at stake.[137] In another letter, this one to Trautmann, Dirksen pursued his favorite plan that Germany should take political advantage of Russia's desire for military aid. How he envisaged this he did not say. Dirksen also pointed out, as Hammerstein had done in his talk with Schubert, that the Russians had offers from other foreign firms which they might accept, if Germany failed to act.[138]

As a result of Hammerstein's urgings, seconded by Dirksen's letters, another telegram was now sent to Moscow, pointing out that a failure of the Rheinmetall negotiations "would have very serious consequences for the mutual relations" between Germany and Russia.[139] It is interesting to note in this connection that the foreign minister himself played no part at all in these negotiations. Shortly after he took office, in November 1929, Curtius had requested a briefing on the Reichswehr's activities in Russia, about which he remembered "from earlier cabinet meetings." [140] This briefing Schubert, "as the only one informed about these matters," promised to give him. But despite Schubert's repeated urgings, Curtius always evaded such a discussion. Finally, in early February, when the Rheinmetall affair became crucial, Schubert brought the matter up again, but Curtius said he hoped he "need not be bothered" with it. He avoided going into the details of the military dealings with Russia when Schubert approached him after the talk with Hammerstein, and again later when the Rheinmetall agreement had been signed. Curtius merely said "he hoped that in the near future he would find time to receive a briefing." [141] One cannot help feeling that the foreign minister purposely avoided getting involved in a matter that had caused his predecessor so many headaches.

The preliminary agreement between Rheinmetall and the Soviet government was signed on February 10, 1930.[142] According to Eltze, the final negotiations had been most cordial. General Ludwig had been present and General Uborevich, under the influence of too much vodka, had exclaimed: "Will we not be ready now in two years to carry out the frontier adjustments and to kill the Poles? After all, we must once again partition Poland." The Foreign Ministry warned Eltze that despite the interest it had shown in the matter, it did not officially endorse the agreement, and Eltze confirmed that he had acted entirely on his own.[143] A few days later, Uborevich paid a visit to Germany to inspect some of the materials and weapons that Rheinmetall had promised to deliver. A new chapter in successful Russo-German collaboration seemed to have begun.[144]

But at this point Rheinmetall suddenly began to find fault with the preliminary agreement and refused to ratify it.[145] The firm's representatives and the Russians agreed upon several new drafts, but Rheinmetall's board of directors approved none of them. In a series of urgent telegrams, Dirksen warned against the serious political consequences of continued refusals by Rheinmetall.[146] Uborevich himself, who had just succeeded Unshlikht as assistant commissar of war, stated "with great seriousness and genuine regret that the breakdown of negotiations would be of the most far-reaching and serious consequences for German-Russian economic and political relations." [147] At this point there is a gap in the documentation, but in a letter to Curtius in July 1930, Dirksen wrote: "Voroshilov expressed his deep satisfaction about the signing of the agreement with Rheinmetall and thanked me for my part in the negotiations. The agreement with Rheinmetall [Voroshilov had added] was only a beginning which would be followed by further large orders in Germany." [148]

This ends the story of Russo-German military collaboration during the 1920's, as revealed in the documents of the German Foreign Ministry.[149] Its significance lies not so much in any revelation of new facts, though there are a few, as in the insight it provides into the relationship both between the Reichswehr and the Red Army and between the Reichswehr and Germany's civil authorities. Looked at purely as a military operation, the partnership between Germany and Russia, despite some statements to the contrary, seems to have been mutually beneficial. Had it not been, there were certainly many occasions on which it could have been terminated. But the Reichswehr's military involvement with Russia was not as far-reaching as many people suspected. The twilight of secrecy has a way of magnifying things. Nor was it conducted with the efficiency and singleness of purpose that we have come to expect from the German military. There was an air of uncertainty and improvisation about the Reichswehr's Russian ventures. This, no doubt, was due in part to the secrecy under which it had to operate and to the uneasy feeling that the Russian adventure might some day prove a boomerang rather than a boon to Germany. It was caused, furthermore, by the individual members of the Reichswehr who were entrusted with the conduct of these relations. General von Seeckt, the driving force behind the Reichswehr's Russian projects, was never able to see with his own eyes what his mind had planned. When, after his retirement, he tried to pay a visit to the Soviet Union, he was dissuaded for fear of political repercussions. The actual direction of the Reichswehr's operations in Russia was in the hands of men like Niedermayer or Tschunke, loyal officers who could keep a secret and who, in an emergency, could be disavowed; but they were no match for the Russians with whom they had to negotiate. In the absence of any really outstanding figure among the Reichswehr's representatives in Russia, it devolved upon the German ambassador in Moscow to keep an eye on Germany's military as well as political interests. But since the aims of Germany's civilian authorities did not always agree with those of the military, a further element of uncertainty was injected into the Reichswehr's Russian activities.

If there is one thing the German documents show, it is the fact that the whole German government and not merely its military branch was actively involved in the collaboration with Russia. The degree of involvement and the attitude toward it, as we have seen, differed from individual to individual. While some, like Wirth, Maltzan, Curtius, or even Schubert, tried to avoid becoming initiated into the details of such collaboration because they felt it was easier to deny something of which they had little knowledge, others, like Brockdorff-Rantzau or Dirksen, complained of not knowing enough of the details. There is no evidence that any of the civilian authorities were wholeheartedly in favor of the collaboration for military reasons alone. As a matter of fact, the first reaction of Brockdorff-Rantzau, Stresemann, Ebert, and Curtius was to oppose any military dealings with Russia, and we know that Hindenburg, upon becoming president, breathed a sigh of relief when he learned that Germany had no military alliance with Russia. It was only when they became aware of the possible political or economic advantages that could be derived from the Reichswehr's Russian connections that the politicians became reconciled to, and, in the case of Rantzau, Dirksen, or even Stresemann, advocates of, such relations. There was never a time at which this positive attitude toward Russo-German military collaboration was not balanced by a whole flock of fears: What would happen, both at home and abroad, if the secret leaked out? What if the guns the Germans helped Russia produce would some day go off against the Reich? What guarantee was there that the Russians would live up to their promises and give Germany her share of war materials if and when she needed them? There is no reason to doubt the sincerity of the recurrent wish of almost every responsible statesman during the Weimar period that Germany's military collaboration with Russia might be discontinued or at least decreased. But the army had made commitments which could not be broken without causing a major political crisis. Nor was there any certainty that the Reichswehr might not continue its collaboration behind the back of its civilian colleagues. And there was the definite certainty that Russia, if shown a cold shoulder by Germany, would try to find what she needed elsewhere, especially in France.

The collaboration of Germany's civilian authorities with the Reichswehr's Russian ventures was thus halfhearted, but it was nevertheless close. In their ultimate aims, both military and civilians saw eye to eye. The hope of one day solving the "Polish problem" animated the men who directed Germany's foreign policy as it drew together the Reichswehr and the Red Army. If the diplomats preferred to solve this problem through "peaceful pressure," this was not because of any aversion on their part toward war but because of their realization that a conflict with Poland meant also war with France and thus certain defeat for Germany. To conclude a military alliance with Russia might have encouraged the latter to move against Poland, thus dragging Germany into a war for which she was not ready. The ideal solution would have been to gain assurance of Russian aid in case Poland, as a result of Germany's pressure or even without such provocation, should invade Germany. But such a one-sided arrangement, as we have seen, was not to Russia's taste. Brockdorff-Rantzau's standing complaint, that the Reichswehr did not keep him fully informed of its Russian dealings, was certainly justified, but it is doubtful whether with more information and greater latitude he would have gained the political concessions from Russia that he desired. The truth of the matter is that the German military found their Russian experiences most valuable and a reward in themselves, and this the Russians realized.

Historians, like everyone else, tend to oversimplify issues on which they feel strongly. Critics of Germany thus have presented the Reichswehr's Russian activities as evidence of a German conspiracy of revenge against the West. Defenders of Germany have tried to explain these activities as understandable military maneuvers of which Germany's political leaders were unaware. The truth lies somewhere in between. Germany's politicians were certainly well informed and often lent aid to the Reichswehr's Russian ventures. Their collaboration did not amount to a conspiracy, not because they had any fundamental aversion to it but because they knew that a conspiracy presupposes mutual trust between conspirators. Germany's political leaders realized, as their military colleagues did not, that it was impossible to have such trust in a government whose aims threatened the very existence of friend and foe alike.

NOTES

1. The first full treatment of the subject, Cecil F. Melville, *The Russian Face of Germany* (London, 1932), though based on unofficial sources, is still highly informative. The most recent study is Georges Castellan, "Reichswehr et Armée Rouge 1920–1939," in Jean-Baptiste Duroselle, ed., *Les Relations germano-soviétiques de 1933 à 1939* (Paris, 1954), pp. 137–260.

2. From the Heeresarchiv, Potsdam, these papers are now on microfilm available in the Widener Library, Harvard University.

3. The most important of these are the article by General Helm Speidel, "Reichswehr und Rote Armee," *Vierteljahrshefte für Zeitgeschichte*, 1 (January 1953), 9–45, and the memorandum by Major Fritz Tschunke of September 15, 1939,

"General v. Seeckt nimmt die Verbindung zur Sowjetunion auf," *Der Monat*, 1 November 1948), 48–50 (hereafter cited as Tschunke Memorandum).

4. Speidel, p. 9.

5. Microfilms of these documents, prepared by the German Foreign Ministry Documents Project (sponsored by the United States, British, and French governments), are deposited in the National Archives, Washington, D.C.

6. The memoirs of Herbert von Dirksen, *Moskau, Tokio, London* (Stuttgart, 1949), are typical in this respect. Dirksen, who served as ambassador to Russia from 1928 to 1933, admits the existence of Russo-German military relations but disclaims any knowledge of their details (see p. 81). Yet, as we shall see, Dirksen was intimately acquainted with, and involved in, these relations.

7. Recent accounts of the first postwar years are George W. F. Hallgarten, "General Hans von Seeckt and Russia, 1920–1922," *Journal of Modern History*, XXI (March 1949), 28–34; Edward Hallett Carr, *German-Soviet Relations Between the Two World Wars 1919–1939* (Baltimore, 1951), Chaps. 1–111; Theodor Schieder, *Die Probleme des Rapallo-Vertrags* (Cologne, 1956); Gerald Freund, *Unholy Alliance: Russian-German Relations from the Treaty of Brest-Litovsk to the Treaty of Berlin* (London, 1957), chaps. IV–V. The article by Alfred L. Smith, "The German General Staff and Russia 1919–1926," *Soviet Studies*, VIII (October 1956), adds little and contains serious errors.

8. Carr, pp. 17 ff.

9. Brockdorff-Rantzau Nachlass, Auswärtiges Amt, Germany, microfilm, container 3441, serial no. 9105, frame nos. 234084 ff., National Archives, Washington, D.C. All documents hereafter cited are from the German Auswärtiges Amt collection now on microfilm in the National Archives and will be cited in the following manner: Brockdorff-Rantzau Nachlass, AA, 3441/9105/234084 ff.

10. The statement in Smith, p. 126, that "some definite contacts" existed in 1919 between Seeckt and the Red Army is not convincing. The passages cited from the Tschunke Memorandum, moreover, contain serious errors of translation.

11. Maltzan to Br.-R., Aug. 6, 1920, Brockdorff-Rantzau Nachlass, 3445/9105/237050 ff.

12. The best account of these early negotiations is given in Freund, pp. 92 ff. See also John Wheeler-Bennett, *The Nemesis of Power: The German Army in Politics 1918–1945* (London, 1953), pp. 127–128; Castellan, pp. 151 ff.; Hallgarten, pp. 30–31. These and other accounts of the events of 1921 all show slight differences in fact and interpretation.

13. Tschunke Memorandum, p. 49.

14. Brockdorff-Rantzau Nachlass, 1013/1691/397479 ff.; Herbert Helbig, "Die Moskauer Mission des Grafen Brockdorff-Rantzau," *Forschungen zur Osteuropäischen Geschichte*, II (1955), 309.

15. Memorandum of March 18, 1924, Akten betr. Militärische Angelegenheiten mit Russland, Büro von Staatssekretär v. Schubert, AA (hereafter cited as Militärische Angelegenheiten), 2329/4564/162585 ff. The minister of finance had to be initiated, since his department had to supply the necessary funds for the Reichswehr's activities in Russia.

16. This rumor has already been discounted by several historians: Schieder, p. 41; Hans Rothfels in his introduction to Speidel, p. 10; Hans W. Gatzke, "Von Rapallo nach Berlin: Stresemann und die Deutsche Russlandpolitik," *Vierteljahrshefte für Zeitgeschichte*, IV (January 1956), 4.

17. Most of the documents on Rapallo can be found in Akten betr. Genua vom 10. Apr. bis 26. Apr. 1922, Büro des Reichsministers, AA, 1734/3398/738276–1735/3398/739144.

18. *Ibid.*, 1735/3398/738917.

19. Militärische Angelegenheiten, 2329/4564/162585 ff.

20. An den Herrn Reichskanzler Eigenhändig! Ganz Geheim! July 29, 1923, *ibid.*, 162539 ff.

21. The authorized biography by Edgar Stern-Rubarth, *Graf von Brockdorff-Rantzau, Wanderer zwischen zwei Welten* (Berlin, 1929), hardly does justice to Rantzau's complex personality. The article by Helbig uses some of Br.-R.'s papers and gives valuable new insights. The late German historian Erich Brandenburg, in 1932, had prepared a book on Br.-R., based on the Nachlass, but the Foreign Ministry prevented its publication as contrary to the national interest. The MS of Brandenburg's book is among the Brockdorff-Rantzau Nachlass (container nos. 1012–13), but it is quite incomplete, since many important events in Rantzau's career could not yet be discussed at that time. With the additional material from the complete Nachlass (container nos. 3154, 3429–36, 3438–41, 3443–46), and with the Foreign Ministry documents, a definitive biography has now been planned by Professor Helbig.

22. Br.-R. to Langwerth von Simmern, May 3, 1919, Brockdorff-Rantzau Nachlass, 3443/9105/235265. See also his letter to Ambassador von Romberg, May 18, 1919, *ibid.*, 235289.

23. Draft memorandum, July 1920, *ibid.*, 1013/1691/397293 ff.

24. Draft memorandum, April 24, 1921, *ibid.*, 397303 ff.; résumé of conversation with Ebert, April 25, 1921, *ibid.*, 397309 ff.

25. Letters of Maltzan to Br.-R., August 1920–January 1922, *ibid.*, 3445/9105/236822–27, 237050–54, 237141 ff.

26. Undated memorandum by Br.-R., *ibid.*, 1013/1691/397320 ff.

27. Unterredung mit Ebert am 10. Mai 1922, *ibid.*, 397333 ff.

28. Helbig, pp. 307–308.

29. *Ibid.*, pp. 303–313. See also Freund, pp. 127 ff.

30. Memorandum of Br.-R., January 29, 1923, Brockdorff-Rantzau Nachlass, 3446/9105/237399 ff.

31. Maltzan to Br.-R., December 15, 1922, *ibid.*, 3431/9101/225086.

32. Br.-R. to Rosenberg, March 1, 1923, Akten betr. Russland, Büro des Reichsministers, AA, 1406/2860/552825 ff.

33. Br.-R. to Maltzan, May 16, 1923, Brockdorff-Rantzau Nachlass, 3431/9101/225606.

34. See footnote 32.

35. Br.-R. to Maltzan, April 18, 1923, Brockdorff-Rantzau Nachlass, 3431/9101/224831 ff. See also Br.-R. to Cuno, April 10, 1923, Militärische Angelegenheiten, 2329/4564/162521.

36. Brockdorff-Rantzau Nachlass, 3431/9101/224826.

37. Br.-R. to Maltzan, May 16, 1923, *ibid.*, 225606.

38. Br.-R. to Maltzan, June 13, 1923, *ibid.*, 225527 ff. Additional information about the Hasse and Mentzel missions may be found in Militärische Angelegenheiten, 2329/4564/162539 ff., 162676 ff. The references in Castellan, pp. 155–163, are based primarily on French intelligence reports and are not always clear or correct.

39. Memorandum by Br.-R., September 10, 1923, reporting complaint by Chicherin of June 15, 1923, Militärische Angelegenheiten, 2329/4564/162676 ff.

40. Maltzan to Br.-R., June 28, 1923, *ibid.*, 162738.

41. Memorandum of July 12, 1923, *ibid.*, 162559.

42. Br.-R. to Cuno, June 16, 1923, *ibid.*, 162523; memorandum by Br.-R., September 10, 1923, *ibid.*, 162676 ff. Rantzau felt that a Russian visit to Berlin would implicate the Soviets sufficiently so that they could not ever use the Hasse letter to Rozengolts for blackmail purposes.

43. Br.-R. to Maltzan, June 30 and July 14, 1923, *ibid.*, 162727 ff.

44. According to Gustav Hilger and Alfred G. Meyer, *The Incompatible Allies:*

A Memoir-History of German-Soviet Relations 1918–1941 (New York, 1953), p. 194, Rozengolts was a member of the Revolutionary Military Council and chief of the central board of the Soviet air force.

45. An den Herrn Reichskanzler Eigenhändig! Ganz Geheim! July 29, 1923, Militärische Angelegenheiten, 2329/4564/162539 ff.; memorandum by Br.-R., *ibid.*, 162557 ff.

46. Memorandum of late August 1922, Brockdorff-Rantzau Nachlass, 1013/ 1691/397476 ff.

47. Rantzau had earlier thought of using Russia against Britain in India, memorandum of July 17, 1922, *ibid.*, 397396 ff.

48. Ganz geheime Aufzeichnung, July 31, 1923, signed by Br.-R. and Cuno, Militärische Angelegenheiten, 2329/4564/102550 ff.

49. According to an earlier report by Mentzel, General Lebedev, Soviet chief of staff, had told him that Germany "was too weak for Russia to consider joint military action." Br.-R. to Maltzan, May 16, 1923, Brockdorff-Rantzau Nachlass, 3431/ 9101/225606.

50. Memorandum by Br.-R., September 10, 1923, Militärische Angelegenheiten, 2329/4564/162676 ff.

51. Br.-R.'s memorandum for Stresemann, February 20, 1924, Brockdorff-Rantzau Nachlass, 3432/9101/226805 ff.

52. *Ibid.* Stresemann's and Ebert's stand is confirmed by Stresemann's own statement, in Nachlass des Reichsministers Dr. Gustav Stresemann, Politisches Archiv, AA (hereafter cited as Stresemann Nachlass), 3167/7337/163462. On Stresemann's attitude toward Russo-German military relations see Hans W. Gatzke, *Stresemann and the Rearmament of Germany* (Baltimore, 1954), Chap. IV. The conclusions stated there are amply supported by the Foreign Ministry documents.

53. Br.-R.'s memorandum to Stresemann, February 20, 1924, Brockdorff-Rantzau Nachlass, 3432/9101/226805 ff.

54. Maltzan to *chargé d'affaires* in Moscow, August 13, 1923, *ibid.*, 162731. Teichmann, i.e., Tschunke, headed the *Gefu*, an organization founded by the Reichswehr to direct its military-industrial relations with Russia. The firm of Stolzenberg was negotiating about a poison-gas factory in Russia. Hagen, on his way to or from Russia, became ill and died in a Riga hotel, leaving a briefcase full of military documents which his doctor turned over to the German embassy. *Ibid.*, 162618, 162674.

55. Maltzan to *chargé d'affaires* in Moscow, August 22, 1923, *ibid.*, 162732.

56. Speidel, p. 20.

57. See footnote 32.

58. Br.-R. to Maltzan, April 13, 1923, Brockdorff-Rantzau Nachlass, 3431/9101/ 224853.

59. Br.-R. to Maltzan, November 29, 1923, *ibid.*, 225273. Major Oskar Ritter von Niedermayer, or Neumann, apparently had made far-reaching promises to the Russians about German deliveries of coal, which never materialized and which, in Soviet circles, made the term "Neumann coals" synonymous with unkept promises. Br.-R. to Maltzan, April 13, 1923, *ibid.*, 224853. On Niedermayer's colorful career during World Wars I and II, see Dirksen, pp. 133–134, and Hilger, pp. 194 ff.

60. Maltzan to Br.-R., December 6, 1923, Brockdorff-Rantzau Nachlass, 3431/ 9101/225256 ff.; memorandum by Maltzan, March 18, 1923, Militärische Angelegenheiten, 2329/4564/162588.

61. Hasse to Maltzan, October 4, 1923, Militärische Angelegenheiten, 2329/ 4564/162735; Hasse to Staatssekretär von Schubert, March 1, 1924, *ibid.*, 162584.

62. Br.-R.'s memorandum to Stresemann, February 20, 1924, Brockdorff-Rantzau

Nachlass, 3432/9101/226805 ff. Brown, according to Br.-R., was "a most outstanding businessman and a likable person"; see also Br.-R. to *chargé d'affaires* Radowitz, February 27, 1924, Militärische Angelegenheiten, 2329/4564/162583.

63. Br.-R. to Stresemann, April 3, 1924, *ibid.*, 2329/4564/162591 ff.

64. See footnote 59.

65. Br.-R.'s memorandum of April 4, 1924, Militärische Angelegenheiten, 2329/4564/162594 ff.

66. On the political relations between Germany and Russia during these crucial years, see Gatzke, "Von Rapallo nach Berlin," pp. 7 ff.

67. Tschunke Memorandum, p. 49; Castellan, pp. 163 ff. The Foreign Ministry documents do not provide much new material on these various operations, except for the Junkers works at Fili. Junkers was in a special category since it was subsidized by the German government. Russia's failure to avail herself sufficiently of Junkers' services ultimately led to a crisis in which Junkers threatened to terminate its Russian ventures. For material on Junkers' operations in Russia see Entwicklung der Beziehungen zwischen Junkers und dem Reich bezüglich der Zusammenarbeit in Russland, Junkers geheim, Gesandtschaft Moskau, AA, 3663/9472/273734–843, esp. 273736 ff.; Deutsch-Russische Luftverkehrsgesellschaft "Junkerswerke," 1922–1932, *ibid.*, 3662/9444/273078–309; Akten betr. Unternehmungen der Junkerswerke in Russland, Büro von Staatssekretär v. Schubert, AA, 2331/4564/163752 ff.; Militärische Angelegenheiten, 2329/4564/162622 ff., 162741 ff., 162784 ff.

68. Castellan, pp. 168 ff.

69. For a detailed discussion of these stations, see *ibid.*, pp. 175 ff. Speidel, p. 18, dates Lipetsk from 1924, Saratov from 1927–1928, and Kazan from 1930. The latter, however, seems to have been in operation as early as 1926.

70. Memorandum by Dirksen, December 18, 1925, Militärische Angelegenheiten, 2329/4564/162663; memorandum by Br.-R., January 18, 1926, *ibid.*, 162667 ff.

71. Castellan, pp. 197 ff.

72. It is difficult to determine who was head of Z. Mo. in 1924. Both Thomsen and Niedermayer are mentioned simultaneously as the Reichswehr's representatives in Moscow. Militärische Angelegenheiten, 2329/4564/162659. As late as January 1926, Br.-R. still asked that one single person be charged with the Reichswehr's affairs in Russia. *Ibid.*, 162667 ff. Hilger, pp. 196–197, places Niedermayer at the head of Z. Mo. until 1932 and Thomsen from then on. The documents show, however, that Thomsen was in charge until March 15, 1928, at which time Niedermayer took over. Militärische Angelegenheiten, 2330/4564/163194.

73. Oberst a.D. von der Lieth-Thomsen to Br.-R., May 29, 1926, Brockdorff-Rantzau Nachlass, 3429/9101/223703. See also Helbig, p. 324. Thomsen had been the senior German air force officer in World War I.

74. Br.-R.'s memorandum of April 4, 1924, Militärische Angelegenheiten, 2329/4564/162594 ff.

75. See the series of so-called Fischertelegramme, named after Major Fischer (pseudonym Frank), who was the Reichswehr's liaison with the Foreign Ministry, in Büro von Staatssekretär v. Schubert, AA, 2329/4564/162726 ff., 2330/4564/163508 ff. Liaison for the Foreign Ministry was maintained by Dirksen.

76. Akten betr. Russland, Büro des Reichsministers, AA, 1407/2860/553774 ff., 553783 ff.

77. Br.-R.'s report on a conversation with Trotsky, June 9, 1924, Stresemann Nachlass, 3165/7414/175334 ff.

78. *Ibid.*

79. Telegram from Lieth (i.e., Thomsen) via Rantzau to Frank (i.e., Fischer) via Schubert, Militärische Angelegenheiten, 2329/4564/162758.

80. Schubert to Br.-R., July 28, 1925, Akten betr. Rückwirkung der Garantie-

paktverhandlungen auf die Deutsch-Russischen Beziehungen (hereafter cited as Akten betr. Rückwirkung), Büro von Staatssekretär v. Schubert, AA, 2314/4562/ 155661.

81. Br.-R. to Schubert, July 31, 1925, *ibid.*, 155703.

82. Telegram from Frank-Lieth via Rantzau to Hoffmeister via Schubert, August 24, 1925, Militärische Angelegenheiten, 2329/4564/162821. This conflicts with Speidel, p. 36, who states that the Germans were not given much insight into Russian military conditions. Germany may have been more liberal in initiating Soviet officers into her military planning, but she was also aware of the value of thus indoctrinating Russian officers. Russische Militärangelegenheiten, Handakten von Herrn Min. Dir. von Dirksen, AA, 3668/9481/276403.

83. Akten betr. Rückwirkung, 2313/4562/154859 ff.

84. Memorandum of January 18, 1926, Militärische Angelegenheiten, 2329/ 4564/162667 ff.; memorandum of January 21, 1926, *ibid.*, 162673 ff. Italics in the original.

85. Gatzke, "Von Rapallo nach Berlin," pp. 14–24. The existence of a secret understanding in connection with the Treaty of Berlin mentioned here as a possibility (pp. 23–24) is not supported by the German documents that have become available since the article was written.

86. Hilger and Meyer, p. 202.

87. Militärische Angelegenheiten, 2329/4564/162694 ff.

88. Schubert to Br.-R., April 3, 1926, *ibid.*, 162703 ff., 162711.

89. For details see Akten betr. Deutsch-Russischer Gefangenenaustausch, Büro von Staatssekretär v. Schubert, AA, 2330/4564/163532 ff., 163354 ff., 2331/4564/ 163701 ff.

90. For details of the Skoblevsky case, see *ibid.*, 2330/4564/163576 ff.

91. Br.-R. to Stresemann, July 5, 1926, *ibid.*, 163601 ff.

92. Discussion between Schubert, Gessler, Dirksen, Hencke, Schleicher, and Fischer, July 14, 1926, *ibid.*, 163632 ff.

93. *Ibid.*, 163662–743.

94. Memorandum by Legationssekretär Hencke, July 12, 1926, Militärische Angelegenheiten, 2330/4564/163630.

95. About this phase of Russo-German collaboration, little has been known thus far. See Castellan, p. 159.

96. Castellan, *passim.* See also Report of Generalkonsul Kessler to Br.-R., November 17, 1924, Militärische Angelegenheiten, 2329/4564/162598.

97. Memorandum by Stresemann on conversation with Br.-R., August 11, 1926, Stresemann Nachlass, 3100/7137/149293.

98. Memorandum by Dirksen on talk with Major Fischer, Militärische Angelegenheiten, 2330/4564/163463.

99. *Ibid.*, 163378 ff., 163401, 163415, 163437; Russland—Sowjetgranaten 1926/ 27, Geheimakten 1920–36, AA, 3028/6698/106231 ff. Much of the information came from a memorandum that the firm of Junkers had distributed in the summer of 1926 to present its case in a controversy with the Reichswehr. See *Denkschrift zum Fall Reichsfiskus—Junkers,* June 25, 1926, Akten betr. Unternehmungen der Junkerswerke in Russland, Büro von Staatssekretär von Schubert, AA, 2331/4564/ 163792 ff.

100. Gatzke, *Stresemann and the Rearmament of Germany,* pp. 73 ff.

101. *Ibid.*, pp. 85–87; Militärische Angelegenheiten, 2330/4564/163487 ff., 163491 ff., 163499 ff., 163513 ff.

102. Tschunke Memorandum, p. 49.

103. Militärische Angelegenheiten, 2330/4564/163383 ff. This is Schubert's account of the meeting as told him by Br.-R.

104. This is almost verbatim what Br.-R. had proposed more than two years earlier.

105. Aufzeichnung über die deutsch-russischen militärischen Beziehungen, December 24, 1926, probably by Dirksen, Militärische Angelegenheiten, 2330/4564/ 163465 ff.

106. Aufzeichnung über eine Unterhaltung mit Major Fischer, January 6, 1927, probably by Dirksen, *ibid.*, 163471 ff.

107. Aufzeichnung über den gegenwärtigen Stand der deutsch-russischen militärischen Beziehungen, probably by Dirksen, *ibid.*, 163480 ff.

108. Vermerk, February 9, 1927, probably by Dirksen, *ibid.*, 163486, 163494 ff.

109. *Ibid.*

110. *Ibid.*, 163529–530.

111. *Ibid.*, 2331/4564/163880 ff.

112. Hilger and Meyer, pp. 206–207.

113. Niederschrift über die Besprechung im Reichsfinanzministerium am 4. V. 1928, Russische Militärangelegenheiten, 3668/9481/276292.

114. Discussion between Stresemann, von Schubert, Groener, and Blomberg, February 6, 1928, Militärische Angelegenheiten, 2331/4564/163921, 163924 ff.

115. Russische Militärangelegenheiten, 3668/9481/276183 ff., 276265.

116. *Ibid.*, 3668/9481/276275, 276283 ff. About forty-three Reichswehr members were sent each year to Lipetsk, and the total number sent to Russia in 1929 consisted of twenty-three active and sixty-three inactive officers. Militärische Angelegenheiten, 2331/4564/163924 ff.; 163947 ff.

117. Russische Militärangelegenheiten, 3668/9481/276305 ff.

118. Reise des Chefs des Truppenamts nach Russland (August–September, 1928), signed by Blomberg, *ibid.*, 3668/9480/276183 ff., 276249 ff.

119. Br.-R. to Stresemann, April 12, 1928, Brockdorff-Rantzau Nachlass, 3432/ 9101/226870.

120. Gatzke, "Von Rapallo nach Berlin," p. 26.

121. Hencke to Br.-R., April 28, 1928, reporting on a talk with Stresemann, Brockdorff-Rantzau Nachlass, 3429/9101/223630 ff.

122. Unsigned memorandum, May 1, 1929, Militärische Angelegenheiten, 2331/ 4564/163956 ff.

123. *Ibid.*, 164006 ff.

124. Dirksen to Trautmann, May 7, 1929, *ibid.*, 163960.

125. Dirksen to Schubert, December 19, 1929, *ibid.*, 163978 ff.

126. Memorandum by Trautmann, January 3, 1930, *ibid.*, 163984.

127. *Ibid.*, 163988–89.

128. Trautmann to Schubert, January 6, 1930, *ibid.*, 163990 ff.

129. Köpke to Schubert, January 6, 1930, *ibid.*, 163996 ff.

130. Schubert to Trautmann, January 9, 1930, *ibid.*, 163994.

131. Report by Moltke, January 29, 1930, *ibid.*, 164003 ff.

132. Votum by Trautmann, January 31, 1930, *ibid.*, 164009 ff.

133. Memorandum by Moltke on talk with Eltze, February 7, 1930, *ibid.*, 164011 ff.

134. Schubert to Dirksen, February 8, 1930, *ibid.*, 164016.

135. *Ibid.*, 164018.

136. Memorandum by Schubert, February 10, 1930, *ibid.*, 164022 ff. Uborevich had spent some time in Germany in 1927 where a conscious effort had been made "to influence him in a pro-German direction." See Russische Militärangelegenheiten, 3668/9481/276403.

137. Dirksen to Moltke, February 3, 1930, received February 10, *ibid.*, 164019 ff.

138. Dirksen to Trautmann, January 30, 1930, received February 10, *ibid.*, 164038 ff.

139. Schubert to Dirksen, February 10, 1930, *ibid.*, 164032 ff.

140. Curtius to Vortragender Legationsrat von Blücher, November 25, 1929, *ibid.*, 163983.

141. Memoranda by Schubert, February 10 and 14, 1930, *ibid.*, 164042 ff.

142. Dirksen to Schubert, February 10, 1930, *ibid.*, 164045.

143. Eltze's report to Moltke, February 12, 1930, *ibid.*, 164052 ff.

144. Memorandum by Schubert, February 15, 1930, *ibid.*, 164056.

145. *Ibid.*, 164046 ff.

146. *Ibid.*, 164058 ff.

147. Dirksen to Curtius, *ibid.*, 164062 ff.

148. Dirksen to Curtius, July 19, 1930, Akten betr. Russland, 1416/2860/561791.

149. On the period beyond, see Speidel, *passim,* and Castellan, pp. 202 ff. See also George H. Stein, "Russo-German Military Collaboration: The Last Phase, 1933," *Political Science Quarterly,* LXXVII (March 1962), 54–71.

Stresemann and Locarno

One of the most prominent statesmen of the 1920's was Germany's Gustav Stresemann. Chancellor and Foreign Minister at the time of the Ruhr crisis and Foreign Minister thereafter, he died on the eve of the Great Depression in 1929. During his six years in office, Germany regained stability at home and respect abroad. Much of the credit for this achievement was rightly given to Stresemann. Only when Hitler began to revise the Treaty of Versailles by threat of force rather than persuasion, as had been Stresemann's method, did people begin to wonder whether Hitler's success was not made easier because Stresemann had prepared the ground, and whether the aims of the two men were not basically much alike.

As this chapter shows, the picture of Stresemann remains far from clear. The author is Professor of History at the University of Alberta. Her special field is recent German history. Among her books are Gustav Stresemann: Eine politische Biographie zur Geschichte der Weimarer Republik (Hannover/Frankfurt, 1957), and Flucht in den Mythos: Die Deutschnationale Volkspartei und die Niederlage von 1918 (Göttingen, 1969). This selection first appeared as: "Die Locarnopolitik im Lichte des Stresemann- Nachlasses," in Zeitschrift für Politik, III (August 1956), 42–63. It is reprinted by permission of the author and publisher and has been translated by the editor.

I

WHEN WEST GERMAN Chancellor Adenauer visited Moscow in September 1955, the *Frankfurter Allgemeine Zeitung* commented on the "new style" of diplomatic negotiations between Germany and the Soviet Union: "Cordial relations, declarations of sympathy, good manners—but in the background the toughest and coldest struggle over the issues. This is something new." [1]

In a similar vein, though with much more warmth and enthusiasm, did Germany and the world in 1925 greet the diplomatic collaboration at Locarno as "something new." Applying the above quotation in retrospect to Locarno, we might say that its first part in the course of time has become exaggerated, while the second—Locarno as a tough and cold struggle over issues—has been forgotten. The statesmen at the time, still caught in nineteenth-century terminology, spoke deliberately and with oratorical relish of the "spirit of Locarno." Britain's Foreign Minister Austen Chamberlain called Locarno "a turning point in European history." No wonder, then, that Gustav Stresemann, the initiator of the treaty, used his British colleague's statement and, at the time of the signing of the Treaty of Locarno, gave his own interpretation of this "turning point": "I see the achievement of Locarno not as a juridical construction of political ideas, I see it as the basis of a great future. Statesmen have thus proclaimed their readiness to prepare the way for mankind's longing for peace and understanding." [2] Stresemann's sentences have since been quoted often and with admiration. [3]

The "spirit of Locarno" had been preceded by the "spirit" of the London Agreements. This "spirit," of course, was propagated not only in Germany but abroad, where the three foreign ministers—Chamberlain, Briand, and Stresemann—were awarded the Nobel Peace Prize. The Cathedral of St. John in New York celebrated a thanksgiving service on the day the Locarno Treaty was signed.

But if, from a distance of thirty-one years, we examine the "new style" of Locarno, we find that it was not really so new after all; it was rather a return, after the war and its aftermath, to customs natural to diplomacy since its beginnings. The style was new only if one considers war, hot or cold, as the normal state of international relations. "New" at Locarno was merely that, compared with negotiations before the war, secret diplomacy had been abolished, and that foreign policy was made not only in view of but with the participation of the public. New, especially in Germany, was the fact that the Foreign Minister was no longer a professional bureaucrat of the old school but a parliamentarian and party leader. The consequences of this change were obvious. They were enhanced by the fact that Stresemann was a skilled speaker and writer who already in his younger years had recognized the importance of the press and film as political tools.[4] His every interview was carefully checked, and each sentence was calculated for effect.[5] Similarly, all his speeches and his innumerable signed and unsigned newspaper articles were intended for specific effect. This is so obvious that it would not bear mentioning if Stresemann's biographers had not neglected the historian's wish to know the political intent behind his numerous and often-quoted speeches.

In trying to answer the question of what the "spirit of Locarno" was all about, we must at the same time concern ourselves with the controversial figure who helped create this "spirit" and used it politically. This is no easy task, not only because we are still missing important documents of the German Foreign Ministry [6] (though Stresemann kept many original documents or copies among his private papers), but because it is one of the most difficult, if not impossible, tasks of the historian to do full justice to a historical figure. What Hans Delbrück said in his critique of Emil Ludwig's image of Bismarck also applies to Stresemann: "Each great statesman carries his own legend." [7] Despite all the attacks which Stresemann suffered in his lifetime, his public image today is generally favorable: "from nationalist to European" is the formula that usually describes his life and development. Anyone who knows Stresemann and the Weimar Republic only from a distance is faced with a dilemma when he compares this established view of Stresemann with the impression he gains from the nearly sixty thousand pieces of his private papers. The traditional picture has little in common with the figure that emerges from the documents.[8] In what follows, the Stresemann papers have been used one-sidedly on purpose. The resulting picture of Stresemann does not claim to be "correct." It is, subjective factors aside, based on a specific source, albeit one (private papers) which normally is the most important to a historian writing on events which he did not himself experience. This, then, is not intended to be a new and complete picture, but merely a contribution to the scholarly discussion concerning Stresemann's personality. Even so, this essay remains a "thorny task." As Delbrück remarked when trying to clarify Bismarck's image, "People do not like to have their legends destroyed; they view the scholar who does so as desecrator." Yet the historian cannot evade his duty; because "where historical scholarship is no longer accepted, historical legend will thrive." [9]

Let us therefore try, in looking at the Locarno Pact, to forget the "spirit of Locarno" and the idea of German-French understanding so dear to us. Instead, let us ask dispassionately how the Locarno agreement originated, what aims Stresemann pursued with it, and what he finally achieved by it.

The demand for German-French understanding was first publicly raised by Stresemann in the Reichstag in March and April 1921, when the German government was afraid of Allied entry into the Ruhr.[10] In the worst days of 1923, after the end of passive resistance in the Ruhr, Stresemann, now Chancellor, renewed his demand and proposed some kind of security agreement. His speech of September 2 had been preceded by the offer of his predecessor Cuno to conclude a pact in which Germany, France, Great Britain, and Italy would promise not to wage war with each other without first holding a plebiscite on the issue. This was an awkward proposal, for what guarantee would a plebiscite offer in a country where the rightist opposition was only waiting for a chance at revenge? Poincaré, therefore, had branded the proposal as a "clumsy maneuver" and a "dangerous deceit," and had refused to take it up. Even so, a security pact among the nations interested in the Rhine region remained a frequent subject of discussion between the British ambassador in Berlin, Lord d'Abernon, and the officials of the Wilhelmstrasse.

On January 10, 1925, the first occupation zone of the Rhineland was to be evacuated by Allied occupation troops under Article 429 of the Versailles Treaty, if Germany had faithfully lived up to her obligations to disarm. Already at the London Conference on August 12, 1924, Britain's Prime Minister MacDonald had notified the German delegates —Marx, Stresemann, and Luther—that in December there would be a check on whether or not Germany had fulfilled her disarmament obligations. "We stand by the letter of the Treaty of Versailles," the Prime Minister had said, "and will not deviate from it by a hair." [11] At the same time he advised the German government to appoint a more tactful liaison officer who could get along with the Allied control officers. If that was not done, Germany might suffer. "I do not want to occupy a foot of German soil longer than I have to," he added; "I want to return the region on time. But I do not know how long I shall be in office. If I should still be here in December, I would very much like to clear up this matter, in close collaboration with the German government." MacDonald was pleased by the cordial relations that had developed among the delegates of the London Conference. "We want to cultivate and deepen this spirit," he said. "The next great difficulty, however, will be the question of Rhineland evacuation; and that, in turn, depends upon disarmament." [12] The MacDonald government was replaced on October 29, 1924, by a cabinet under Stanley Baldwin, with Austen Chamberlain as Foreign Minister.

The disarmament check by the Military Control Commission, which began on September 8, met with great popular resistance and with passive resistance from the Reichswehr.[13] Although it was rumored in the foreign press that the results of the check were by no means satisfactory and that, as Lord Curzon stated in the House of Commons on December 18, the evacuation of the Rhineland could only be decided after a report from the Allied Control Commission, Germany clearly expected the evacuation by January 10, 1925.

On December 28, however, the Conference of Ambassadors, after receiving a preliminary report from the Allied Control Commission, decided to postpone the evacuation. Already, on December 20, a meeting of the German cabinet had dealt with these impending events. There was great concern over possible opposition from the right if the Rhineland were not evacuated. Stresemann demanded that the fight for evacuation on January 10 be continued, even if a postponement until May might seem bearable.[14] In a second cabinet meeting on December 29, he insisted that if "Germany were notified of the nonevacuation in the manner already reported in some French newspapers, and especially if an indefinite further occupation were planned, this would mean the bankruptcy of the London policy, and the three German Ministers, who had participated in the London negotiations, would have to ask themselves whether in view of this blow (*Faustschlag*) against their policy they could still belong to the cabinet and face parliament." [15]

What did Stresemann mean by *"Faustschlag* against their policy"? He was obviously referring to Germany's acceptance of the Dawes Plan which, to Stresemann, meant primarily an international loan and the postponement of reparations, and which he viewed as no more than "an economic armistice for a few years." [16] Thus if Stresemann here speaks of a *Faustschlag,* he identifies himself with the views of his opponents, who accused him of being a "proponent of fulfillment" (*Erfüllungspolitiker*) par excellence.[17] He repeatedly insisted that the German government had loyally lived up to its obligations under the London Agreements and the Dawes Plan and that the failure to evacuate the Rhineland violated the "spirit" of the London Agreements, to which Britain's Prime Minister had also referred.

The next day Stresemann addressed the kind of audience with which he was always a great success and which he therefore liked best—the foreign press. He skillfully explained what he understood by "loyal fulfillment." As a term, it was "not very precise," and he interpreted it vaguely and evasively. "Loyal fulfillment" could not possibly mean living up to every detail of every provision; the important thing was whether Germany was disarmed or not. "If one wanted to interpret the term differently, one might hold that because Germany had one rifle more than permitted, the Allies could remain in the Cologne zone." [18] Stresemann instead appealed to the "spirit" of the London Agreements: their purpose had been not merely to solve the reparations question; with its solution there was to come "a period of international understanding. The Dawes Plan is to be the foundation of Germany's freedom, guaranteed by treaty." The London Conference, he added, was "a fight of trust against distrust." All who had supported the Dawes Plan were thus affected. What did 20,000 or even 100,000 rifles matter against the fact that Germany was completely disarmed! Germany could not even wage a defensive war. Stresemann skillfully belittled possible Allied objections. "These are things that can be cleared up in a short time, were it not for material differences such as whether an existing powder factory can produce more powder than Germany is permitted under the Treaty of Versailles and whether, therefore, it must be dismantled. It has been objected that the Krupp firm has lathes that are larger than permitted . . ." and so on. At the end of his speech Stresemann touched on the question of police, whose large number and billeting in army barracks was among Allied objections. Stresemann ridiculed the idea that a policeman directing traffic on the Potsdamer Platz might turn out to be a military commander because of his knowledge of strategy. He closed his speech saying: "There must be certainty about the facts: presentation and examination of material evidence by both sides; if there are wrongs, the German government must correct them. But I would like to warn against a policy which would disavow those who have honestly worked for and believed in a policy of understanding, which is essential not only for Germany's, but for Europe's future."

On January 3, 1925, Stresemann brought the impending nonevacuation and expected Allied note before the Foreign Affairs Committee of the Reichsrat:[19] "With respect to the actual situation, if one looks at the facts—let me first speak purely theoretically—the position created by Allied suspicions is very difficult." It was difficult because Stresemann realized that the Allies were in the right, at least as far as the letter of the treaty was concerned, and because Germany did not wish to live up to certain demands. As Foreign Minister he refused, however, to answer the question how far the Allied objections concerning disarmament were justified. He *did* say that the objections concerning the General Staff were nonsense.[20] As for temporary army volunteers, it was generally known that Germany had needed them during the Ruhr crisis. Germany's domestic situation had made this necessary. Stresemann, of course, knew very well that the temporary volunteers and the "Black (i.e., secret) Reichswehr" had not existed only in 1923. Ludwig Quidde and Professor Walter Schücking had informed him about the training of volunteers (in Marburg, for instance), and had asked what he intended to do about his "policy of understanding," for which the German people could only be grateful, "being sabotaged by other groups, if not systematically, nevertheless in fact."[21]

The "Nachlass" contains no reaction of Stresemann to this inquiry, nor any evidence that he acted on it. The papers show rather that Stresemann again and again tried to belittle these matters without doing anything about them. To be sure, as E. H. Carr notes,[22] it is customary for a Foreign Minister to reject attacks against another government department. But there is no doubt that Stresemann agreed with, and thus indirectly supported, the activities of the Reichswehr and various patriotic associations so long as they did not interfere with his diplomatic negotiations.[23] In an emergency he could always use the "communist danger" as an excuse, as he did especially with England and America.[24] With the French, on the other hand, he preferred to dwell on the deplorable danger of Europe's Americanization.[25] But the Foreign Minister was again more farsighted and realistic than his domestic opponents. Allied fear of German rearmament, whether justified or not, was a fact to be taken into account. Stresemann therefore seized upon the remark by Herriot to the German ambassador in Paris, von Hoesch, that France feared for her security. The German Foreign Minister countered by appealing to a "policy of understanding." "I warn against any movement that brings us into a new Ruhr struggle," Stresemann said. "To make a gesture is worthless. If one does, it must be followed by a deed; else it serves no purpose." [26]

On January 5, 1925, the Allies gave official notice that they would not evacuate the first zone of the Rhineland by January 10, because Germany had not fulfilled the conditions of Versailles. The violations of which Germany was accused were not spelled out in detail. In return the German note of protest, while not accusing the Allies of "treaty violation," nevertheless spoke of "disloyal execution of the treaty." [27] When the Lord Mayor of Cologne, Konrad Adenauer, notified Stresemann that he planned to make a statement about the nonevacuation in the name of the Cologne city council, Stresemann agreed, but warned the Mayor not to take issue with any alleged German violations. He should emphasize instead that Germany's recovery under the Dawes Plan was thus being endangered. Germany was ready to take on the London obligations; but to do so she also needed "psychological satisfaction" (*seelische Befriedigung*). Stresemann realized that Germany would be the loser in any specific discussion of violations and thus shifted to the vague ground of the "spirit" of the London Agreements and the *seelische Befriedigung* of the Germans.

In the meeting of the Reichsrat's Foreign Affairs Committee, Stresemann had proposed "to give in on the industrial questions and to destroy the lathes and steel furnaces because," as he put it, "if they [the Allies] insist, I want to force them to meet our argument: it is not possible to bring about maximum German production and export, if the industrial means for peaceful production are destroyed on such flimsy pretext. Should the time come when we have to pay $2\frac{1}{2}$ instead of 1 billion and we cannot do so,[28] we must be able to point out that present policy was responsible." [29] The Mayor of Cologne spoke as Stresemann had suggested.

Germany's notes of protest did not improve an already tense situation. The German government had complained especially that it had not been told of specific violations. This failure to specify Allied objections in fact created an uncomfortable situation for the government. The defense of an accused who knows that he is guilty but does not wish to mend his ways is difficult as long as he does not know for which of his misdeeds he is being accused. In a private letter,[30] a poor translation of which is among Stresemann's papers, Britain's Foreign Minister complained about the "illconditioned" first, and the "even more stupid" second note of the German government. If Germany fulfilled her obligations, he wrote, the British would fulfill theirs. "I would have thought that it would have been valuable for the German government to take notice of this pledge. . . . Their second note is full of complaints. Even in the matter of formulating Allied complaints, I am surprised they never thought of the fact that this hesitation stemmed from a wish on the part of the Allied governments to examine the military report carefully and to distinguish between those violations which are essential and must be corrected, and those which are unimportant and thus might be summarily passed over. . . . Maybe I don't understand the German mentality; but the Germans never understand the mentality of others."

It must not, of course, be forgotten or underestimated that a large part of Stresemann's and Chancellor Luther's difficulties came from the fact that for the first time the German National People's party was participating in the government. Luther's major concern was to keep his cabinet together.[31] When the German government at last was officially notified, on June 4, 1925, of the specific Allied objections,[32] Luther took the position that small demands should, if possible, be met, but more important ones should be turned down.[33] This agreed with Stresemann's statement in the Reichsrat's Foreign Affairs Committee on January 3.

These events, which Hans W. Gatzke has already mentioned, are told here because there was a close connection between Germany's failure to disarm, the resulting nonevacuation of the Cologne zone, and the initiative for a security pact. This connection has been neglected by earlier research into the history of Locarno. In a speech to the Foreign Affairs Committee of the Reichstag on March 11, 1925, Stresemann dealt with the background of the memorandum of February 9, 1925, in which Germany had proposed a German-French Security Pact. Under such a pact, Germany, France, and Belgium were to forgo any change of their frontiers by force and were to recognize the status quo of Versailles in the west. This was to be likewise guaranteed by England and Italy. Stresemann's speech told what had led to this German initiative. "It was in December of last year. I may perhaps briefly describe the situation. It was characterized for one thing by official announcements that an evacuation of the Cologne zone on January 10 of this year would not take place. The reason given was the same we are still hearing today— no specific evidence as yet on German violations, such material could not be presented; but that a still-to-be-published report will prove these German violations. But I still do not believe that the nonevacuation of the northern Rhineland zone is solely due to this issue." [34]

Another consideration in connection with the Security Pact was how much the fate of the "Geneva Protocol" had been responsible for non-evacuation. "This raises the question of what we can do about this Allied worry over the occupied region and the Rhineland, so as to avert the consequences for us of continued occupation and its effects on the whole future of the Rhineland. Our concern that Anglo-French proposals might tend in the direction [of continued occupation] was increased by the fact that the present British Foreign Minister, while very cool toward us, belongs among the advocates of an *entente cordiale* with France and the believers in an Allied Security Pact which would doubtless be directed against Germany. In view of England's difficulties in the Orient, her acquiescence to France on this question would simply be a compensation for France's support of England in the Orient, so that the differences between the two *entente* powers would be settled on our back. Those were the considerations which led us to consider whether it was not a good idea to take the initiative ourselves and to state our position on these events, rather than simply to await developments." The withdrawal of military occupation from the Rhineland, Stresemann said, had been left out of the memorandum of February 9 on purpose; but the "logical connection" was there. One of the main reasons for Germany's initiative had been Herriot's statement that the question of security was at the center of all his considerations. Since France was thus chiefly concerned about security, one could try to satisfy her in this manner without having to live up fully to the embarrassing disarmament obligations.

Here we have an outline of the "spirit of Locarno" half a year before Locarno. Stresemann thus could later say with full justice: "I place far less value on the paragraphs of Locarno than on the political-psychological consequences of this collaboration." [35] He was entirely correct in his interpretation of the Locarno Treaty. The psychological-political consequence of which he spoke was the liberation of the Rhineland, without Germany's fulfilling in return all the Allies' demands.[36] It began with the evacuation of the first zone on the day the Locarno Treaty was signed. The Ambassadors' Conference which had reached this decision on November 14 thus wished to show that a new chapter had begun in relations between Germany and the Allies. Stresemann's assumption that the nonevacuation of the Cologne zone was due not solely to Germany's failure in her treaty obligations, but was also related to the general problems of security, especially for France, was thus proved right.

So much for the internal discussions of the Security Pact and its relation to demilitarization. Such a pact, however, meant more for Germany than merely the avoidance of continued occupation. To understand this we must consider the world's economic situation at the time. Germany urgently needed foreign credits, while the United States was in the midst of an economic boom and was accumulating excess gold. The $800 million loan had been one of the conditions on which the German delegation in London had accepted the Dawes Plan in August 1924. In a meeting of the Reichstag's Foreign Affairs Committee on July 17, Stresemann explained: "If we do not win cooperation from the financially strong nations, especially America, who is on England's and France's side in these issues, I predict an economic collapse with unforeseeable consequences." [37] A few weeks earlier, the financial leaders of England, America, and Germany—Montagu Norman, Strong, and Schacht—had met to talk about some kind of joint capital trust.[38] The governor of the American Federal Reserve Bank apparently had warned Stresemann at that time that America would not grant any loans to Germany if the Security Pact failed because of Germany.[39] Stresemann had been sufficiently worried to write a long letter to the American ambassador in London, Houghton, with whom he was on close terms since the latter's years in Berlin. The letter told about the negotiations concerning demilitarization, raising once again the communist specter; but it also dwelled on Houghton's good relations with Germany, stressing the fact that Stresemann had accepted the Dawes Plan at the time because of Houghton. Now Stresemann was worried that Germany had perhaps overestimated her strength, and urgently needed further loans.[40] The Dawes Plan and Locarno thus were closely related. Locarno was the necessary political sequel and supplement to the Dawes Plan if the economic policy of loans was to be continued. Stresemann hoped that foreign economic support for Germany, especially from the United States but also from England, would automatically tie the creditors' interests more closely to Germany and thus bear political fruit.[41] In discussing the Locarno Treaty with his party colleagues, Stresemann repeatedly stressed the relationship between a Security Pact and American loans.[42]

The last, but by no means weakest, motive for Stresemann's seeking the Security Pact was the recovery of the lost territories in the east.[43] Public opinion in France, as in Poland, feared that Germany, through a Security Pact in the west, merely wanted a free hand in the east. The French therefore demanded a Security Pact with the eastern states as well. But this Stresemann categorically refused. Just as Bethmann Hollweg during the First World War had turned down all annexations in the west while reserving a change of frontiers in the east, so Stresemann now declared that the frontiers in the east had not been settled and therefore could not be guaranteed. England and the United States looked favorably upon Germany's demand for a revision of eastern frontiers. France, however, declared that a Security Pact that affected the interests of her allies, especially Poland, was out of the question. But instead of the requested guarantee of the eastern frontier, Germany only concluded arbitration treaties with Poland, Czechoslovakia, and France.

The Treaty of Locarno was called a "treaty of renunciation" (*Verzichtvertrag*) by Stresemann's opponents, especially those on the right, and the German National People's party asked its ministers to leave the government after Stresemann and Luther returned from Locarno. The agitation against Stresemann took on unusual and threatening forms. But unless the purpose of the opposition was to prevent the hated Republic from stabilizing itself with an improvement of its international relations, such opposition is incomprehensible. For at Locarno nothing was "renounced" that Germany had not already lost by the Treaty of Versailles. But only by conceding that Germany recognized existing conditions in the west was it possible openly to state that she did not accept her eastern frontiers. Locarno, as Stresemann emphasized again and again, was not *Verzichtpolitik* [44] but rather the first step toward "undermining" (*auszuhöhlen*) the Treaty of Versailles. The cornerstone of the whole Versailles system was being demolished. Locarno was Germany's first successful step toward a revision of Versailles.

II

A few weeks before Locarno, where Stresemann (according to Henry Bretton) went as a German proposing a German solution to the problem of peace and from where he returned as a "European," [45] he wrote his famous letter to the German Crown Prince.[46] This letter actually says nothing much new. If it did not exist, Stresemann would hardly appear different. With little effort one can document its statements from other sources. The letter is significant because it contains all of Stresemann's aims in a single document and because it uses Metternich's term *finassieren,* which means "to play dirty tricks" or, as Srbik says in his biography of Metternich, "devious deceit of enemies under the cover of friendship." [47] Was this word only aimed at the Crown Prince, to make Locarno palatable to him? Stresemann often used the term in referring, if not to Metternich, at least to the organizers of the Wars of Liberation, Stein and Hardenberg.[48] His statements cannot simply be waved aside with the regret that Stresemann ever wrote such letters and the claim that this letter was not very important.[49] To be sure, its interpretation poses difficult problems, and it cannot yet be decided whether Stresemann's true thoughts and aims were expressed in his eulogy of the "spirit of Locarno" at the signing of the Locarno Treaty, or in his letter to the Crown Prince. But why should the alternative be "European" or "nationalist"? Why not say simply that Stresemann, more akin to Metternich than he knew and wanted to be, was a "master of politics"? Such a man would necessarily be different in the twentieth century than in the eighteenth or early nineteenth. He had to conduct, methodologically, a quite different policy, *with the public,* and hence with the "spirit of Locarno." One need not therefore share the pessimism of Hirsch: "There would be no hope of ever having real peace in the Old World if it could be proved that the only German statesman who won the Nobel Peace Prize and who was generally believed to be a good European, was merely a front for the sinister tendencies of the German General Staff, and that all of his protestations of sincerity were hollow phrases cleverly designed to deceive his colleagues in Paris and London." [50] Politics, Stresemann once said, is a "business deal" (*Geschäft*), and relations with other nations must be built upon common interests.[51] Locarno, too, was a *Geschäft,* which had to serve the interests of all concerned and with which the three foreign ministers—Stresemann, Briand, and Chamberlain—were well satisfied. But would the "political-psychological consequences," that is, the unsaid purposes and aims of Locarno, in the long run turn out to be to the common interest of Germany and France? Were they not rather opposed to each other and mutually exclusive? Stresemann saw Locarno as a means of speeding up the revision of the Treaty of Versailles, to make Germany again what she once had been. His aim, in the last analysis, was "to fight France's aggressive policy" [52] and to drive her back "from trench to trench" (*von Schützengraben zu Schützengraben*).[53] His friend and partner Briand, on the other hand, wanted to use the Locarno Treaty and his European policy to stabilize the Europe of 1918. Germany's aim was equality, France's aim security. Was it not mixing fire and water to try to satisfy both aims at once?

In the name of Europe, with emphasis on the friendly sentiments of European statesmen (who had not even made a concession on the issue of the "war guilt clause" [54] which was so important for Stresemann's domestic position), and with enthusiastic support from the neutral states, the "spirit of Locarno" was cultivated and cited far more by Stresemann than by his foreign partners. This was necessary because in practice the "spirit" was quite ineffective. It remained merely a semblance, an illusion which nonetheless was used by Stresemann whenever he encountered difficulties and when the liberation from the "shackles" of Versailles went too slowly. He knew that at Locarno he had made not a political but only a psychological sacrifice; but as a true statesman he used this psychological sacrifice in international negotiations as well as in anonymous articles in which he appealed to the "spirit of Locarno." "The ordinary person [he once wrote] thinks as follows: Through the

Locarno Treaty, peace between France and Germany is secured. Why, then, are there still troops in the Rhineland? Through the Kellogg Pact, the nations have renounced war as a political instrument. Why, then, do the troops remain in the Rhineland? In the League of Nations all powers have equal rights. Why, then, is the territory of one of the members being occupied? When Germany joined the League, Briand said: Away with cannons and machine guns! But why do they remain in the Rhineland? The opponents of the Locarno policy point to these things as weaknesses in Stresemann's policy, and he himself admits that these objections are just and that he has nothing to say in return." [55] Stresemann, however, did not really want to say anything in return because, as he had said in an off-the-record speech to a select audience, the government and the Foreign Minister had to try very hard "not to let a success appear as such, but to paint a sombre picture even when we do not think it is appropriate." [56] The constant appeal to Locarno finally had its effect. In the late summer of 1929, Stresemann was able at the Hague Conference to extract from Briand a final date for the evacuation of the Rhineland, five years ahead of the date set in the Treaty of Versailles.

III

Let us now look at the man whose name is most closely associated with Locarno. To do so, we must go beyond the subject of this chapter, so as to judge the relation and importance of Locarno to the rest of Stresemann's policy.

The traditional German view of Stresemann is centered on the great "transformation," the "Damascus" in his life. The date for this is variously given as 1918, 1922, 1923, or as late as 1925,[57] each time with a different event as cause. These differences by themselves indicate that the "Damascus" may exist more in the mind of the observer than in Stresemann himself. But even if there was no sudden change, there remains the question whether Stresemann underwent a basic change from nationalist to European gradually. This also requires a definition of what Stresemann's biographers mean by "European." Stresemann was forty years old at the time of the collapse of 1918; he was forty-three when he first spoke of the need for German-French understanding; and he was forty-seven when he took the road to Locarno. These are times of life when men do not usually undergo a basic change in their political views.

It is important for Stresemann's political development that only in the last ten years of his life, under a new constitution, did he enjoy wider influence, and that only in the last six years did he gain a position of political responsibility. The fact that he was ready thus to participate distinguishes him favorably from the German Nationalists, who preferred to remain in opposition. While the Nationalists remained party politicians, Stresemann grew into a responsible statesman and diplomat. Already, as a party politician during the World War, he had shown the ability not only to adjust to "new circumstances" but to move in a new direction in order to appear "progressive" and "not get run over" (*nicht unter den Schlitten zu kommen*).[58] This he had done in 1917, when he came out for electoral reform in Prussia, and again in January 1918, when he demanded equal franchise, even though he did not favor it.[59] In the summer of 1917, he had also—somewhat vaguely but no more dishonestly than the initiator of the Peace Resolution, Erzberger [60] (with whose character and political development Stresemann had much in common)—come out for a "peace of understanding." How elastic the term "peace of understanding" was becomes clear if we compare what the Germans understood by it in 1917 and in 1918. In 1917 it was still a concept which could later lead to Brest-Litovsk; in 1918 it was a nebulous Wilsonian "peace of conciliation." What Stresemann really expected from a peace based on Wilson's Fourteen Points he had written on October 26, 1918, to Friedberg: "Wilson's Fourteen Points, in my opinion, entail the possibility of loss of Alsace-Lorraine, Upper Silesia, Posen, and parts of West Prussia, and in addition an unlimited amount of reparations, which may easily turn into a war indemnity, even if dressed up differently." [61] When this prediction came to pass, however, with the publication of the peace conditions in May 1919, Stresemann branded it a "world fraud" (*Weltbetrug*) since peace "was to be based on quite specific conditions." [62] The indignation against the Treaty of Versailles was less because of its "immorality" than because those who had thought of themselves as Romans suddenly found themselves Carthaginians.[63]

In discussing war aims during the last two years of the war, as also in the question of electoral reform, we are faced for the first time with the problem that Stresemann said different things to different people on the same subject, and in doing so made a distinction between "deeply committing oneself" (*bekennen*) and "publicly advocating" (*öffentlich dafür eintreten*). It was a contrast between theory and practice. No one will criticize an important political figure for not holding rigidly to party dogma, or for acting pragmatically in the best interests of his country—or what he thinks are the best interests. In Stresemann's case, his "adjustment" after 1918 was the less "blameworthy" since (with the exception of the Kapp *Putsch,* where he once more bet on the wrong horse) the "facts" to which he adjusted appear in retrospect as the only possible and sensible ones. This made him unpopular with his old friends and popular with his former opponents—the Democrats, Social Democrats, and the Center, even with some pacifists—though they never quite trusted him. His policy also earned him great prestige abroad, for while the bourgeois governments of the West did not like Germany's bourgeois nationalists, they nevertheless preferred a bourgeois to a socialist government. Cooperation with Stresemann was the easier because the numerous industrialists and economic leaders engaged in foreign affairs all were seized by the fear of bolshevism. The American Ambassador Houghton [64] and Lord d'Abernon were foremost among them. The lack of politically able men in Weimar Germany made Stresemann by necessity the only possible negotiating partner.

It is difficult for an outsider to understand Stresemann the man. He liked to apply to himself a saying which, of course, anyone can apply to himself:

> I'm not a clever book of fiction,
> I am a man of contradiction. [65]

To be sure, there was much contradiction in him. As in each important statesman, one finds in Stresemann the two faces of a Janus, or even the constantly changing figure of a Proteus. On the one hand we have the shrewd politician, a man of affairs, of business—matter-of-fact and without a sense of humor [66]—who adjusts his policy to the way people are and not the way they ought to be. On the other hand we have, it seems, an emotional politician of great personal sensitivity, a man whom his contemporaries and friends found good, generous, helpful, and loyal, with a touch of the typical German bourgeois (*Biedermann*) and philistine (*Bildungsphilister*).

He was an excellent speaker, less because of the wealth of his ideas than the eloquence of his speeches. But then, the speeches of a politician are intended for the moment and for a specific purpose, and are not meant for the edification of future generations and of historians. For the latter, however, the problem arises—what is rhetoric and show and what is conviction, where does the one end and the other begin? Does he speak from conviction when he tries to win the German Nationalists to his side; or does he speak from conviction in Geneva or before any other international forum, to gain the world's trust for his own and Germany's policy, so that his national aim, liberation from the Treaty of Versailles, will be achieved? Or does he perhaps identify always with those he is addressing, so that neither the speeches to the one nor the other audience can be used as sources for his convictions or confessions? From his earlier days we know that to "commit himself" always meant to him to "commit himself behind closed doors." Might he suddenly have changed this fundamental attitude and, from his forty-seventh year on, that is from the time of the Locarno Conference, proclaimed in Geneva a kind of political testament? [67] One must distinguish with Stresemann, as was done so acutely by the editor of this journal in his obituary,[68] between what he was and what he wanted to be. If he wanted to be or become a great statesman, Grabowsky writes, that may mean that he was not really a great statesman. But one does him perhaps greater justice and wins more sympathy and recognition for him by acknowledging his efforts.

In this light, Stresemann's literary attempts, his juxtaposition of Goethe and Napoleon, appear less dilettantish and awkward. On the other hand, one must not take these literary ambitions too seriously, for they also suggest how well he understood his German public to realize that it is always effective to cite Goethe to them and to speak of culture, learning, and spirit (*Kultur, Bildung und Geist*). Stresemann, in his readiness to quote as well as in his adaptability, comes perhaps closest to Prince Bülow, for whom he had great admiration. To be sure, Stresemann liked to talk in the *Bühnenklub* and in literary groups, but one wonders with whom he talked and with whom he exchanged his countless letters. A man who in retrospect has often been described as spiritual (*vergeistigt*) and "Western" (*abendländisch*) ought to have had contact with some persons of rank and achievement. But Stresemann's papers and letters show a man who, outside of politics, was quite average, a man who through his speeches and letters again and again had the misfortune to be misunderstood, though he claimed always to have expressed himself so very clearly. No one, certainly, will make demands upon a politician and statesman which he need not fulfill and which do not belong to his metier. But here, too, others have tried, as with his premature death,[69] to employ fairy tales which do not stand up to critical examination but which the legend seems to demand,[70] so as to make the hero appear greater and more attuned to German needs—then and now.

In so doing, one really renders Stresemann no service. For it is unjust to demand of a man more than his talents as well as his times and surroundings permit him. His achievements in politics, of which he was a master, remain unimpaired, because they were extraordinary. The skill and agility, as well as the calculation, with which he mastered a political discussion, be it with politicians of the German National People's party or with his diplomatic opponent Briand, make us suspect that when he expressed himself vaguely and indistinctly, when he couched his aims in passionate and emotional language, when he was misunderstood—it was not the working of a muddled, emotional mind prone to illusions but of a calculating intelligence.

He was a politician with extraordinary instinct for what was politically necessary and possible, a man of "finesse" (*Finassieren*). It is certainly no accident that he used this word of Metternich's and that he repeatedly referred to the statesmen of the Wars of Liberation, for he sensed strongly the parallelism of events. Just as Wagram and Schönbrunn deeply affected Metternich's internal and external development, so the lost war had its impact on Stresemann. "Cool waiting, soft step, and careful advance"—these were Metternich's and Stresemann's methods. One might say of Stresemann's policy what Srbik writes of Metternich's: "It is perfect and statesmanlike if it recognizes that 'one cannot fight against necessity' and if, with undeviating aim, it awaits the day of decision with patience, subtlety, and keenness, in order to intervene strengthened and with full power." [71] Different as these two men were, and little as Stresemann would have chosen the unheroic Metternich as a model—his models were Napoleon and in Germany Stein and Hardenberg—nevertheless in the weakness of the two men as well as in their strength there was much similarity. Both possessed great optimism, unusual adaptability, and a great measure of self-assurance which, on Stresemann's part, because of an inferiority complex, was at times exaggerated, at times deflated. Just as Metternich was ready to fulfill the conditions of his peace treaty so as to avoid any suspicion of hostile intentions against France, and to win Napoleon's good will for Austria so as to lead his country out of its misery, so Stresemann needed for the same long-range goal the "armistice" of the Dawes Plan and the "armistice" of Locarno. His undeviating aim was to revise, undermine, and liquidate the Treaty of Versailles.

Where might his policy finally have led? [72] History does not allow us to travel with assurance any road other than the one it has taken. It became the world's tragedy that the consistent execution of the aims pursued by Stresemann at Locarno fell to the National Socialists.

NOTES

1. *Frankfurter Allgemeine Zeitung*, September 15, 1955.

2. Gustav Stresemann, *Vermächtnis*, II, 253.

3. The speech had been too *pathetisch* even for Chancellor Luther, who was to have given it. This had led to a long argument the night before, the result of which was that Luther gave a different speech, and Stresemann delivered the above.

4. Germany, Auswärtiges Amt, Politisches Archiv, "Nachlass des Reichsaussenministers Dr. Gustav Stresemann," microfilm, National Archives, Washington, D.C. Cited by numbers of film roll, serial, and frame: "Nachlass," 3104/7158/153456, no date: "It is necessary that we make use of every modern means to influence public opinion." Even the film *Aschenbrödel* (*Cinderella*) was to give "other nations a better understanding of the German people's soul." "Nachlass," 3106/7166/155161: "Dr. Stresemann über die Aufgaben des Films," *Film Kurier*, February 2, 1924.

5. See Annelise Thimme, "Gustav Stresemann, Legende und Wirklichkeit," *Historische Zeitschrift*, CLXXXI, No. 2 (April 1956), 335, note 4.

6. On one question these documents can supply important information: What was the relationship between Stresemann and the Foreign Ministry? Stresemann had little personal knowledge of foreign countries, personalities, conditions, and forces. That also explains his relations to sometimes rather dubious nonofficial go-betweens, as for instance the participant in the Kapp *Putsch*, Waldemar Pabst, and the eagerly pushing industrialist Arnold Rechberg.

7. Hans Delbrück, "Von der Bismarck-Legende," *Historische Zeitschrift,* CXXXIII (1926).

8. I have discussed this with several younger historians who have worked in the Stresemann papers and have found my views confirmed.

9. Gerhard Ritter, "Gegenwärtige Lage und Zukunftsaufgabe deutscher Geschichtswissenschaft," *Historische Zeitschrift,* CLXX (1950), 1.

10. "Nachlass," 3094/7002/142293: Stresemann to his brother-in-law Sorge, April 21, 1921. *Le Journal* of May 4, 1921, writes: "On the verge of seeing the Ruhr occupied, Mr. Stresemann suddenly discovers that we have common interests and therefore proposes an economic entente for the betterment of the world. This is either too late or too soon, but in any case, it is suspicious."

11. "Nachlass," 3119/7175/156816–24: "Tagbuch der Londoner Konferenz 4.–19. August 1924, geführt von der Reichskanzlei. Herrn R. M. Dr. Stresemann. Streng vertraulich, Nr. 2, 19 Anlagen. Anlage Aufzeichnung über ein Gespräch zwischen MacDonald und der deutschen Delegation Marx-Stresemann-Luther, 12. August 2:30 Uhr in Downing Street."

12. *Ibid.*

13. See Hans W. Gatzke, *Stresemann and the Rearmament of Germany* (Baltimore, 1954).

14. "Nachlass," 3111/7125/147227ff.

15. "Nachlass," 3120/7179/157829–32: Excerpt from the minutes of the cabinet meeting on December 29, 1924.

16. "Nachlass," 3119/7176/156946f.: Draft letter to the King of Bulgaria, no date, probably September 1924. See also Thimme, "Gustav Stresemann," pp. 312–14.

17. The *Deutsche Tageszeitung,* on August 13, 1926, called Stresemann a "fulfillment politician to the bitter end" (*Erfüllungspolitiker bis zum Äussersten*).

18. "Nachlass," 3129/7179/157838: Stresemann before the foreign press on December 30, 1924. See also *Vermächtnis,* I, 619ff.

19. "Nachlass," 3120/7180/157879–96: Reichsaussenminister Stresemann im Auswärtigen Ausschuss des Reichsrates am 3. Januar 1925. See also *Vermächtnis,* II, 12ff.

20. This concerned the reproach that the German General Staff, which was to be abolished, had actually been restored in a different guise.

21. "Nachlass," 3106/7167/155388–90: Schücking to Stresemann, March 6, 1924.

22. Carr, *German-Soviet Relations Between the Two World Wars, 1919–1939,* p. 89.

23. See Gatzke, *Stresemann,* and Wheeler-Bennett, *The Nemesis of Power.*

24. Stresemann to Houghton, June 4, 1925: "We do not intend to let us be driven into revolution by the entente and to be deprived of the means [i.e., the police] which enable us to combat communism at home." Stresemann, *Vermächtnis,* II, 260.

25. On this Stresemann saw eye-to-eye even with Poincaré. See his talk with Poincaré on August 27, 1928: Stresemann, *Vermächtnis,* III, 357ff.; "Nachlass," 3116/7150/151363ff.

26. "Nachlass," 3120/7180/157890–91.

27. "Nachlass," 3120/7180/157904–06: Stresemann to Konrad Adenauer, January 7, 1925. The German-Allied exchange of notes is published in *Schulthess' Europäischer Geschichtskalender,* 1925.

28. In his letter to the Crown Prince on September 7, 1925, Stresemann mentioned that reparations under the Dawes Plan would probably become unpayable already in 1927: *Vermächtnis,* II, 553. He said the same in his speech to the

"Arbeitsgemeinschaft deutscher Landsmannschaften" on December 14, 1925: "Nach-lass," 3144/7323/160745ff.

29. "Nachlass," 3120/7180/157879–96.

30. "Nachlass," 3166/7312/158672–74: Copy of a letter from Chamberlain to Countess Seherr Thoss. The Countess appears to have been the very pro-German daughter of the American ambassador Henry White; see Alfred Vagts, "Henry White," *Europäische Gespräche*, IX, 1931.

31. Luther, "Vor 25 Jahren war Locarno—was ist heute?" Vortrag am 5. Dezember 1950, 20 Uhr, im Hotel Atlantic, Hamburg. Amerika-Gesellschaft e.V. Hamburg.

32. These were mainly complaints already mentioned in the note of January 5: restoration of the General Staff, training of volunteers, failure to convert factories from war production, and the housing of police in army barracks.

33. "Nachlass," 3114/7133/148794–801: Niederschrift über den Ministerrat am 5. Juni 1925, mittags 12 Uhr, im Hause des Reichspräsidenten.

34. "Nachlass," 3114/7135/148981–149010; see also *Vermächtnis*, II, 73ff.

35. "Nachlass," 3113/7131/148386f.: Stresemann to Wolgast, December 13, 1925.

36. See Gatzke, *Stresemann*, the chapter "From Ruhr to Locarno."

37. Stresemann, *Vermächtnis*, II, 149.

38. *Ibid.*, p. 154.

39. *Ibid.*, p. 222.

40. *Ibid.*, pp. 257ff. See also Felix E. Hirsch, "Stresemann, Ballin und Amerika," *Vierteljahrshefte für Zeitgeschichte*, January 1955.

41. "Nachlass," 3113/7131/148392–439: Speech to the "Arbeitsgemeinschaft der deutschen Landsmannschaften," December 14, 1925.

42. "Nachlass," 3113/7131/148313ff.

43. Stresemann to von Keudell, November 27, 1925: "I see in Locarno the preservation of the Rhineland and the possibility of the recovery of German lands in the east." *Vermächtnis*, II, 246. See also Thimme, "Gustav Stresemann," p. 316.

44. See, for instance, "Nachlass," 3165/7415/175681ff.

45. Henry Bretton, *Stresemann and the Revision of Versailles* (Stanford, 1953), p. 13. Is it really credible that a man of forty-seven, who had gone through the bitter and painful experience of a lost war and who, in constant conflict with the opposition of the right and with his own party, had lost many illusions, that such a man would return from a conference different from when he went?

46. For details see Thimme, "Gustav Stresemann."

47. Srbik, *Metternich: Der Staatsmann und der Mensch* (1925), I, 114.

48. See, for instance, Stresemann to Mrs. L. Fahlberg, September 30, 1922: "He [Stadtler] knows only the concept power and force, which is all very beautiful, but which at present has no meaning. Prussia would never have risen if, in the period from 1807 to 1813 she had not pursued a careful, and thus nationally successful, policy." "Nachlass," 3096/7017/144401, and 3169/7322/160637. See also Stresemann, *Vermächtnis*, II, 94f. and elsewhere. There remains the question, What do all these allusions to the policy of Stein and Hardenberg signify? Are they solely tactical, as was obviously the case in a speech before the members of the iron and steel industry in 1924 (see Thimme, "Gustav Stresemann," p. 334) or are, as was so often the case with Stresemann, tactics and "conviction" so intermingled that it is no longer possible to distinguish one from the other? It is at least clear that Germany *at the time* could pursue no policy other than peace and compliance. This frequently recurring "at the time" is equivalent to "until Germany has regained her strength." This reservation, whether its purpose was tactical or not, must be noted.

49. Thus Felix E. Hirsch, "Locarno—25 Years After," *Contemporary Review,* November 1950.

50. Felix E. Hirsch, "The Portent of Stresemann," *Commonweal,* March 1945.

51. "Nachlass," 3113/7131/148392: Stresemann's speech to the "Arbeitsgemeinschaft der deutschen Landsmannschaften," December 14, 1925.

52. Stresemann, *Vermächtnis,* II, 172: September 14, 1925.

53. *Ibid.,* p. 61: Stresemann to Generalleutnant K. von Scheuch, July 27, 1925.

54. A retraction of this clause by the Allies was so difficult because while initially it had nothing to do with moral guilt (see Annelise Thimme, *Hans Delbrück als Kritiker der Wilhelminischen Epoche* [1955], p. 146, note 6), it was tied up with the reparations chapter of the Treaty of Versailles. A retraction, therefore, meant not only an accommodating gesture which would have restored the "honor" of the German people, but it would have meant the legal cancellation of Allied reparations demands.

55. "Nachlass," 3101/7155/151883–96: "Die Vertrauenskrise des Locarnopaktes," undated manuscript.

56. Speech to the "Arbeitsgemeinschaft der deutschen Landsmannschaften," December 14, 1925.

57. See Thimme, "Gustav Stresemann," p. 290, note 1.

58. "Nachlass," 3066/6878/131727–31: Stresemann to List.

59. Stresemann to Friedrich Thimme. Original in author's possession.

60. Max von Baden, *Erinnerungen und Dokumente* (1927), p. 114. Erzberger defended the form, contents, and timing of the Peace Resolution with the words, "What do you want, highness; with it I shall get Briey and Longwy through negotiation."

61. "Nachlass," 3068/6889/133563–67.

62. Stresemann, *Von der Revolution bis zum Frieden von Versailles,* p. 168.

63. *Ibid.*

64. Houghton once expressed his surprise to A. Mendelssohn-Bartholdy that a decent German could be the enemy of Stresemann, since he was obviously leading Germany toward a better future. He could understand the communists, but not the members of the German National People's party or even some of the People's party. They were, after all, conservatives who should know their best interest and thus should realize that a warlike revision of Versailles, which they obviously desired, would not proceed in a conservative manner but would necessarily lead to a collapse, which would benefit the "Reds." Houghton thought it a typical German paradox when Mendelssohn replied that true conservatism, as a force for peace, could only be found among Social Democrats. Not because they, or Mendelssohn, thought the Treaty of Versailles good, but because they considered nonpeaceful revision too expensive and catastrophic. (Information to the author by Dr. Alfred Vagts, who was present at the exchange.)

65. *Ich bin kein ausgeklügelt Buch,*
Ich bin ein Mensch mit seinem Widerspruch.

66. Many of his biographers praise Stresemann's humor. Those who have worked through the sixty thousand pages of the "Nachlass" have been struck by his complete lack of humor and wit and by his petulance.

67. Thus O. Hauser, "Der Plan einer deutsch-österreichischen Zollunion von 1931," *Historische Zeitschrift,* CLXXIX, No. 1 (1955).

68. Grabowsky, "Stresemann," *Zeitschrift für Politik,* XIX (1930), 369ff.

69. See Thimme, "Gustav Stresemann," p. 337 and note 3.

70. See Delbrück, "Von der Bismarck-Legende."

71. Srbik, *Metternich: Der Staatsmann und der Mensch,* I, 123f.

72. Hirsch, in "Locarno—25 Years After," *Contemporary Review* (1950), writes: "If he were still alive, he and Winston Churchill would have fought side by side

for the same lofty cause at the Strasbourg meeting of the Council of Europe last August." O. Hauser writes: "That he strove to make his suffering country strong and *bündnisfähig* again, and therefore tried to undermine the Treaty of Versailles and to push back France 'from trench to trench,' that is, step by step and not through a major attack, that he desired the *Anschluss* of Austria and the restitution of colonies in due time, and that he was convinced that with a strong army one could more successfully make foreign policy than without, these are rights and convictions which one will have to grant Stresemann just as any other responsible statesman." This is doubtless true; but in our judgment of Stresemann we are not merely concerned with understanding him and "granting" him his policy, but with finding out what he wanted and where his policy might have led.

F. G. STAMBROOK

The German-Austrian Customs Union Project of 1931: A Study of German Methods and Motives

One of Stresemann's long-range aims was the union of Germany and Austria, which the Allies had refused at the time of the Peace Conference because they feared that such an Anschluss *would substantially increase Germany's power and potential threat to peace. The same fear moved the Allies, notably the French, to oppose a project for an Austro-German customs union, which Germany and Austria sprang upon the world in 1931. Such an economic union, it was felt, might ultimately lead to political union. Defenders of the scheme, on the other hand, presented it as a move born of economic necessity and as an effort to boost popular morale at the time of the Great Depression.*

The following article, based on new German documentation, shows that foreign apprehension concerning Germany's ultimate aim was not unfounded and that the customs union project provided a significant link between the policies of Stresemann and Hitler. Professor Stambrook teaches history at the University of Manitoba. Among his other writings are European Nationalism in the Nineteenth Century *(London, 1968); and "Das Kind—Lord D'Abernon and the Origins of the Locarno Pact,"* Central European History, *I (1968), 233–63. The present chapter first appeared in the* Journal of Central European Affairs, *XXI (1961), 15–41. It is republished with permission of the author and the publisher.*

94

THE DECISIONS reached at the two Hague Conferences of August 1929 and January 1930, providing as they did for a settlement of the reparations question and for the evacuation of the Rhineland by French troops by the end of June 1930, together with the death of Foreign Minister Stresemann on October 4, 1929, form a turning point in German foreign policy. The evacuation of the Rhineland five years prior to the time-limit laid down in the Treaty of Versailles was a triumph for Stresemann's policy of "fulfillment," a triumph he was able neither to enjoy nor to make the basis for Germany's future policy. The conduct of German policy passed into other and less skillful hands, and within eighteen months of Stresemann's death, in March 1931, the outside world was suddenly confronted with the proposal for a German-Austrian customs union, a proposal presented in such a way as to make it appear that the technique of foreign policy by surprises, abandoned under Stresemann, was once more being employed.[1]

Stresemann at no time made a secret of the fact that he regarded a settlement of the reparations problem and the evacuation of the Rhineland as a prerequisite for any future foreign policy[2] and therefore as justifying the great attention bestowed upon them. It is thus somewhat ironical that the reproach was leveled at him by his successor Curtius that these two problems had taken up so much of Stresemann's time and that of his collaborators that other aspects of foreign policy and relations with certain other states had suffered.[3] Curtius, with little experience in foreign policy and lacking Stresemann's broader outlook and his skill, was determined to force the pace. It had long been his conviction, he subsequently wrote, that it would be necessary to "intensify" Germany's relations with East and Southeast Europe as soon as a settlement in the West had been reached. In particular he thought that a new approach to Austria was essential.[4] The customs union of 1931 was the outcome of this new approach.

It was a question hotly debated at the time, and also subsequently, whether the proposed customs union was designed as a measure to relieve the growing economic emergency or whether it harbored more long-term designs.[5] It was thought then, and also later, that the German government was influenced by considerations of domestic policy in seeking for some success in foreign affairs,[6] a contention which has been angrily rebutted by Curtius.[7] The suggestion was made at the time,[8] and has been maintained,[9] that the proposed union was a measure for economic recovery within the framework of the Briand Plan for European Union,[10] and indeed that it would promote rather than restrict Austria's political independence.[11] It was also argued that there had been no intention of creating a *fait accompli* and that it was only because a leakage had occurred in Vienna and/or because the Organization Committee of the League's

Commission of Enquiry for European Union decided to meet in Paris on March 24, 1931, that hasty notice was given to the other powers on March 21 instead of adhering to the original schedule, which called for the other powers to be notified during the May session of the Commission of Enquiry.[12] Hitherto the main sources for the study of the German-Austrian plan, apart from the statements made in public at the time, have been the two books by Curtius [13] and the documents published in Documents on British Foreign Policy.[14] The German diplomatic documents which, in the form of photostats or microfilm, are now available to researchers at the Public Record Office, London, and at the National Archives, Washington, cast fresh light on the subject and make it possible to provide more substantial answers to these questions.[15] It is on these German records that the present account is primarily based. It should, however, be noted that the files of the German Foreign Ministry on this topic are not complete. In particular the most important series of files, *Handel 13A Österreich (geheim)*, the working files of Department II [16] on the customs union, is missing, except for Volume 17. Missing, too, are the *Handakten* of Ministerial-Direktor Ritter,[17] the economic expert of the German Foreign Ministry, on the customs union. Fortunately, however, there are frequently several copies of documents, and the author was able to search for relevant documents in the files of the Foreign Minister, State Secretary, and other departmental files, as well as in those of the Reich Chancellery. Moreover, Curtius, before he relinquished his post in October 1931, compiled a collection of copies of and extracts from documents to which he wrote a linking commentary. Documents no longer to be found elsewhere in the Foreign Ministry files have been traced there and the commentary, too, sheds light on otherwise obscure events.[18]

Following the attempts made in 1918 and 1919 by the newly constituted Austrian Republic to join the German Reich, Article 80 of the Treaty of Versailles imposed upon Germany an obligation to respect Austria's independence. Article 88 of the Treaty of St. Germain declared that Austria's independence was inviolable, except with the consent of the League of Nations, and Austria undertook, in the absence of such consent, to abstain from any act which might directly or indirectly "or by any means whatever" compromise her independence. This undertaking was reaffirmed in the first of the three Austrian reconstruction protocols signed at Geneva on October 4, 1922, by which Austria undertook to refrain from any negotiations or from any economic or financial engagement calculated directly or indirectly to compromise her independence, and not to violate her economic independence by granting to any state a special regime or exclusive advantages calculated to threaten this independence.[19] That the conclusion of a customs union between Germany and Austria would, under the terms of the Treaty of St. Germain and of the Geneva Protocol, require the consent of the Council of the League of Nations appears to have been recognized both in Vienna and in Berlin during the 1920's. The German view was expressed in a dispatch of February 4, 1930, from Schubert, the State Secretary of the German Foreign Ministry, to the German Minister in Vienna. This stated that although there might be doubt as to whether the conclusion of customs and economic alliances in the form of terminable treaties of fixed duration was to be regarded as a limitation of the political and economic independence of the countries concerned, there could scarcely be any doubt that the signatories of the Geneva Protocol would regard the conclusion of a customs union between Germany and Austria as a measure which would endanger the economic independence of Austria, and would therefore withhold their consent.[20] The binding nature of the Geneva Protocol on Austria would therefore appear to have been clearly acknowledged, else there would have been no mention of the need for the consent of the signatory powers. The Austrian view was stated by the Austrian foreign trade expert Schüller; it was a clear acknowledgment that the other powers would regard a customs union as prohibited in the same way as the political Anschluss. In any case, Schüller said, the Geneva Protocol entailed no commitments which were not already contained in the peace treaties.[21]

While it was thus recognized that there were considerable difficulties in the way of implementing either an Anschluss or a customs union with Austria, the Anschluss remained "the obvious aim of German policy." [22] But if, during the 1920's, the political Anschluss was regarded as impracticable because, for Germany, a settlement of the Western questions had priority as a political aim and because nothing must be done which might jeopardize the evacuation of the Rhineland,[23] the utmost care was nevertheless taken to ensure that no additional barriers were placed in the way of an eventual Anschluss. From this arose Germany's concern to prevent the question of Austria from being brought into the Locarno negotiations.[24] Conversely, everything which might harm the Anschluss idea in Austria was studiously avoided; hence Germany's refusal to make a fresh affirmation guaranteeing the Brenner frontier between Austria and Italy and her concern not to make any statements regarding the South Tyrol which might be construed as a sign of approval of conditions there.[25] On the other hand, the Anschluss concept was fostered in various ways. Cultural exchanges were promoted, preparatory work was done on the coordination of the legal systems of the two countries, and steps were taken to assure the propagation of the Anschluss idea both in the press and through various organizations in Austria.[26] While demonstrative advocates of the Anschluss movement were apt to be discouraged,[27] constant and quiet preparations and propaganda were carried on, and it appeared evident that the settlement of the reparations question and the evacuation of the Rhineland, by allowing greater freedom to German policy, would, as Stresemann had told Seipel in 1927,[28] enable Germany to bring up the two territorial demands—the Polish Corridor and the Austrian Anschluss—at much the same time.

Although it was subsequently argued that the customs union was purely economic in nature and not a forerunner of a political Anschluss, no such distinction appears to have been made within the German Foreign Ministry. There the customs union was regarded as a prelude to, and a temporary substitute for, the Anschluss. A Foreign Ministry brief prepared for Curtius prior to the Austrian Chancellor's visit to Berlin in February 1930 stated that, as the Anschluss was out of the question for the time being, Germany had all the more interest, for political and economic reasons, in maintaining very close economic ties with Austria and that the closest of all ties would be a customs union.[29] "The Anschluss," so Curtius told the Cabinet on March 16, 1931, "is politically not ripe, but it can be decisively furthered on the economic plane." [30] The axiom "Commercial policy is an instrument of diplomacy" was familiar to German diplomats; the use of economic and financial means to achieve political ends was no novelty at a time of Germany's political weakness,[31] and the possibility of furthering the Anschluss by economic agreements with Austria had been considered before Curtius became Foreign Minister. The subsequent State Secretary, von Bülow,[32] at a time when he was still Deputy Director of Department II, wrote in the early summer of 1929:

> . . . Normally we would be able to hope that the Rhineland will be evacuated by the spring of next year and that the other problems which keep us and France apart will have been settled or postponed. If the British Labour Party is then still in power and, as seems probable, pursues an active foreign policy, then the moment will perhaps have arrived for us also to embark on a greater activity. The questions of the Corridor and of Upper Silesia as well as the Anschluss question are the problems which will then force themselves to the fore. Coming to grips with Poland would, for practical reasons, deserve priority, because if we were to wait much longer it could happen that all the Germans would have been driven out of the occupied territories. But it could be that the time for raising the Eastern problems may not be ripe, and that we must tackle the Anschluss question in some form or other. For my own part I am not here thinking of an Anschluss in the fullest sense of the word, but rather of active steps in respect to preferential tariffs and similar things.[33]

How Stresemann would have conducted German policy after the evacuation of the Rhineland is a matter of hypothesis and outside the scope of this article. The stage was, however, set for his successor who, by his own account, had long been convinced of the need to pursue an active policy in the Southeast and especially toward Austria. Two factors, apart from the settlement in the West, appeared from the outset to favor the course Curtius had in mind. In the first place, the new Austrian Chancellor, Schober, was a nonparty man who was regarded as a "good German" as well as a "good Austrian" [34] and was in any case not tainted by the suspicion that he was at best lukewarm about the Anschluss such as clung, in German eyes, to the personality of Ignaz Seipel, who had long been the dominant figure on the Austrian political scene.[35] Of equal if not greater importance was the fact that Austria was in serious economic difficulties. This was held to be conducive to the Anschluss, and throughout the period of preparation of the customs union project the Foreign Ministry maintained the view that pro-Anschluss feeling in Austria was in the main due to direct material interests and essentially the outcome of economic depression.[36]

Three other factors made the closer attachment of Austria to Germany not only desirable but of the greatest importance at that time. These were the Heimwehr movement, that same economic depression which, in its other aspect, was favorable to the Anschluss concept, and the Pan-Europe idea which the French Foreign Minister, Briand, had advocated in Geneva in September 1929. The Heimwehr movement appeared to be of particular importance during the constitutional conflict which threatened Austria during the autumn of 1929. Its attitude toward the Anschluss was ambiguous and undefined, and inasmuch as it strove to promote Austrian national sentiment it could become an obstacle to the Anschluss. Moreover—so the German Minister in Vienna, von Lerchenfeld, reported—its complete victory would render inevitable a semi-fascist dictatorship and, because this would involve firm commitments to the Italian-Hungarian bloc, would very seriously threaten "the development of German-Austrian relations." [37] The economic depression, too, while providing a pro-Anschluss attitude in Austria, also contained elements of danger for German policy. If pro-Anschluss sentiment was essentially an outcome of economic depression, it was nourished by the conviction that this could be overcome only by alignment with the Reich.[38] Should it become apparent that Germany was unable to provide effective help, then Austria would have to turn elsewhere for the assistance of which she was in need. This could only be toward either Czechoslovakia and France or toward Italy and Hungary, and, as will be seen, both possibilities were equally unwelcome to Germany. Third, it was known that France was preparing a plan for the organization of Europe which, it was thought, would attempt to secure the political and territorial *status quo*. Such a development, so Bülow warned in August 1929, might have an adverse effect on Germany's opportunities in Central Europe.[39]

Curtius' convictions could therefore only have been strengthened by a letter of December 25, 1929, from Lerchenfeld in Vienna. Lerchenfeld pointed out that the Hague Conference, due to be held the following month, would give Curtius an opportunity for making contact with Schober, the "good German" and "good Austrian," and to hold conversations which could be of great significance. "Austria," so Lerchenfeld continued, "is one of the few truly active factors on our political horizon. At the moment the Austrian economy is aiming at a customs and economic union [with Germany]. Business circles are by nature opportunist and have to be so. The political extension of our mutual relationship cannot come about without the economic. This view is held both by Schober and by [Finance Minister] Juch. From this there emerges the possibility of an active policy which can, in its outward appearances, be presented as being based on international or Pan-European principles." [40]

An invitation to Schober to visit Berlin as the guest of the German government had already been issued on December 21, 1929. In his reply to Lerchenfeld Curtius stated that he had already had the intention of approaching Schober at the Hague and that he would follow Lerchenfeld's advice, but he expressed concern at the fact that Schober had agreed to visit Rome before coming to Berlin. [41] Curtius has since stated that during their discussions at the Hague in January 1930 both he and Schober were thinking of a customs union. [42] Schober also informed Curtius that he had successfully resisted French attempts to get him to renounce the Anschluss or otherwise to draw this question into the negotiations. [43] But if Curtius had already decided on the customs union project, he either failed to inform his senior officials of his decision or there developed a difference of opinion, or at least of emphasis, between himself and his State Secretary, Schubert. In the dispatch of February 4 which has already been cited Schubert instructed Lerchenfeld that, in reply to any Austrian inquiries and in order to remove any misconceptions, he should state that Germany regarded a customs union as very desirable but not feasible at that time, as Austria was bound by the Geneva Protocol, whose signatories would doubtless regard a customs union with Germany as incompatible with Austrian independence and would therefore refuse their consent. Lerchenfeld was also to say that "a solution of the question would therefore be possible only by means of a carefully prepared understanding [with other states?] which would take these external political factors into account. To bring this about was Austria's affair." Consequently there was no need at that time to enter into a discussion of the technical issues involved in the creation of a customs union. [44]

Austria's serious economic difficulties and the possibility that these might cause her to be drawn into the orbit of France or of Italy aroused considerable concern in Berlin. The brief drawn up for Curtius by Department II in preparation for the Austrian Chancellor's visit stressed

Germany's interest, at a time when the Anschluss was out of the question, in very close economic ties with Austria; the closest of all such ties would be a customs union. The memorandum continued: "From a political point of view its conclusion would be of the greatest value, as only thus could we ensure that German and Austrian foreign policy interests would no longer seriously diverge, and the danger that Austria would be drawn into a closer, and to us undesirable, relationship with other states would thereby be avoided." The technical problems posed by a customs union were stated to be great though not decisive, but the political impediments created by the Geneva Protocol still remained. The memorandum therefore recommended that, at any discussion of a customs union, it should be made plain to the Austrians that, while Germany would in principle welcome this, the agreement of the other powers signatories to the Geneva Protocol would first have to be obtained.[45]

Other information subsequently reaching the Foreign Ministry may, however, have convinced Curtius, if he had not already determined on this course, that it was essential for him to take the initiative in order to obtain a binding commitment in favor of the customs union from Schober and to embark on a joint study of the technical problems involved. In the collection of documents which Curtius compiled he noted, in connection with Schober's visit, that Austria expected a decisive step to be taken on economic integration with Germany, especially as overtures to Austria from her neighbor states and from Italy were again to be expected.[46] For this statement Curtius cited a letter from Herr Karl Lahm to Dr. Paul Goldmann of February 11, stating that the majority of Austrian industrial circles wanted a customs union with Germany and that this opportunity, which might not recur for many years, ought not to be missed,[47] and one from Herr von Loesch to Senior Counselor Reinebeck urging that Germany take the initiative in order to forestall Czechoslovak overtures to Austria.[48]

Two days before Schober's arrival, the German Cabinet approved the concessions to be made to Austria in the trade treaty negotiations which had been dragging on for two years. Speaking in support of these concessions, Chancellor Müller stressed the relative unimportance of the difficulties which had arisen in the trade negotiations when compared with the great political issues involved, especially the Anschluss question. No mention was made, however, of a customs union.[49]

Schober's visit to Berlin took place on February 22–24, 1930; discussions between Chancellor Müller and Curtius on the one hand and Schober on the other were held on the 22nd and 24th;[50] the intervening day, a Sunday, was passed in consultations between the accompanying experts, largely on the trade negotiations. The general political situation, especially the Pan-Europe movement, the affairs of the Little Entente, and Schober's recent visit to Rome, took up much time on the first day, but when the conversation turned to economic matters the subject of a customs union speedily came up, being broached somewhat tentatively by Schober and then more particularly by the Austrian economic expert Schüller. In Austria's view, the latter said, a customs union was not feasible, as the Entente considered it to be prohibited in the same way as the political Anschluss; this had also, he said, previously been the view of the German government. Curtius, while recognizing that the former Allies would interpret the peace treaties to Germany's and Austria's disadvantage, strongly urged that preparatory discussions on a customs union should be begun soon. The decision, he said, must be taken in principle, and although the present political scene was not favorable for such action they "must be prepared for the future." Both Schüller and Ritter, the German economic expert, opposed this suggestion, the former because he was doubtful about the feasibility of a customs union, the latter because he feared that the negotiations could not be kept secret and because once it became a political possibility technical negotiations could be completed in six to eight weeks. No decision was thus reached on the first day, but Curtius returned to the charge on February 24 and suggested that it be agreed to begin preparatory work. He had, he said, no fears regarding lack of secrecy; there were good grounds for thinking that the peace treaties were not a decisive obstacle, as it could be argued that a terminable customs union was not a renunciation of independence. A favorable moment must, of course, be chosen for this struggle (*Kampf*), and political and diplomatic preparations made. He wanted some decision that day as to whether and how the whole problem could be tackled. It should not be put off, as the political constellation was capable of very sudden change; if the overall European situation provided an opening they must be able at once to make use of it (*"Wenn die gesamt-europäische Konstellation eine Lücke bietet, müssen wir sofort hineinstossen können"*). Schober now gave a warm welcome to Curtius' statements and, after a discussion of the technical problems which would arise, it was agreed that the question of the customs union should be studied, although Chancellor Müller's final words on the subject contained no mention of the "great speed" to which Schober had explicitly referred and which Curtius had implied.[51] In conversation with Schubert later that day both Secretary General Peter and Schober expressed their satisfaction at the decisions which had been reached, Schober adding, "If we effect the customs union we will thereby get the whole Balkans."[52]

The immediate result of this acceptance in principle of the customs union, a decision evidently taken by the politicians in the face of the misgivings of their officials, was meager enough, for during the ensuing months there were developments in Austria's foreign as well as domestic affairs which boded ill for Curtius' policy. Particular anxiety was felt in Berlin when Schober visited Paris at the end of April 1930, for it was feared that, in connection with Austria's search for financial assistance, Schober might again be pressed to renounce the Anschluss. No such renunciation appears to have been made, but Curtius was not wholly reassured when Schober wrote to him to say that the Anschluss had not been discussed in either Paris or London, which he also visited, for the Austrian Chancellor added that Briand had constantly spoken of an "independent" Austria and had assured him that, to facilitate Austria's existence as an independent state, France would continue to exercise her influence on the Little Entente with a view to obtaining concessions for Austrian trade. Curtius sent only a brief reply to Schober's letter.[53] Lerchenfeld, too, reported that in the official memorandum on Schober's conversation with Briand (of which he had been shown an extract by Schober) there was no mention of the Anschluss but merely constant reiteration of the advantages of Austrian independence. To this Curtius minuted "Independence—no Anschluss." [54]

There were fears too that the Briand Plan for European Union, which had been communicated to the other powers in May, was designed to restrict Germany's freedom of action. In a memorandum of May 21, 1930, Bülow wrote:

> . . . Accordingly the purpose of the whole plan seems to be to yoke us with new chains by making use of the fact that the consolidation of Europe is, in the prevailing view, only possible on the basis of the *status quo*. . . . At stake here are not only the territorial *status quo* but also all obligations arising out of the peace treaties . . .[55]

The consolidation of the political structure of Europe would rule out the possibility of the Anschluss, and the closer economic contacts and greater stability at which the Briand Plan aimed might well render even a customs union between Germany and Austria superfluous. There was also constant concern on another score, for it was feared in Berlin that Austria might be changing her policy with regard to a Danubian confederation, and Lerchenfeld too, in a report of June 4, stated that there were renewed attempts, by the former French Minister Loucheur and others, to bring about closer economic relations between Austria, Hungary, and the successor states. Such plans, he said, were motivated by the political aim of drawing Austria away from Germany, and France's ability to promote her plans by providing capital made the situation very dangerous. Although some satisfactory assurances were received on this account from the Austrian Minister in Berlin at the end of June, the German fears were revived in a slightly altered form in August, when Lerchenfeld reported that, while no great importance had previously been attached in Austria to the various economic conferences of the successor states, the attitude toward the conferences of the agrarian states had now changed significantly.[56]

In his report of June 4, Lerchenfeld had also drawn attention to an improvement in relations between Austria and Italy, for which the Austrian Heimwehr movement was constantly pressing, and to an increase in legitimist activity. State Secretary Bülow was much perturbed by Schober's negotiations with the Heimwehr and the pro-Italian trend which this might entail, and when Lerchenfeld wrote that Prince Starhemberg, the Heimwehr leader in Upper Austria, had visited Mussolini at the end of July with the approval of the Austrian government, Bülow feared that this might indicate Schober's capitulation to the Heimwehr.[57]

Thus it came about that, despite urgings from both those who knew of the conversations in Berlin in February and those who did not, the customs union project made no outward progress. A warning that pro-Anschluss feeling in Austria was at a low ebb, owing to Germany's failure to give the requisite assistance in order to relieve the complete economic stagnation which prevailed there, and that if no German help were forthcoming there would be a serious danger of such feeling disappearing altogether, came from the Secretary General of the German Center party, who added that even Austrian quarters which were on the whole hostile to the Anschluss were sympathetic to the idea of a customs union. Lerchenfeld too, in the report of June 4 which has already been cited, pointed out that Germany could counter Austrian receptiveness to French plans only through the press and by overcoming dissatisfaction with the German-Austrian Trade Treaty through closer economic relations with a customs union in view; and in his report of August 9 he again suggested that the time had come for Germany and Austria jointly to examine the preconditions for the establishment of a unified economic area. It is no doubt not without significance that there are heavy sidelinings by Ritter against the passage urging joint consultation on the customs union.[58]

But such urgings were in truth not necessary, for it was realized in the German Foreign Ministry that Austria's economic recovery through Germany's help and through close ties between the Austrian and German economies was the best and most effective guarantee against Austria's entering into relationships with other states which were unwelcome to Germany.[59] But such close links could not be imposed upon the Austrian government against the latter's will. Thus it was German policy, at a time when the Austrian government appeared to be displaying little or no interest in the decisions reached in Berlin, to seek to preserve Austria's independence and to prevent her, if possible, from entering into closer association with other states or groups of states; for only thus would the way be left open for the conclusion of the Anschluss or of a customs union at some more favorable opportunity. In a circular dispatch to various missions dated June 4, 1930, Curtius was at pains to make reassuring statements regarding Austrian policy under Schober, saying that he had not entered into any fresh commitments and that his policy to date had not run counter to Germany's interests; but he went on to state that further attempts to influence Austrian policy in a direction unwelcome to Germany were to be expected, and he instructed the missions to keep a close watch on Austrian policy. Regarding Germany's policy, he wrote that, while it was true that every measure of stabilization and every step toward economic recovery fostered Austria's national pride and harmed the Anschluss idea, Germany must nevertheless welcome such recovery for political reasons because an internally divided and economically disrupted Austria would necessarily fall into the French or Italian net. As long as Germany was unable to effect the political Anschluss, she wished Austria to maintain her political and economic independence which, he stated, was threatened by France's aim to set up a Danubian confederation and by Austria's need for financial aid, which forced her to turn toward France.[60]

But internal preparation of the customs union was not neglected. Ritter made a careful study of the question in the spring of 1930 and, on June 20, presented his conclusions in the form of a memorandum.[61] On July 3—just three days after French troops left the Rhineland—Ritter wrote to Schüller suggesting that they should at long last meet to give effect to the decisions reached at Berlin, but he met with no positive response and the two did not in fact meet until the League Council's and Assembly's sessions at Geneva in September. Curtius ascribed this delay to vacations and other pressing business (which he did not specify).[62] It seems most likely that the Austrians had not exhausted other means for assuring their economic recovery. We now know that in Paris Schober had indicated to Briand that, if Germany declared herself ready to enter into a close economic alliance with Austria, he would be unable to decline, and that this obvious attempt to use the German bogy had elicited from Briand the statement that he would do his utmost to prevent Austria from being placed in such desperate straits as to be forced into acceptance, and had led to Schober's being given a preview of the Briand Plan.[63] Possibly analogous efforts to procure financial and economic aid were made elsewhere too, for, as will be seen, Schober subsequently told Curtius of Italian and Hungarian attempts to enter into closer relations with Austria. Moreover, so the Austrian Finance Minister, Juch, told Lerchenfeld, there was passive resistance in certain Austrian government departments to the idea of a customs union with Germany. In the same conversation Juch also hinted that it would be desirable for Germany to urge Schober to more decisive action on the customs union question, a view which Lerchenfeld strongly supported.[64]

Juch's approach to Lerchenfeld might be taken as an indication that the Austrian government was now ready to enter into further negotiations with Germany on the customs union, or it might merely have been a move occasioned by divisions of opinion inside the Austrian Cabinet. But the next initiative came very definitely, and for the only time, from the Austrian side; for on August 27 Schober told Lerchenfeld that the line of economic integration decided upon in Berlin should now be energetically pursued. Schober suggested that the efforts of the Eastern states, especially Yugoslavia and Rumania, should be made the point of departure in the German-Austrian discussions.[65]

But if Curtius expected that when he and Schober met at Geneva in September the Austrian Chancellor would come out unequivocally for the customs union, he was disappointed. It was agreed that Curtius should pay a return visit to Vienna at the end of October, but then Schober went on to speak at some length of Austrian discussions with Hungary (Schober had visited Budapest in June) and with Italy, and especially of an Italian suggestion that Austria should act as a kind of trustee in the exchange of agricultural produce and manufactured goods between Austria, Hungary, Germany, and Italy. Schüller would discuss this with Ritter and would probably not be as frank as he, Schober, had been. In these circumstances, so Schober continued, he thought it desirable that German-Austrian negotiations of an economic approach (*Annäherung*) should begin. At Curtius' request they then discussed the tactical treatment of the Pan-Europe question, and Curtius stated that he found considerable identity of views.[66] It was at Geneva, too, that Schober delivered a speech in which he suggested that regional economic agreements might eventually lead to European union.[67] In view of Schober's statements to Curtius, of subsequent Austrian attempts to conclude customs unions simultaneously with both Italy and Germany, and of the conclusion, albeit at a time when Schober was no longer in office, of preferential economic agreements with Italy and Hungary—it would appear not unlikely that Austrian policy, especially as expounded by the Austrian economic expert Schüller, was aiming at achieving a preferential treatment for her trade with most of her immediate neighbors, and it is in this light that Schober's speech at Geneva should perhaps be viewed.[68]

What passed between Ritter and Schüller at their meeting on September 22 cannot be ascertained at present, as no record exists in the German archives. Curtius states that they both appeared to agree on essentials regarding the form which the projected customs union should take, and that careful internal studies were made subsequently.[69] In any case the basis on which the proposed customs union was founded was abruptly shattered when the Schober government, brought down by a scandal involving an appointment in the Austrian Federal Railways, resigned on September 25. From Germany's point of view this was most detrimental, for not only did it put a stop to Curtius' projected visit to Vienna but, as Lerchenfeld reported, "the move toward the intensification of economic relations between Germany and Austria has also been temporarily broken off." [70] The new government, with Vaugoin as Chancellor and Seipel as Foreign Minister, was not auspicious for Curtius' plan. Seipel, indeed, took pains to stress the continuity of Austrian policy, but with the motto "no combination without Germany," [71] which was not likely to arouse confidence in Berlin. Vaugoin was regarded as a supporter of the Habsburg monarchy and as "extremely Austrian," [72] and Seipel was always viewed with extreme suspicion by Curtius, who blandly states that "Seipel steered away from Germany on a Hungarian-Italian course." [73] This assertion was not substantiated in a memorandum on the foreign policy aims of the Vaugoin-Seipel Cabinet which Curtius ordered prepared for him before he left office in October 1931, for this stated that there was no basis for such a supposition. But, the memorandum continued, "the very fact that an Austrian government was formed in which a personality like Seipel had complete responsibility for foreign policy was bound to give cause for concern in pro-Anschluss quarters in Austria and in the Reich. Whatever the true intentions and wishes of Seipel for Austria's future may be, he is certainly no friend of the Anschluss concept." [74] Thus, even when Seipel expressly identified himself with the policy of his predecessor and requested that the personal contacts which had been discussed in Berlin should now be brought about between special delegates of the two foreign ministries,[75] this evoked no response in Berlin. During the Vaugoin-Seipel government's two months' period of office the customs union project, apart from any internal preparations in the German Foreign Ministry, was simply placed in cold storage.

At the beginning of December, however, a new Austrian government was formed with Ender as Chancellor and Schober as Vice-Chancellor and Foreign Minister. This enabled the former contacts to be re-established; Curtius states that Schober very speedily telephoned him to suggest that negotiations on the customs union be resumed and brought to an early conclusion.[76] At the turn of the year Ritter paid an unobtrusive visit to Vienna and, on January 2, 1931, he handed Schüller his draft of the customs union agreement.[77] Three days later Schüller expressed his approval of the draft as a whole, and also asked Ritter some questions concerning it, two of which are of particular interest. In the first place he asked whether Ritter was serious in proposing that other states too might be included in the customs union. In reply Ritter explained that this provision had been incorporated because the Geneva Protocol prohibited Austria from restricting her economic independence by granting exclusive advantages to any other state; it was therefore necessary to anticipate possible objections by stating that the mutual concessions were not necessarily confined to the two countries. Besides, he said, Germany was not in principle opposed to the inclusion of other countries, and Hungary would probably be forced to seek admission to the new union. In reply to another question, Ritter stated that he had included a provision that the customs union could be terminated "at any time" because Schober and Schüller had said in Berlin the previous year that Austria must safeguard her "independence." [78] But, Ritter added, he had in any case incorporated safeguards to ensure that no precipitate use would be made of the right to terminate the union.

Ritter and Schüller agreed that the details of the draft agreement should be considered further and discussed, in the strictest confidence, with experts from other departments. But if agreement in essence had thus been reached, as far as technicalities were concerned, the political question of whether Austria wished to conclude a customs union with Germany and, if so, when she thought the time would be right, presented more difficulties. Schüller was very vague and attempted to push the decision on to the German government; the German and French foreign ministers, he said, should first discuss the matter. Ritter countered that it was Austria, not Germany, who was bound by treaty obligations. Secretary General Peter, whom Ritter saw the following day, refused to comment on the question of whether and when a customs union should be concluded.

On the same day, January 6, Ritter saw Schober, who also approved the draft text. Unlike his civil servants, Schober stated himself to be, in principle and without qualification, in favor of a customs union; he was moreover of the opinion that the time had now come to take active steps toward this end. But, said Schober, he was opposed to the idea that Germany and Austria might "one fine day surprise the world by concluding a customs union" and he thought that diplomatic preparations should be made. Ritter, in reply, explained that the whole plan had so far been shrouded in secrecy because the Geneva Protocol imposed on Austria the obligation not even to enter into negotiations which might directly or indirectly compromise her independence. In any case Curtius would like to discuss the matter with Schober in Geneva.

Schober's favorable views having thus been ascertained, the negotiations now moved from the private to the official plane. In Berlin Curtius, evidently only because his senior officials urged that this was necessary, informed Chancellor Brüning of his intention to engage in official conversations with Schober on the subject of the customs union and received his assent.[79] At Geneva, in the course of a lengthy conversation on January 15, Curtius and Schober reached agreement on a number of points. Schober agreed that the negotiations, and especially the Austrian reply to the German draft text, which had previously been handled in a dilatory fashion, should be accelerated, so that an overall picture might be available at the end of February, when Curtius and Brüning were to visit Vienna. The whole project was to be kept secret until the negotiations between the governments were concluded, and in particular Schober now concurred with Curtius' view that the time was not opportune for a discussion of the customs union with the other powers. Curtius also explained to Schober that Germany could not take the initiative in informing the other powers, as this might give the impression that she was bringing up the Anschluss question. "The initiative must therefore come from Austria and it would be advisable to place the whole action within the framework of Pan-Europe"; this would moreover be natural in view of Schober's previous statements on regional cooperation. To this, too, Schober agreed.[80]

Preparations were now set afoot in Berlin for Curtius' visit to Vienna. Strict secrecy was still observed, the Cabinet was not informed of the scope of Curtius' discussion with Schober when he presented his report on his activities at Geneva; [81] only a restricted circle in the Foreign Ministry knew of the plan and there appears to have been no consultation with officials in other Ministries. But one senior diplomat to whom preliminary information was given in strict confidence at an early date, and this because he might not otherwise be informed in good time, was Ambassador Prittwitz in Washington. On January 20 Bülow wrote to him:

> . . . There is, however, a plan, which can perhaps be implemented, to enter into an economic union with Austria, which would probably very speedily lead to the accession to it of Czechoslovakia and Hungary. . . . It is quite possible that it may lead to political conflicts, although we will dress the whole matter up in a Pan-Europe cloak [*obwohl wir der Angelegenheit ein paneuropäisches Mäntelchen umhängen werden*]. . . .

The plan, Bülow stated, would probably be brought up at the earliest in May.[82]

The legal situation was now subjected to renewed scrutiny. Gaus produced a lengthy memorandum in the course of which he examined the provisions of the peace treaties and of the Geneva Protocol, explained how and why certain provisions of the customs union agreement had been drafted in order to try to obviate the need to obtain the express consent of the Council of the League of Nations or of the states signatories to the Geneva Protocol, and advocated that it would be advantageous to conclude only a *pactum de contrahendo* rather than a final treaty. But, Gaus warned, it would be dangerous, even with the careful formulation which he had chosen, to allow the League Council to refer the matter to the International Court at The Hague; Germany would be in a better position if the plan could be discussed in the Commission of Enquiry for European Union, where the economic aspects and the connections with the new "European" endeavors could be placed in the forefront.[83]

Further economic and technical preparations, too, were made at this time, but no details of these have been found. Much attention was naturally also focused on the general international situation, and especially on the reaction which the project might be expected to evoke in France. Franco-German relations appeared to have reached an impasse. Curtius has ascribed this to the effect on France of the Reichstag elections of September 14, 1930, at which the National Socialists increased their representation from 12 to 107. German diplomats in Paris, however, discerned an additional reason, the German failure properly to appreciate the French evacuation of the Rhineland five years before the time fixed in the Treaty of Versailles, and regretted the resultant bitterness and misunderstandings.[84] Curtius and Bülow, however, appear to have thought— and this at a time when disarmament negotiations were believed to be imminent and when Germany was anxious to secure further concessions in the reparations question—that the successful conclusion of a customs union with Austria, to which other states too might well be obliged to adhere, would put sufficient pressure on France to force her to negotiate on general questions and to resume her old policy of understanding (*Verständigungspolitik*). It is clear, however, that there was no intention of using the customs union with Austria as a bargaining counter which might be given up if France made suitable concessions in any general negotiations which might ensue.[85]

Curtius has claimed that he summoned the heads of mission in France, Czechoslovakia, and Italy to inform them of the plan in good time and to seek their advice, and that he received their concurrence, or at least no warning. The Ambassador in Paris, von Hoesch, in particular, is described as being much in favor of the proposed course and as welcoming it as an opportunity to get away from the stagnation which had set in in Franco-German relations. In fact, only Hoesch and the Ambassador in London, von Neurath, were asked for their views before Curtius visited Vienna, and doubts were later raised as to whether they had been consulted in the full sense of the word.[86] No direct record has been found of Curtius' conferences with Hoesch and Neurath, but on his return to Paris Hoesch submitted a long exposé in which, so he wrote to Köpke, he repeated the views he had put forward in Berlin. If Hoesch's account is accurate, then the opinions which Curtius has ascribed to him are either a complete invention on Curtius' part or are based on a colossal misunderstanding. In his exposé Hoesch discussed the six major problems confronting German foreign policy—reparations, the Eastern frontier, disarmament, the Saar, Austria, and colonies. He saw no prospect of successful discussions with France on the Anschluss question at that time, nor, for that matter, on the other questions either. But he counseled patience and moderation. "*Without* France," he wrote, "let alone *against* France, none of the problems facing us can be solved," and he concluded with the hope that Germany would continue to follow the path of *Besonnenheit, Geduld,* and *Klugheit.*[87]

Although the exact nature of the advice given to Curtius by the officials of his own Ministry cannot be determined, warning notes were sounded there too. Gaus had pointed out (see above) that the legal situation was not altogether secure. On the political side, Counselor von Heeren, the official in charge of Central European affairs, is said to have repeatedly and strongly urged in February and March that the plan should be abandoned.[88] Köpke, the Director of Department II, claimed that he too had repeatedly voiced the misgivings of his department to Curtius.[89] A memorandum of February 21, drafted by Heeren and signed by Köpke, clearly outlined the political implications and dangers of the proposed action and contained an explicit warning of the strength of the opposition to be expected from France and Czechoslovakia. Although not openly opposing the plan, the memorandum sought to show that Austria would have less to lose than Germany if the attempt should fail, and for this reason must not be regarded as an altogether steadfast partner. The utmost care in the preparation and timing of the project was therefore advocated.[90]

In the meantime the date for the Foreign Minister's visit to Vienna had been fixed for March 3–4, and Brüning had decided that it would be more prudent not to accompany Curtius.[91] No definite information was as yet given to the Cabinet. Curtius merely informed his colleagues that he intended to discuss disarmament, the Pan-Europe negotiations, and related economic matters; within this framework, he said, negotiations on assimilating tariffs (*Zollannäherung*) appeared likely to succeed.[92]

Very few details regarding Curtius' visit to Vienna, which in fact lasted from March 3rd to 5th, are known. Curtius tells us that he became convinced of Austria's willingness and determination to proceed with the plan, even in the face of opposition. The Austrian President, Miklas, and Chancellor, Ender, showed themselves to be fully informed, and approved the project. Curtius and Schober agreed on the text of the customs union agreement, and also that it should be presented in the form of a preliminary agreement and not as a final treaty. They also decided that the consent of the two cabinets should be obtained during the following three weeks and that the statesmen of the interested nations should be informed during the May session of the Commission of Enquiry for European Union.[93] Thus far Curtius. From an account given shortly afterward by Schüller to Ambassador Schubert in Rome, however, it would appear that it was not all quite such plain sailing. Schüller said that he had voiced his doubts both as to the timing and as to the wisdom of proceeding in the absence of any other diplomatic activity on questions of international importance; he had therefore suggested that the project be postponed until during the Disarmament Conference the following year, but Curtius had said that "the affair could be managed (*dass die Sache gemacht werden könne*)." [94]

Curtius has maintained that the date on which the other powers were to be notified of the German-Austrian agreement had to be brought forward from May to March 21 because of an indiscretion in an Austrian newspaper on March 17. This, he said, made it necessary to inform the other powers before the Organization Committee of the Commission of Enquiry for European Union met in Paris on March 24, and he has angrily denied Schuschnigg's charge that the Germans took Schober by surprise.[95] Yet it was on March 9—a week before the first leak—that the legation in Vienna was instructed to tell Schober that the German Cabinet would approve the customs union protocol on March 21 and that the joint démarches should take place on March 27. The following day Curtius suggested to Schober that the démarches should take place at the beginning of the week starting March 23, because the Organization Committee would meet in Paris that same week, and on March 12 the legation in Vienna was further instructed to suggest to Schober that the démarches should take place on March 21 or at the latest on March 23. On March 13 the legation in Vienna reported Schober's approval of this suggestion.[96] But it had been known in Berlin in February that the Organization Committee would meet in Paris in March, and if the Germans nevertheless agreed at the beginning of March that the project should be communicated to the other powers in May, it would seem that their subsequent justification was disingenuous and that, as Schober told the British Minister, Sir Eric Phipps, Austria's hand had been forced by Germany.[97]

The Austrians, indeed, appeared ill prepared for this advance of the date of notifying the other powers. Differences of opinion also existed on the mode of making this notification and on the text of the declaration which was to be made to the other powers. Austria endeavored to restrict the first information to vague intimations of the two countries' intentions, while the Germans contended that specific information should be imparted on the occasion of the démarche, together with the text of the customs union protocol. The Austrians proposed, too, that the declaration which should be made should state that Germany had made an offer to Austria to conclude a customs union with her within the Pan-Europe concept, and that Austria had accepted this offer; this formulation was naturally rejected in Berlin. It was, however, agreed that Germany should take the first step in Paris, and Austria in London and Rome.[98] In fact, however, the Austrian envoys were not as well briefed as their German colleagues and, although they were able to transmit the agreed declaration, they were without instructions as to how it should be interpreted and they did not at that time know the text of the customs union protocol.[99] Schüller told Schubert that this was due to two reasons—that the instructions would not have arrived in time and that experience had shown that such instructions often shattered the faith in his own cause ("*das Glauben an die gute Sache*") of the diplomat concerned.[100]

In Berlin active preparations were in full swing. Very brief and strictly confidential information on the outcome of Curtius' negotiations in Vienna was sent on March 9 to the missions in Paris, London, Rome, Budapest, and Prague.[101] A memorandum of the previous day examined the economic consequences of the customs union and spoke of the advantages which would accrue to Germany. It is estimated that the reduction of foreign imports into Austria and the decrease in Austria's own production would in due course lead to an increase in Germany's exports to Austria of between a half and one milliard marks; but whereas this increase would be brought about partly at the expense of Austria's own industries, an increase in Austrian exports to Germany would be achieved mainly at the expense of other foreign competitors. In conclusion, the memorandum did not fail to point out that the customs union would effectively avert the danger of Austria's being drawn into some form of Danubian or Southeast European economic unit or into dependency on Italy, and thus of becoming a barrier instead of an outlet to the Southeast.[102]

Mention has already been made of the German insistence on bringing forward the date of notifying the other powers and efforts to ensure that analogous statements should be made by the Austrian and German diplomatic representatives. All these activities took place before the German Cabinet was informed of the proposed action, for it was not until March 16, when Curtius presented his report on his visit to Vienna, that the ministers heard for the first time of the lengthy negotiations. Curtius stated that the Austrian government had at first been very lukewarm toward the proposal, but now welcomed it. Austria had turned away from the idea of a Danubian economic confederation, and this situation must be turned to account. The Anschluss, he said, was politically not ripe, but it could be decisively furthered on the economic plane. The draft protocol [103] was explained to the Cabinet by Ritter. Curtius then described the proposed diplomatic action. The form of a protocol had been chosen so as not to give offense to the interested governments. Czechoslovakia and France would probably be hostile and a difficult phase of diplomatic discussion was to be expected. Brüning congratulated Curtius on his achievement, but added that the timing was perhaps not entirely fortunate. But this, Brüning remarked somewhat cryptically—and erroneously—had not been chosen by Germany. The ensuing discussion revealed general agreement in principle, but misgivings were voiced on particular aspects by various ministers, each speaking solely from the point of view of his own department. There was, however, general rejection of a clause in the draft text providing for the reference of disputes to the

Hague Court. At Brüning's suggestion it was decided that departmental experts should study the proposals on the following day and that the Cabinet should consider them again on March 18. At this resumed Cabinet session Ritter reported that the Austrians had agreed to the deletion of the clause providing for reference to the Hague Court. Various ministers now spoke of the need for Germany to retain in her own hands leadership and preponderance in the union, and after Curtius had stressed the domestic political advantages which the German initiative might be expected to have, the Cabinet gave their unanimous consent to the project.[104]

The instructions to the German missions were by this time already drafted and ready for dispatch. The démarches were to be carried out on March 21 if possible, and, besides directions as to language to be held, the missions were also sent the final text of the customs union protocol and a memorandum dealing with legal aspects. The protocol, however, was not to be handed over until March 24 or 25. Hoesch in Paris was instructed to stress the connection with the Pan-Europe movement, Schubert in Rome to promise German cooperation with Italy in dealing with the economic problems of the Balkans. No special aspects were to be stressed in London, mainly because British interests were not directly affected. Nothing was to be said that might in any way suggest that the German government was asking the other powers for their consent. There could be no question of this, Curtius wrote, for the German and Austrian governments were convinced that their intention of concluding a customs union did not violate any international commitments and that no foreign state had the right to hinder them.[105] Bülow supplemented this dispatch with identical letters to Hoesch and Neurath in which he warned that no member of their embassies must show any signs of a bad conscience over the plan or the mode of its presentation. Germany, he said, had every right to take the action on which she was now embarking, even if it involved what he called a "play with Article 80 of the Treaty of Versailles," and she had a greater right than other powers to look after her own interests.[105a]

On March 19 Ritter informed Schüller by telephone of the outcome of the German Cabinet's discussion and of the text of Curtius' letter to Schober formally notifying him of the German government's consent to the plan. The Austrian Cabinet reached its decision a day later than the German, and Schober hastened to send formal intimation of their approval to Curtius.[106] On March 19, too, the Germans received the text of the declaration which the Austrians proposed to make in London (and with minor amendments, in Rome) and decided that there was no need to make such a formal declaration in Paris, although Hoesch was authorized to make use of the ideas expressed therein. That day, too, Schubert was instructed, at Curtius' request, to postpone his interview with Grandi, the Italian Foreign Minister, until March 23 so that, in Rome at least, Austria's initiative in the whole matter might be made to seem more obvious; but this Schubert declared himself unable to do, as he had already arranged to see Grandi on March 21.[107]

The formal notification of the three Great Powers duly followed on March 21, but by then the cat was out of the bag. The Czechoslovak Minister in Vienna called on Schober on March 18 to inquire about the rumors which were by then current in Vienna, and, on receiving an evasive reply, he gave warning that there were likely to be serious repercussions. By March 20 the French Foreign Minister was addressing requests to the British and Italian governments asking that the signatories of the Geneva Protocol of 1922 instruct their ministers in Vienna to remind Austria, on March 21 if possible, of the engagements into which she had entered in that Protocol. No such action was evidently taken by the British government, while in Rome Grandi told Schubert that, acting on the basis of reports from the Italian Minister in Vienna, he had declined to associate Italy with such démarches, although he had asked for further inquiries to be made in Vienna.[108]

Thus inauspiciously was the customs union project launched into the public arena, without either that prior consultation with the other Great Powers which the Austrians had desired or the achievement of that element of surprise which the Germans seemingly hoped for.

A distinguished historian has written that it is scarcely to be doubted that Curtius, in pressing forward with the customs union plan, was motivated more by considerations of domestic than of foreign policy, and that it was a mistake, arising mainly from these considerations of domestic policy, to attempt to spring a surprise on the world.[109] But from many German points of view the project appeared eminently desirable. It accorded well with ideas long held both by Curtius and by State Secretary Bülow; Bülow told the British Ambassador that he had long had some such customs union in mind and believed that it would provoke less opposition on the part of other powers than two other questions of urgent interest to Germany—reparations and the Eastern frontier.[110] If in its inception the plan was more than just a move on the chessboard of domestic politics, its realization, as Curtius did not fail to point out to the Cabinet, would ease the position of the whole government, which, together with Curtius' own position as Foreign Minister, had grown steadily more precarious during the long period of planning and negotiation.[111] But the plan was more than the culmination of ambitions, however long-cherished, of the Foreign Minister and the State Secretary, or the outcome of the exigencies of domestic politics. The basic reasons for the attempt in 1930 and 1931 to conclude this customs union with Austria must rather be sought in the field of foreign policy. It accorded with the long-term objectives of German foreign policy, as seen in the Foreign Ministry, in that it would at the same time link Austria securely to Germany and forestall efforts to include Austria in some form of regional Danubian association or to bring her into a closer relationship with Italy. This consideration remained paramount throughout the year of preparation. The customs union and eventual Anschluss, moreover, would open the way to the Southeast and, together with the tariff preference treaties which Germany was at that time negotiating with Rumania and Hungary and which she had also proposed to Yugoslavia and Bulgaria,[112] would ensure German dominance in the Danube Basin and the Balkans.

Germany also hoped, by presenting the plan in the year following the Briand Memorandum on European Union, by "dressing up the whole matter in a Pan-Europe cloak," and by stressing its economic aspects, to ensure a favorable intellectual response throughout Europe and a tactical advantage in the diplomatic repercussions which were expected. Moreover, advantage could be taken of the favorable political constellation in Austria as represented by Schober's leading position in the government and by the desperation arising from the economic crisis. In the mind of one of the principal advocates of the project, however, there was yet one further motive. Bülow elaborated his ideas regarding the ultimate aim of the customs union with Austria in a letter of April 19 to Koch, the German Minister in Prague, a letter interesting also for the confidence it expresses in Germany's ability to bring about this union. Czechoslovakia, so Bülow wrote, would quickly be forced to join the German bloc, and Germany would be able to secure the dominant position in Southeast Europe. If, in the meantime, Germany's economic ties with the Baltic states had been strengthened, then a solution might in due course be found to a problem which otherwise appeared insoluble—namely, that of Germany's Eastern frontier. Poland, with her unstable economy, Bülow continued, would be surrounded and in the grip of a vise, and would perhaps be willing to make political concessions in return for tangible economic advantages.[113]

Thus the German-Austrian customs union, far from being conceived as a step within the framework of the Pan-Europe movement and purely to give aid to Austria at a time of economic crisis, was a long-planned project designed to achieve at one stroke the realization of Curtius' ambition. This envisaged attaching Austria irrevocably to Germany, ensuring to Germany the dominant position in Southeast Europe and, in so doing, disrupting the Little Entente, and, finally, bringing about, in the long run, a situation in which Poland could be forced, by the application of economic pressure, to make territorial concessions to Germany.

NOTES

1. How far even French statesmen and diplomats were from suspecting the imminent announcement may be gathered from Briand's remarks on the receding danger of an Anschluss and Austria's increasingly solid consciousness of her own nationality during a debate in the French Chamber of Deputies on March 3, 1931 (*Journal Officiel, Débats Parlementaires, Chambre,* p. 1525), and from the statements made by the French Ambassador in Washington (see *Foreign Relations of the United States, 1931,* 1 [Washington, 1946], 571).

2. Cf., for example, his statements to Seipel during his and Chancellor Marx's official visit to Vienna in November 1927 (memorandum by State Secretary Pünder, November 22, 1927; 3086/D614241–60).

3. Julius Curtius, *Bemühungen um Oesterreich, das Scheitern des Zollunionsplans von 1931* (Heidelberg, 1946), p. 10. Curtius used much the same words in May 1930 when suggesting to Grandi that there should be closer German-Italian relations (memorandum RM 701, May 15, 1930; 4679/E224462–65).

4. Curtius, *Bemühungen,* p. 11.

5. For a contemporary account of the German-Austrian project see *Survey of International Affairs, 1931* (London, 1932), pp. 297–323. For a recent German account see Ludwig Zimmermann, *Deutsche Aussenpolitik in der Ära der Weimarer Republik* (Göttingen, 1958), pp. 407–415; for a French view see Maurice Baumont, *La Faillité de la Paix* (Paris, 1951) pp. 411 ff., who tersely heads this short section "La tentative d'Anschluss en 1931."

6. See E. L. Woodward and Rohan Butler, eds., *Documents on British Foreign Policy, 1919–1939* (hereafter cited as *DBFP*), 2nd Series, II, No. 34, and André François-Poncet, *Souvenirs d'une Ambassade à Berlin* (Paris, 1946), p. 19.

7. Curtius, *Bemühungen,* p. 33.

8. Cf. Article I of the Customs Union Protocol (for an English text of which see *DBFP,* 2nd Series, II, No. 3, encl. 1), and *ibid.,* No. 2, encl. 2, and No. 21.

9. See Oswald Hauser, "Der Plan einer deutsch-österreichischen Zollunion 1931 und die europäische Föderation," in *Historische Zeitschrift,* CLXXIX (1955), No. 1, 45–92.

10. For the Briand Plan see *Survey, 1930* (London, 1931), pp. 136–142.

11. Cf. the argument by the Austrian advocate, Prof. Kaufmann, before the International Court (Permanent Court of International Justice, Series C, XXII Session —1931, No. 53, *Customs Regime Between Germany and Austria* [Leyden, 1931], pp. 100 and 312), and Curtius, *Bemühungen,* pp. 31 and 57 ff.

12. See *DBFP,* 2nd Series, II, Nos. 6, 8, 21, and 28, encl.; see also Zimmermann, *Deutsche Aussenpolitik,* p. 410, and Hauser, "Der Plan," pp. 66–67.

13. Julius Curtius, *Bemühungen um Oesterreich* (see footnote 3 above) and *Sechs Jahre Minister der deutschen Republik* (Heidelberg, 1948).

14. The British documents also reveal contemporary German efforts to indicate that, while the subject of a customs union had often before been discussed, all the negotiations for the 1931 project had been carried out during Curtius' visit to Vienna at the beginning of March (*DBFP,* 2nd Series, II, No. 28, encl., and No. 34; cf. also M. J. Bonn, *So macht man Geschichte* [Munich, 1953], p. 312 and footnote 1). In his two books Curtius has already shown that these negotiations had a longer history.

15. Material from the German Foreign Ministry and Reich Chancellery is here identified by the serial and frame numbers allotted to the documents by the German Documents Project; these serial and frame numbers enable reference to be made to the relevant German text both in the films and in the original files. The serial number, which was allotted to a file or series of files on filming, consists of two,

three, or, more usually, four numerals, which may be preceded by the letter K or M. Each page of every filmed document is identified by a frame number stamped on the original at the time of filming. Frame numbers consist of six (sometimes only five) numerals, which may be preceded by the letters D, E, H, K, L, or M, or may be without such prefix. In the document cited in footnote 3 above, the number 4679 is the serial number and the numbers E224462–65 are the frame numbers.

16. The German Foreign Ministry was at this time organized into a number of geographical and a number of functional departments. Department II dealt with the political and economic affairs of West, South, and Southeast Europe, as well as with disarmament problems and League of Nations affairs. The Director of Department II was Gerhard Köpke.

17. Dr. Karl Ritter, head of Sonderreferat W., which dealt with reparations as well as with general economic and financial matters.

18. Curtius sent one copy of his collection of documents to the Foreign Ministry, another to the Reichsarchiv, at the beginning of 1932. In March 1932 the Foreign Ministry requested, and the Reichsarchiv agreed, that it should be regarded as secret and that no reference should be made to its existence (K928/K234451–52). The collection in the custody of the Foreign Ministry has been filmed on Serial K49.

19. For the text of the first Austrian Reconstruction Protocol of October 4, 1922, see League of Nations, *Treaty Series*, XII, 386–389.

20. Schubert to Vienna, dispatch II Oe.136, February 4, 1930 (4938/E266582–85). Karl von Schubert was State Secretary of the German Foreign Ministry from December 1924 to June 1930 and German Ambassador in Rome from October 1930 to October 1932.

21. Agreed record of the German-Austrian conversations in Berlin on February 22 and 24, 1930 (3086/D614740–80). This undated and unsigned record is based on the Austrian record (K59/006680–724), which bears insertions embodying the German Foreign Ministry's suggestions for additions to the record. These additions were approved by the Austrians (K59/K006779).

22. Undated and unsigned memorandum II Oe.293 of 1931 (K920/K229674–77). The Austrian Federal Chancellor, Seipel, insisted in November 1927 that any public German pronouncement on foreign policy should not include a reference to the Anschluss (memorandum by Pünder, November 22, 1927; see footnote 2 above).

23. Stresemann and Chancellor Marx to Seipel, *ibid.*

24. Köpke to Rome, telegram No. 125, May 7, 1925 (3086/D614020–21); Stresemann to Rome, telegrams Nos. 139, May 15 (3086/D614038–39) and 150, May 23, 1925 (3123/D643290–96); Schubert to Paris, telegram No. 702, June 2, 1925 (4509/E126478–84). For expressions of later German fears lest Austria's independence be guaranteed by Italy or by a general agreement preserving the *status quo* in Central Europe, see Schubert to Rome, telegram No. 32, January 29, 1926 (6038/E445006–08); Hoesch (Paris) to Berlin, telegram No. 183, February 17, 1928 (5972/E438918–20) and Hoesch to Berlin, telegram No. 304, April 20, 1929 (K450/K131290–93).

25. Minute by Counselor Toepke, September 11, 1920 (K442/K126198); Vienna Report A 460, November 10, 1926 (K430/K124185–87).

26. Among the newspapers which at one time or another in receipt of subsidies from the German Foreign Ministry were the *Wiener Neueste Nachrichten* and the *Reichspost* (memoranda by Counselor Redlhammer, November 15, 1929 [4576/E173741–44] and January 28, 1930 [4576/E173953–55]). Among the organizations subsidized directly by the Foreign Ministry and the Reich Ministry of the Interior were the *Oesterreichisch-Deutscher Volksbund* and the *Deutsch-Oesterreichische Arbeitsgemeinschaft*. Both these bodies were organized in Austria and in Germany; Reich funds were transmitted to the German branch, sometimes with the condition that part should be forwarded to the Austrian organization. The

amounts involved in these cases were comparatively small; relevant documents have been filmed on Serials K55 and K56.

27. Cf. Chancellor Müller to Reichstag President Loebe, letter of September 25, 1928 (K1064/K273227–29); memoranda by Schubert, February 10 and February 24, 1930 (4576/E174–007–08 and E174116–22).

28. Memorandum by Pünder, November 22, 1927 (see footnote 2 above).

29. Unsigned memorandum II Oe.171, February 12, 1930 (3086/D614671–90).

30. Minutes of the Conference of Ministers held on March 16, 1931 (3575/D786142–47).

31. "Wirtschaftspolitik ist Instrument der Diplomatie" (Hans Riesser, *Haben die deutschen Diplomaten versagt?* [Bonn, 1959], p. 30). As an instance of this may be cited the German efforts, through the governor of the Bank of England, to prevent the raising of loans for Poland's effective economic rehabilitation in 1926 (London reports A 492, March 1 [4569/E168585–93], A 644, March 19 [4569/E168605–14], A 689, March 30 [K160/K019878–81] and A 754, April 8 [K160/K019886–96], all of 1926, and Stresemann to London, dispatch RM 644, April 19, 1926 [4569/E168665–71]). See also Zimmermann, *op. cit.,* pp. 339–340, which does not, however, give a complete picture.

32. Bernhard Wilhelm von Bülow, the Foreign Ministry's expert on League of Nations affairs, Deputy Director of Department II, 1928–1930, and State Secretary, June 1930–June 1936.

33. Bülow to Counselor of Embassy Smend, Rome, letter of June 5, 1929 (4607/E193757–59).

34. Lerchenfeld (Vienna) to Curtius, letter of December 25, 1929 (3086/D614605–11). Schober's government, a coalition of the Christian Social, *Grossdeutsche,* and *Landbund* parties, was formed on September 26, 1929.

35. Seipel had been Austrian Chancellor, with one interruption in 1926, from May 31, 1922, to April 3, 1929, and remained thereafter the most powerful man in the Christian Social party. In the autumn and winter of 1929 he was, however, not active in political life owing to illness. For a sympathetic treatment of Seipel's often contradictory utterances on the Anschluss see *Geschichte der Republik Oesterreich,* H. Benedikt, ed. (Vienna, 1954), pp. 330–331. Curtius' antipathy to Seipel is reflected throughout his writings; cf. especially *Bemühungen,* p. 13.

36. Memorandum II Oe.293 of 1931; see footnote 22 above. The Anschluss appeared in the programs of all Austrian parties, but only for the numerically weak *Grossdeutsche* party was it a matter of principle; see also *Geschichte der Republik Oesterreich,* pp. 384–390.

37. Vienna report A 435, November 21, 1929 (K921/K230973–80); cf. also Innsbruck report 33, January 30, 1930 (K926/K233370–72), and *Innsbrucker Nachrichten* of the same date (K926/K233373–74).

38. Memorandum II Oe.293 of 1931; see footnote 22 above.

39. Memorandum by Bülow, August 2, 1929 (L1508/L444666–68); cf. also his memorandum of August 7, 1929 (L1508/L444661–65). Briand was charged with the preparation of a memorandum on European Union in September 1929. Briand had first mooted his idea to Stresemann during the Madrid session of the League Council in June 1929 (memorandum by interpreter Schmidt, RM 911, June 11; 2406/D507172–78); Stresemann spoke appreciatively of Briand's initiative at Geneva on September 9 (League of Nations, *Official Journal,* Special Supplement No. 75, pp. 67–71).

40. Lerchenfeld to Curtius, letter of December 25, 1929 (see footnote 34 above).

41. Curtius to Vienna, telegram No. 43, December 21 (K924/K231933), Curtius to Lerchenfeld, letter of December 31 (3086/D614612–13); the invitation appears to have been issued at Lerchenfeld's instigation and after a hint from Schober, who is said to have regarded a visit to Berlin as an essential counterweight

to his visit to Rome (Vienna report A 485, December 10; Vienna telegram No. 54, December 14; K924/K231930–32).

42. Curtius, *Sechs Jahre Minister*, p. 119. This claim is not made in his earlier and more detailed book on the customs union.

43. Curtius, *Bemühungen*, pp. 12, 17; unsigned memorandum, January 4, 1930 (3086/D614620–24), memorandum by Curtius, RM 65, January 14 (3086/D614626–27). Neither of these memoranda indicates that Curtius and Schober discussed a customs union; nor is there any such indication in Schubert's brief minute of January 3 (4498/E110024) in which the State Secretary recorded what Curtius told him regarding his first conversation that day with the Austrian Chancellor. No memorandum by Curtius on this conversation has been found.

44. Schubert to Vienna, dispatch 11 Oe.136, February 4 (see footnote 20 above).

45. Memorandum II Oe.171, February 12 (see footnote 29 above); an earlier version is dated February 1 (4576/E173967–80).

46. Curtius commentary (K49/K004861).

47. The extract in Curtius' collection is K49/K004862; a fuller extract, initialed by various officials of Department II on February 18, is K920/K229614–18. Goldmann was Berlin correspondent of the Vienna *Neue Freie Presse* and was in regular contact with the German Foreign Ministry; it is not known to whom he transmitted Lahm's letter, but Lahm had asked him to bring it to the attention of the Foreign Ministry. Lahm was Vienna correspondent of the *Vossische Zeitung* and a member of the *Arbeitsgemeinschaft* (see footnote 26 above). He stated that he was acting on behalf of this and various other pro-Anschluss organizations and also for Herr Richard Riedl, one of the principal exponents of the idea of Central European economic integration.

48. Letter of February 20, submitted to Curtius the following day (3086/D614710–12; the excerpt in Curtius' collection is K49/K004863–65). Loesch was head of the *Deutscher Schutzbund,* one of the main organizations for the promotion of Germanism; Reinebeck was the Foreign Ministry official in charge of German internal affairs.

49. Record of the Cabinet session of February 20, 1930 (3575/D782804–20). The collection of Cabinet protocols in the files of the Reich Chancellery is almost complete, but it lacks the full record of a Conference of Ministers, held on the same day, of which only a brief extract (3575/D782837) has been found. In view of the secrecy which attended the final negotiations in 1931, it is most unlikely that the Ministers were given an indication of Curtius' intentions. No record of the Cabinet's being informed of the outcome of the conversations with Schober in Berlin has been found, and again it is highly improbable that they were told.

50. Others taking part were, on the German side, State Secretaries Pünder (Reich Chancellery) and Schubert, *Ministerialdirektoren* Köpke and Ritter of the Foreign Ministry, and the Minister in Vienna, Lerchenfeld; on the Austrian side, Secretary General Peter of the Foreign Affairs Department of the Federal Chancellery, *Sektionschef* Schüller of its economic section, Minister Junkar, the Austrian *Chef de Protocol,* and the Austrian Minister in Berlin, Frank.

51. Agreed record of the conversation (see footnote 21 above). Bülow, who had not taken part in the discussions, rightly noted that the record shows that it was Germany who demanded preparations for a customs union and that the Austrians consented only very reluctantly; this, he claimed, did not correspond to what he had heard from the participants (minute of April 30, 1930; K59/K006729).

52. Memoranda by Schubert, February 24, 1930 (4576/E174110–15, 116–22).

53. Schober to Curtius, letter of May 14 (3086/D614834–37). Curtius to Schober, letter of May 23 (3086/D614842). Cf. also marginalia by Curtius on p. 1 of Paris telegram No. 453, May 1 (K1090/K281224; the full telegram is K1090/K281215–21) and Rome report I 810, May 8 (K1090/K281267–76).

54. Vienna report A 240, May 12, with Curtius' marginalia (K1090/K281283–84).

55. Memorandum by Bülow, May 21, 1930 (L1712/L503550–56); cf. also Curtius' circular dispatch of June 10 (L1712/L503685–91).

56. Memoranda by Köpke, June 3 (3241/D702696–97), June 6 (3086/D614850–51), and June 30 (3086/D614866–68), by Curtius, June 14 (3086/D614853–55), and by Bülow, June 28 (3086/D614864–65); Vienna reports A 285, June 4 (K1101/K282833–36) and W 623, August 9 (K2103/K572689–92). Conferences of agrarian states, with varying participants, were held at Bucharest and Sinaia in July and at Warsaw in August 1930.

57. Vienna report A 415, August 8 (K921/K231162–66), Lerchenfeld to Bülow, letter of August 8 (4620/E198649–55), minute by Bülow, August 14 (4620/E198668).

58. Memorandum by Counselor Heeren, May 24, on his conversation with Dr. Vockel (3086/D614844–46); for the Vienna reports of June 4 and August 9 see footnote 56 above.

59. Memorandum by Köpke, May 8 (3086/D614828–32); cf. also the Vienna report of June 4 cited in footnote 56 above.

60. Curtius dispatch II Oe.938, June 4, 1930 (K59/K006781–90); the same dispatch also forwarded for information a shortened version of the record of the Berlin conversations (see footnote 21 above), omitting all mention of the customs union.

61. Curtius commentary (K49/K004878); the memorandum of June 20 has not been found.

62. *Ibid.* (K49/K004879); neither Ritter's letter of July 3 nor any reply has been found.

63. This follows the account given by Schober to Curtius in May 1931 and recorded by the latter in November 1931 (Curtius commentary; K49/K005134). In his letter to Curtius, May 14, 1930 (see footnote 53 above), Schober implied that the Briand Plan had not been discussed. The Embassy in Paris reported on July 23, 1930, that despite Briand's best endeavors, French participation in a loan to Austria had not come about (Report A 2652; K1090/K281300–02).

64. Lerchenfeld to Bülow, letter of August 20 (4620/F198659–62).

65. Lerchenfeld to Bülow, letter of August 29 (4620/E198665–67). Yugoslavia and Rumania agreed at Sinaia at the end of July to set up permanent commissions to work out plans for cooperation in the marketing of cereals and for the establishment of a customs union.

66. Memorandum by Curtius, September 7 (4679/E224498–501).

67. For the text of Schober's speech of September 12, 1930, see League of Nations, *Official Journal, Special Supplement* No. 84, pp. 60–61.

68. For Austrian negotiations with Italy immediately after the announcement of the German-Austrian customs union project, see Bülow to Rome, telegram No. 78, March 28, 1931 (5269/E324469); undated memorandum by Ritter on his discussions in Vienna, April 11–13, 1931 (5269/E324681–92); and Rieth (Vienna) to Bülow, letter of April 25, 1931 (4620/E199580–90). These negotiations were viewed with great disapproval by the Germans. For the published texts of the three protocols signed in Rome in March 1934, see League of Nations, *Treaty Series*, CLIV, 281–303; see also *Documents on German Foreign Policy*, Series C, II, Nos. 332–334. No texts are available of the so-called Brocchi Agreements of 1931 and 1932, which had the effect of establishing a system of preferential tariffs between Austria, Hungary, and Italy. Schüller took part in the preparation of all these agreements. As the Austrian foreign trade expert for two decades he had a vast fund of experience at his disposal and, as far as can be judged from the German documents, tended rather toward links between Austria and Italy and Hungary than between

Austria and Germany. His influence cannot yet be adequately assessed. Lerchenfeld once described him as an official who, in the last resort, did as he was told, but who also knew that Austrian governments tended to be short-lived (Lerchenfeld to Curtius, letter of December 25, 1929, see footnote 34 above).

69. Curtius commentary (K49/K004879–80).

70. Vienna report A 487, September 26, 1930 (K921/K231212–18).

71. Vienna telegram No. 40, October 6 (3086/D614902).

72. Memorandum by Heeren, II Oe.892, May 24, 1930 (6401/E474764–66).

73. Curtius, *Bemühungen*, p. 28.

74. Memorandum by Köpke, e.o. II Oe.2119, September 25, 1931 (K1101/K282866–70); cf. also Curtius commentary (K49/K005187–91).

75. Lerchenfeld to Curtius, letter of November 15, 1930 (3086/D614908–13).

76. Curtius, *Bemühungen*, p. 28.

77. This and the account which follows are based on Ritter's memorandum, January 7, 1931, on his negotiations in Vienna (K49/K005109–15); the draft text of the customs union agreement has not been found.

78. In quotation marks in the original.

79. Retrospective memorandum by Ritter, February 17, 1932 (K1148/K294596–98).

80. Geneva (Delegation) telegram No. 2, January 16, 1931 (4622/E202511–14). Memorandum by Bülow, January 17, recording information from Curtius (4619/E197056–58). Schober also told Curtius of negotiations between Austria and Hungary on a hidden preferential system.

81. Minutes of the Cabinet meeting of January 28, 1931 (3575/D785726–32).

82. Bülow to Prittwitz, letter of January 20, 1931 (4620/E199138–44).

83. Memorandum by Gaus, February 23, 1931 (K1168/K299826–39). Gaus was Director of the Legal Department of the German Foreign Ministry. The draft of the customs union agreement which Gaus appended to his memorandum has not been found; from the memorandum itself it emerges that Gaus's draft differed on some points from the text Ritter had discussed in Vienna, and it was probably not much different from the text submitted to the Cabinet on March 16 (see footnote 103 below). It is a tribute to Gaus's skill as a draftsman that the customs union agreement so nearly withstood the scrutiny of the International Court.

84. Curtius, *Bemühungen*, pp. 30–31; Paris report A 3393, October 10, 1930 (K936/K240381–86); Paris telegram No. 53, January 13, 1931 (K936/K240571–73). Cf. also Curtius, *Sechs Jahre Minister*, p. 137, Hauser, *op. cit.*, p. 53, and Zimmermann, *op. cit.*, p. 393.

85. Curtius, *Bemühungen*, p. 32, where this opinion, with which Curtius obviously concurred, is ascribed to Hoesch; Bülow to Hoesch, letter of January 23, 1931 (4620/E199035–41). Bülow, writing before Hoesch was informed of the customs union project, spoke merely of "independent steps in Central Europe in the direction of an economic union."

86. Curtius, *Bemühungen*, pp. 29–30, 32; Curtius commentary (K49/K005275); Köpke subsequently noted that these consultations took place, some immediately before Curtius' visit to Vienna and some only just prior to the publication of the plan, at a time "when the heads of mission were entitled to assume that in view of the advanced stage of the action the purpose of the consultation was in the main purely informatory, and that it was no longer their comment on the question 'whether' but only on the question 'how' which was expected." (Memorandum by Köpke, February 24, 1932 (K1148/K294599–603).) Schubert (Rome) noted that he was "informed" of the content and aim of the impending German and Austrian démarche by Curtius and others in the Foreign Ministry on March 13, 14, and 15 (memorandum, March 17, 1931; 5269/E324233). Koch (Prague) did not arrive in Berlin until March 19.

87. Memorandum by Hoesch, forwarded to Berlin under cover of his report A 820 of March 6, 1931 (K936/K240609–26); Curtius initialed this on March 14. Cf. also Hoesch to Köpke, letter of March 6 (K936/K240607–08). Nowhere in Hoesch's exposé does the phrase "customs union" appear.

88. Memorandum by Ritter, February 17, 1932 (see footnote 79 above); it is not known at what stage Heeren was drawn into the small circle which knew of the project.

89. Memorandum by Köpke, February 24, 1932 (see footnote 86 above).

90. Memorandum by Köpke, February 21, 1931 (K51/K005880–86).

91. Bülow to Curtius, letter of February 16, 1931 (4619/E197113–14).

92. Minutes of the Conference of Ministers held on February 28, 1931 (3575/D786070–80).

93. Curtius, *Bemühungen*, pp. 36 ff.; Curtius commentary (K49/K005245–264).

94. Memorandum by Schubert, March 29, 1931 (5269/E424490–92).

95. Curtius, *Bemühungen*, pp. 39 ff.; Kurt von Schuschnigg, *Dreimal Oesterreich* (Vienna, 1937), p. 169. See also footnote 12 above.

96. Curtius commentary (K49/K005264 and 276); the only reason for advancing the date which Curtius gives in his commentary was the fear that secrecy could not be long preserved after the two cabinets were informed. While this was likely, and in fact borne out by events, this factor too must have been appreciated when Curtius agreed to the May date.

97. Item B of the memorandum of February 24, 1931 (K59/K006864–79), prepared for Curtius as a brief for his visit to Vienna; *DBFP*, 2nd Series, II, No. 6.

98. Memorandum by Ritter, March 14, on a telephone conversation with Schüller (K49/K005277–80); on this occasion Schüller also stated that the first Austrian Cabinet session on the subject of the customs union had been satisfactory.

99. For the communication made in London on March 21 by the Austrian Minister, see *DBFP*, 2nd Series, II, No. 2 and encl. Evidence of the lack of proper instructions to the Austrian Ministers in Rome and Paris is contained in Schubert's memoranda of March 19 (5269/E324305–10 and 313–17) and in Bülow's memorandum of March 20 on a telephone conversation with Hoesch (3086/D614995–96).

100. Memorandum by Schubert, March 23, 1931 (5269/E324410–13).

101. Dispatch II Oe.303, March 9 (3086/D614971).

102. Unsigned memorandum, March 8 (K49/K004881–87). The memorandum expressed some concern at the detrimental effect of the customs union on Austrian industry and suggested that German firms be advised to make private arrangements with Austrian ones, at least for an interim period, to afford the latter some protection. But this, it was stated, would be feasible only with some industries, and despite protective treatment of this sort, German industry would gradually push under (*zurückdrängen*) a section of Austria's industry. For another estimate see Herbert Gross, *Industrie-wirtschaftliche Wirkungen einer deutsch-österreichischen Zollunion* in *Schriften des Weltwirtschaftsarchivs Kiel*, cited in Hauser, *op. cit.*, p. 55, fn. 2, where the economic advantages for Austria were estimated at 600 million marks and those for Germany at 500 million.

103. This draft (3575/D786148–61), which was the text agreed on in Vienna, contained the provision (said by Curtius to have been a German proposal which need not be upheld) that disputes arising out of the customs union should be referred to the International Court at The Hague; otherwise it differed only very slightly from the final text (see footnote 8 above).

104. Minutes of the Conferences of Ministers held on March 16 (3575/D786142–47) and at four P.M. on March 18 (3575/D786165–71).

105. Curtius to Hoesch, Neurath, and Schubert, dispatch II OE.352, March 18 (K49/K005284–306) with enclosures (K49/K005307–33). Cf. also Curtius' dispatch to various other missions of the same date (K49/K005281–83). An earlier

draft of the dispatch to the principal missions, handed to Schubert during his visit to Berlin (5269/E324236–54), differs in some respects from the final instructions.

105a. Bülow to Hoesch and Neurath, letter of March 17 (4620/E199091–94; 130–33).

106. Memorandum by Ritter, March 19 (3086/D614976); Schober to Curtius, letter of March 19 (3086/D614994); Vienna report A 162, March 20 (5002/E284343–44).

107. Ritter to Paris, telegram No. 133, March 19 (K1168/K299843–45), Ritter to Rome, telegram No. 58, March 19 (5269/E324369–71), Schubert to Berlin, telegram No. 54, March 20 (5269/E324373); for the text of the Austrian declaration made in London see DBFP, 2nd Series, II, No. 2, encl.

108. Memorandum by Ritter, March 19 (see footnote 106 above); DBFP, 2nd Series, II, No. 1; Schubert to Berlin, telegram No. 56, March 21 (3086/D615008–10).

109. Erich Eyck, Geschichte der Weimarer Republik, II (Zürich, 1956), 405–406.

110. DBFP, 2nd Series, II, No. 34; cf. also Bülow's letter to Smend quoted in footnote 33 above. Bülow has often been regarded as the real author of the customs union (DBFP, ibid., No. 262, where Ritter's name is coupled with Bülow's; Eyck, op. cit., p. 379; and Herriot in Ère Nouvelle, May 7, 1931), but it would appear that the original initiative, and especially the determination to get an agreement in principle from the Austrians in February 1930, came from Curtius. It is, however, curious that Bülow's name does not appear in Curtius' book on the customs union.

111. Bülow described Curtius' precarious position in a letter to Hoesch, December 12, 1930 (4620/E198591–94), stating that the majority of Curtius' party no longer wished to be represented in the Cabinet and that there was a tendency to concentrate the government in fewer hands. It was therefore necessary for Curtius to cut a good figure in public at Geneva. See also DBFP, 2nd Series, I, No. 326.

112. See also League of Nations, Official Journal, Special Supplement No. 86, pp. 47–49, where, however, no countries are specifically named. The texts of the treaties concluded on June 27, 1931, with Rumania and on July 18, 1931, with Hungary have been filmed on Serials K2107 and 9841, respectively. The treaties were, however, not implemented under the Weimar Republic because of opposition from the United States (cf. Foreign Relations of the United States, 1932, II, 338–349).

113. Bülow to Koch, April 19 (4620/E199512–15). Koch, in his reply, April 22 (4620/K199520–22), stated that he did not share the view that economic difficulties would sooner or later force Czechoslovakia to align herself with Germany.

CHARLES BLOCH

Great Britain, German Rearmament, and the Naval Agreement of 1935

Hitler's rise to power in January 1933 caused much apprehension abroad. To project a peaceful image, he embarked on a series of conciliatory moves, notably the Concordat with the Holy See of July 1933, and the Non-Aggression Pact with Poland of January 1934. He also joined the Western powers in the abortive Four-Power Pact in June 1933 for the peaceful revision of Versailles. At the same time, however, there were ominous signs of a more recalcitrant German attitude: in October 1933, Germany left the Disarmament Conference and the League of Nations, and in July 1934 she was suspected of complicity in an unsuccessful attempt at a Nazi takeover in Austria. It was not until March 1935 that Hitler committed his first open violation of Versailles by proclaiming German rearmament.

The author of the following selection is Professor of Modern History at Tel Aviv University. His special field of interest is Nazi Germany. Among his books are Hitler und die europäischen Mächte 1933/34: Kontinuität oder Bruch *(Hamburg, 1966), and* La nuit des longs couteaux *(Paris, 1967), which deals with the "Blood Purge" of 1934. The present chapter first appeared as "La Grande-Bretagne face au réarmement Allemand et l'accord naval de 1935," in* Revue d'Histoire de la Deuxième Guerre Mondiale *(1966), No. 63, pp. 41–68. It is reprinted by permission of the author and publisher and was translated by the editor.*

IN LATE 1934 and early 1935, Nazi Germany, compared with France, appeared virtually isolated. France was about to conclude a military alliance with the Soviet Union and was drawing closer to Italy, who did not yet favor German revisionism and at the same time was worried over Austria. But Hitler was not intimidated. In March 1935 he announced the creation of a German air force and reintroduced compulsory military service, thus flagrantly violating the Treaty of Versailles. This *coup* provoked no serious reaction from the victors of 1918, chiefly because of Great Britain. As a matter of fact, three months later, Britain sanctioned rearmament by signing the Naval Agreement with Germany on June 18, 1935. To Hitler this was "the happiest day of his life"; he thought he had attained a goal to which he had aspired since 1923.

Early on, Hitler had thought of cooperation, even an alliance, with England, and at least until 1936 he adhered to the idea. In doing so he continued the policy of the Weimar Republic which, with brief intervals, had relied on Great Britain to bring pressure on France.

Certain Englishmen sympathized with the Third Reich. Among them at the time were Lloyd George and especially his former chief secretary, Lord Lothian, as well as Lord Rothermere, owner of the *Daily Mail*. Even the *Times*, sometimes considered the organ of the British government, advocated good relations with Berlin. Its editor, Geoffrey Dawson, had been hostile to France since 1922. No wonder, then, that the majority of British opinion was more favorable to Germany than to France, even though Englishmen were shocked by certain actions of the Hitler regime—the persecution of the Jews, the restrictions imposed on the churches, and the Blood Purge of June 30, 1934.[1] In addition to the above men, there were certain military figures such as Colonel MacCaw, adviser to the Secretary of War, who maintained close ties with Alfred Rosenberg, head of the Foreign Policy Office (APA) of the Nazi party. MacCaw and some of his colleagues, notably the influential Colonel Conwell-Evans, fostered a pro-German state of mind in the British Legion (Britain's veterans' organization). Similar currents, we shall see, were manifest in the Admiralty. In the Coalition Cabinet, headed by Ramsay MacDonald, the Secretary for Air, Lord Londonderry, represented the same tendency. More discreet, but also more important, was the support given the Third Reich until the war in 1939 by the Governor of the Bank of England, Montagu Norman. His attitude reflected the majority view of the City. Nor must we forget the Prince of Wales, the future Edward VIII, who on every occasion showed his Germanophile sentiments.

Hitler's wish to bring about good relations with Great Britain was thus not illusory, even though only a minority of Englishmen were favorably disposed toward his regime. These positive feelings were reinforced, however, by more general tendencies: First of all, the principle of the "balance of power" which since 1918 had worked against France, whom most Britishers considered the imperialist power par excellence, imbued with memories of Louis XIV and Napoleon I,[2] an impression that prevailed in England until 1936. Then there was England's bad conscience vis-à-vis Germany, who was generally viewed as the victim of the harsh and unjust peace of 1919, which in turn had been responsible for the revival of German nationalism and the advent of the National Socialist regime. The excesses of the latter must not prevent British policy from repairing the wrong committed at Versailles. This state of mind was found especially among the Liberal opposition (e.g., the *News Chronicle*) and the Labor opposition. Prime Minister MacDonald, though he had left the Labor party in 1931, still maintained this attitude. The same circles were also firm partisans of disarmament. They were joined by numerous Conservatives, to whom a decrease in military spending was indispensable after the great economic crisis that had struck England in 1931. All these tendencies had one direct effect: they created an almost universal dislike of taking on new obligations on the continent, especially for the security of France, and even less for that of Central and Eastern Europe. Even the obligations assumed at Locarno in 1925 were considered excessive and ways were to be found to get out of them.[3] The advantages which German policy could derive from this state of mind are obvious.

Yet not all British politicians favored concessions to the Third Reich. Two great statesmen, former ministers, did not cease to warn against the rising danger—Austen Chamberlain and Winston Churchill. But they were rather isolated in the House of Commons. Military and diplomatic figures, and especially high functionaries in the Foreign Office, notably Permanent Under-Secretary of State Sir Robert Vansittart, echoed their warnings. But they were disregarded by the government because the minister responsible for foreign affairs, Sir John Simon, held entirely different views. Having, like MacDonald, been opposed to Britain's entry into the war in 1914, Simon favored an accord with Germany and urged France in the same direction, although he, too, was appalled by Hitler's excesses. His assistant, Anthony Eden, sincerely desired Franco-British collaboration; but he was comparatively young and did not have much influence at the center. MacDonald, as we have seen, was generally favorable toward Germany. But beginning in 1934 his declining health restricted his activities. The actual direction of affairs came to rest with Stanley Baldwin, who sometimes listened to Eden but more often to persons favorable to Germany. Above all, he was not much interested and took little initiative in foreign affairs. More and more Neville Chamberlain, well known for his later appeasement policy toward Hitler, became the "strong man of the government." Among the most pro-German and anti-French members of the government was the friend of Lord Lothian, Sir Samuel Hoare, Secretary of State for India, who was to succeed Simon in the Foreign Office in the ministerial re-organization of June 7, 1935. His colleagues, especially Neville Chamberlain, as well as Geoffrey Dawson of the *Times,* preferred him to Eden, who was considered too hostile to the Third Reich.[4]

The pro-German and anti-French attitude that prevailed in leading British circles made itself especially felt in naval questions. This had been so since the Washington Naval Treaty of 1921–1922, which France had accepted only with reluctance. She had never concealed her intention not to renew it at its expiration on December 31, 1936. Naval rivalry among England, France, and Italy had taken a particularly sharp turn at the time of the Disarmament Conference of 1932–1933. Great Britain, supported by the United States, at the time refused to reduce her naval forces until the next conference, scheduled for the end of 1935; but she demanded that France diminish hers, so that Italy would have almost obtained parity with her, while Paris hoped to maintain always a 50 per cent superiority with respect to Italy.[5] Opposition to England led France's naval experts, supported by Minister of the Navy Georges Leygues (whose chief of military cabinet was Vice-Admiral François Darlan), to seek contact with their Italian colleagues, despite reservations on the part of the Quai d'Orsay, committed to close cooperation with London. The beginnings of a Franco-Italian rapprochement were interrupted after the visit of Sir John Simon to Rome in January 1934. In the course of 1934, Franco-British differences became deeper and deeper. The policy of Barthou, trying to erect a security barrier against Nazi Germany that would include both Italy and the USSR, was disapproved of by Britain's government and the majority of her public. Barthou's visit to London in July brought only apparent reconciliation. Naval problems were broached only on the periphery of the conversations. Each of the two parties stuck to its position—the British wishing an increase of the German Navy from 100,000 to 200,000 tons (at a time when France's whole policy aimed at preventing German rearmament), and for the rest the maintenance of the terms of the Washington Treaty, which France wanted abolished. At the same time, Britain's Admiral Hector Bywater published a book entitled *A Searchlight on the Navy,* in which he preached close naval cooperation between England and the United States, especially against France and, to a lesser degree, against Italy. Under the circumstances, French naval circles induced the new Minister of the Navy, F. Piétri, who was by no means anti-British, secretly to encourage Japan to denounce the Washington Treaty on December 29, 1934. (Tokyo, as we shall see, showed no gratitude to Paris for this diplomatic support.) Four days later, on January 2, 1935, France in turn addressed a note to the signatories of the Washington

Treaty, leaving no doubt that after 1936 she would no longer feel bound by that convention.

Meanwhile, Pierre Laval had become Foreign Minister in place of Barthou, who had been assassinated on October 9, 1934. From his predecessor he inherited, above all, the idea of a Franco-Italian rapprochement. In pursuit of this aim he went to Rome, where he and Mussolini signed the Accords of January 7, 1935. It is possible that this rapprochement caused some uneasiness in London. To dispel it, Pierre-Etienne Flandin, then President of the Council, visited the British capital, together with Laval, where they talked with members of the British government on February 1–3, 1935.[6] France's announced intention of no longer holding to the Washington Naval Treaty at first, perhaps, threw a shadow over the conversations. But their result could only please the British, considering France's concessions on the subject of German rearmament.

This latter question was of burning importance. Germany for some time had demanded rearmament by insisting on "equality of rights." But she had not dared return to the subject since France's firm note of April 17, 1934. She then waited several months so as not to jeopardize the return of the Saar to the Reich. After the plebiscite in that territory, however, she presented the victorious powers of 1919 with a *fait accompli* in the rearmament field.

Actually, Hitler had already begun to lay the diplomatic groundwork with England for his *coup,* in order to separate her from her former allies. In doing so he had combined tempting offers with intimidation. On the one hand, he informed the British in November 1934 that he wanted only 35 per cent of the British Empire's naval tonnage for the German Navy. He confirmed this offer, apparently sincerely, in a secret instruction to the German Admiralty. At the same time he sent his confidential aide, Ribbentrop, to London to agitate for an Anglo-German rapprochement in face of the Franco-Soviet alliance then being negotiated.

At the time of his visit to the British capital, Ribbentrop also broached the subject of air armament. This was the area in which Britain felt most vulnerable. Government circles and public opinion were much concerned over it, as was shown in frequent parliamentary debates. But Hitler did not wish to make specific commitments in this area. On the contrary, he let rumors get about that Germany's secret air armaments were already far advanced. Absolutely fantastic figures on this subject circulated across the Channel. Actually, Germany had apparently only between seven hundred and a thousand planes,[7] of which only a few hundred were first-line. But MacDonald and Baldwin, until the spring of 1935, were victims of propaganda.

At the end of January 1935, Hitler received two pro-German British personages in Berlin—first the Laborite Lord Allen of Hurtwood, and then the Liberal Lord Lothian, accompanied by Colonel Conwell-Evans. To these visitors he repeated his "offer" of a 35 per cent ratio for Germany's navy to that of Britain, and he even talked of the possibility of an international convention for the limitation of armaments. Concerning aviation, however, Hitler spoke only in vague terms about parity between the Reich and neighboring powers. Immediately upon his return to London, Lord Lothian published two articles in the *Times* in favor of Anglo-German cooperation. He also reported his talks to Simon. Thus briefed, Simon, on January 31, spoke in very conciliatory terms to Germany's ambassador in London, von Hoesch, assuring him that England would not enter into any unilateral engagement with France. The next day, Flandin and Laval arrived in London. In return for some vague promises from their British counterparts about Franco-British solidarity and mutual consultation, the French ministers abandoned all of Barthou's German policy in order to accept the principle of German rearmament; so it was confided by a French diplomat in London to his German colleague.[8] The final communiqué of February 3, among other things, spoke of a projected air pact among the five signatories of Locarno, providing for mutual assistance in case of unprovoked aggression,[9] something close to Britain's heart. This proposal was communicated to Berlin in mid-February, where Neurath's first reaction was mostly favorable. It was agreed, therefore, that Simon and Eden would pay a visit to the German capital.

But the British ministers did not wish to face Hitler in a position of weakness. Thus the London government, on March 4, 1935, published a *White Book* on German secret rearmament, especially airplane production, in order to obtain increased military funds. The *White Book* was violently criticized as "inopportune" by the pro-German press, especially the *Daily Mail* and the *Observer,* as well as by "pacifist" papers of Labor and Liberal tendencies, such as the *Daily Herald,* the *News Chronicle,* and the *Economist.* In the House of Commons, Labor's chief delegate, Clement Attlee, led the attack, seconded by the Liberal Herbert Samuel; but their motion of censure against the government was defeated.

Hitler did not let himself be intimidated by this show of force on the part of the British government. The day after the publication of the *White Book,* March 5, Neurath informed London that the visit of Simon to Berlin, already scheduled for March 7, had to be postponed, since "the Führer suffered from a cold." On March 9, Göring revealed to the correspondent of the *Daily Mail* the German government's decision of February 26 to set up a military air force under a special ministry. The creation of the Luftwaffe was thus made official. Before the victorious powers of 1918 could react to this violation of the Treaty of Versailles, it was followed by another one of much greater import:

on March 16, using the vote for two-year military service in the French Chamber of Deputies as a pretext, the Reich's government unilaterally declared Part V of the treaty, dealing with questions of armament, abolished; at the same time it reintroduced compulsory military service and, in a single stroke, created an army of thirty-six divisions, or 500,000 to 550,000 men. This exceeded the most far-reaching and audacious demands Germany had made to date.[10]

Hitler knew the risk he was taking was not very great. The accommodation shown by Flandin and Laval since the Saar question and their visit to London, not to mention other discreet overtures to Berlin, had shown him that the days of Barthou were over. Italy was always afraid of a forcible German move against Austria. But she was now preparing for the Ethiopian War and, under the circumstances, wished to avoid an increase of tension with the Reich. Above all, it was the attitude of England which reassured the Führer. On March 14, the day after the parliamentary debate on defense, Simon, without mentioning the creation of the Luftwaffe, and despite the insult of Hitler's "diplomatic cold," had again approached von Hoesch about the British visit. He told the ambassador that the British government had sufficient influence in Europe "to explain the German point of view" to the other European powers and thus have them endorse the Reich's demands.[11] While France and even Italy, as a matter of form, protested loudly against the violations of the Treaty of Versailles, the note handed Berlin on March 8 by Britain's ambassador, Sir Eric Phipps, was far more moderate. The visit of Britain's ministers to the German capital was still planned— to the great displeasure of Paris, because the united front of the powers against Hitler's provocation was henceforth clearly ruptured. Still, as on previous occasions, France submitted to the moderating influence of Britain. She was content to bring the matter before the League of Nations, and placed her hopes in the Anglo-French-Italian conference that was to meet at Stresa on April 11.

Part of the British public and a majority of the press showed even greater understanding toward Germany than the government. This was true of the most influential and widely read papers, such as the *Times,* the *News Chronicle,* the *Daily Mail,* the *Daily Mirror,* and the *Daily Express* (organ of the Canadian Lord Beaverbrook, who preached British "isolationism"; Britain was to disinterest herself in the affairs of the European continent and devote herself entirely to problems of her Empire). The *Daily Herald,* organ of the Labor party, went so far as to say that Hitler's declarations at the time of the creation of the new Wehrmacht constituted an invitation to general disarmament. The whole press criticized even France's decision to bring the matter before the League of Nations. Many Britishers charged that Germany had been forced to act because of France. In 1934, Hitler had only demanded an army of 300,000 men and an air force half that of France; but the Doumergue-Barthou government had rejected that proposal by its note of April 17, 1934. According to these British circles, Hitler's offer could have led to limited and controlled German rearmament within the framework of a general armaments convention. It was thus France who was responsible for the breakdown of the Disarmament Conference at Geneva, and not Germany, though the latter had left the conference in October 1933. But there were also other voices, though few, like the Liberal *Manchester Guardian,* which had been favorable toward Germany until 1933, and the Conservative *Morning Post* and *Daily Telegraph,* the latter close to certain officials of the Foreign Office and following a line similar to that of Eden. These papers condemned Germany and approved France's policy.

On March 19 and 23, von Hoesch sent two dispatches to Berlin, stating that Germany was threatened by an encirclement of France, Italy, and the USSR. Such a coalition, however, would not be complete without England. Yet within the British government, only a minority, represented by Secretary for War Lord Hailsham and Duff Cooper, favored such a course, while Eden, who had a certain influence on Baldwin, was beginning to waver. The majority of ministers, led by Simon, who was supported by MacDonald, were firmly opposed to any policy of encirclement and wished to reach an accord with Germany on the basis of international cooperation and the maintenance of European peace. The government in Berlin must make their task easier and must lend itself to such cooperation, must even return to the League of Nations and consent to a limitation of armaments—on condition, of course, that it would apply to all states without exception. If, on the other hand, Germany embarked on unlimited rearmament, British public opinion, thus far hostile to encirclement, would change and demand Britain's adherence to the coalition led by France, perhaps even a rapprochement with the Soviet Union. Then the Reich would be surrounded by enemies on all sides.[12]

These dispatches had an effect on Hitler quite different from what their author had expected.[13] Far from leading him to make concessions, they only increased his distrust of diplomatic (as also of military) professionals, because they "did not understand the dynamics of National Socialism" and "were deeply tied to liberal and pacifist prejudices." For Hitler, the Anglo-German cooperation which he desired with all his heart was to be based on a fundamental identity of interests between the two powers against their common enemies, France and especially Russia, as well as on a delimitation of spheres of interest. There was no room for "silly pacifism," unworthy of two great peoples of Germanic race, or for a return to the "babbling" of Geneva. These slogans were all right to mislead public opinion in other countries, notably France, already decadent and undermined by pacifist propaganda, or a small minority in Britain, represented by Eden (whom von Hoesch had recommended for special attention).

It is in this light that we must interpret the proposals Hitler made to the British ministers during their Berlin visit, on March 25–26. They were a mixture of truths and lies. As Hoesch had foreseen, Simon opened discussions by saying that England wanted cooperation among all European states and wished above all to avoid the formation of two hostile blocs. British public opinion was troubled by certain German actions— the exit from the League of Nations, the threats against the independence of Austria,[14] and the unilateral violation of the Treaty of Versailles. But in principle Britain was not anti-German. Of Simon's statements, Hitler remembered especially the last. The rest in his eyes was merely propaganda addressed to the pacifists of Western Europe. He pretended to "play the game" and replied that Germany desired no territories from her neighbors. She was ready to conclude nonaggression pacts with them, even with Austria, on condition, however, that other countries (Italy and the "Little Entente") would no longer interfere there. Hitler added even that he wanted by no means to separate England from France, a declaration which Simon noted with satisfaction.[15] On the other hand, Hitler came back again and again to the danger of communism for all of Europe and to the alleged aggressive designs of the Soviet Union. On this point his two discussion partners differed in their reactions: while Simon did not pursue the charge and placed the accent on the air pact which should be concluded without Soviet participation, Eden replied that the USSR, which was involved in grave domestic difficulties, had neither the desire nor the power to attack any country. He added that anti-bolshevik propaganda in the style of Alfred Rosenberg made a bad impression in England.

Hitler did not move an inch from his already fixed position. He did not wish to go back to the League of Nations, nor consent to a genuine limitation of armaments. When the British ministers remarked that the new army of 550,000 men henceforth assured Germany's predominance on the European continent and that she had additional forces in the paramilitary formations of the SA, the SS, and the "Labor Service," Hitler declared all these forces indispensable for the security of the Reich, in view of the armaments of France, Czechoslovakia, and especially the USSR, who would conclude an alliance with each other and encircle Germany. For that reason she needed the same material as the other powers, including heavy weapons (tanks, airplanes, and so forth), which had been forbidden her by the Treaty of Versailles. As for aviation, Britain's main concern, Hitler gave evasive answers. He declared himself ready to conclude the proposed air pact, but raised (not without justification) the problem of Russian and Japanese aviation. He added that the Reich had already attained equality in the air with Great Britain (later, on November 19, 1936, he was to boast to Austria's Foreign Minister, Guido Schmidt, that this had been a bluff to intimidate the British ministers and make them conclude the naval accord).[16] Germany would reserve for herself, moreover, the right to increase her air fleet if the USSR did the same and also to attain equality with France (including her colonial aviation).

Yet Hitler was sincere, in the sense indicated above, when he proclaimed his desire to achieve close cooperation with England. In this context he recalled that it was thanks to the aid of Blücher that Wellington had been able to defeat Napoleon at Waterloo. Touching, in quite a vague manner, on the colonial problem, Hitler hinted at the possibility of a German contribution to the defense of Britain's overseas possessions, that is to say, a global alliance between the two powers (an idea to which he was to return at the end of August 1939, a few days before the outbreak of the war). But seeing that the British ministers were not attracted by his "offer," Hitler did not insist. Instead he dwelled extensively on naval matters, underlining the fact that he definitely recognized Britain's supremacy at sea. That is why he was ready to restrict Germany's naval tonnage to 35 per cent of that of the British Empire. Simon's first reaction was negative. He found Hitler's proposal excessive and feared that it would lead to an armaments race, especially on the part of France who, he knew, would not accept the naval equality with Germany which Hitler desired. But instead of being consistent and refusing all discussion on this basis, Simon invited a German delegation to come to London to negotiate a naval agreement. In thus accepting the principle of a bilateral accord, Simon abandoned his initial stand of wanting to link all armaments problems, especially those of an air pact, so as to achieve a collective agreement on general limitations. This would also have been consistent with the Franco-British communiqué of February 3, 1935, and with the assurances Eden had repeated to Paris on the eve of his arrival in Berlin.[17]

Hitler thus rightly felt he had achieved a first success. Perhaps his assumptions were exaggerated, for he thought he had won Simon over entirely to his view. That was how Neurath presented it in his March 29 circular to the German ambassadors in the various European capitals, because Simon, after all, had expressly regretted at the end of his talks with Hitler that no accord had been reached on the most important questions. But in his report to Commons on March 28, Simon spoke of "considerable differences of view between Germany and Great Britain," and he was still more explicit in his personal notes.[18] We are thus faced with an extremely important psychological phenomenon which starts at this time and which gathered momentum to assume abnormal proportions during the war: Hitler hears what he wants to hear. In some respects he creates for himself a British policy in his own image. Later on, reality will surprise him.

But "in some respects" only. Because while Simon had spoken of differences, he was not the man to draw conclusions from them. Fundamentally, he always clung to his master plan—to achieve an entente with Germany. It is also permissible to assume that (together with other influential British personalities) Simon did not remain entirely unaffected by Hitler's anti-bolshevist argument. He had restricted his visit to Berlin and had left his deputy, Eden, whose authority was much less than his, to continue to Moscow (and then to Warsaw and Prague), where his talks with Stalin, Molotov, and Litvinov could only be in the nature of simple exchanges of views. The Soviet leaders showed respect and good will toward Eden; but they did not hide their distrust of British policy in general, which they suspected of trying to give Germany a free hand for expansion to the East.[19] In the same way the Soviet press had already criticized Britain's weak reaction to the creation of the new German air force and army.

Hitler was annoyed by Eden's trip to Moscow. He had not failed to note the differences between Simon and his deputy. On March 25, after the first conversation with Hitler, Eden had written in his diary that Germany's old nationalism was being resurrected. Great Britain must under no condition permit a German attack upon Russia; because once victorious, she would turn against England.[20] On March 27, Eden sent a dispatch to the Foreign Office, warning not to give in to Germany's blackmail by making excessive concessions. The great powers, desirous of peace, must strengthen their mutual ties and, above all, must not abandon the small states to German imperialism. Eden found the support of Vansittart, but not that of the majority of his colleagues in the government.[21] The Prince of Wales, on April 11, told von Hoesch of his disapproval of the Foreign Office's anti-German attitude.[22]

Hitler had thus succeeded with his tactics of intimidation. Simon was much impressed with his declaration that Germany had already achieved aerial parity with Great Britain. He even feared German superiority, and the majority of British ministers shared this fear. Public opinion also was much disturbed. On April 3–4, 1935, a conference met in London under the auspices of the British League of Nations Union, presided over by the aged Lord Cecil. It was attended by politicians of all persuasions, as well as by military and academic figures. The most diverse views were expressed. In the name of the government, Under-Secretary of State for Air Sir Philip Sassoon stated that British aviation was in effect incapable of large-scale action, since England held only fifth rank among aerial powers, after the USSR (whose military aviation he estimated at two thousand planes), France, the United States, and Italy. She also risked being soon overtaken by Germany. To meet this situation of inferiority, the British government planned two measures:

(1) Accelerated airplane construction, to put into service shortly 41 new squadrons and to gain ultimately 129 small squadrons with 1,750 planes.

(2) The conclusion of an air pact among the five Locarno powers.

It was mainly in the hope of making progress on this latter project that MacDonald and Simon, accompanied by Vansittart, went to Stresa on April 12–14 to meet Flandin, Laval, and Mussolini.

This conference was meant to confirm Anglo-French-Italian solidarity, but from the start it appeared that Great Britain was keeping her distance.[23] It quickly became clear that the conference could not conclude an air pact, which presented a complicated problem requiring long negotiation, but could merely approve its principle.

In their final communiqué the three governments reaffirmed their mutual obligations under the Treaty of Locarno, and censured Germany's unilateral treaty violations and her creation of an air force and the new Wehrmacht. This Platonic censure was repeated three days later, on April 17, by the Council of the League of Nations, which unanimously adopted a resolution introduced by France, supported by England and Italy, with only Denmark abstaining. Despite the harmless character of these declarations, French public opinion, even so serious a paper as Le Temps, made itself illusions about their significance and considered Stresa as manifest proof of solidarity among the three powers against the German menace. In reality, the British government, even less than Italy, had not taken on any obligations. British public opinion, as could be seen from the majority of newspaper comments, would not have allowed it.

Berlin knew well that nothing need be feared from Great Britain. Far more serious might have been the conclusion of a Franco-Soviet alliance, following Laval's visit to Moscow on May 13–15, and the signing of the alliance between the USSR and Czechoslovakia, if the Franco-Soviet treaty had become effective. We cannot here go into the details of this important event, about which much has already been written,[24] though it still calls for a deeper analysis based on documents not yet published. Let us merely point out that, contrary to the original plan of Barthou, Laval subordinated the application of the alliance to the Treaty of Locarno (following a request by Simon),[25] as was obvious from the official commentary in Le Temps of May 9, which went over the text paragraph by paragraph. This meant that the right to decide whether the casus foederis existed between France and the USSR devolved upon England and Italy. A reading of the Paris governmental press shows that France attached much more importance to the solidarity, however vague, with these latter two powers, than to her alliance with Soviet Russia, even though the latter called for mutual assistance in case of a German attack. Under these circumstances, the value of the alliance was limited from the start. Even so, Germany, in a note of May 25, protested against the Franco-Russian treaty as contrary to the spirit of Locarno. Neurath invoked the treaty to delay the opening of talks on the air pact, which was to fit into the framework of Locarno, obviously hoping to turn England against the Franco-Russian alliance and to sow discord between London and Paris.

We still lack the documents to ascertain exactly Britain's reactions to the alliance. It seems that the Foreign Office in its majority approved it, to judge from the comments in the *Daily Telegraph*. Among ministers, Baldwin gave a speech that showed understanding for France's security needs, as did Eden. The paper of MacDonald (who at the end of his career seemed to have a change of heart) published an article along the same lines. The attitude of Simon was more complex. Answering an interpellation by Herbert Samuel, he said (full of the assurances Laval had given him) that England did not risk becoming involved in a European war through the alliance—a statement which the *Times* registered with satisfaction. Samuel Hoare and Neville Chamberlain made no statement. Violent criticism of the alliance came from the Liberal and Labor opposition, which charged that the pact was unilaterally directed against Germany and was contrary to the spirit of collective security. The strongest hostility naturally came from pro-Hitler, anti-Soviet, and anti-French elements. According to the German military attaché in London,[26] anger was especially great in the War Ministry (though the Minister himself, Lord Hailsham, generally adopted a quite different attitude) and in the British General Staff, as doubtless also in the Admiralty. These circles were the first to push for a naval accord with Germany, which they saw as a reply to the Franco-Soviet alliance.

Cautious contacts regarding this subject had not ceased since Simon's and Eden's visit to Berlin, and they had continued through April. Despite the hesitations of the Wilhelmstrasse, Admiral Raeder allowed his subordinates to communicate certain information concerning German naval construction to the Admiralty, apparently with the aim of impressing the British and making them amenable to Berlin's wishes. This maneuver was successful, it seems, even though French Minister Piétri, who visited London on May 1, tried to dissuade his British colleague, Sir Bolton Eyres-Monsell, from concluding a separate naval agreement with the Reich on France's back.[27] British naval circles decided to go ahead. They tried to hide their contacts with Germany from the Foreign Office, which they accused of trying to sabotage the agreement. They were especially anxious to obtain data on submarines. Raeder informed them that twelve light submarines were under construction, but he concealed the steps that had been taken to build a secret base at Heligoland. Moreover, Germany planned construction of a 35,000-ton battleship. This information soon leaked out and caused a certain stir in England. Simon complained to von Hoesch about this indiscretion, which made the negotiations more difficult, and he asked that the German government show greater understanding for his delicate position vis-à-vis British public opinion. It was now decided to postpone further discussions until Hitler had taken his next official stand on all current political problems.

This stock-taking came in form of a major Reichstag speech by the Führer on May 21, 1935.[28] Hitler again went over the points he had already expounded to Simon and Eden on March 25–26. Pro-Germans and "pacifists" noted especially the German dictator's alleged agreement to reciprocal arms limitation and the prohibition of especially dangerous weapons as well as bombardment of civilian populations. The Labor party called the speech "constructive" and demanded acceptance of the German proposals. That was also the reaction of the great majority of the press, with the exception of the *Daily Telegraph,* the *Morning Post,* and the *Manchester Guardian.* The Labor opposition proposed a new motion of censure against the government when Baldwin, on May 22, insisted in Commons on the need to increase Britain's air power. But on this occasion he admitted that in 1934 he had much overestimated Germany's air strength and had been misled by the propaganda of the Third Reich and its friends. Lord Londonderry, Secretary of State for Air, estimated the German air force more or less correctly at eight hundred planes. At the end of the month, Berlin officially submitted to London its proposed air pact, which referred not only to the Treaty of Locarno but also to the League of Nations, of which Germany was no longer a member. This was clearly designed to create a favorable atmosphere for the negotiations of a naval agreement, which now entered their decisive stage.

Such an agreement was favored not only by political forces in England but also by the most influential leaders of the British Empire. The chiefs of Dominion governments were reunited in London for the jubilee of George V in May 1935. With Britain's ministers, they deliberated on all major political problems, and without exception they advised a conciliatory attitude toward Berlin, stressing their countries' opposition against involvement in a new war. They were especially attracted by the idea of a naval treaty which would limit Germany's forces so that she would be incapable of threatening overseas nations.

On May 23 the German Admiralty issued the following top-secret instructions for the London talks:

(1) Germany demanded the right to build all categories of ships and

the same fortifications as all other powers; all contrary provisions of the Treaty of Versailles, including the demilitarization of Heligoland, were to become invalid.

(2) Germany limited herself to 35 per cent of Britain's tonnage. This percentage would only be attained between 1942 and 1946 (this was to be the answer given to possible British questions). This ratio was to be the criterion for German naval construction regardless of what decisions might be reached at the next naval conference in late 1935. On the other hand, no ratio would be fixed with the French fleet. Germany, moreover, was concerned over the relation of this percentage to global tonnage and would feel free to build more ships of one category and less of another. Even if ratios should be fixed for different categories, she must remain sufficiently flexible to permit certain transfers. Germany wished to have the maximum of capital ships and would start their construction on January 1, 1937. The conference of late 1935, therefore, must be prevented from proclaiming an interruption of naval construction.

(3) Along the same lines, the German naval budget must not become an object of discussion.

(4) Germany must reject any British demand to concentrate her navy in the Baltic, so as to keep it away from England's coasts. Since the Reich's chief commercial centers were along the North Sea, they were in need of naval protection. (Perhaps the German Admiralty wanted to use this argument as a bargaining point.)

(5) Germany will share in any increase in the number of submarines, if such is decided by the next naval conference. She will, however, consent to any regulation of submarine warfare which applies to all powers. To please England, Germany might make certain concessions on this point.[29]

Several days later the German delegation was officially appointed. Distrustful of professional diplomats, especially von Hoesch, Hitler placed at its head Ribbentrop, friend of Himmler, who had already, since April 1934, undertaken certain missions in France and especially in England, where he had tried to win sympathies for Nazi Germany, chiefly through anti-communist propaganda. Hitler believed in Ribbentrop's success and made him "ambassador extraordinary," with precedence over all other diplomats. Ribbentrop was assisted by Councillor of Legation Erich Kordt and interpreter Paul Schmidt. Admiral Schuster was assigned as naval expert. In addition, the naval attaché in London, Captain Wassner, who had excellent relations with the British Admiralty, was to play a major role in the negotiations. Before leaving for London, the delegation received its last instructions on May 31, in an interministerial council presided over by Hitler, and including von Neurath,

General Blomberg, and Admiral Raeder. On the British side, the negotiations were led by the chief of the American Department of the
Foreign Office and expert in naval questions, Sir Robert Craigie, seconded
by Admiral Little, the captain of the ship *Danckwerts,* and others.[30]

The discussions began on June 4. The first session was opened by
Simon. In his inaugural speech he welcomed Hitler's declaration against
any future Anglo-German rivalry. But it was also important, he added,
to prepare the ground for the next conference of all the major naval
powers, so as to prevent an armaments race. For that reason it was not
enough to limit tonnages; it was also necessary to eliminate certain
categories of particularly dangerous vessels. Experience had shown, moreover, that the quota system adopted at the Washington Conference in
1922 had not proved very helpful. These British arguments ran counter
to Germany's wishes. In his reply, Ribbentrop insisted that England
accept in advance the 35 per cent ratio; it was the Führer's final offer, to
prevent forever all possibility of war between Great Britain and Germany. The British protested against the German method of imposing
preliminary conditions on the negotiations, which would make the conclusion of a general treaty with the other interested powers very difficult. Simon left the room red with anger. His place was taken by
Craigie, who in a firm manner formulated Britain's objections. But
Ribbentrop remained immovable, and the impasse appeared complete.
At this moment the two admirals, Little and Schuster, who had quickly
developed a mutual sympathy, took charge and succeeded in bringing
about a *détente.* Ribbentrop explained that Germany would stand by
her 35 per cent ratio, no matter what France's building program would
be and despite the danger to European peace created by the Franco-
Soviet alliance. This statement made a favorable impression. Even so,
Craigie asked for a delay in order to consult the other powers. Ribbentrop refused flatly, and the British diplomat did not insist.

This first British retreat was ratified the next day, June 5, in a series
of private meetings: first between Craigie and Ribbentrop; then between
the two admirals, Little and Schuster; and finally at a dinner in the
German embassy. The British accepted the 35 per cent principle but,
referring to the assurances Ribbentrop had given the previous day, asked
that in case of France's decision to increase her navy, Germany and
Great Britain should work together to dissuade her.[31] The naval agreement from the start thus took on the form of a tacit agreement against
France. The Germans, furthermore, agreed that the 35 per cent figure
would in principle apply to different categories of vessels, and only a
small part, about 25 per cent, could be transferred from one category
to another (the details were to be settled later). But this was only a
partial concession, because the Reich reserved the right to build submarines—at least if the next international naval conference did not find

a solution to this problem—at an accelerated rate, beginning on January 1, 1937, in order to attain parity with the other powers.

The treaty was thus almost ready. On June 6, Simon returned, all smiles, and said that the British government accepted Hitler's offer and confirmed the unofficial agreement which the two delegations had arrived at the previous day. He asked only for a brief interruption of the negotiations, so that he could "inform the other powers and give them a chance to make observations." But in reply to a question by Ribbentrop he made clear that England would not consider their possible objections; she would thus face them with a *fait accompli*.[32]

That was Simon's last act as Foreign Secretary. The next day he was transferred to the Ministry of the Interior in the governmental shuffle in which Baldwin replaced MacDonald as Prime Minister. His successor, Sir Samuel Hoare, was no less eager to arrive at an understanding with the Reich and especially to bring about the naval accord. Certain officials of the Foreign Office, however, appeared not to share this point of view and tried to question the results already obtained.[33] But this opposition was not unanimous. Even Vansittart, usually so watchful against danger from the Reich, resigned himself to the naval agreement, thus hoping to limit the strength of the German Navy and to gain time until England had rearmed in turn.[34] The Prince of Wales, on June 11, greeted the delegation of the British Legion which was to visit Germany in July in terms that were scarcely compatible with the reserve to which members of the royal family are generally confined. Fortified by these supports, Hoare had the outlines of the agreement ratified by the Cabinet on June 11, before he had even received the responses from the other signatories of the Washington Treaty to the communication which he had addressed to them. The next day he obtained the assent of the United States and Japan (which he confidentially communicated to Ribbentrop). Nevertheless, he justified the accord to his colleagues by the necessity to send certain units of the British fleet to the Pacific because of Japan's expansionist designs. In his first conversation with von Hoesch, on June 13, Hoare was much preoccupied with the threat of conflict in the Far East and in Ethiopia, and he emphasized his interest in the naval agreement with Germany.

To dispel any last uneasiness, Raeder softened Ribbentrop's statements concerning submarines and claimed only 45 per cent of Britain's strength (after having stated in a secret memorandum of June 12 that Germany would be incapable for some time to build more).[35] On June 13 he wired instructions along this line to the delegation in London. The road was thus clear for finishing the agreement. Beginning on June 14 the *Times* prepared public opinion, saying that England had no choice. The Disarmament Conference and efforts for a general agreement having failed (because of France, of course), a bilateral agreement with

Germany, limiting the latter's armaments in an area essential to British security, had thus become indispensable. Most other English papers agreed.

Official negotiations were resumed on June 17 in London. The same day, France presented London with her formal objection to the accord, which envisaged an exchange of naval information between Germany and Great Britain, while no similar arrangement existed between the latter and France. The Paris government pointed out that this British action was contrary to the spirit of the Franco-British communiqués of February 3, 1935, and of the Stresa Conference.[36] But the British government took no notice of these objections, nor of those from Italy. The agreement was officially concluded the next day, June 18, 1935, the 120th anniversary of the battle of Waterloo (which brings to mind Hitler's statement to Simon on the brotherhood of arms between Blücher and Wellington). The exchange of notes, signed by Hoare and Ribbentrop, repeated the points on which the two delegations had agreed. They stipulated that Germany would fix her naval tonnage at 35 per cent of that of the British Commonwealth; for submarines the ratio was 45 per cent. These percentages were to be independent of the naval construction of other powers. Only if these were to overthrow completely the world's naval balance could Germany ask England to re-examine the situation and especially to permit the increase of her submarines up to parity with England. In their closing statements, Hoare and Ribbentrop declared that the Anglo-German Naval Agreement was to facilitate the conclusion of a general treaty on armaments, especially naval forces. It was Ribbentrop who stressed the rapprochement it represented between Great Britain and the Reich.[37]

After Ribbentrop's departure from London, the agreement was completed by a series of negotiations between Captain Wassner and his British counterparts. Even more than the official phase of the negotiations, these talks showed how much the accord was directed against France. This came out especially in the deliberations on capital ships. The British were much interested in preventing construction of the battleship *France* (which never took place). Germany thus must not furnish a pretext for it by premature construction before January 1, 1937. If France nevertheless insisted on her intentions, one could place responsibility for the naval race on her.[38]

In summary one can say that by the accord of June 18, 1935, Germany realized all her aims as they had been laid down in the secret memorandum of May 23. She obtained the right to build a fleet of 420,000 tons, instead of the 144,000 tons which the Treaty of Versailles had left her (while Sir Bolton Eyres-Monsell, on February 7, had spoken to the French naval attaché in London of a maximum of 200,000 tons).[39] The only concession she had made concerned the transfer of tonnage

from one category to another. In a circular of July 15 to Germany's
high naval officers, the contents of which were repeated and elaborated
in an unsigned Wilhelmstrasse memorandum of August 28, 1935,[40]
Admiral Raeder expressed his full satisfaction and stressed that the
Reich would not be able to achieve the quota it had been granted for
another ten years.[41] In the long run this interdependence of the British
and German navies could obviously create difficulties for Germany, if
other powers increased their forces without England following suit.
But this was most unlikely. Germany counted on Great Britain: she
would guard her interests and would build new units herself, which
would allow Germany to do the same. The significance of the agreement
was chiefly in the political sphere. The danger, quite real at the Stresa
Conference, that the other maritime powers at the next naval conference might conclude a new agreement unfavorable to Germany, had
been averted. Above all, the act of June 18 excluded any possibility
of future antagonism between Great Britain and the Third Reich.

The agreement was made public the evening of its conclusion. The
first reaction of British public opinion was almost universally favorable.
Approval by the known Germanophile elements was to be expected.
They were joined by the Admiralty, whose official organ, *The Naval
Review,* published an article in July (anonymous, but probably by a
high-ranking person), saying that Germany had recognized British
supremacy at sea and consequently was assured of Britain's friendship
as long as she kept the agreement. The Treaty of Versailles and the
Franco-British alliance of 1914–1918 were dead. Sir Bolton Eyres-Monsell,
on June 22, spoke in moderate terms to the House of Commons, saying
that all Anglo-German rivalry was henceforth excluded and that the
agreement restricted German naval rearmament already in progress (this
was also the view of the commander-in-chief of the British Navy, Lord
Chatfield).[42] Even politicians and newspapers generally hostile to the
Third Reich and advocating resistance to its demands, made an exception this time. Only a minority of public opinion revised its stand after
a few days. Besides Winston Churchill who, in a resounding speech,
condemned the agreement as damaging to Britain's security, other persons
found the concessions to the Reich excessive, especially with respect to
submarines. After several interpellations and ministerial responses, parliamentary debate finally started on July 11. Hoare defended his policy:
referring to Sir Bolton Eyres-Monsell's statements of June 22, he said
correctly that it had been the Admiralty that had pushed the agreement.
He added that France had no reason to complain, since the agreement
left her with a margin of naval superiority over Germany. Besides,
France had concluded for her own security an alliance with the Soviet
Union. Opposition critics, like Churchill and Austen Chamberlain, as
usual had no effect. The government's parliamentary majority remained

considerable, and it was supported by the majority of public opinion. Several days after the Commons debate, on July 15, the delegation of the British Legion visiting Germany was received by Hitler, after its leader, Major Fetherton-Godley, had declared that England would not repeat the mistake of 1914 and fight Germany.

The Naval Agreement between Great Britain and the Third Reich naturally caused great excitement elsewhere, especially in France, the country most hurt. Anger was general, the more so since, despite secret information that had reached Paris, most political circles had nourished until the end the illusion that England would remain faithful to the solidarity solemnly proclaimed at Stresa. This was borne out by the semi-official comments of *Le Temps*. When the bitter truth became known even this paper, usually so measured in tone, gave free rein to its disappointment and did not fail to call attention to the fact that the accord had been reached on the 120th anniversary of Waterloo. Elsewhere reaction was still more violent, and not only in traditionally anti-British circles which, incidentally, were small. Especially those people most attached to Franco-British friendship, like Herriot and the Secretary-General of the Foreign Ministry, Alexis Léger,[43] did not hide their bitterness at the fact that the London government had unilaterally sanctioned the violation of the Treaty of Versailles, thus reneging on its earlier declarations, and had delivered a heavy blow to collective security. This was also the almost unanimous verdict of the press, from such diverse sources as the socialist *Populaire* on the left and *L'Echo de Paris* on the right. The soothing British reply of June 22 to the French note of the 17th did not calm matters. A pertinent point made in many French circles was that the transaction between Germany and Great Britain, far from serving the cause of peace, actually encouraged an armaments race. This was so because, on the one hand, it was not to be expected that the other powers would remain idle in the face of the Reich's growing naval power; and, on the other, Germany, having obtained satisfaction in the naval sphere, would be far more reluctant to limit her land and air forces. The Naval Commission of the Chamber of Deputies, and subsequently that of the Senate, after hearing a report by Naval Minister Piétri, denounced the Anglo-German Agreement on June 25 and demanded that France resume her freedom of action at sea. Two days later Piétri inspected a naval squadron at Brest and gave a speech announcing that this was exactly the government's intention. He repeated his criticism of the agreement, saying that he did not doubt Britain's friendship but rather her traditional prudence. French ship-building actually accelerated. In 1935 the *Dunkerque* was launched, followed the next year by the *Strasbourg,* each of them 25,000 tons, then by the *Richelieu* and the *Jean-Bart,* each 35,000 tons (which were not finished at the start of the war in 1939), as well as by a number of submarines.

Naval circles—and not only those who believed in a traditional rivalry with England—were naturally the most indignant. It seems quite likely that the Anglo-German accord had a decisive influence on the political evolution of the future Admiral of the Fleet Darlan, in the sense of increasing his distrust of England. This also applied to Laval (see note 6 below), though his reaction to the pact seems to have been more equivocal.[44] The event may not have been irrelevant to the behavior of the two men after 1940.[45]

It should be pointed out, however, that most other French political circles soon forgot their anger. On June 26-27, Eden was again in Paris, on his way back from Rome, where he had been unable to dissuade Mussolini from his plans for war against Ethiopia. Embarrassed, he defended an agreement of which he inwardly disapproved and in which he had taken no hand, and did his best to appease his French interviewers. The next day Le Temps wrote that despite the blow which Britain had dealt the idea of collective security, Franco-British cooperation remained intact. The other papers, especially those of the left, followed suit. The tradition of the Entente Cordiale which, with brief intervals, had determined French policy for thirty years, was too deeply rooted to be overthrown by an event which, after all, was judged minor. This was especially the attitude of the Quai d'Orsay, which induced the somewhat hesitant naval circles to re-establish contacts with England in the summer of 1935. The new naval conference of the five Washington Treaty powers began in London on December 9. On January 15, 1936, Japan walked out in order to regain her freedom of action. Two weeks later, the Laval government fell. Thereafter, France became more amenable and on March 25, 1936, joined England and the United States in a new tripartite naval treaty to which Germany adhered on July 17, 1937, and Italy not until April 16, 1938.[46]

In June and July 1935, Italy took an ambivalent attitude toward the Anglo-German Naval Agreement. To be sure, the semi-official periodical Affari Esteri published an anonymous article (generally attributed to Mussolini), stressing Franco-Italian solidarity and accusing Great Britain of duplicity and departure from the Stresa front. But this strident tone can be explained by the failure of Eden's mission to Rome, which marked the beginning of Anglo-Italian tension during the Ethiopian War. It was, in fact, Ethiopia which at the time preoccupied the Italian government and made it decide also to resume freedom of action in naval affairs. Under the circumstances, Italy made an effort to maintain her entente with France (while at the same time sending out feelers to Germany so as not to burn her bridges there) and to exploit French anger against

England. That is why Italy protested against the June 18 agreement, albeit in quite a moderate tone. She criticized less the accord as such than the manner in which it had been negotiated. Basically she was not dissatisfied, because she rightly saw the accord as a prize given by England for the unilateral violation of international treaties. If Germany could so easily free herself from the Treaty of Versailles, might Italy not attack with impunity Ethiopia, despite the Covenant of the League of Nations? Japan drew an analogous conclusion and felt encouraged, as we have seen, to withdraw from the London Naval Conference in January 1936. She had agreed to the Anglo-German accord on June 10, considering herself not directly affected. In the United States, the *New York Times* published an article disapproving, in rather Platonic terms, an accord to which Washington had nevertheless given its consent.

Together with France, it was the USSR which showed the most violent reaction. The Anglo-German Naval Agreement confirmed all of Russia's suspicions about Great Britain which Eden's visit to Moscow had not been able to dissipate. The Soviet press (*Pravda,* Karl Radek in *Izvestia,* the *Red Star,* organ of the army) held that a faction of Britain's ruling classes wanted Germany to strengthen her navy in the Baltic Sea in order to attack Russia, while at the same time encouraging Japanese aggression in the Far East. Litvinov spoke in the same vein to the American ambassador in Moscow, William Bullitt.[47] The fear of a coalition among England, Germany, Poland, and Japan, encircling the USSR, had not ceased to haunt the minds of Soviet statesmen since 1933–1934. It is thus understandable that they wished to make the alliance with France as effective as possible and to gain also the sympathies of the United States.

Apprehension was not limited to Moscow. The small states of Eastern Europe also began to feel that they were being left at the mercy of the Third Reich. This sentiment was particularly strong in the Balkans. The first to draw her conclusions was Yugoslavia. On June 23, 1935, five days after the naval accord, Stoyadinovich succeeded the Francophile Yevtich as President of the Council and Foreign Minister. While this change was initially due to domestic considerations, it was not slow in having its influence upon Yugoslavia's external policy. It was in a direction favorable to Germany, and clearly as a result of the nonreaction to German remilitarization and of the Anglo-German accord.

In conclusion, we must sum up the motives which led the two powers to conclude the agreement on June 18, 1935, and look at its effects.

The motives of Great Britain were evidently quite diverse. Still, the naval agreement fitted in very well with Britain's general policy at the time, namely her desire for an entente with Germany. In 1935 special factors increased that desire: the imminent conflict in Ethiopia and the latent tension in the Far East forced England to concentrate the bulk of her naval forces in the Mediterranean, and to a lesser extent in the Pacific. She therefore wanted to disengage herself as much as possible from the North Sea and be reassured as far as Germany was concerned. A bilateral accord seemed the only possible way, since negotiations for general disarmament had failed. To this was added a trace of anti-French feeling. As we have seen, it was France whom many Britishers held responsible for the breakdown of the Geneva Conference. Hoare repeats this argument in his memoirs.[48] We have already seen how widespread this state of mind was in the British Army, Navy, and elsewhere. These circles—not large, but very influential—always looked upon France and not Germany as the first power on the continent, the one to which the principle of a "European equilibrium" need be applied. Despite all the assurances which Laval had given on this subject, they were especially agitated by the Franco-Soviet alliance, which in their eyes upset that equilibrium still further (anti-communism, in part due to Nazi propaganda, also played its part). It seems possible, though there is as yet no documentary evidence, that the British viewed the naval agreement as an answer to that alliance. To a lesser degree this also seemed to apply to the rapprochement between France and Italy, which just at that time appeared very active, with visits to Rome by the chiefs-of-staff of the French Army and Air Force, Generals Gamelin and Denain, where they concluded military conventions with their Italian colleagues. This displeased the British circles mentioned above which, in the past, had tried to prevent such rapprochement. Franco-British naval rivalry, France's refusal to renew the Washington Treaty of 1922, and her secret encouragement of Japan to denounce the treaty, all had their effect upon Britain's attitude, especially in the Admiralty.

The question is, What did Britain gain by the agreement? Germany's naval threat at the time certainly was not very great, far less than danger from the air, which the British rightly feared. Yet the theory that the naval accord was the result of blackmail from the air, as Hitler told Guido Schmidt later on (see above, p. 134), does not hold. Baldwin's declarations to the House of Commons on May 22, a month before the accord, show that he had already recovered from his 1934 panic on this subject. More likely, the British considered the naval agreement a precedent for, and a step toward, a general arms convention, especially an air pact. But this hope was disappointed. Once the naval agreement was assured, the Reich no longer was in any hurry to proceed with air negotiations. In this field a bilateral agreement between Great Britain and Germany was not desired by either side, because it would have been insufficient. The two powers, at least according to contemporary estimates, occupied only fifth and sixth place among air powers. The pact, therefore, would have had to be multilateral and especially to include France. The latter wanted to link it to a general system of security in the air and to an Eastern pact. The Foreign Office vainly asked Berlin to adopt a more positive attitude toward such a pact and to agree to it on certain conditions, in order to facilitate air negotiations. But Germany was not ready to make such concessions, nor to agree in advance to limit her aviation. British policy would have done better, perhaps, to make the naval agreement dependent on concessions in the air. For England, after having hurt France by the accord with the Reich, could for the moment exert no more pressure on the Paris government.[49] In the question of aviation, so essential for England's security, the naval agreement thus in effect worked against her. Air negotiations never started, and the air pact was never concluded. In the naval field the accord—though it was maintained until 1939—had only a limited usefulness.

Germany, on the other hand, profited from it, the more so since she had made no real concessions, being unable in any case to reach her assigned quota for another ten years. By permitting her nearly to quadruple her fleet, Great Britain had officially voided the military clauses of Versailles, something Germany had hoped to do for sixteen years. The Reich, in addition, had succeeded in beating France two-fold: by sowing discord between her and England, at least temporarily; and by gradually detaching from France her traditional allies in Eastern Europe. (This latter process had actually begun in 1934, with the conclusion of the nonaggression pact between Germany and Poland; it now seemed counterbalanced by the Franco-Soviet alliance.)

Still, Hitler probably exaggerated the importance of the June 18 agreement. All witnesses agree that he thought he had won a genuine alliance with England on the basis he had always dreamed of: domination of the European continent by Germany in return for recognition of Britain's maritime and colonial supremacy. That is why he called that date "the happiest day in his life." Yet it is doubtful that even the most Germanophile Englishmen saw the accord in that light (see note 37 below). Later on, realizing that he had made himself illusions, Hitler was to experience great disappointment and anger, even real hatred, toward England.

Another error, for which the German dictator was to pay still more dearly, concerned British psychology. Hitler was convinced that he had obtained the naval agreement through intimidation. Emboldened by this, he was to repeat his tactics again and again, only to get in the end the opposite of what he wanted. In August 1939 he concluded the nonaggression pact with the Soviet Union, hoping to make England retreat and consent to his expansionist plans. But he merely strengthened British resolve to come to the aid of Poland. Thus came about the war between England and Germany, which Hitler basically had always wanted to avoid.

Hitler was confirmed in his fatal illusion by Ribbentrop, who reported the same impression from London, reinforced by the behavior of Simon between June 4–6. The Führer henceforth was to put great confidence in his negotiator, whose prestige increased at the expense of the Foreign Minister and the professional diplomats. There were many among the latter who saw things correctly and warned Hitler against his mistakes, emphasizing his chances for success if he showed moderation. But Ribbentrop, now powerful, closely followed the Führer's line, finally becoming Foreign Minister himself on February 4, 1938. Eighteen months later the war began. The naval agreement, even though its importance must not be exaggerated, was one of the landmarks on the road to that catastrophe.

NOTES

1. A. Eden, *Memoirs*, I, 225.
2. *Ibid.*, p. 152.
3. The Peace Ballot, organized by the League of Nations Union, in which more than ten million Britishers favored sanctions against a possible aggressor, had no influence on Britain's German policy but only affected the Ethiopian War.
4. Eden, *Memoirs*, I, 219.
5. For details, see Rear-Admiral Belot and A. Reussner, *La puissance navale dans l'histoire*, III, 153–156, and Espagnac du Ravay, *Vingt ans de politique navale française*, pp. 93–133. The latter, published at Grenoble in 1941, has a preface by Admiral of the Fleet F. Darlan and contains numerous secret memoranda by him. It was apparently edited under his close supervision. The book is violently anti-British and should be used with caution. Still, it contains interesting details. See also the article by M. F. Piétry, "La marine d'hier," *Revue des Deux Mondes*, August 1, 1957, pp. 425–428.
6. No document has thus far been published concerning these London talks. It is possible that Laval already harbored a certain suspicion toward England and wanted first of all to strengthen ties between France and Italy. This is the version—subject to much caution—of Flandin, *Politique française (1919–1940)*, p. 166. But until the French diplomatic documents for the period and Laval's personal papers have been published, there is no proof that Laval intended to pursue a systematic anti-British policy prior to the conclusion of the Anglo-German naval treaty and the Ethiopian War. See also A. Mallet, *Laval*, I, 53–63.
7. G. Castellan, *Le réarmement clandestin du Reich (1930–1935)*, p. 501.
8. *Documents on German Foreign Policy (A.D.A.P.)*, Series C, III, No. 483.
9. We will not here analyze the air pact project. Let us merely point out the paradoxical attitude of French policy which was ready to conclude a collective agreement for assistance in the air, including Germany, but not as yet the Soviet Union, at a time when France was negotiating for a military alliance with Russia against Germany. In any case, the air pact would have been incomplete without the USSR, whose air force at the time was considered to be the world's first (see above, pp. 135–136).
10. According to Hitler's former military adjutant, F. Hossbach (*Zwischen Wehrmacht und Hitler*, pp. 95–96), the Führer notified his military chiefs only at the last moment of a decision which he took on his own initiative. They had reser-

vations, especially the Minister of War, General von Blomberg, who feared military sanctions by France and her allies. These fears proving unfounded, the prestige of Blomberg and of military professionals in general began to decline in Hitler's eyes.

11. *A.D.A.P.,* C, III, No. 528.

12. *A.D.A.P.,* C, III, Nos. 542, 552.

13. According to F. Hesse, *Das Spiel um Deutschland,* pp. 35–36, Hitler was so annoyed by these dispatches that he thought of recalling the ambassador. Hesse had been named London correspondent of the official German news agency, D.N.B. He was thus in the confidence of Goebbels, Minister of Propaganda. His memoirs, which show a taste for the romantic, must be used with great caution and have been the object of numerous denials. Still, they contain some interesting and believable details, since the author obtained much firsthand confidential information.

14. On the subject of Austria, Simon said that England wished to maintain the independence of the country, without, however, attaching the same significance to it as in the case of Belgium. Hitler must have rememberd this in March 1938.

15. This remark of Hitler's contains both truth and falsehood. His whole policy at the moment, notably the conclusion of the naval accord, tended toward a bilateral entente with England on the back of France. But, on the other hand, he was very much interested in maintaining the "moderating" influence of London upon Paris.

16. *A.D.A.P.,* D, I, No. 181.

17. *A.D.A.P.,* C, III, Nos. 555–564; P. Schmidt, *Als Statist auf diplomatischer Bühne,* pp. 300–304.

18. After his talks with Hitler, whom he described unsympathetically, Simon wrote in his diary: "The practical result of our Berlin visit is to establish that Germany greatly desires a good understanding with Britain, but that she is determined to go her own course in rearmament; that she expects in time to get all Germans within her borders, including Austria; that she does not fear isolation and has no intention of joining in collective security; and that she wants the ex-German colonies back before returning to the League of Nations. All this is pretty hopeless; for if Germany will not cooperate for confirming the solidarity of Europe, the rest of Europe ought to cooperate to preserve it in spite of Germany. This may not prevent an ultimate explosion, but it will delay it. We may see the curious spectacle of British Tories collaborating with Russian Communists, while the League of Nations thunders applause. There may be no other course, but will it ensure peace? I most gravely doubt it." Simon, *Retrospect,* pp. 202–203. This passage shows Simon hesitant and torn: on the one hand he distrusts Germany, on the other he does not believe that a coalition against her can save the peace, and he shrinks from the thought of cooperation with the Soviet Union.

19. Eden, *Memoirs,* I, esp. 145–152.

20. *Ibid.,* pp. 138–141.

21. *Ibid.,* pp. 142–143, 170–172.

22. *A.D.A.P.,* C, IV, No. 27.

23. It is impossible to analyze exactly the deliberations of the Stresa Conference. No authentic British, French, or Italian document has been published thus far. Among writers of memoirs, Simon and Eden (who was not there) say little, and the account of Flandin (*Politique française,* pp. 172–173) is both incomplete and suspect.

24. The best book, to my knowledge, on the subject to date is William E. Scott, *Alliance Against Hitler: The Franco-Soviet Pact* (Durham, N. C., 1962).

25. Scott, *Alliance Against Hitler,* p. 258.

26. Geyr von Schweppenburg, *Erinnerungen eines Militärattachés,* pp. 76–78.

27. In February 1935, England had notified France that she would discuss naval

questions with Germany, but strictly within the framework of Versailles (Espagnac du Ravay, *Vingt ans de politique navale française*, pp. 147–148).

28. See the complete text in one of the collections of Hitler's speeches.

29. *A.D.A.P.*, C, IV, No. 100.

30. For details of the negotiations, see *A.D.A.P.*, C, IV, Nos. 131, 132, 135–137, 141, 148, 154, 156, 161, 176, 177, 181, 182, 187, 193, 273, 275; Raeder, *Mein Leben*, I, 301–309; P. Schmidt, *Als Statist auf diplomatischer Bühne*, pp. 311–315; F. Hesse, *Das Spiel um Deutschland*, pp. 35–43; E. Kordt, *Nicht aus den Akten*, pp. 100–113; Templewood (Sir S. Hoare), *Nine Troubled Years*, pp. 138–146; Admiral E. Chatfield, *It Might Happen Again*, pp. 73–76; D. C. Watt, "The Anglo-German Naval Agreement," *Journal of Modern History*, XXVIII (1956), 155–175; W. Malanowski, "Das deutsch-englische Flottenabkommen vom 18. Juni als Ausgangspunkt für Hitlers doktrinäre Bündnispolitik," *Wehrwissenschaftliche Rundschau*, V, 1955, 408–420; R. Ingrim, *Hitlers glücklichster Tag*, pp. 129–154. See also Espagnac du Ravay, *Vingt ans de politique navale française*, pp. 147–154.

31. *A.D.A.P.*, C, IV, No. 135.

32. *Ibid.*, No. 141.

33. Raeder, *Mein Leben*, I, 301–302.

34. R. Vansittart, *The Mist Procession*, pp. 525–527.

35. *A.D.A.P.*, C, IV, No. 148.

36. E. Herriot, *Jadis*, II, 559–563.

37. According to Hesse (*Das Spiel um Deutschland*, pp. 43–47), Ribbentrop, on Hitler's orders, offered Hoare on June 18 military and air aid for the defense of the British Empire, in return for Germany's freedom of action in Central and Eastern Europe. But Hoare is said to have categorically rejected the idea of an alliance between the two countries, even saying that the danger of war between the two was by no means impossible, despite the naval agreement. This statement of Hesse's is naturally subject to caution.

38. *A.D.A.P.*, C, IV, Nos. 176, 177, 181.

39. Espagnac du Ravay, *Vingt ans de politique navale française*, pp. 147–148.

40. IMT Nuremberg, Vol. 41; Raeder, 12, pp. 3–5; *A.D.A.P.*, C, IV, No. 275.

41. Actually, at the start of the war in 1939 the German Navy was still quite inferior, not only to the British but to the French Navy as well.

42. Chatfield, *It Might Happen Again*, pp. 74–75.

43. Herriot, *Jadis*, II, 559–563; Templewood, *Nine Troubled Years*, pp. 144–145.

44. See Templewood, *Nine Troubled Years*, pp. 144–146; Eden, *Memoirs*, II, 230–235. It is possible that Laval was unhappy because the British had beaten him to a bilateral treaty with Germany, a goal that he had set for himself.

45. This is merely a hypothesis, short of the publication of authentic documents and the private papers of Laval and Admiral Darlan (on the latter, however, one should consult Espagnac du Ravay, *Vingt ans de politique navale française*).

46. For details see Espagnac du Ravay, *Vingt ans de politique navale française*, pp. 154–165, and Belot and Reussner, *La puissance navale dans l'histoire*, III, 158–166.

47. *Foreign Relations of the United States, 1935*, II, 168. See also *Ambassador Dodd's Diary*, pp. 258, 261–265.

48. Templewood, *Nine Troubled Years*, p. 145.

49. *A.D.A.P.*, C, IV, Nos. 113, 117, 140, 152, 201, 207.

HENDERSON B. BRADDICK

The Hoare-Laval Plan:
A Study in International Politics

Not all international crises of the 1930's were centered on Hitler—although he knew how to take advantage of disturbances caused by others. Mussolini's invasion of Ethiopia did much to sow dissent between Italy, France, and England, a situation from which Hitler profited when he reoccupied the Rhineland. The Ethiopian crisis also brought home the failure of the League and of collective security. It was the most blatant example to date of Britain's appeasement policy. Its lessons were not lost on Hitler.

Professor Braddick teaches international relations at Lehigh University. He is currently at work on a book dealing with the Italo-Ethiopian crisis which will incorporate much new material, especially from British Foreign Office sources. The following article was first published in the Review of Politics, XXIV *(July 1962), 342–364. It is republished with the author's and publisher's permission.*

T HE AGREEMENT between British Foreign Minister Sir Samuel Hoare and Pierre Laval, French Premier and Foreign Minister, in early December 1935, was a major turning point in European international politics during the interwar period. It placed a premium on fascist aggression in Ethiopia by proposing that Italy be given actual or *de facto* control over huge slices of the African country. Several volumes of memoirs published in the last few years throw new light on some aspects of the proposal itself and on the policies of Great Britain, Italy, and France toward the Italo-Ethiopian conflict, policies which at the height of the international crisis produced the Hoare-Laval Plan. In addition, the State Department documents, published and unpublished, are a mine of information on these matters.

Standard accounts of European international relations during the period tend to neglect the power politics which lay behind the Plan.[1] And even in the most extensive treatments of the crisis, there are important gaps in this respect.[2] It has been maintained, for example, that France prevented England from leading the League of Nations in imposing an oil sanction against Italy.[3] The evidence, however, indicates that the British were just as reluctant to support this measure as the French.

The Hoare-Laval proposal for the settlement of the Italo-Ethiopian War cannot be understood without reference to the main lines of British, French, and Italian policies in the crisis as it developed. Ethiopia had been a target of Italian expansionism for many decades and, beginning in 1928, the fascist government had pursued a policy of economic and political penetration with considerable vigor, though with little success. Indeed, by the end of 1934, the Italians believed that British influence in the country was becoming so powerful that within a few years they might virtually be forced out. They had information concerning negotiations between Ethiopia and Great Britain about the establishment of a British protectorate and the cession of part of Ethiopia to British Somaliland. Moreover, there is evidence that British authorities supported an Ethiopian military demonstration in November 1934 before Wal Wal, a military outpost which the Italians had held for a number of years near the disputed Ethiopian-Italian Somaliland frontier. The demonstration was made by a large Ethiopian military escort of a joint Ethiopian-British commission, engaged in surveying the boundary between British Somaliland and Ethiopia. While Wal Wal was located some fifty miles from the Italian Somaliland frontier according to most maps, even Italian ones, it was also about one hundred miles from the Ethiopian-British Somaliland frontier as it then stood.

Immediately after the Wal Wal incident, Mussolini ordered his military forces to be ready for a campaign against Ethiopia to begin not later than October 1935. The possibility of such action had been considered seriously by the Duce since 1933; and although military preparations had been begun in 1934, it was apparently the Wal Wal affair that precipitated his decision. Of course, he would have been satisfied if the other powers had handed Ethiopia to him; he had no desire to waste limited Italian resources on protracted military campaigns. In any event, he had to show that he meant business.[4]

On their side, the British became concerned about the implications of the steady Italian military buildup in Africa. This concern, however, related less to an independent Ethiopia than to the security of British interests in East Africa and the Near East. While there was anxiety over the safety of the headwaters of the Blue Nile at Lake Tsana in Ethiopia, Italian preparations suggested that Mussolini intended to pursue the grandiose policy which he had publicly proclaimed in March 1934:

> I could give you the details of a plan up to 1945 but I prefer to point out to you the historical objectives towards which our generation and the generations to follow should be directed during the present century. Let us calmly consider a plan that reaches the nearby millennium, the year 2000. It is only a question of sixty years. The historical objectives of Italy have two names: Asia and Africa. South and East are the cardinal points that should excite the interest and the will of Italians. There is little or nothing to do towards the North and the same towards the West, neither in Europe or beyond the Ocean. These two objectives of ours are justified by geography and history. Of all the large Western Powers of Europe, Italy is the nearest to Africa and Asia. A few hours by sea and much less by air are enough to link up Italy with Africa and with Asia.[5]

For generations Britain had assiduously extended and consolidated her influence in the Near East and East Africa; the maintenance of her predominance there was an imperative of British foreign policy. Thus, the Italo-Ethiopian controversy led to a crisis between fascist and British imperialisms, for British imperial and commercial policy could not countenance a substantial augmentation of Italian power in these areas or in the Mediterranean.[6]

It was of importance to Mussolini that some sort of understanding be worked out with Britain if possible, because the vital logistical line from Italy to Somaliland and Eritrea was vulnerable to British sea power along most of its length, especially at the bottleneck of Suez. While Italian military strength in Africa accumulated, spokesmen in Rome made statements to the effect that Italy did not intend to interfere with British interests. Such statements were probably discounted in Whitehall and produced little more than a warning against the use of force.[7]

The British Foreign Office did not consider Italy as a first-rate diplomatic power; the Italian international political position was particularly weak at the moment because of German pressure on Austria, where Italian influence was paramount. In London, Mussolini was regarded as having an intense dislike and fear of Hitler. Furthermore, it was believed that the Italians were apprehensive about the possibility of German forces on the Brenner. After all, had not an Italian military demonstration at the northern frontier saved Austria from Hitler in 1934,[8] and would the Duce risk the Austrian *status quo* by committing Italian arms in Ethiopia? In any case, there was considerable doubt in London whether Italian financial and military resources could sustain an overseas adventure.[9]

It is likely that Sir John Simon, British Foreign Minister during the first half of 1935, felt no need to bargain with Italy, an inferior power, about the developing Anglo-Italian problem in Africa. Simon's strategic plan in the existing situation was evidently to maintain freedom of action and a measure of the initiative *vis-à-vis* Italy by refusing to inform the Italians as to what Britain would do about Italian ambitions in Ethiopia. At the same time, he exerted considerable diplomatic pressure on the Fascist government, particularly in the League of Nations, to settle the Wal Wal incident and other differences with Ethiopia peacefully. In this way he demonstrated the predominance of British power in Anglo-Italian relations to the peoples of Africa and the Near East. With regard to Ethiopia itself, there is good evidence that the country was rapidly and quietly moving into the British orbit. Simon's international policy and League action gave the impression that Britain had won the first round in an Anglo-Italian diplomatic contest. Instead of weakening before this pressure, Mussolini mobilized further military resources and sent several divisions to Libya, near the Egyptian frontier. He instructed his delegate at the League to maintain an attitude of complete intransigence.[10]

This was the situation confronting Sir Samuel Hoare, who succeeded Simon as British Foreign Minister in early June 1935. He decided that an effort had to be made to deal with the Italian leader. It was not successful. In the first place, the decision to send Anthony Eden, then Minister for League of Nations Affairs, as the emissary to carry the British proposal to Mussolini, was not a happy one. Mussolini regarded the Geneva organization as primarily an instrument of British and French politics and Eden as the British minister charged with the mission of enlisting League support for British policy against him. The proposal would have given Ethiopia the important commercial advantage of an outlet on the Red Sea through British Somaliland. But in return, Italy was to receive only the desert province of Ogaden and undefined economic concessions. Mussolini rejected the idea out of hand. In fact, Rome interpreted the proposal as likely to advance British political and economic interests in Ethiopia and not those of Italy. The result was an exacerbation of Anglo-Italian relations, rather than an amelioration of tension. Eden said that he had been treated like a pickpocket, while the Italian view was that the proposal was a trap. Furthermore, secret documents which Mussolini's agents had purloined from the British Embassy reinforced his suspicion that London was playing a double game with him over Ethiopia.[11]

Mussolini was infuriated by the attitude of the British. He argued that he merely intended to do in Ethiopia what they had done in Egypt or the French in Morocco: he was particularly angered at their policy of pressure against him but of condoning Japanese expansion in Manchuria. Japanese grievances against the Chinese in Manchuria evoked considerable sympathy in England and were in many respects similar to those held by Italy against the Ethiopians. In both cases, the weaker states violated existing economic agreements.[12] Chiang Kai-shek and Haile Selassie had made progress in unifying and strengthening their countries, a development that might diminish foreign privileges. Japanese in China and Italians in Ethiopia were subjected to indignities, the Japanese because of hate, the Italians because of scorn. "There is a large Ethiopian party," reported the American Minister in Addis Ababa, "which looks with contempt on the Italians and believes, probably fatuously, that it is more than a match for any Italian army if but given the chance to fight. This Ethiopian contempt for the Italians will doubtless survive through the present and perhaps through another generation." [13] He also wrote that to "mislead an Italian is probably the Ethiopian idea of a highly satisfying practice and diversion, particularly as Italian resentment does not appear since the Battle of Adowa in 1896 to have taken any positively threatening or potentially dangerous form." [14]

Following the Duce's rejection of their June proposals, the British attempted to align France behind British policy. As might be expected, Laval had his own ideas on this matter. Earlier in the year he had concluded an agreement with Mussolini to defend the independence of Austria and led the Italian dictator to believe that he could proceed with his intended penetration of Ethiopia. There is evidence that Laval even made promises of French financial assistance for the enterprise. Details of an Italo-French military agreement, apparently regarding Austria, were worked out shortly thereafter. Also, Laval had entered into a defensive military understanding with Soviet Russia. Though he had been successful in organizing the Continent against Germany, it is not clear whether Laval's activities were designed entirely for the purpose of containing German expansion. There are indications that he may have had in mind the alternative of bargaining with Hitler, for example over Eastern and Central Europe, from a more powerful situation of strength.[15]

Meanwhile, the British had concluded a naval agreement with Germany. This accord permitted German naval construction (in violation of the Versailles Treaty) up to 35 per cent of British strength in being. Such action can be explained in part as an effort to "restore" the Continental balance of power and as a manifestation of British isolationism.

The naval agreement strengthened the German position with regard to the French alliance system and suggested to Mussolini that Italy must look to its own devices for protection against German expansionism.[16] Under these conditions it could hardly be expected that Laval would respond with great enthusiasm to British proposals for French cooperation against the Italian Duce. While the naval agreement strengthened the German position against France, the Italo-French understanding strengthened Italy against Britain in East Africa and against Germany over Austria. British Conservative leadership, 1934–1938, had no particular objection to an alteration of the Austrian *status quo,* provided it was not accomplished by violence. Nazi penetration of Austria, it was believed, would accentuate Italian dependence on England. With regard to the Austrian question, the Franco-Italian agreement tended to prevent the British from assuming an advantageous middle position between Italy and Germany.[17]

Following orthodox British policy, Whitehall would press Italy only as far as it could lead another Continental power. But France under Laval had no intention of seriously endangering the Franco-Italian alliance or of risking war with Italy for the sake of British interests in the Mediterranean and Africa. On the other hand, the French Premier saw in the situation possibilities of promoting French interests, as he interpreted them. He hoped to maintain the Italian commitment against Germany intact while extracting a guarantee of Austrian independence from the British, the *quid pro quo* for a measure of support against Italy in the present crisis. His cynical maneuvers alienated both London and Rome. The British had no more intention of exposing themselves to the danger of fighting Germany for the French position in Central and Eastern Europe than did Laval of fighting Italy for British interests. Furthermore, Britain exploited her middle position between France and Germany by telling Laval flatly that if France did not cooperate against Italy, Britain might withdraw from Continental affairs. This was a threat; it was also very close to being a policy. The British were protected by the Anglo-German Naval Treaty, and there was a conviction that the direction of German dynamism lay in East and Southeast Europe where British interests were minor. Laval felt compelled to make some concessions to British demands. Italy hardly posed a mortal danger to Great Britain, but a remilitarized Germany did positively threaten France. But close cooperation between Britain and France was virtually impossible because each government suspected the other. Mussolini made the most of Anglo-French differences and worked hard to prevent Laval from going completely into the British camp.[18]

Such were the national policies of the three powers when another effort was made in August 1935 to settle the Italian dispute with Ethiopia by peaceful means. On this occasion, Britain and France proposed a scheme that would have permitted Italian colonial settlement in parts of Ethiopia and a measure of Italian political and economic penetration of the rest. These last privileges were to be exercised under the supervision of the League, a body in which French and British influence was paramount. Consequently, Mussolini sensed another trap and flatly rejected the proposal; his anger at Laval and antipathy for the British increased proportionately.[19]

Mussolini's attitude led the British Cabinet to apply more pressure against Italy, using the British fleet and the collective security apparatus of the League of Nations. A large armada of warships was sent into the Mediterranean and Sir Samuel Hoare made an electrifying speech before the League; apparently proponents of collective security action against Italy had found a champion. However, the fleet which steamed into the Mediterranean had only a short supply of anti-aircraft ammunition and Valetta, the capital of Malta and only a short distance from Italian airfields, was without air defense. There was concern in London about the maneuverability of heavy British vessels in narrow seas. Consequently, the British Chiefs of Staff advised the Cabinet that the country was not prepared to fight Italy. This warning came before the fleet was sent into the Mediterranean and before Hoare's speech. In a word, therefore, the dramatic naval show of force was simply bluff.[20]

There are indications that British policy in the League of Nations was not only that of bluff, but Machiavellian as well. On the day preceding Hoare's speech before the League Assembly, he and Laval had agreed that the League should take no action that would bring the danger of war with Italy.[21] In any case, Whitehall believed that the League states probably would not follow British leadership in the matter anyway because few of their immediate and vital national interests were involved in the crisis.[22] Why then did the British foreign policy planners decide to place the matter before the League and risk a rejection of British policy? The risk was taken because the political strategists of the Conservative party were convinced that the government had to endorse collective security against Italy in order to win an immediately forthcoming general election. Moreover, there is strong evidence that the Conservative leaders expected or even hoped that Hoare's efforts in the League would fail. The views of both Hoare and Neville Chamberlain on this point are most instructive. Apparently Chamberlain helped Hoare draft the League of Nations speech. The two men told L. S. Amery that sanctions would not involve the danger of war with Mussolini because only mild economic measures would be taken and that either Mussolini would succumb to British pressure or the French would back out. Chamberlain told Lord Lloyd virtually the same thing, adding that anything was better than being drawn into a war in which Britain was too weak to fight. Should the sanctions program collapse, the Conservative party could tell the electorate that it had done its best. However, as an instrument of collective security, the League of Nations would be destroyed.[23]

While the British exerted themselves to mobilize the League in the name of collective security, they also made further efforts to bargain with the Duce. New proposals for the settlement of the Italo-Ethiopian dispute at the expense of Ethiopia were made to Mussolini between September 12 and 18. In this carrot-and-stick politics, while the stick became heavier, the carrot also became sweeter, but not appetizing enough from the Italian viewpoint. Mussolini buried the proposal by calling it "not only unacceptable but derisory." [24] Consequently, there was no settlement and Fascist Italy invaded Ethiopia on October 3. Britain led the League in adopting a program of limited economic sanctions.

The British objective was to isolate Mussolini politically and make him more amenable to a settlement on British terms. But neither Britain nor France had any intention of adopting measures which might bring hostilities with Italy. On the other hand, because of the Anglo-French public commitment to collective security, an opportunity was presented to the smaller states to press for really effective sanctions. And the question of an embargo on oil and other strategic raw materials was raised by small power delegates at Geneva in mid-October. The small states tended to support collective security through the international organization because it offered a measure of protection for them against predatory great powers. League support for British leadership gave Whitehall some surprise. Britain and France were faced with the possibility that their hands might be forced.[25] They had gone on record in support of an oil sanction, but Mussolini let it be known that the imposition of this sanction would bring an attack on the British fleet in the Mediterranean. He later boasted to the Germans that he was convinced that the British, a satiated and pacifistic people, would not risk a showdown with him. But Mussolini's politics were largely the politics of prestige; and it is more likely that the only way out, as he saw it, was to risk marching forward. Whatever Mussolini's motivations, his policy presented an acute dilemma to the British policy-makers. The Conservative party was returned to power in the election of November 14 partly because of its platform of support for League action against Italy, but, as has been noted, British service chiefs warned the Cabinet that Britain was not prepared for war. There was a further difficulty in the minds of some. Anglo-Italian hostilities might lead to the fall of Mussolini; Fascist Italy was looked on as a bulwark against a Red Italy.[26]

By November, it was clear that the whole matter would soon come to a head, probably when the League met to decide on the oil sanction proposal. The obvious resolution of the British dilemma was to achieve a negotiated settlement with Italy beforehand, procure the acquiescence of Ethiopia, present it to the League as an agreement among the three powers and Ethiopia, and confidently expect ratification. In this way the principal internal and external political objectives of the government in the situation would be achieved. Since negotiations leading to an agreement would be authorized by the League and the arrangement ratified by the League, sufficient *pro forma* and procedural support for the Covenant would be given to fulfill the election promise of the Conservative party.

If the position of the British leadership in the developing crisis was dangerous, that of the Italian Duce was precarious. Influential groups in Italy were working for his overthrow. Except for France under Laval, Italy was nearly isolated in the international community: Britain had been successful in aligning the League states behind its public policy, and the American administration was doing what it felt it could to encourage effective League action against Italy. Responsible officials in Washington intimated that in the event of hostilities between Italy and England growing out of the Italo-Ethiopian War, the provisions of the Neutrality Act would not be extended to England.[27] Hitler went so far as to offer German war equipment to the British. He probably wanted a bargain giving German support for sanctions against Italy in return for British support of his designs on Austria. There was some sympathy for this idea in London.[28]

The Italians were aware that Laval was not to be relied upon in spite of his undertakings made at Rome earlier in the year, and it is clear that he intended to extract the maximum advantage for himself and for France from the crisis. His political position had been strengthened by the fact that both Britain and Italy had acquiesced in his role as an intermediary.[29] Knowing that Laval was subjected to enormous pressure by the British, Rome renewed assurances that Italy would stand at the side of France against Germany. The Italians also heavily subsidized sections of the French press in order to influence French public opinion. To this pressure, Laval responded in kind. He gave the British the impression that he was pro-Italian, while causing the Italians to fear an Anglo-French deal at their expense.[30] By this strategy, he sought to force each side to lower its demands so that a peaceful settlement, which was his objective, could be achieved. This would give all three powers more freedom of action to face the greatest threat to Europe: German militaristic revisionism.

Peaceful settlement of the Anglo-Italian dispute and of the Italo-Ethiopian War was in accordance with the interests of all three governments, as interpreted by those chiefly responsible for foreign policy formulation. And negotiations to this end began in Paris late in October 1935, continued intermittently in November, and finally concluded with the Hoare-Laval Plan in early December. Consideration of oil sanctions by the League was postponed at the initiative of Laval to permit the working out of an agreement.[31] During this period, each of the powers increased pressure on the others for the purpose of maximizing the satisfaction of national interests in a settlement. Britain urged the adoption of an oil sanction against Italy as a political tactic and, to guard against the possibility of an Italian "mad dog" attack against their fleet, sought to form a naval coalition in the Mediterranean with France as a member. The formation of such a coalition, however, was undesirable from Laval's standpoint because it would greatly strengthen the British hand in the Anglo-Italian crisis and diminish his influence as holder of the political balance of power between the two. There was apprehension in Paris that mobilization of the French fleet might bring serious internal disturbances; Laval, however, warned Mussolini that France would come to the assistance of Britain in case of an Italian attack. At the same time, he refused to make any positive commitment to Britain. On their part, the British attempted to increase their bargaining power in Paris by refusing consistently to give significant support for French security against Germany beyond that already on the books. They warned Laval, as already noted, that failure to support British policy against Mussolini might result in their withdrawal from Continental affairs.[32]

Mussolini countered the British threat of oil sanctions with his own threat against the British fleet. He was fully aware of the danger of an oil embargo to his campaign in Ethiopia and told Hitler in 1938 that had one been imposed, he would have had to withdraw in a week.[33] The Duce made strenuous efforts to prevent an Anglo-French agreement at his expense. Laval was informed that Italy stood squarely behind the Franco-Italian accord of January against Hitler, but that it would be a dead letter if Laval made a deal with England in the present crisis. On his side, Laval told the Italian negotiator in Paris that unless Italy agreed to British proposals, he would resign.[34]

Such were the pressures exerted by the three powers on each other during the course of the conversations in Paris that led to the Hoare-Laval Plan. Sir Maurice Peterson, head of the Ethiopian Department of the Foreign Office, began negotiations on the British side. He was authorized to offer the concessions Mussolini had turned down in August, but began the discussions by proposing a solution, even less favorable from the Italian point of view, based on the plan which the Duce had rejected in June.[35] Obviously, nothing could be accomplished on this basis and Peterson was given a new set of instructions. By this time, Whitehall was convinced that Mussolini would win in Ethiopia and the General Staff felt that there was nothing the Army could do about it. Possibly the British were impressed by the fact that General Badoglio, frequently regarded as the finest staff officer in Europe, was taking over command of the Italian forces in Africa.[36]

In Paris, bargaining began in greater earnest. Mussolini had already let Laval know his minimum terms; but the latter, in dealing with the British, raised them. Because of their distrust of Laval, the British made an attempt in the first days of December to deal with Mussolini directly and sent more acceptable proposals to Rome.[37] The decisive negotiations, however, continued in Paris where Sir Samuel Hoare and Sir Robert Vansittart took over from Peterson.

There is no need to make a detailed examination of the Hoare-Laval Plan here. An analysis of its provisions can be found in Arnold Toynbee's *Survey of International Affairs, 1935,* Volume II.[38] With one minor exception, Italy was permitted to annex all the territory she had occupied in the north and southeast of Ethiopia. In addition, she was given a vast area in the south and central part of the country for economic exploitation. At the last moment, Laval insisted that this area be larger than even Mussolini demanded in his minimum terms. Peterson had tentatively set the western boundary of the zone of economic exploitation along the 40th meridian. The French negotiator St. Quentin had advocated the 38th, while Mussolini demanded the 37th. Then Laval suddenly insisted that Hoare agree to the 35th as he did. Finally, the proposal envisaged that Ethiopia should receive the port of Assab in Eritrea, an adjacent Italian colony, together with a strip of territory connecting the port with Ethiopia. There is evidence of an Anglo-French understanding, at Laval's insistence, that the Ethiopians were not to build a railroad in this corridor, since it would compete with the French-owned Addis Ababa–Djibouti line, Ethiopia's only railway contact with a seaport.[39]

Such were the principal provisions of the Hoare-Laval Plan. It gave the aggressor more than he had, but less than he could take. The taking, however, would require a substantial investment of men, time, and money. Laval was in frequent telephone communication with Mussolini, and it was understood that the Duce was favorably inclined toward the proposal. It marked the collapse of the British politics of rigorous pressure against Italy. Mussolini had called the British bluff, and the British were unwilling to run the risk that he was not bluffing. Settlement of the Anglo-Italian crisis would very likely have proceeded according to the Plan or something close to it, but Laval himself arranged matters so that it was leaked to the press.[40] Vansittart suggests that Laval's purpose was to destroy the proposal by exposing it to public opinion, which he anticipated would be hostile. However, Laval was perturbed and apparently surprised by the adverse reaction in Great Britain, and called Vansittart to the Quai d'Orsay in the middle of the night to explain the situation. If Laval was indeed responsible for the leak, it was more likely that he feared a bilateral settlement of the crisis without French participation. He knew that both governments were angry with him; he could hardly have been ignorant of the London-Rome exchange of views just a few days before. Therefore, he might have considered it expedient to have the proposal publicized as promptly as possible so that he could make the maximum capital in domestic and international politics of his successful role as mediator between Italy and England. In any case, a certain amount of Anglo-Italian animosity was probably desirable to Laval; it gave him an advantageous bargaining position with respect to both.[41]

The Hoare-Laval Plan was accepted by the British Cabinet, then rejected following an explosion of public indignation against it. After all, the new government had been elected on the basis of a platform which included a promise of support for collective security through the League. Hoare became the scapegoat and resigned, but was soon back in the Cabinet as First Lord of the Admiralty, and a few years later joined Neville Chamberlain, Sir John Simon, and Viscount Halifax as a member of the Inner Cabinet which shaped the course of British foreign policy in the year before World War II.[42]

The victory of Mussolini in the crisis with England firmly established Italy as a great power. This status was acquired in the usual way: by inflicting a defeat on another great power. Here the defeat was political; it was nonetheless real, for the political battle was fought with great intensity on both sides. The outcome of the crisis could hardly have been more tragic. Formulation of the Hoare-Laval Plan destroyed the League as a collective security organization, for it showed that British and French support for collective action against Italy was largely a sham. Thereafter, small states in the League became more fearful of being drawn into the games of the big powers; they looked outside the League for security. The Plan's premature exposure in Paris, as well as the orientation of French policy in the crisis, confirmed opinions in London that France was unstable and untrustworthy. Repudiation of the Plan prevented a possible reconciliation between Italy and the Western powers. It was Hitler who exploited these divisions, marching into the Rhineland in March 1936. Thereafter he maneuvered to maintain them, for unity of policy against him would have frustrated his grandiose dreams. Following the collapse of the Plan, the oil sanction proposal was gradually shelved and Mussolini's legions entered Addis Ababa in May 1936. In the meantime, Japan took advantage of the turmoil in Europe to make a further penetration of North China.[43]

Is it possible to account for the failure of British policy which was manifested in the Hoare-Laval Plan and its reception in England? A hypothesis can be suggested on the basis of available evidence. It is that the foreign policy decision-making process was impaired by amateurism, debility, and indifference in high places, the willingness of politicians to use foreign policy matters as expedient tactics in domestic politics, and the disparity between the public and private attitudes of British leaders toward the crisis. There was a tendency in London not to take the Italians very seriously—politically, economically, or militarily. Apparently the Conservative policy-makers believed that Italy must inevitably bend before the British will.[44] The history of English relations with Italy since unification would indeed tend to support this view; as late as 1923, Mussolini had evacuated Corfu following British pressure. Nevertheless, this was more supposition than a calculated evaluation. It would appear that the attitude prevented a realistic appraisal of Mussolini's determination and Italian strength in 1935 until after the Cabinet had made a public policy commitment based on an invalid estimate of Italian weakness. Then the election promises of the Conservatives and press campaigns in both countries made an alteration of this policy very difficult. Hence the secrecy of the Anglo-French conversations in Paris and the uproar which in England followed the disclosure of the Plan.

In the first months of the crisis, Ramsay MacDonald, the Prime Minister, was so infirm that at times he was practically inarticulate; his mind, writes Vansittart, being "no longer equal to public tests." [45] MacDonald's Foreign Minister, Simon, would not say either yes or no to the Italians regarding their ambitions in East Africa. British prestige was so high that there was no need to bolster its military underpinnings; complacency was general in 1935. A change in the government was imminent and Simon's foreign policy drifted along. MacDonald was succeeded by Stanley Baldwin who was more willing to endorse foreign policy as a tactical maneuver in domestic policies to win an election than to give direction to foreign policy matters *per se*. He had little interest in, or knowledge of, foreign affairs and was inclined to temporize when faced with difficult policy decisions. According to A. L. Rowse, he said some years later that he was physically incapable of holding office.[46] When Hoare left for Paris in early December 1935 to negotiate the Plan, the burden of Baldwin's instructions was to prevent war by whatever means. This was not foreign policy; it was an acknowledgment of political bankruptcy.[47]

Such being the attitudes and capabilities of Baldwin, it was particularly unfortunate that his Foreign Minister, Hoare, came to office with little experience in the foreign field. Secretary of State for India in the preceding MacDonald Cabinet, he was utterly exhausted after guiding the Government of India Act through the House of Commons. The critical negotiations with Laval in December were conducted by a man so overworked that he was subject to what Baldwin called "fainting fits." As a matter of fact, Hoare stopped in Paris while en route to Switzerland for a rest leave to repair his health.[48] This inexperienced and exhausted Foreign Secretary found himself in the fall and early winter of 1935 face to face with the most serious challenge to British imperial and prestige interests by a European power since World War I. He had little guidance from his chief, whose eyes were fixed on the November elections. Moreover, the same preoccupation prevented the Cabinet from giving much attention to the crisis in the critical months of October and November.[49]

Hoare did have the assistance of Anthony Eden, then Minister for League of Nations Affairs. But there is no evidence that Eden played a prominent role in foreign policy-making during this period. He was the government's spokesman in Geneva for the public policy of support for the League. The Permanent Under Secretary in the Foreign Office was Sir Robert Vansittart, a man of exceptional brilliance and experience who wrote at the end of his life that "I can recall no major issue on which my advice was taken." [50] The principal preoccupation of Vansittart during this period was to prevent Austria from falling into the hands of Hitler. He had long since taken the measure of Nazism as an ominously powerful and disruptive force in European affairs, as evidenced by an extraordinary memorandum which he wrote shortly after Hitler came to power. While he was anti-German, he was certainly not pro-Italian and furthermore was among those who in the first part of the crisis held a dim view of Italian capabilities. When it became evident, however, that Mussolini regarded the danger of an imminent Nazi penetration of Austria as less serious to Italian interests than a failure of the Ethiopian adventure, Vansittart was willing to sacrifice Ethiopia to Mussolini in the hope that the latter would resume his role as the protector of Austria. Actually, Mussolini probably regarded his position against Germany over Austria as stronger in 1935 than in 1934 because of the alliance with Laval's France. During the Austrian crisis of 1934, neither Britain nor France gave much political support to his military demonstration at the Brenner. The Duce believed that Hitler would require several years more to complete his war preparations. This would give Italy a short time in which to augment her power and prestige through colonial enterprises in order to face the international crisis he saw looming over the European horizon. In the meantime, he threatened to deal with Hitler by making it clear that Italy, alone, would not undertake the preservation of Austrian independence.

When the crisis came to a head in early December 1935, therefore, Baldwin wanted compromise and peace with Italy at almost any price for want of a policy, while Vansittart accepted compromise to support a policy of promoting the containment of Germany. He thought it vital to prevent Austria from falling into Hitler's hands either through Italian weakness or an Italo-German bargain.[51] Compromise and settlement with Italy, however, were made impossible because the British public had elected a government which had publicly committed itself to the coercion of Italy through the League. British policy therefore fell between two stools. One difficulty was that the collective security commitment of the government was more domestic than foreign policy and that it could not be openly and dramatically repudiated. Another was that the global security requirements of Britain exceeded by far its existing military strength. This was a principal malaise of the democracies during the 1930's. Anglo-Italian hostilities in the Mediterranean might have permitted either Japanese action in North China, an area of important British commercial interests, or German aggression in Europe. But it was not until late October or early November that such military considerations became decisive factors in policy formation. Until that time it was felt that Italy could be coerced into a settlement in spite of military deficiencies.

This account must close on a tentative note. The failure of British pressure on Mussolini at Paris is largely to be explained by the unwillingness of Britain to test his threat of armed reprisal in the event of an oil sanction. British military unpreparedness was undoubtedly the prime factor here. However, it is to be noted that while Baldwin received an authorization to rearm in the November elections, he proceeded very slowly in this direction. One is struck, moreover, by the totality of Hoare's capitulation in the Paris negotiations. There are indications that more subterranean currents were at work in shaping policy. At the end of November and in the first days of December, British industrial and financial interests exerted strong pressure on the Cabinet to avoid a conflict and the oil sanction which might precipitate it. The identity of such interests can only be the subject of speculation. But it may be noted that the International Petroleum Cartel, which had controlled roughly 75 per cent of the Italian market since 1928, would certainly be apprehensive about the upsetting effects of an oil sanction.[52]

NOTES

1. For example: Chester V. Easum, *Half Century of Conflict* (New York, 1952), pp. 479–484; René Albrecht-Carrié, *A Diplomatic History of Europe Since the Congress of Vienna* (New York, 1958), pp. 484–491; Walter Phelps Hall and William Stearns Davis, *The Course of Europe Since Waterloo* (New York, 1957), 4th ed., pp. 737–738; Carl H. Pegg, *Contemporary Europe in World Focus* (New York, 1956), pp. 215–223.

2. Arnold J. Toynbee, *Survey of International Affairs, 1935* (London, 1936), II; Gaetano Salvemini, *Prelude to World War II* (New York, 1954).

3. G. M. Gathorne-Hardy, *A Short History of International Affairs, 1920–1939* (London, 1952), 4th ed., pp. 414–415.

4. On these matters see: Addis Ababa to Washington, December 14, 1934, 765.84/111 (unpublished State Department documents will be cited by file number), April 3, 1935, 765.84/282; Rome to Washington, December 8, 1934, 765.84/89, October 18, 1935, 765.84/2244; Memoranda, December 10, 1934, 765.84/166, January 8, 1935, 765.84/121, June 14, 1935, 765.84/400; July 25, 1936, *Foreign Relations of the United States, 1936* (Washington, 1953), III, 83 (hereafter cited as *Foreign Relations*); Ambassador Long in Rome to President Roosevelt, October

30, 1935, President's Personal Files, Breckinridge Long Folder, Franklin D. Roose-velt Library, Hyde Park, New York (hereafter cited as Roosevelt Library); Emilio De Bono, *Anno XIII* (London, 1937), pp. 13, 116–117, 202; Istituto per gli studi di politica internazionale, *Il conflitto Italo-Etiopico, documenti* (Milano, 1936), I, 273; Baron Aloisi, *Journal* (Paris, 1957), pp. 200–201; Giorgio Pini e Duilio Susmel, *Mussolini, l'uomo e l'opera* (Firenze, 1955), III, 314; L. S. Amery, *My Political Life* (London, 1955), III, 172; Lord Templewood, *Nine Troubled Years* (London, 1954), pp. 150–151; George Martelli, *Italy Against the World* (New York, 1938), p. 8; Toynbee, *Survey of International Affairs, 1935*, II, 133–136; Kurt Schuschnigg, *Austrian Requiem* (New York, 1946), p. 115; Mario Toscano, "Eden's Mission to Rome on the Eve of the Italo-Ethiopian Conflict," in A. O. Sarkissian, *Studies in Diplomatic History and Historiography in Honor of G. P. Gooch* (London, 1961), p. 136.

5. Memorandum, April 7, 1939, 865.002 Mussolini Speeches/4.

6. London to Washington, August 20, 1935, *Foreign Relations, 1935*, I, 633; Rome to Washington, October 16, 1935, 765.84/1870; Ambassador Long to Presi-dent Roosevelt, September 6, 1935, President's Secretary's Files, Breckinridge Long Folder, Roosevelt Library; Ottavio Dinale, *Quarant'anni di colloqui con lui* (Milano, 1953), p. 162; Templewood, *Nine Troubled Years*, p. 152; Aloisi, *Journal*, p. 290; Toynbee, *Survey of International Affairs, 1935*, II, 249–252.

7. Rome to Washington, February 15, 1935, 765.84/176, August 31, 1935, 765.84/1171, September 4, 1935, 765.84/1216, September 13, 1935, 765.84/1341; Paul Gentison, *Défense de l'Italie* (Lausanne, 1949), p. 23; Martelli, *Italy Against the World*, pp. 63–64; Raffaele Guariglia, *Ricordi, 1922–1946* (Napoli, 1949), pp. 214–217; Hugh R. Wilson, *Diplomat Between Wars* (New York, 1941), p. 308.

8. Memorandum, commenting on letter, Ambassador Long to President Roose-velt, December 15, 1933, President's Secretary's Files, Italy Folder, Roosevelt Library; Templewood, *Nine Troubled Years*, pp. 152–153; Lord Vansittart, *The Mist Procession* (London, 1958), pp. 502–503, 516, 518.

9. London to Washington, August 20, 1935, *Foreign Relations, 1935*, I, 634, August 28, 1935, *ibid.*, 640, September 16, 1935, *ibid.*, 650–651; Rome to Wash-ington, September 18, 1935, 765.84/1971; Amery, *My Political Life*, III, 172.

10. Rome to Washington, July 5, 1935, 765.84/543; Geneva to Washington, May 28, 1935, 862.20/1042, September 26, 1935, 765.84/1384; memorandum, July 6, 1935, *Foreign Relations, 1935*, I, 726; Guariglia, *Ricordi*, p. 255; Aloisi, *Journal*, pp. 259, 270, 273, 275–279; Templewood, *Nine Troubled Years*, pp. 156–157. The silence of MacDonald and Simon was particularly pointed at the Stresa Conference in April 1935: Pietro Quaroni, *Ricordi di un ambasciatore* (Milano, 1954), p. 125; Winston Churchill, *The Gathering Storm* (Cambridge, 1948), pp. 132–134; Giu-seppe Bottai, *Vent'anni e un giorno* (Milano, 1949), 2nd ed., pp. 124–125; Thomas Jones, *A Diary with Letters* (London, 1954), p. 193; Vansittart, *The Mist Proces-sion*, p. 520; Amery, *My Political Life*, III, 166; Vansittart, *Lessons of My Life* (New York, 1943), pp. 40–42.

11. Rome to Washington, June 27, 1935, 765.84/472, July 2, 1935, 765.84/429, July 5, 1935, 765.84/543; memorandum, November 18, 1935, 765.84/2905½; Aloisi, *Journal*, p. 282; Templewood, *Nine Troubled Years*, pp. 152–153, 155–156; Amery, *My Political Life*, III, 167; Reynolds and Eleanor Packard, *Balcony Empire, Fascist Italy at War* (New York, 1942), p. 13; Toscano, "Eden's Mission to Rome," p. 135; Vansittart, *The Mist Procession*, pp. 516–519; Elizabetta Cerruti, *Ambassador's Wife* (New York, 1953), pp. 227–228.

12. Rome to Washington, August 31, 1935, 765.84/1171, August 19, 1935, *Foreign Relations, 1935*, I, 740, September 17, 1935, *ibid.*, p. 757; Italian Ambas-sador Rosso to Under Secretary of State Phillips, September 20, 1935, *ibid.*, p. 764;

De Bono, *Anno* XIII, p. 5; Istituto per gli studi di politica internazionale, *Il conflitto Italo-Etiopico, documenti,* I, 169.
13. Addis Ababa to Washington, March 6, 1929, 765.84/17. See also memo-randum, September 25, 1934, 765.84/52.
14. Addis Ababa to Washington, December 12, 1932, 765.84/40.
15. Rome to Washington, February 19, 1935, 765.84/185, June 30, 1935, 765.84/420, September 13, 1935, 765.84/1416½; Istanbul to Washington, June 24, 1935, 765.84/592; London to Washington, May 2, 1935, 756.84/334; October 5, 1935, 765.84/1586, September 16, 1935, *Foreign Relations, 1935,* I, 650; Geneva to Washington, September 4, 1935, *ibid.,* p. 641; memorandum, May 27, 1935, 765.84/1342; Ambassador Long to President Roosevelt, February 15, 1935, President's Secretary's Files, Breckinridge Long Folder, Roosevelt Library; Letter to Mr. Roosevelt, September 6, 1935, 765.84/1148; Letter to Assistant Secretary of State Dunn, September 5, 1935, 765.84/1278; Rome to London, December 24, 1938, *Documents on British Foreign Policy, 1919–1939* (London, 1950), 3d. ser., III, 490; memorandum, October 10, 1934; *Documents on German Foreign Policy, 1918–1945* (hereafter cited as *German Documents*) (Washington, 1959), ser. C, III, 472; Count Jean Szembek, *Journal, 1933–1939* (Paris, 1952), pp. 72, 83, 130–131, 142; William Phillips, *Ventures in Diplomacy* (London, 1955), p. 85; Hubert Lagardelle, *Mission à Rome: Mussolini* (Paris, 1955), pp. 106, 111–115; J. Paul-Boncour, *Entre Deux Guerres* (Paris, 1946), III, 14–16; Pierre Laval, *The Unpublished Diary of Pierre Laval* (London, 1948), p. 34; Vansittart, *The Mist Procession,* pp. 515–516, 518; Paul Schmidt, *Hitler's Interpreter* (New York, 1951), p. 31; Arnold Toynbee, *Survey of International Affairs, 1935* (London, 1936), I, 72, 146; William C. Askew, "The Secret Agreement Between France and Italy on Ethiopia, January 1935, *Journal of Modern History,* XXV (March 1953), 47–48; Lord Vansittart, *Lessons of My Life,* p. 39; Toscano, "Eden's Mission to Rome," p. 136.
16. Churchill, *The Gathering Storm,* p. 139; D. C. Watt, "The Anglo-German Naval Agreement of 1935: An Interim Judgment," *Journal of Modern History,* XXVIII (June, 1956), 155–175.
17. Geneva to Washington, June 29, 1935, 765.84/419, April 16, 1935, *Foreign Relations, 1935,* I, 257; London to Washington, April 17, 1935, *ibid.,* p. 945; Gentison, *Défense de l'Italie,* p. 136; Guariglia, *Ricordi,* pp. 255–256; Churchill, *The Gathering Storm,* p. 133; Vansittart, *The Mist Procession,* pp. 518–520; Toynbee, *Survey of International Affairs, 1935,* I, 121–123.
18. Geneva to Washington, September 5, 1935, 765.84/1045, September 12, 1935, 765.84/1133, September 16, 1935, 765.84/1198; Paris to Washington, August 15, 1935, *Foreign Relations, 1935,* I, 626–627; London to Washington, August 20, 1935, *ibid.,* p. 633, August 22, 1935, *ibid.,* p. 636, August 23, 1935, *ibid.,* p. 638; The Hague to Washington, April 2, 1935, *ibid.,* p. 217; Geneva to Washington, September 4, 1935, *ibid.,* pp. 640–641; Report by Under Secretary of State Welles, March 7, 1940, *Foreign Relations, 1940,* I, 61; Viscount Simon, *Retrospect* (London, 1952), p. 203; Vansittart, *The Mist Procession,* pp. 518, 532, 539; Vansittart, *Lessons of My Life,* p. 39; Stephen Heald, ed., *Documents on International Affairs, 1935* (London, 1937), II, 304–307; Aloisi, *Journal,* pp. 290–291, 303. By the middle of August, Laval was convinced the British government was determined to avoid war with Italy. *Ibid.,* p. 295.
19. Geneva to Washington, September 11, 1935, 765.84/1117; Rome to Washington, July 17, 1935, 765.84/556, July 18, 1935, 765.84/718; Templewood, *Nine Troubled Years,* pp. 171–172; Aloisi, *Journal,* pp. 287, 289, 290, 297; Lagardelle, *Mission à Rome: Mussolini,* p. 204; Toynbee, *Survey of International Affairs, 1935,* II, 174.
21. London to Washington, August 19, 1935, 765.84/874, 765.84/3737; Geneva to Washington, December 12, 1935, *Foreign Relations, 1935,* I, 709; Paris to Wash-

ington, August 16, 1935, 765.84/926; Vansittart, *The Mist Procession*, pp. 522–523, 531, 533, 538, 544; Jones, *A Diary with Letters*, pp. 159–160; Wilson, *Diplomat Between Wars*, pp. 317–320; Gentison, *Défense de l'Italie*, p. 129; Templewood, *Nine Troubled Years*, p. 177; Churchill, *The Gathering Storm*, pp. 171, 173; Heald, ed., *Documents on International Affairs, 1935*, I, 101–102; Iain Macleod, *Neville Chamberlain* (London, 1961), p. 187.

21. Vansittart, *The Mist Procession*, p. 532; Templewood, *Nine Troubled Years*, pp. 168–169.

22. Geneva to Washington, November 4, 1935, *Foreign Relations, 1935*, I, 682; Paris to Washington, December 9, 1935, *ibid.*, p. 700; Vansittart, *The Mist Procession*, p. 522; Templewood, *Nine Troubled Years*, p. 166.

23. Memorandum, September 20, 1935, 765.84/1281; Geneva to Washington, September 5, 1935, 765.84/1070, November 4, 1935, *Foreign Relations, 1935*, I, 681–683; London to Washington, August 20, 1935, *ibid.*, pp. 633–634, August 28, 1935, *ibid.*, pp. 639–640, September 16, 1935, *ibid.*, pp. 649–650; Rome to Washington, September 30, 1935, *ibid.*, pp. 661–662; Geneva to Washington, March 11, 1936, *Foreign Relations, 1936*, I, 231–232; Oslo to Washington, March 18, 1936, *ibid.*, p. 254; Geneva to Washington, April 11, 1936, *Foreign Relations, 1936*, III, 119–120; memorandum, June 24, 1939, *German Documents*, ser. D, VI, 783; Colin Forbes Adam, *Life of Lord Lloyd* (London, 1948), pp. 268–269; Keith Feiling, *The Life of Neville Chamberlain* (London, 1947), pp. 265, 268; Toscano, "Eden's Mission to Rome," p. 146; Amery, *My Political Life*, III, 173–174, 176; Templewood, *Nine Troubled Years*, pp. 164–166; Vansittart, *The Mist Procession*, p. 532; Guariglia, *Ricordi*, p. 219. Iain Macleod contests Amery's opinion that Chamberlain's attitude toward sanctions was "frankly cynical." However, the evidence he gives is not convincing. It is taken from Chamberlain's diary which was obviously written with an eye on the public record. Apparently Chamberlain, even late in the crisis, expected Mussolini to back down, while others did not. Macleod, *Neville Chamberlain*, pp. 187–188. Washington was warned that British public policy might change after the elections. London to Washington, August 8, 1935, 765.84/771, October 18, 1935, 765.84/1955; Rome to Washington, October 24, 1935, 765.84/2104, November 6, 1935, 765.84/2391, November 12, 1935, 765.84/2507; Washington to Paris, October 12, 1935, *Foreign Relations, 1935*, I, 845.

24. Rome to Washington, September 6, 1935, 765.84/1058; Geneva to Washington, September 9, 1935, 765.84/1083; Paris to Washington, September 9, 1935, 765.84/1084; Aloisi, *Journal*, pp. 304, 306–307; Stephen Heald, ed., *Documents on International Affairs, 1935*, II, 106–110; Toynbee, *Survey of International Affairs, 1935*, II, 192–195.

25. Geneva to Washington, September 5, 1935, 765.84/1070; Nicholas Mansergh, *Survey of British Commonwealth Affairs, Problems of External Policy, 1931–1939* (London, 1952), pp. 116–117; Templewood, *Nine Troubled Years*, p. 177; Gwendolen M. Carter, *The British Commonwealth and International Security: The Role of the Dominions, 1919–1939* (Toronto, 1947), pp. 216–225; Vansittart, *Lessons of My Life*, p. 44.

26. London to Washington, August 19, 1935, 765.84/874, November 26, 1935, 765.84/2749; Geneva to Washington, December 12, 1935, *Foreign Relations, 1935*, I, 709; Rome to Washington, August 19, 1935, *ibid.*, p. 742, September 17, 1935, *ibid.*, p. 757; Paris to Washington, October 29, 1935, *ibid.*, p. 676; London to Washington, January 29, 1936, *Foreign Relations, 1936*, III, 100; memorandum, October 2, 1937, *German Documents*, ser. D., I, 3; Maurice Peterson, *Both Sides of the Curtain* (London, 1950), pp. 118, 122; Templewood, *Nine Troubled Years*, pp. 163, 177–179; Vansittart, *The Mist Procession*, p. 533; Amery, *My Political Life*, III, 186; Toynbee, *Survey of International Affairs, 1935*, II, 280; A. L. Rowse, *All Souls and Appeasement* (London, 1961), p. 26.

27. Washington to Rome, October 3, 1935, 765.84/1562A; memoranda, August 28, 1935, *Foreign Relations, 1935,* I, 789, September 11 and 12, 1935, *ibid.,* p. 746; Statements to the press by Secretary of State Hull, September 12 and November 15, 1935; Letter, Ambassador Dodd to President Roosevelt, April 1, 1936, President's Secretary's Files, William E. Dodd, 1933–37 Folder, Roosevelt Library; Aloisi, *Journal,* p. 312.

28. Ambassador Dodd to Secretary Hull, August 22, 1935, 765.84/916; Amery, *My Political Life,* III, 173; Templewood, *Nine Troubled Years,* pp. 189–190; Goering testimony, International Military Tribunal, *Trial of the Major War Criminals* (Nuremberg, 1947), IX, 295.

29. Aloisi, *Journal,* p. 315; Vansittart, *Lessons of My Life,* p. 46; Templewood, *Nine Troubled Years,* p. 167.

30. Geneva to Washington, October 8, 1935, *Foreign Relations, 1935,* I, 641; Martelli, *Italy Against the World,* p. 114; Aloisi, *Journal,* pp. 294, 312.

31. *Ibid.,* pp. 310, 315, 318–319; Toynbee, *Survey of International Affairs, 1935,* I, 277–279. Mussolini was perfectly willing to make a negotiated settlement, provided, of course, that he got most of Ethiopia: Rome to Washington, September 6, 1935, 765.84/1058, September 12, 1935, 765.84/1338, October 24, 1935, 765.84/2104; London to Washington, November 26, 1935, 765.84/2749.

32. London to Washington, December 16, 1935, *Foreign Relations, 1935,* I, 713, January 29, 1936, *Foreign Relations, 1936,* III, February 13, 1936, *Foreign Relations, 1936,* I, 198; Geneva to Washington, December 13, 1935, 765.84/3069; Letter, Hugh R. Wilson to Secretary Hull, December 5, 1935, copy to Mr. Roosevelt, President's Secretary's Files, Diplomatic Correspondence, Great Britain, 1933–38, Roosevelt Library; Laval, *Unpublished Diary,* p. 13; Vansittart, *The Mist Procession,* pp. 533, 538; Templewood, *Nine Troubled Years,* pp. 164, 171, 179; Aloisi, *Journal,* p. 317; Feiling, *Neville Chamberlain,* p. 267; Toynbee, *Survey of International Affairs, 1935,* II, 257–267.

33. London to Washington, November 26, 1935, 765.84/2749; Geneva to Washington, December 12, 1935, *Foreign Relations, 1935,* I, 709; Peterson, *Both Sides of the Curtain,* pp. 118, 122; Aloisi, *Journal,* pp. 292, 315, 317, 325; Vansittart, *The Mist Procession,* p. 533.

34. Aloisi, *Journal,* pp. 316–317; Toynbee, *Survey of International Affairs, 1935,* II, 265–266.

35. Vansittart, *The Mist Procession,* pp. 537–538.

36. Templewood, *Nine Troubled Years,* pp. 177, 181–182; Peterson, *Both Sides of the Curtain,* p. 117; Vansittart, *The Mist Procession,* p. 544.

37. *Ibid.,* p. 538; Templewood, *Nine Troubled Years,* p. 169; Aloisi, *Journal,* pp. 318–319, 326–327; Vansittart, *Lessons of My Life,* pp. 47, 49.

38. Pp. 295–300. See also Peterson, *Both Sides of the Curtain,* pp. 116–117.

39. Vansittart, *The Mist Procession,* pp. 539–540; Templewood, *Nine Troubled Years,* pp. 179–182.

40. London to Washington, January 29, 1936, *Foreign Relations, 1936,* III, 101–102; Aloisi, *Journal,* pp. 329, 331; Guariglia, *Ricordi,* p. 294ff.; Jones, *Diary with Letters,* p. 159; Amery, *My Political Life,* III, 184; Peterson, *Both Sides of the Curtain,* p. 119; Vansittart, *The Mist Procession;* Templewood, *Nine Troubled Years.*

41. Vansittart, *Lessons of My Life,* pp. 50–51.

42. Jones, *Diary with Letters,* p. 161; Templewood, *Nine Troubled Years,* pp. 184–185, 291. Cf. Simon, *Retrospect,* p. 214.

43. Letter, Ambassador Wilson to Secretary Hull, December 15, 1935, copy to Mr. Roosevelt, President's Secretary's Files, Diplomatic Correspondence, Great Britain, 1933–38 Folder, Roosevelt Library; Geneva to Washington, December 11, 1935, *Foreign Relations, 1935,* I, 701–702, December 12, 1935, *ibid.,* pp. 707–708; Paris to Washington, January 9, 1936, *Foreign Relations, 1936,* III, 86; Rome to

Washington, January 17, 1936, *ibid.*, p. 90; London to Washington, January 18, 1936, *ibid.*, pp. 92–93; Geneva to Washington, January 23, 1936, *ibid.*, pp. 97–100, April 11, 1936, *ibid.*, pp. 119–120; Paris to Washington, April 15, 1936, *ibid.*, pp. 120–121; London to Washington, February 13, 1936, *Foreign Relations, 1936,* I, 196–198; Geneva to Washington, March 11, 1936, *ibid.*, p. 231; Oslo to Washington, March 18, 1936, *ibid.*, p. 254; Brussels to Washington, November 10, 1937, *Foreign Relations, 1937,* IV, 176. See my article, "A New Look at American Policy During the Italo-Ethiopian Crisis, 1935–36," *Journal of Modern History,* XXXIV (March, 1962), 64–73.

44. Vansittart, *The Mist Procession,* p. 515; Vansittart, *Lessons of My Life,* p. 48. The British policy-makers showed little disposition to compromise with Mussolini until the end of October, when the Ethiopian military position had deteriorated. Peterson, *Both Sides of the Curtain,* p. 115.

45. Vansittart, *The Mist Procession,* p. 519.

46. Lagardelle, *Mission à Rome: Mussolini,* p. 124; Churchill, *The Gathering Storm,* p. 221; Templewood, *Nine Troubled Years,* pp. 35, 135, 163–164, 167, 291; Vansittart, *The Mist Procession,* p. 517; Amery, *My Political Life,* III, 176; Rowse, *All Souls and Appeasement,* p. 55. As early as the spring of 1935, Italian Ambassador Grandi in London wrote Mussolini that for the English government European politics counted primarily as instruments in election tactics. Guariglia, *Ricordi,* p. 219.

47. Geneva to Washington, December 12, 1935, *Foreign Relations, 1935,* I, 709; Peterson, *Both Sides of the Curtain,* p. 118; Vansittart, *The Mist Procession,* pp. 538–539; Jones, *Diary with Letters,* p. 159; Wilson, *Diplomat Between Wars,* pp. 160, 317–320. *Cf.* Simon, *Retrospect,* pp. 213–214.

48. Jones, *Diary with Letters,* p. 158; Templewood, *Nine Troubled Years,* pp. 108–109, 177–178; Feiling, *Life of Neville Chamberlain,* p. 273.

49. Templewood, *Nine Troubled Years,* pp. 176–177.

50. Peterson, *Both Sides of the Curtain,* p. 118; Vansittart, *The Mist Procession,* pp. 522, 530, 550.

51. Ambassador Bingham in London to President Roosevelt, December 24, 1935, President's Personal Files, Robert W. Bingham, 1933–38, Roosevelt Library; Paris to Washington, December 9, 1935, *Foreign Relations, 1935,* I, 699–700; London to Washington, December 16, 1935, *ibid.*, pp. 711–712; Rome to Washington, February 2, 1935, *ibid.*, p. 188; July 17, 1935, 765.84/556, May 25, 1935, 765.84/71; Jones, *Diary with Letters,* p. 159; Vansittart, *The Mist Procession,* pp. 518, 522, 540; Vansittart, *Lessons of My Life,* p. 42; Peterson, *Both Sides of the Curtain,* p. 121; memorandum, April 7, 1934, *Documents on British Foreign Policy, 1919–39* (London, 1957), 2nd ser., VI, 975–990.

52. Letter, Ambassador Wilson to Secretary Hull, December 15, 1935, copy to Mr. Roosevelt, President's Secretary's Files, Diplomatic Correspondence, Great Britain, 1933–38 Folder, Roosevelt Library; London to Washington, December 11, 1935, *Foreign Relations, 1935,* I, 700; oral communication, British Embassy to the State Department, December 5, 1935, *ibid.*, pp. 871–872; Select Committee on Small Business, United States Senate, *The International Petroleum Cartel* (Washington, 1952), p. 345; Templewood, *Nine Troubled Years,* p. 196; Peterson, *Both Sides of the Curtain,* p. 117.

JOHN C. CAIRNS

March 7, 1936, Again:
The View from Paris

The most crucial event on the road to World War II was Germany's reoccupation of the Rhineland on March 7, 1936. Had it been met with the resistance of England, France, Belgium, and Italy which the Treaty of Locarno called for, Hitler might have been halted in time and Europe and the world might have been spared a major war. Among Allied mistakes that contributed to the origins of World War II, the Rhineland crisis of 1936 looms large.
John C. Cairns is Professor of History at the University of Toronto. His major interest is recent French history, on which he has written a number of articles and a small book, France *(Englewood Cliffs, New Jersey, 1965). He also edited* The Nineteenth Century, 1815–1914 *(New York, 1965). The following selection was first published in* International Journal, xx *(Spring 1965), 230–246. It is reprinted by permission of the author and the publisher.*

LOOKING THROUGH a large volume of diplomatic documents * covering a very short period of time is somewhat like looking at the wreck of a house one has known from the outside for a long time. The essen-

* Ministère des Affaires Etrangères, Commission de Publication des Documents Relatifs aux Origines de la Guerre 1939–1945, *Documents Diplomatiques Français 1932–1939, 2e série (1936–1939), I (1er Janvier–31 Mars 1936),* (Paris, Imprimerie Nationale, 1963).

tial mystery is at least partly dispelled. The demolition has almost obscenely revealed the interior, exposing the bad taste one suspected or unveiling an ornamentation one had not suspected. Fixtures and furnishings are at once starkly banal and compellingly of interest. It is all very much what one supposed and a little surprising; it both confirms and adds a dimension to one's knowledge. But it is a ruin, only remnants and traces. Much has been removed; the actors are gone; the life that inhabited this former structure has long since departed. Condemned by time, the building is both accessible and only a part of what once it was. Made available by the passage of time, the collection of papers is only a fragment of a vaster deposit, a part cut out of a larger human exchange, most of it ephemeral and gone forever. This sense of observing a cross-section of some inaccessible whole, either destroyed or still closed off from full view, is particularly marked with the first volume of a projected series, which is itself only a segment of the whole period to be covered by other series.

And yet, in the case of the French documents concerning the origins of the war of 1939–1945 (as indeed of all the national diplomatic papers thus far published for the years between the two wars), so much was known before, so many "secrets" were leaked at the time, so many memoirs have been published, so much of the century's diplomacy was conducted in less than cameral conditions, that an already elaborate setting against which to consider these fresh revelations has long existed. All the interest is to compare what one knew or guessed or believed with official (and perhaps more reliable) evidence now revealed. In the case of this volume, all the interest derives from the fact that it deals principally and in some detail with an event which was considered widely, both at the time and since, as marking a turning point in the fortunes of Europe and, as it happened, of the world.

On Saturday, March 7, 1936, in violation of the imposed conditions of the Treaty of Versailles and of the freely negotiated terms of the Treaty of Locarno, Adolf Hitler sent troops into the demilitarized zone of the Rhineland. Since that day there has been something approaching consensus among statesmen and historians that the act itself and the failure of the Western democracies to compel its withdrawal consolidated the domestic triumph of the German leader, destroyed finally the commanding position France had enjoyed in Europe since 1918, and subordinated this Third Republic thereafter to a position of satellite in tow of Great Britain. Nothing thus far made public, including the present papers, seriously contradicts this general verdict. A. J. P. Taylor's brilliant argument that in fact March 7 was not "the last chance" to stop the Third Reich short of war, but rather the beginning not only of Hitler's external successes but also of his vulnerability to attacks is a characteristic exception to prevailing interpretation.[1] There are others of course, if only asserting, as Jacques Chastenet has asserted, that it was by no means certain that Hitler would not have resisted attempts to expel him and, backed by an aroused German national sensibility, have precipitated war then and there.[2] All things are possible when one plays games with the past. But the prevailing opinion has been, as, for instance, Stuart Hughes put it, that "The first—and the best—opportunity had been lost for nipping Nazi aggression in the bud. After the crucial year 1936 it was too late." [3]

Presented with the French documents dealing with this crisis, then, every reader will ask of them what they can tell about French policy and (in the continued absence of the relevant British documents still to come) British policy. For if it is true that Great Britain called the tune after March 1936 and gave such directions as it had to the remnant of the Entente created by Delcassé and Lansdowne a generation before, how did this come about? Still another generation later, the question still nags. Many answers have been given already. Perhaps all are doomed to seem unsatisfactory. Quite certainly no collection of diplomatic papers will furnish all the elements of a general explanation. One thing is sure: there is no simple answer to the question. And it is a misfortune that knowledgeable men and serious historians should mislead us, the more so when they are skillful writers of popular books. Thus we must throw out of court George F. Kennan's verdict: "The French wished to resist this move by military action. They certainly had at that time the power to do so. The British dissuaded them." [4] It would be difficult in notably nonpolemical literature more succinctly to confuse the issues, inject half-truths, and distribute responsibilities so unfairly. Better to admit we know nothing than to sum up so crudely an interplay of ideas and men, motives and intents, action and paralysis so dimly perceived and so complicated as to defy anything but the most tentative, qualified summation. This is doubtless an unhappy admission, but life and history are like that.

What can be learned from the French materials? In what ways do they advance an understanding of this critical step Hitler took and the other Locarno powers accepted? First of all, even though the volume begins as late as January 1, 1936, one is struck by the repeated warnings of, and constant preoccupation with, the possibility of denunciation of Locarno. Day after day the probability of this action was driven home to Paris and London. It has long been known that on May 2, 1935, General von Blomberg issued the first order in preparation for eventual remilitarization of the zone.[5] That happened to be the day the Franco-Soviet Treaty of Mutual Assistance was signed at the Quai d'Orsay, an instrument which Hitler was constantly to declare incompatible with Locarno, ratification of which on February 27, 1936, finally permitted him to allege the necessity to act on March 7. Years ago General Gamelin recounted how from the autumn of 1935 the Army's Intelligence and Deuxième Bureau provided warnings of what lay in store and how he or his staff wrote to the Prime Minister, Pierre Laval, October 21, advising that the possibility of repudiation of the Rhineland settlement should be envisaged "before the autumn of 1936 at the latest." The Ambassador in Berlin, André François-Poncet, told of his warnings that November of 1935.[6] But what strikes one now is the weight of evidence pouring in on Paris, from Berlin, Cologne or Berne, months before Hitler took his decision in February 1936. Though the Führer began the New Year with the banality for François-Poncet that "he had no intention of bringing into question again the validity of the 1925 agreements," [7] the Ambassador, aware of the German Army's unwillingness to run risks, informed Paris that the Nazis controlled both Army and policy and observed that the press campaign against Locarno was mounting ominously.[8] The date and the method were uncertain, but the inevitability of repudiation seemed sure. Thus before his fall, January 23, Laval was fairly alerted and had passed along his concern to Stanley Baldwin's government in London.[9] The succeeding French cabinet of Albert Sarraut was no less troubled by this alarm, despite conflicting reports that Hitler might negotiate rather than strike.[10] Indeed, the French Consuls General in Düsseldorf and Cologne were more convinced of an imminent remilitarization than was the Ambassador in Berlin.[11] François-Poncet's interview with Hitler on March 2 (the day the Führer ordered his military men to be ready on Z-day to move three infantry battalions across the Rhine, and so forth) [12] led him to conclude only that it was "probable" that Hitler would try to gain time and to await at least the French Senate's vote on ratification of the Franco-Soviet Treaty (approved by the Chamber of Deputies, February 27). Still, he did also warn that it would be "completely vain" to have "the least illusion" about determination to end or modify status of the zone during 1936.[13] But through the final week, he held to the view that Hitler did not intend to pounce, qualifying this on the eve of the coup: "In actual fact, it is still unknown who, the partisans of moderation or those of violence, have finally prevailed in the councils of these last days." [14] Early on the Saturday morning this was revealed.

How were these uncertain warnings interpreted in Paris? Seriously enough to cause a multiplication of assurances to Hitler and his servants that the Franco-Soviet Treaty was pacific and compatible with Locarno, and that the proposed Anglo-French talks were directed specifically at possible action on behalf of the League of Nations in the case of the Ethiopian war.[15] And seriously enough by the French Army to make it conclude that "reoccupation" of the demilitarized zone was certain sometime that year.[16] These documents reveal, however, that the Army was far less resolute and bold than Gamelin tried to suggest.[17] An anonymous note, dated January 27, 1936, found in the Army archives, warned against the consequences of ratification of the Franco-Soviet pact: pretext for German "reoccupation" of the Rhineland and alienation of Poland and Belgium. Undoubtedly this was the view of much military opinion then; almost certainly it was held by both Gamelin and the Minister of War, General Maurin.[18] Obviously both of these men were reluctant to propose any measures which might offer Germany what they called a "valid pretext for conflict." Routine measures of cover and alerting of active units in the event that Hitler should send in troops were the limit of Maurin's suggestions on February 12. He threw the ball back to the Foreign Minister, Pierre-Etienne Flandin, arguing that governmental decisions and a concerting of policy with Great Britain and the other Locarno powers must occur before further measures were contemplated.[19]

No less deftly, Flandin pressed the Minister for information as to what steps the Army would eventually intend, not only to oppose a *fait accompli* but to forestall it, and which could be communicated to the British ahead of time. Moreover, he inquired, did the Army consider that it would be possible to negotiate a liberalization of the Rhineland statute without sacrificing the essential principle of demilitarization? [20] The question might have taxed an oracle more ancient and more experienced than Maurin. Nevertheless, his reply, February 17, was classic: in event of violation of the zone, the French should avoid making good "our right to occupy the demilitarized zone" lest they appear as "the aggressor" and be left "alone face to face with Germany." Rather, the case should be taken to Geneva. Detailed measures of defense would be taken, and (this of course was the thrust to the heart of the civilians) meantime the government must consider the need to provide further credit with which to improve the military position. As for negotiations beforehand (the notion was put forward by the British government), they would be "extremely dangerous" and it would be best to avoid them or, at most, simply to stand firmly on the settlements of 1918 and 1925.[21] What all this seems to have added up to was the bleak recognition that if political action with Great Britain was impossible or ineffectual, a German violation of Locarno without any attack upon French soil proper would certainly have to be endured.

To put it crudely, the Army had very cold feet. Maurin's note of February 17 had all the earmarks of the subtlety and political finesse of the Chief of Staff, General Gamelin. How hopelessly at sea they all were is suggested by Gamelin's murky analysis of the position during a chiefs of staff conference, February 19: on the one hand, he did not think that they had to consider the case of France acting alone; on the other, they must do "everything" to maintain the demilitarized zone at least until 1940 or 1942; and then, again, he did not think that you could indefinitely prevent Germany from doing what she liked within her own frontiers. . . . [22] In his memoirs, Gamelin told how on February 25 Maurin wondered aloud whether it might not be best to postpone still further the ratification of the Franco-Soviet Treaty, so as to avoid provoking both Adolf Hitler and the British who were very cool to the agreement; in the interval, the text of the treaty could be submitted to the Hague Court or the League to determine whether it did or did not collide with the undertakings of Locarno. The fruits of this notion were a second anonymous note handed to the Political Director at the Quai, René Massigli, that very day. Gamelin's explanation was that the matter was of such urgency that the text of the note was not submitted to him before being delivered to the Ministry.[23] How so intelligent a man could have expected this tale to be taken at face value, one does not know. Suffice it to say that nothing of such magnitude was drawn up and sent in the name of the Army without this most sensitive of politically aware soldiers passing upon it. The flight from responsibility was so flagrant that the document in question, now printed (and with a deadpan editorial note saying that its origin and destination remain obscure),[24] must dispel any lingering mystery at once. Moreover, Gamelin's unworthy insinuation that his predecessor (and, of course, in 1940, successor) General Weygand's notorious hostility to the treaty may have been at the origin of the note is a non sequitur. Beyond these few scraps, the volume contains no further direct indication of the attitudes prevailing at the Ministry of War. Gamelin himself has told of the failure of this "mysterious" initiative to bring about deferment of ratification, and of Maurin's categoric statement to the Council of Ministers that, short of general call-up and industrial mobilization, France must limit herself to a defensive stance. The silence of this volume appears to confirm that account and, like the general's own memoirs, to give the lie to his incredible protestation, "I therefore had every reason to think that the Government was moving toward a vigorous conclusion." [25]

And what of the Quai in all this? So far as can be told from these papers, the Political Director and, presumably, the Secretary General, Alexis Léger, and his staff were all quite clear that everything depended upon concerting measures beforehand with the Baldwin government.[26] They were similarly cautious about making any move which might precipitate Nazi action (everyone was perfectly aware of *existing* violations by the Germans in the *Landespolizei* matter), unless it was absolutely certain what support London and Brussels would offer and what policy would be adopted in the event of unilateral denunciation of demilitarization by Berlin.[27] Unless attacked, France could not "think" of operations against Germany without prior assurance that such action would be "understood" in London at least.[28] Officialdom believed that economic sanctions could have serious consequences for the German economy and the Nazi regime,[29] but there is nothing here to show that, beyond issuing a general warning to all that France would not accept unilateral repudiation of the treaties, it had any clear policy. Massigli complained about the lack of precision in General Maurin's statement of what the Army proposed, pointing out that he gave no indication of how it proposed "to intimidate the enemy or to make him retreat." [30] But if the Ministry of Foreign Affairs had any concrete suggestions, they have not been recorded in this volume at least.

In all, then, the Army chose to see the affair as involving a necessary prior political accord with Great Britain and, should the government be so rash as to decide upon action in the field, mobilization of men and resources. The Quai saw it as necessitating a prior agreement by London to French military measures, which, it became clear, the Ministry of War would not spell out beyond insisting (one may read "threatening") that they would be dependent upon a general call-up and large new credits. On the eve almost of parliamentary elections—coming in April and May—such credits were obviously not to be had. Small wonder, therefore, that the Council of Ministers decided, February 27, that France would not act alone but rather concert her action with that of the other Locarno powers and assume a defensive attitude. The British and Belgian foreign ministers were so informed.[31] Without seriously considering what the strength might be of the German forces that would have to be met in the case of "flagrant violation," everyone appears to have accepted the Army's tacit assumption that any action would probably mean war and that, as of that moment, the French military establishment was in no position to entertain it.

If the Army's attitude turns out to have been far more disheartening than heretofore realized, what of the friends and neighbors of France? In a word, these papers do nothing to refurbish the reputation of the Baldwin government in international affairs. Largely preoccupied with the frightful sanctions imbroglio at Geneva, and considerably at odds with France over that unhappy episode of hypocrisy, cant, and vacillation, the Foreign Office that winter of 1935–1936 seems to have been covered by a thick fog which even a French Ambassador's dispatches (and how few there are here!) could not dispel. There is an indication here of British concern about Hitler's intentions,[32] but no document (the editors say that none could be found) on any discussion between Flandin and the Foreign Secretary, Anthony Eden, on the occasion of George V's funeral. Thus, apart from Flandin's brief account, we still have only Lord Avon's recollection that they agreed that Mussolini's fortunes were deteriorating—not too helpful a conclusion so far as an impending Rhineland crisis was concerned—and that "it seemed improbable" that Hitler would act precipitately. Avon claims to have got the impression that Flandin was merely sounding out British attitudes and preaching the virtues of consultation ("hardly the attitude or language of a man determined to fight for the Rhineland") and did not expect ratification of the Franco-Soviet Treaty to cause "any undue stir." He rightly sized up the French stance as one of refusal to re-negotiate the Rhineland situation and reluctance to fight for its continued demilitarization. Eden's follow-up instructions to Ambassador Sir George Clerk in Paris were ice-cold: France and Belgium must first decide "what value" the zone had for them and "what price" they would pay to keep it; should Flandin return to the subject—the exact words were "in the event of M. Flandin returning to the subject," which somehow communicate nicely the now scarcely credible frivolity of it all beneath the frozen formalities of tradition—he must be told "that, in the first instance, we expect to be told the views and intentions of his own Government, and you should not give him any encouragement to hope that His Majesty's Government would be prepared to discuss the matter on the basis of the British attitude." The Earl of Avon's subsequent explanation was that he was trying to avoid a situation where Flandin might be tempted to blame inaction on others. Though doubtless true, the interpretation is not wholly convincing. Eden's own conclusion was that Great Britain and France should negotiate away their rights in the zone, "on condition," and "while such surrender still has a bargaining value." [33] He must have known that his refusal to discuss common action before France revealed her intentions explicitly was all the Sarraut government needed to extinguish any flickering will to fight if need be for the retention of the treaties and the zone. His attitude was commentary enough on the relations prevailing in the Entente; his language to Clerk was eminently suitable for communication to a wayward chief of some Hottentot tribe.

It would be satisfying to have the French view of all this, but the volume is almost silent. Yet if Avon's account is substantially accurate, Ambassador Charles Corbin's report of a talk Eden had with Foreign Minister Maxim Litvinov at about the same time must be reliable also: Great Britain, Eden said, would not be able to take effective military action for "quite a few years"—the original is *plusieurs,* and thus something more than "several." [34] Very cool toward the Franco-Soviet Treaty, London shrouded itself in silence and Corbin (so often accused of anglophilia) suggested flatly that the British wanted to see France take responsibility for ratification, so that in the event of Hitler causing trouble they would be covered in evading their legal obligations. In Great Britain, he reported in mid-February, the Rhineland zone had "a completely secondary role" and did not constitute "a major interest." [35] Thus was the essential rift in the Entente perceived well before the event. But the game of blindman's buff went on until Hitler struck. When the British military attaché in Paris asked Gamelin's principal aide, Commandant Petitbon, point blank, "What do you expect to do alone, or together with us, if the Germans reoccupy the left bank of the Rhine?", he was smoothly invited to drop by some day for a chat with the Army staff or with the General's entourage.[36] And when the staff drew up a paper (February 18) on possible Franco-British co-operation in that horrid contingency, Gamelin's deputy, General Georges, wrote on it, "political matter," and "Fully agree, but everything depends on England's willingness to bind herself to France. . . . Will 1914's example be of profit? Is English opinion ready? . . ."[37] The question so directly put by the attaché was embarrassing, and to judge by the minutes Admiral Abrial took of the chiefs of staff meeting, February 19, no one had anything but the sketchiest idea of what to reply.[38] (It is of interest that here, as elsewhere, the editors have had to resort to naval minutes for such meetings, the Army archives yielding nothing, though whether through the depredations of interested parties or the misfortunes of war one does not know.)

So Anthony Eden never got the answer to his question, nor Flandin to his, nor the military attaché to his, nor Georges and the chiefs of staff to theirs. And the days ran out. Reports poured in: the German generals were hostile to any overt action; the blow was impending; now Hitler was hesitating; now Great Britain was at last getting worried. . . . At Geneva, on March 3, Eden was informed by Flandin that France would not take any action alone, and thus the fundamental independence of French policy was surrendered once and, as it turned out, for all. Flandin's account of this talk to Corbin is short and plain. Annexed to it is an interesting *aide-mémoire,* interesting because Lord Avon recalled that "On March 3rd Flandin presented me with a document asking the British Government for an undertaking that they would fulfil their engagements under the Locarno Treaty, if necessary alone." The implication is perhaps deliberate; it is certainly far more startling than the language of the French document will support, and the implied allegation now falls away.[39] Even skillful memorialists do things which they must know the fuller record will one day refute.

Suddenly on March 6 the telegrams were flying, and on the morning of the 7th the deed was done. Across the more than two months covered here, through the four hundred pages of documents, the great majority of which bear on the Rhineland question, the major conclusions are clear: Great Britain had indeed ruled out any intention of stopping or helping to stop Hitler from another assault upon the Treaty of Versailles and the destruction of Locarno; bewildered France, taunted to declare her intentions of acting alone (or with Belgium), chose subordination to the government in London which apparently was concerned more to rescue the dregs of British prestige from the Ethiopian catastrophe and to slap (but not too hard) Mussolini's wrists than to

risk adventure in order to maintain a national indignity imposed at
gunpoint and reaffirmed voluntarily and publicly, but with the *arrière-
pensées* which all but the willfully blind had discerned for years.

As London and Paris foresaw taking no action, so, when the event
came upon them earlier than had been reckoned, they took none. If
François-Poncet proposed "energetic reaction," [40] Eden's first counsel to
Corbin that Saturday morning was "that no action irremediably compromising the future be undertaken before the governments concerned
and particularly those of France and Great Britain have been able to
consult." [41] Considering Flandin's words just four days earlier and their
own determination to do nothing, what could the Baldwin Cabinet have
possibly feared? An outburst in either France or Great Britain? There
is no knowing. But even this firm advice from the Foreign Secretary
will not suffice to buttress the interpretation that Great Britain held
France back. The known record of weakness and indecision in Paris
that day [42] and thereafter is not demonstrably altered by these papers.
Here are the formal protests,[43] the complaints that Great Britain did
not understand the full gravity of the situation, the refusal to discuss
Hitler's peaceful proposals in return for abandoning the principle of
the zone, [44] the appeal to the League,[45] the really shameless stalling of
Eden,[46] and the French chiefs of staff agreeing that entry into the zone
would mean war and thus general mobilization and that neither England
nor Italy (and what unlikely allies *they* were!) could give anything but
moral support at best.[47]

Again, the military men cut a worse figure than their memoirs have
informed us. On the lamentably confused Council of Ministers proceedings [48] there is no fresh light here. Of intransigence at the Quai ("Our
allies," Léger evidently told Gamelin, "would be obliged to follow
us." [49]) there is scarcely a trace. From Cologne Jean Dobler urged some
strong riposte and held out the hope of a resulting collapse of the Hitler
regime [50]—but, after all, who read the telegrams from Cologne? From
Berlin the Ambassador lashed out at "the clergymen, the old ladies, the
pacifist organizations, the intellectuals, and the socialist electors across
the Channel" with "their latent germanophilia, their desire to recover
the sheep strayed from the fold" who had played Hitler's game, while
"it is France alone who would be left to foot the bill." [51] So the hours
went by, and Hitler's nervousness and jitters ("What saved us," he
boasted years after, "was my unshakable obstinacy and my amazing
aplomb"), the tension von Blomberg and his officers felt, were needless
and soon over.[52] The meeting in Paris of the Locarno powers, March 10,
was useless, despite Flandin's effort to put a good face on things,[53] and
his instructions to prepare some project for the possible seizure of some
German *prise de gage, "without firing a shot,"* [54] make as stupefying
reading now as they must have made maddening reading to the soldiers

and sailors then. Indeed, Vice-Admiral Durand-Viel's letter on the subject of this request to Vice-Admiral Robert is contemptuous of the
civilians and quite despairing: "It goes without saying that the whole
thing means taking risks; thus it would be well to weigh everything
and to put forward nothing, so far as we are concerned, without fully
thinking it through." [55] As for the Army, its waffling reply (vastly over-
rating the German strength moved into the zone) has been known
through Gamelin's memoirs. But it is interesting to see now that he
omitted a crucial line from the document which stipulated that the
measures he envisaged should be taken "by the entire body of powers
represented at Geneva." [56] Impossible condition for an improbable action
in which, four days after the coup, no one really had any belief. Intelligent, civilized, and circumspect to a degree, the chief of staff thought of
everything. One wonders if Mars ever had a more reluctant disciple.

The implication of this impasse seemed clear at the Quai. "The question now confronting us," Massigli noted for Flandin, March 12, "is
whether or not Europe will become German." [57] But there is no trace
here of the firm words the Foreign Minister evidently delivered in
London those next few days,[58] only Corbin's or Massigli's attempts to
put the best possible interpretation upon the British stand revealed in
the Locarno meetings and in the House.[59] One sees so clearly that the
ball—there was certainly no torch—had been passed to the British.
Whatever warnings Flandin gave his allies, obviously he took no consistently firm line. The documents here are grey, the veriest reflection
of a purpose abandoned. One of the most compelling is the superb note
drawn up for or by Gamelin, March 28, on the possibility of sending
French troops into the Rhineland.[60] Every eventuality is covered in a
careful manner and the conclusion is, in effect, "For Heaven's sake, don't
even think of it!" All in all, not much is left of Gamelin's watchword of
March 10: "At all costs, people must not be able to say that the Army
didn't dare to march." [61] It revealed everything, the revealer included,
and these papers confirm the revelation.

About British policy there has been no mystery. It has been made
much clearer because of the greater British willingness to permit private
papers and biographies to be published. By comparison there is nothing
on the French side to set aside the ingenuous directness of, say, Neville
Chamberlain's thoughts. Thus his diary, four days after the German
coup: "Everyone agreed that we could not contemplate war, but we
must make every effort to avoid repudiation of Locarno." [62] Or his talk
with Flandin next day, "emphasizing that public opinion here would
not support us in sanctions of any kind. His view is that, if a firm
front is maintained by France and England, Germany will yield without war. We cannot accept that as a reliable estimate of a mad dictator's
action." [63] Or this on March 28: ". . . and I can't help hoping that

Ribbentrop will have warned Hitler that if he persists in refusing to make any contribution, he may lose the sympathy of England, and find that he has driven us into an alliance with Belgium and France." [64] Such were the most horrible possibilities of it all as seen from London— though not quite: at a slightly less official level was Violet Markham's cry of alarm, March 22: "I am simply in despair about the European situation. Germany was, of course (as always), utterly wrong in method though right in fact. But she has flung us into the arms of France in a deplorable way; you have seen how the French are exulting over the military guarantee which England has now entered. Flandin triumphed all along the line in London. . . ." [65] This spectacularly deformed estimate must have seemed a bit much even in London where, as Tom Jones noted a few days later, the Prime Minister "was tired but not rattled," and the country was considered "pro-English, rather fed up with France than actively pro-German, but more pro-German than the Cabinet." [66]

Could the French or any other documents shed new light on this situation? Probably not, and perhaps that is why the editors here did not try. Or did Charles Corbin not reveal the awful truth? Or, more mercifully, did he not know it? At all events, it is not to be seen in this volume. It is merely implicit all the way through.

What of the other powers in this affair? In general, there is not much fresh information. Italy, as a major guarantor of Locarno, is shown to be almost wholly preoccupied with the outcome of the Ethiopian war,[67] but willing to consider reconstitution of the Stresa front of 1935, provided that sanctions were dropped.[68] Mussolini's bombast that winter was muted, though his threats of blackmail were blatant and incessant.[69] Even serious statesmen were reported as believing that his fall was in the offing (January 1936), so poorly was the campaign going,[70] and Pius XI advised him to accept offers to regulate the matter peacefully.[71] It was a godsend, therefore, to have March 7 shift attention dramatically away from his difficulties. "Mussolini has been lucky," the Pope remarked to François Charles-Roux some days later, "very lucky." [72]

On the famous meeting of the Duce and Pierre Laval in Rome, January 1935, there is no evidence here, naturally enough, but there is a personal letter to Mussolini, dated January 23, 1936 (i.e., as Laval abandoned office), in which the Frenchman recalled all he had done to bring about good relations between them, from renunciation of certain French interests in East Africa to proposal of the ill-fated Hoare-Laval Plan. Was it mostly for the record that he insisted that if he had used the term "a free hand" in a loose way during their private talk on January 6, 1935, at the Palazzo Farnese, he had certainly never given approval for war? Here one sees that extreme reluctance to abandon the play already lost, the unwillingness Laval would show all his life thereafter (nine years) to admit that the Rome accords had not represented "the sound and durable basis for Franco-Italian friendship and at the same time an essential factor of European peace." [73] But then, in January 1936, Laval was finished. His successors had to evaluate the combination of threats and appeals which wrapped the enigma of Italy's position in Europe. "I can assure you that today there is absolutely nothing of a political nature between Germany and me," the Duce remarked to the French Ambassador on February 27. ". . . France and England would be wise not to reject me." [74] He was still opposed to the idea of *Anschluss*,[75] insisted upon his coming victory in Africa, and on March 27 he predicted (quoting Hitler as saying two years before at Venice that German youth would never be sent to slaughter against the Maginot Line) that the March 7 stroke meant Germany would build fortifications there and "your two countries will remain shut up opposite each other, each within frontiers equally impenetrable." The prediction was not less Machiavellian for being accurate. And in noting too that such a German fortification would render the operation of the French alliance system a difficult proposition, Mussolini put his finger on the critical wound to France and to the whole of Europe.[76]

Thus Great Britain was opposed to any action, and Italy, under sanction for transgressions of the public law, was an unlikely defender of treaties outraged. There was no help to be had from any other quarter. The Belgians had (contrary to the common view that their neutralist stance followed upon the events of March 7) made their position clear before the blow fell. They would be *"prudent,"* as the Foreign Minister, Emile Vandervelde, was reported to say, leaving it up to France and Great Britain.[77] Protestations by Prime Minister Paul van Zeeland to the contrary,[78] Belgium was moving toward a policy of neutrality. If her sentiments were correct on and after March 7, her attitude was closer to London's than to that of Paris. The pacifist, anti-French currents among the Flemings [79] were prodromes of the diplomatic and military withdrawal to come. The comfort offered by Brussels was perfunctory. In Prague the reaction to Hitler's move was much firmer. Aligning himself with Paris rather than London, President Beneš believed that strong economic and financial sanctions would compel Hitler to withdraw if not bring about his downfall. Here we see him vainly urging France to take this course of action.[80] Instead, both he and his French allies stood watching the disintegration of the Little Entente. If Yugoslavia remained formally linked to France and her eastern friends, the German commercial pressure, Belgrade's desire to restore better relations with Italy, and suspicions of Austrian intentions troubled the mood of Paris and Prague.[81]

As for Poland, the documents underline again the unhappy relationship existing between her and France. Ambassador Léon Noël's view of

Colonel Beck remained consistently hostile. For him the Foreign Minister was unreliable, subject to German flattery, wholly unscrupulous, and increasingly prepared to gamble on a deal with the Third Reich despite the wishes of Army and nation for rapprochement with France.[82] On March 7 Beck expressed himself correctly toward his French ally, insisting that good relations with Germany did not affect general policy. But Noël's suspicions of Beck's opportunism should France not succeed in forcing Hitler to back down were quickly realized.[83] Doubtless Noël was swift to take offense, too readily inclined to mark Beck down as an amoral cynic, and too little sympathetic to the peculiar plight of the Polish Republic, but it was a fact (as René Massigli suggested from the Locarno meeting in London) that the Poles were bound to assume a strong position *vis-à-vis* Germany only if France gave a vigorous lead. And as the days passed, the miserable reaction of French civilians and military was not lost upon the Polish soldiers or their government. Confronted by Beck's request that France and Poland put their relations on a formal footing of the "pre-war alliance" type, the French waffled hopelessly. Noël might point to the divisions in Warsaw caused by the Colonel's opportunism, but there could be only one conclusion for all Poles: France could or would be able to do little for their country.[84]

From the Soviet Union little was hoped for, nothing expected or desired. That January the Chairman of the Council of People's Commissars, Vyascheslav Molotov, had sounded the note of polite good relations with France but insisted upon the Soviet determination to depend on Russian strength alone. The opposition to Foreign Minister Litvinov's line was evident, and Litvinov's references to those espousing another policy were frank.[85] Like the Poles, the Soviets watched their reluctant, newly refound French allies with critical eyes, swallowed their pride over the much delayed ratification of the May 1935 Treaty, and drew the inevitable conclusions after March 7. In a sense, everything which would be revealed over the next three and a half years is here in embryo, even the Russo-German trade talks and the tentative betterment of relations between Moscow and Tokyo.[86] There would be many shiftings, of course, and it would be wrong to propose that this isolated volume reveals a grand fatality of events. But with the wisdom of hindsight one discerns portents of grave developments to come.

In short, these papers demonstrate again how crucial was this turning point of March 7, how it really was a moment of high decision, and how infinitely much harder it would be for France (and for them all) to recover the ground already lost should she fail to make a stand then and there.

Other matters are covered. Many documents bear upon the Italo-Ethiopian war, reflecting the dark view of Mussolini's position held by Hitler and his generals that winter,[87] the Vatican's hopes for a negotiated settlement,[88] the dogged British hostility to the enterprise,[89] and the endless debate upon, the fears expressed about, and the Italian threats made concerning sanctions.[90] It all adds up to reconfirmation of the embarrassment which the halfhearted, unpopular effort to apply the Covenant long after it had ceased to have any reality caused almost everyone associated with the League. Sarraut's government tried to tread the narrow way between obligations to Geneva and the policy of a revived Stresa front. Flandin's attitude was both correct and incapable of producing results.[91] For Mussolini there could be no retreat.

French views of both American and Japanese policies during these months are of interest, a useful commentary on familiar events. If Laval was hopeful that the neutrality legislation implied less than the letter of the law suggested, Ambassador de Laboulaye quickly disabused him. After the March coup, he assured Flandin that, whatever the feelings of Cordell Hull, American opinion was thankful to have been put beyond these fresh European difficulties.[92] Eleanor Roosevelt's column in the Scripps-Howard press, insisting on the unjustness of Versailles, on the need for treaty revision, and on the unwisdom of negotiating after the coup did not go unnoticed either.[93] The correspondence with Tokyo suggests again the fears of a German-Japanese pact,[94] the unsettled nature of the Japanese domestic scene (government by assassination),[95] and the concern of the Emperor's ministers lest the Franco-Soviet Treaty create additional worries for them by reassuring the Russian position in the West.[96]

Still in 1936 that incongruous subject of the limitation of armaments is mirrored in the resumption of naval talks. Having demanded parity, the Japanese left the discussions after a few days. The French government, opposed to any general naval accord with the Third Reich at that time, became more anxious for an agreement à quatre, so that Germany would eventually find herself bound by these same undertakings whenever the time should come to include her. In fact, however, there was no four-power pact: Italy abstained and the signatures on March 25 were those only of Great Britain, France, the United States, and some Dominions. François-Poncet's remark about the notorious June 1935 Anglo-German naval agreement ("Sooner or later it will have the same fate as the Locarno pact. How it is that the English do not see this?") applied to this negotiation and to them all.[97]

Diplomatic documents, however unsensational their major revelations may be, always offer minor sidelights to sustain the reader's interest. One such here is Pius XI's conversation with François Charles-Roux, March 16, when the Holy Father declared flatly, "If you had at once moved 20,000 men into the zone re-occupied by the Germans, you would have done the world an immense service." And to the Ambassador's unctuous rejoinder that this had not been done out of France's attachment to peace, the Pope replied (with at least the possibility of irony, which this humorless report to Paris did not detect), "Yes, and that's commendable on your part. Moreover, you doubtless reckoned that you would not be followed by the English, and still less by the Italians. But I say again, had you done that, you would have rendered everyone a very great service. There now, isn't that an unexpected opinion coming from a man Maurras calls germanophile!" [98] Another small and hardly unrelated *aperçu* into the Papacy, which must now seem like a foreshadowing of more terrible days and dilemmas to come, was the conversation the Ambassador had some days earlier with Cardinal Pacelli and his secretary. Charles-Roux was so bold as to inform them that it was the Vatican's duty to insist upon the principles of, and respect for, international law. "Both of them pointed out to me that the relations of the Holy See with the German Government were so bad that the least pretext would be enough to unleash the worst persecutions of Catholics in the Reich." [99] Pius XI, of course, had still to launch *Mit brennender Sorge,* but the views of the Cardinal Secretary of State appear, in the light of this conversation, to have had a character before the election of 1939 consistent with those of the Pope thereafter.

The scope of this collection is ample and admirable. One might look for more material bearing upon Spain, for instance, and yet what the four documents printed show is that no one in Madrid was especially upset and worried in these winter months. As Ambassador Herbette reported on February 21, the dispatch of General Franco to the Canaries and of General Goded to the Balearics had exiled "the two generals whose attitude had in recent days occasioned certain anxieties." [100] What is missing from the record, however, and what one hoped to see, is more of the internal memoranda of the Quai. Owing to the cooperation of René Massigli, who provided some papers, this sort of thing is not wholly absent. But the editors say plainly that they obtained little cooperation from private individuals. There is virtually nothing here from or about Alexis Léger, a very great gap in the record, if it is not indeed an irreparable loss. The editors also say that the losses of documents, owing to the destruction ordered by Léger and/or Paul Reynaud (Reynaud, it may be recalled, once indicted Léger alone for this [101]), to enemy action, and to fire during the liberation of Paris, are particularly serious for the years 1930–1939 and in the area of Foreign Ministry materials which naturally cannot be reproduced from the French Embassy archives in various capitals. Unless or until more personal documents are made available by individuals from their personal holdings, the guessing game about who made French policy will have to go on.

The best documented personality here is François-Poncet. He is the star of the volume. But even the large quantity of his communications printed here represents a mere fragment of the total outpouring from

Berlin. The Ambassador went on record years ago with his complaint that no one paid much attention to his views. Count Ciano noted at the time that François-Poncet thought Léger a "sinister man." [102] But whatever the truth about the charges of ignorance and isolation laid against the officials at the Quai, the sheer bulk of François-Poncet's reportage must almost have stunned them—let alone foreign ministers who might read as they ran. A mere three-month period cannot reveal the whole man, but the Ambassador perceived in this volume was no appeaser.[103] His predictions changed, he hedged, he defended himself, but his gaze into the gangland around him was largely unblinking. In January 1936 he considered that war must come in two years.[104] In these lengthy reports (analyses of the press, of the Reich's personalities, of the public mood—journalism of a frank character, one might say, rather shapeless but by no means dull) he showed himself a Hitlerologist of the first order. In the March crisis he was an accurate observer of the Führer's forty-eight hour uncertainty. A diplomatic prima donna he may well have been, but the French documents alone will assure him of a place in the history of those times. If he was capable of such a lapse as imagining that Hitler was secretly counseled by men such as Lord Lothian,[105] the provocations suffered from Englishmen were after all enough to make the mind wander. And though the source might not be the purest, he enjoyed the highest reputation with General Göring, who remarked at lunch in Warsaw one day when someone mentioned François-Poncet, "France has diplomats; Germany doesn't have any." [106]

Present in these pages and yet somehow missing is Charles Corbin. Colorless and unrevealing in the main, his dispatches are few in number. The discrepancy between the reporting from London and the avalanche of papers from Berlin is astonishing. Corbin's telegrams have been the more eagerly awaited because the man died without revealing anything at all. Posthumous publications there may be, but this record is slight, dry, not very helpful really. One would gratefully have exchanged not a few of Berlin's outpourings for some accounts of what went on in London. Unfortunately the reader is likely to surmise that the Republic's Ambassador to the Court of St. James lived a secluded life, shut off from society, from the press, and from almost everything else but a torpid official round.

In conclusion, one must grant that the French documents are off to a good start. Not startling, sometimes disappointing, but substantial in scale, balanced in proportion (if one accepts the primacy of March 7 and the German problem), and, as usual with French diplomatic papers, edited with an excellent—though not infallible—analytical table of contents. The editors have been excessively sparing with their gloss (for instance, they could, and certainly ought to, identify the mysterious military note on February 25, 1936, more closely than they have). But on the whole, the volume is most excellent. It is a pity that the Fifth Republic did not provide more fitting paper and binding, even if the memory now of the Third Republic is not held in the highest esteem. But all who are interested in the years between the wars will be profoundly grateful to Pierre Renouvin and his committee and their researchers, as to those who have worked to reconstitute the fragmented archives of the Quai d'Orsay. They will await the rest of the great collection with the best patience they can muster.

NOTES

1. A. J. P. Taylor, *The Origins of the Second World War* (London, 1961), pp. 100–101.

2. Jacques Chastenet, *Histoire de la Troisième République*, 7 vols. (Paris, 1952–63), VI, *Déclin de la Troisième 1931–1938*, 137.

3. H. Stuart Hughes, *Contemporary Europe: A History* (Englewood Cliffs, N.J., 1961), p. 282.

4. George F. Kennan, *Russia and the West Under Lenin and Stalin* (Boston, 1961), p. 286. Lest there be any suspicion, the view represents no special anti-British bias. Cf. the similarly summary position of the English historian Anthony Wood: "Flandin, the French Foreign Minister, was determined on resistance, but the British Government, more concerned over the Abyssinian war at this time, held him back from presenting an ultimatum and insisted that the question should be settled at a diplomatic level" (*Europe 1815–1945* [London, 1964], p. 426).

5. *Nazi Conspiracy and Aggression*, 8 vols. (Washington, 1946), VI, 951–952. See C. Waldron Bolen, "Hitler Remilitarizes the Rhineland," *Power, Public Opinion, and Diplomacy: Essays in Honor of Eber Malcolm Carroll by His Former Students*, Lillian Parker Wallace and William C. Askew, eds. (Durham, N.C., 1959), p. 246.

6. Général Maurice Gamelin, *Servir*, 3 vols. (Paris, 1946–47), II, *Le Prologue du Drame (1930–Août 1939)*, 194, 195; André François-Poncet, *Souvenirs d'une Ambassade à Berlin, Septembre 1931–Octobre 1938* (Paris, 1946), pp. 236–251.

7. *Documents*, No. 1 (hereafter, unless otherwise indicated, all references are to documents in the volume by number).

8. Nos. 17, 21, 24.

9. E.g., Nos. 27, 36, 63, 75, 77, 82, 91, 92.

10. E.g., Nos. 95, 96, 122, 126, 144.

11. E.g., Nos. 147, 175, 188, 189, 213.

12. *Nazi Conspiracy and Aggression*, VI, 974–976.

13. Nos. 265, 272.

14. Nos. 286, 287, 289, 294.

15. Nos. 11, 18.

16. Nos. 62, 82, 83.

17. See Gamelin, *Servir*, II, 197–198.

18. No. 166.

19. No. 170.

20. No. 186.

21. No. 196; cf. Gamelin, *Servir*, II, 197.

22. No. 203.

23. Gamelin, *Servir*, II, 198.

24. No. 227.

25. Gamelin, *Servir*, II, 199–200.

26. E.g., Nos. 53, 78.

27. Nos. 105, 125.

28. No. 143.

29. No. 169.

30. No. 241.

31. Nos. 243, 283; cf. Gamelin, *Servir*, II, 199.

32. No. 29.

33. The Rt. Hon. The Earl of Avon, K.G., P.C., M.C., *The Eden Memoirs* (London, 1962–65), I, *Facing the Dictators*, 325, 332–335. Cf. Pierre-Etienne Flandin, *Politique Française 1919–1940* (Paris, 1947), pp. 194–195. See also the allusion to the talks in No. 184, *Annexe*.

34. No. 112.

35. Nos. 163, 165, 184.

36. No. 187.

37. No. 202.

38. No. 203. See Flandin, *Politique,* pp. 195–197.

39. No. 283; Avon, *Eden Memoirs,* I, 329; Flandin, *Politique,* p. 197.

40. No. 299.

41. No. 301. Cf. Avon, *Eden Memoirs,* I, 341.

42. See Gamelin, *Servir,* II, 200–202; Joseph Paul-Boncour, *Entre deux Guerres: Souvenirs sur la Troisième République,* 3 vols. (Paris, 1946), III, *Sur les Chemins de la Défaite, 1935–1940,* 32–38; Flandin, *Politique,* pp. 197–200.

43. No. 310.

44. No. 317.

45. No. 321.

46. No. 322. Cf. Avon, *Eden Memoirs* I, 341–347.

47. No. 334. Cf. Gamelin, *Servir,* II, 202–203.

48. Flandin, *Politique,* pp. 198–200; Paul-Boncour, *Entre deux Guerres,* III, 33–36; Gamelin, *Servir,* II, 203; Jean Zay, *Souvenirs et solitudes* (Paris, 1945), pp. 65–67; Pierre Lazareff, *Deadline: The Behind the Scenes Story of the Lost Decade in France* (New York, 1942), pp. 117–119; Paul Reynaud, *In the Thick of the Fight 1930–1945* (London, 1955), pp. 126–132.

49. Gamelin, *Servir,* II, 202. Cf. No. 391. Léger supposedly threatened resignation if Flandin did not take a firm line. Géneviève Tabouis, *They Called Me Cassandra* (New York, 1942), p. 274.

50. No. 333.

51. No. 350.

52. *Hitler's Table Talk 1941–1944* (London, 1953), pp. 258–259; William L. Shirer, *Berlin Diary: The Journal of a Foreign Correspondent 1934–1941* (New York, 1943), pp. 39–47; John W. Wheeler-Bennett, *Nemesis of Power: The German Army in Politics 1918–1945* (London, 1954), pp. 350–353; Raymond Cartier, *Hitler et ses Généraux* (Paris, 1962), pp. 56–60.

53. No. 380. Cf. Avon, *Eden Memoirs,* I, 347–354.

54. No. 390.

55. No. 391.

56. No. 392. Cf. Gamelin, *Servir,* II, 204–211. This sentence was also omitted when the document was printed by the committee established in 1947 by the National Assembly to investigate responsibilities for events in France during the Hitler era. France, Commission d'Enquête Parlementaire, *Rapport fait au nom de la commission chargée d'enquêter sur les événements survenus en France de 1933 à 1945 par M. Charles Serre,* I, *Les Evénements du 7 Mars 1936* (Paris, n.d.), 51–52. Did the committee take this document from Gamelin's memoirs? The fact that the text reproduced in *Documents* came from the Navy archives suggests that this was

so, that the Army archives contain no text, and that the General (or his staff) altered the text in his possession.

57. No. 407.

58. See Flandin, *Politique*, pp. 205–209; Winston S. Churchill, *The Second World War*, 6 vols. (New York & London, 1948–54), I, *The Gathering Storm*, 195–198 (U.S.), 153–155 (Br.); Avon, *Eden Memoirs*, I, 355–360.

59. E.g., Nos. 410, 414, 454, 496, 516, 529.

60. No. 525. Also in the Serre *Rapport*, I, 53–56.

61. Gamelin, *Servir*, II, 203–204.

62. Iain Macleod, *Neville Chamberlain* (London, 1961), pp. 189–190.

63. *Ibid.*, p. 190, and Keith Feiling, *The Life of Neville Chamberlain* (London, 1946), p. 279.

64. Feiling, *Life*, p. 280.

65. To Thomas Jones, in Jones, *A Diary with Letters 1931–1950* (London, 1950), p. 183.

66. Jones to Lady Grigg, April 4, 1936, *ibid.*, p. 185.

67. E.g., No. 378.

68. Nos. 524, 526.

69. E.g., No. 145 and *Annexe*.

70. No. 38.

71. No. 278.

72. No. 447.

73. No. 99.

74. No. 239.

75. No. 248.

76. No. 518.

77. Nos. 123, 136, 137, 146, 167.

78. No. 282.

79. Nos. 330, 361, 381, 462, 468.

80. Nos. 343, 344, 373, 385, 402, 424, 476, 482.

81. E.g., Nos. 20, 42, 52, 60, 100, 140, 156, 164, 360, 377, 422, 476, 510.

82. Nos. 128, 179. All this kind of thing is to be found in Léon Noël, *L'Agression allemande contre la Pologne: Une Ambassade à Varsovie 1935–1939* (Paris, 1946), *passim*.

83. Nos. 303, 325, 327, 331, 408, 488.

84. Nos. 445, 455, 487, 497, 506.

85. Nos. 43, 46, 156, 366.

86. Nos. 8, 41, 364, 426, 451, 470.

87. Nos. 1, 21.

88. E.g., Nos. 35, 114, 278, 447.

89. E.g., No. 165.

90. See the *table méthodique* here, pp. xlviii–l.

91. No. 259.

92. Nos. 13, 26, 158, 161, 463.

93. No. 464.

94. E.g., Nos. 62, 80, 532.

95. Nos. 230, 244.

96. Nos. 285, 356, 374, 427, 528.

97. No. 435. On the naval question see the *table méthodique*, pp. lxx–lxxi.

98. No. 447.

99. No. 342.

100. No. 210.

101. In *La France a sauvé l'Europe* (Paris, 1947), II, 131; withdrawn in his *Au*

Coeur de la mêlée 1930–1945 (Paris, 1951). It is asserted in Paul Baudouin, *The Private Diaries (March 1940 to January 1941)* (London, 1948), p. 31, and denied in Pertinax, *The Gravediggers of France* (Garden City, N.Y., 1944), p. 238. Elizabeth Cameron, after talks with Léger, revealed no conclusion about this: "Alexis Saint-Léger Léger," in Gordon A. Craig and Felix Gilbert, eds., *The Diplomats 1919–1939* (Princeton, 1953), p. 402, fn. 76.

102. François-Poncet, *Souvenirs,* pp. 12–13; see his testimony in *Les Evénements survenus en France de 1933 à 1945: Témoignages et documents recueillis par la Commission d'Enquête parlementaire* (Paris, n.d.), 11 vols., III, 767, and that of Jean Dobler, *ibid.,* II, 499–506. The Ciano interview was on May 27, 1940. *The Ciano Diaries 1939–1948* (Garden City, N.Y., 1946), p. 255.

103. Already, then, Franklin L. Ford's essay, "Three Observers in Berlin: Rumbold, Dodd, and François-Poncet," in *The Diplomats,* pp. 460–476, needs modification.

104. No. 62.

105. Nos. 436, 438.

106. No. 212.

DAVID VITAL

Czechoslovakia and the Powers, September 1938

The most written-about event of pre–World War II diplomacy is the Sudeten crisis of 1938. Since the Munich Agreement did not prevent but merely postponed war, historians have often asked: what would have happened had the Great Powers stood firm and resisted Hitler's threats? Would there have been war, and if so what would have been its outcome? In such speculations the central object of the crisis—Czechoslovakia—is often neglected. Yet since she would have had to bear the immediate brunt of German aggression, her readiness and ability to resist are important factors in any assessment of the military situation in September 1938.

Professor Vital is chairman of the Department of Political Studies at Bar-Ilan University in Israel. He has written two books: The Inequality of States: A Study of the Small Powers in International Relations *(Oxford, 1967) and* The Making of British Foreign Policy *(New York, 1968). The following article first appeared in the* Journal of Contemporary History, *1 (October 1966), 37–67. It is republished with the permission of the author and the journal.*

T HE PRESENT article is concerned with two closely related questions: why did the Czechoslovak government accept the terms of the Munich Agreement, and to what extent was the alternative of rejecting the Agreement a feasible course of action?

At the foundation of Czechoslovak foreign policy lay the alliance with France, and the cornerstone of that alliance was Czech military power. Masaryk and Benes may have been, in their way, rather old-fashioned liberals, but they were not pacifists and they were, on the whole, unsentimental in their appreciation of world affairs. During World War I they conceived and formed the Czech Legions to serve two ends: to embody in the most tangible way the still unrecognized nationhood of their country and at the same time, by contributing to the general effort, to lay a claim on the loyalty and recognition of the Allies. After the establishment of the Czechoslovak state, much the same purposes underlay the very great effort put into the armaments industry and into the Army itself. A small nation, they reasoned, surrounded by greater and lesser enemies, needs great friends. Tradition, political philosophy, the Versailles settlement, common interests, and sentiment all dictated that the alliance with France be made as secure as possible. The some two score Czech divisions were conceived as a contribution that no French General Staff could ignore; nor could the Skoda plants at Brno and Pilsen; nor the possibility of all this military wealth falling into the hands of the Germans.[1] Finally, there was Czechoslovakia's geographical situation, the spearhead in Germany's side or, as Hitler put it on another occasion, the "aircraft carrier" in the heart of Europe.

While active French interest in Czech military power tended to evaporate with the general failure of French nerve in the face of resurgent Germany, this last advantage, the geographical one, attracted them to the end. Facilities for French bomber squadrons were maintained in Czechoslovakia, whence Berlin could be bombed at a distance shorter than that between Paris and the German frontier at the nearest point.[2]

There was no question of the Czechs refusing the French the use of these facilities, and there was no question that in the event of war between France and Germany they would enter it. This was axiomatic; it was the price they had to pay for their own security. In 1933 and again in 1936 the Germans offered the Czechs a nonaggression pact. On both occasions Benes stood firm.

On the other hand, if it was the Czechs who were attacked, it was not expected that the French would rush to assist them actively. What was expected was that the French would declare war on Germany. That alone would immobilize a substantial part of the German Army. The Czechs, for their part, would defend themselves against the rest. The main thing was for the Germans to realize that a war with Czechoslovakia implied a general war.

It was a simple, brave theory, easily translated into an even simpler national policy: everything must be subordinated to the interests of the French alliance, which with time acquired a certain sanctity. It was rude to question it. "How dare you say such things of your country, you a

Frenchman?" said an indignant Benes to his good friend Hubert Beuve-Méry in the spring of 1938, when the latter came to warn him that he should not put absolute reliance on France.³ The indignation was sincere. "I know the history of France. She has never failed her word. She will not begin today."

The nub of the matter, however, was that the Czechs founded their belief in the permanence of their alliance with the West on the undoubted fact that both they and the French were beneficiaries of the Versailles settlement. They were among the first to recognize that Hitler was intent on the destruction of Versailles, and Benes and his colleagues made the greatest possible efforts, over a period of years, to convince all who cared to listen that the victor powers and their clients must stick together. Germany was bent on destroying Versailles, and the key to the Versailles arch was Czechoslovakia. It was therefore in the interests of the British and the French to help Czechoslovakia to help itself. By doing so they would enhance their own power. It was a good case, sincerely held. It was persisted in to the end:

> Even if the Czechoslovak Government were resigned to the proposed sacrifices, the question of peace would in no way be settled. . . . To paralyse Czechoslovakia would entail a profound political change for the whole of Central and South-east Europe. The balance of forces in Central Europe and in Europe in general would be upset; and this would not fail to produce important consequences in every other state and particularly also in France. . . . Czechoslovakia has always remained faithful to treaties and has carried out engagements arising from them. . . . She has been and always is ready to honour treaties in all circumstances.⁴

Thus the central argument of the initial Czechoslovak reply to the Anglo-French proposals of September 19, rejecting the demand that the frontiers be redrawn on a basis of self-determination. But by then, unfortunately, the foundation of the case (and of the alliance) had long since collapsed. In 1938 the maintenance of Versailles was no longer the first priority of the French, still less of the British. The two governments were now concerned with one matter above all others: the avoidance of war. And they held to this with great tenacity. In contrast, the central purpose of the Czechoslovak government during the months leading from the Anschluss to the September crisis—and during September itself practically to the end—was to maneuver a return to the *status quo ante*. At the very least they hoped to salvage something of substance from the wreckage. To this end they agreed to a series of very substantial concessions to Western pressure, the efficacy of which was vitiated from the outset by the divergent purposes and outlook of the two sides. These concessions were demanded by the British and French as steps toward the settlement of the Sudeten German problem and, of course, more generally as a means of appeasing *Germany*. The Czechs, on the other hand, saw them exclusively as concessions in the interests of preserving their relationship with the *West*. But in this the West had already lost much of its interest.

Nevertheless, the concessions were of the highest importance as stages by which the Czechs progressed toward a situation in which, once placed, they believed themselves compelled to capitulate. And, indeed, by September 18, when the Anglo-French ministerial conference opened in London and the crisis was unmistakably upon them, they had added up to a great deal.

On July 23, 1938, the Czech government agreed to the arrival of Lord Runciman as "mediator." On September 5 they conceded self-government to the Sudeten Germans. On September 15 Benes made a point of mentioning to the British Minister in Prague, Newton, that at the Paris Peace Conference he, Benes, had personally been in favor of excluding certain German-speaking areas from Czechoslovakia. This was duly reported to London, as it was certainly meant to be. A day later, the Prime Minister, Hodza, hinted to Newton that if some territorial cession was insisted upon it might be possible to surrender the area Benes had had in mind. Lest there be any mistake, the British Military Attaché, Lieutenant Colonel Stronge, was on the following day given to understand that the Army would not object to such a transfer.[5] (All this was taken to concern a fairly substantial area inhabited by from 800,000 to one million people.) Thus by the time Chamberlain had returned from Berchtesgaden and was meeting the French ministers in London on September 18, the assembled ministers and their advisers were aware that step by step, under their own heavy pressure, the Czechs had made two vital concessions. They had accepted the Western Powers as their interlocutors in their conflict with Germany, rather than deal with the Germans themselves. They had accepted, too, that they must offer a territorial sacrifice. These were, of course, the two fundamental elements of the Munich Agreement.

The consequence was that when the ministerial conference opened in London the participants had no reason to contemplate too seriously a Czech refusal of what Hitler and Chamberlain had ostensibly agreed upon at Berchtesgaden, i.e., that the solution of the problem they were formally considering would be based on the principle of self-determination. Nor did they.

Daladier could be even more specific. He told Chamberlain privately, before the formal conference began, that he had received a confidential intimation from Prague that the Czechs would agree to concessions.

"So you see there is nothing we can do." Chamberlain replied, "Prague itself recognizes that." [6]

In the course of the London discussions it was readily conceded that the Czechs would reject the idea of holding a plebiscite in the disputed areas. It would open the floodgates to demands from other neighbors. On the other hand, a straightforward cession of territory was in a different case. "If friendly pressure were brought to bear on Prague, pointing out all the difficulties and stressing the necessity of giving up some portion of Sudeten territory," then, Daladier felt, the Czechoslovak government might agree.[7]

Thus by the time the crisis opened with the presentation to the Czechs of the Anglo-French proposals (to accept the Berchtesgaden formula with all its implications), the Czech position *vis-à-vis* the Western Powers had been thoroughly eroded. And as the crisis developed and as further *démarches,* maneuvers, and concessions followed, it became increasingly difficult to reverse the direction of events.

The Anglo-French proposals of September 19, if implemented, would have meant very nearly as substantial an amputation of Czechoslovak territory, wealth, and military installations as later followed at Munich. So while the Czechs had resigned themselves to ceding territory—limited, they hoped, to a palatable minimum—they now saw that they had miscalculated. Their first reaction was to temporize and to suggest a watering-down, specifically to return to what they themselves had already offered the Sudeten leaders, and, at the same time, to invoke their Treaty of Arbitration with Germany. But the pressure that accompanied the proposals was so intense that in very nearly the same breath the Czechs indicated that this was not their final answer. Meanwhile they debated what to do—almost continuously from the early afternoon of September 19 to the afternoon of September 21. Before them was the uncompromising demand that they give a positive answer without delay. Chamberlain was due back at Godesberg for his second meeting with Hitler on September 22 and "it might be disastrous if he should have to go without any answer from Prague." [8]

The special horror of the trap they had helped to prepare for themselves lay in the fact that there was now no difference, except in tempo, between what the Germans demanded and what the British and the French required. The alliance with the West had been turned inside out and upside down. Instead of easing the German pressure on Czechoslovakia, the British and the French were adding to it. And because of the historical, ideological, and doctrinal aura the alliance bore in Czech eyes, the Western pressure was, if anything, more painful and more effective than the German.

Three courses of action were now open to the Czechoslovak government:

(a) They could defy the Great Powers, rest on their arms, and await developments in the full expectation of war with the Germans.

(b) They could appeal either to the Russians or to the League of Nations or both and meanwhile proceed as in (a).

(c) They could give in to Western pressure and seek to salvage what remained of the traditional foreign policy and orientation.

To encourage the Czechs to adopt the third course, the Western Powers had baited their demand with the offer of guarantees. Thus the British Minister in Prague could argue, quite plausibly, that from the point of view of the future of the country it seemed to him

> that the choice lay between worse than loss of everything acquired in 1918 and on the other hand the retention backed by a British guarantee of nearly everything which they had gained in so far as concerned the unity and independence of the Czechs and Slovaks themselves and the territories in which they were a majority.

This was shrewd and concise. Benes retorted that the guarantee he already possessed had now proven valueless. Yet Newton felt he could report his impression that "President Benes is more likely to accept than to refuse and is very receptive to any reason which will help him justify acceptance to his people."

It is, indeed, characteristic that even at this early stage, namely the initial presentation to Benes of the Anglo-French proposals at 2 P.M. on September 19, Newton already had something more substantial to go on than his "impression" that the President would probably accept them. The same morning (and therefore before the interview with the President) the British Military Attaché had visited the General Staff and had discovered that the substance of the proposals was already known. He was also told that it was not proposed to resist and that "every officer . . . would obey the orders of the Chief of the General Staff." [9] It is almost inconceivable that this conversation should have taken place without authority. Furthermore, in view of the general attitude of the Army to the issue in question, there is every reason to suppose that the authority in question was the political one.

For these reasons it is hard to escape the conclusion that the first two courses were never seriously considered by the political leaders. Subsequent developments tended to bear this out, and in view of Benes' profound influence on events, it is readily understandable.

By 1938 Eduard Benes had been responsible for the foreign relations of his country for nineteen years, as President in the later years no less than as Foreign Minister in the earlier period. He was a most experienced diplomat and a professional statesman of the highest order. Hardworking, intelligent, educated, possessed of a first-hand knowledge of men and events that was almost unrivaled in his time, he was regarded, not without justification, as a consummate negotiator. In this he was strengthened by a gift that Wickham Steed—who knew him well— thought exceptional:

> Especially striking was his ability—an ability he shared with Masaryk —to put himself in the place of any foreign statesman with whom he might have to deal, and to think out his own problems in terms of that statesman's interests or prejudices. Thus he saved many a minister or politician in Allied countries from irksome mental effort.[10]

Such an ability has been an essential part of the equipment of the weak when dealing with the strong in all times; Wickham Steed was probably right in ascribing to it much of Benes' success throughout the years. Yet this kind of sophistication can be dangerous. It can lead to too great a stress being laid on diplomacy and to a tendency to believe that by diplomatic techniques the statesman can do more than bridge minor and marginal gulfs and differences betwen states. There is a tendency in the successful diplomat—and Benes was nothing if not that—to persist in believing that always, somehow, somewhere, there is a solution waiting to be conjured up by a sufficiently gifted operator. This is perfectly natural; the alternative is for the diplomat, like a doctor at the deathbed, to retire and call in a representative of another profession. Loyalty, professional reflexes, and a sense of responsibility are usually all too strong for that.

Since the alternative to acceptance of the Anglo-French proposals was war with Germany, something must be said about the relative state of the German and Czech forces. The question of Soviet assistance will be considered separately; in any case it was conditional in the first instance on Czech resistance, quite apart from the problem arising from the formal Soviet undertaking to aid the Czechs provided the French fulfilled *their* obligations.

The Czechoslovaks devoted between 15 and 20 per cent of their annual state budget to defense. In the record year of 1938, planned expenditure rose to 44 per cent. These are official figures, and it is not clear whether they fully reflect acquisition of aircraft from abroad. They are nevertheless indicative of the effort made, and by the time of the crisis there was a good deal to show for all that money.

The peacetime strength of the Czechoslovak Army [11] was seventeen infantry divisions and four motorized divisions, and this could be rapidly expanded upon mobilization. When mobilization was decreed on September 23, 1938, some thirty-five divisions were formed; but even this did not represent the full strength available, as over and above the divisional formations there were some 60,000 special fortress troops, bringing the land forces up to the rough equivalent of forty divisions. Furthermore, the September mobilization was not complete. A second-line reserve equivalent to another ten divisions could have been called up, but as it is not clear whether there were sufficient arms for them, the total of forty divisions of land troops may be taken as a measure of the effective strength immediately available. Thus:

Land forces

1,250,000 men organized in 15 army corps of 35 or 34 divisions, of which at least seven were of special troops, i.e., armored, mountain, or cavalry formations; plus fortress troops
   30,000 motor vehicles
      700 tanks
       16 armored trains
  200,000 horses
Over 1,000,000 rifles
   60,000 light and heavy machine guns
    2,200 field guns (one source gives a figure of 3,200) of all calibers ranging from light field pieces to 305mm howitzers
    2,500 anti-tank guns

Air forces

      60 wings equipped with 1,200 aircraft; of these 600–700 were first-line craft

The principal deficiencies were in anti-aircraft and heavy artillery. (The German forces will be dealt with below, but to put these figures in perspective it may be mentioned here that the German plan of attack provided for the employment of thirty-seven divisions organized in ten corps.)

The Czechoslovak Army was a hardy, sober, and disciplined force. It was well trained and its officers were well qualified for their tasks, though some foreign observers had doubts about the professional capacity of those generals who still survived from Legion days. Its morale was high, and the September mobilization demonstrated very amply both the discipline and the loyalty of the reserves. Cases of German or Magyar troops failing to answer the call or sabotaging it were extremely rare. In any case, the great majority of the troops were Czechs and Slovaks and the officer corps overwhelmingly so. Even the noncommissioned officers were 85 per cent Czech or Slovak. No unit had non-Czechoslovak troops in a proportion higher than 15 per cent, and even then minority troops did not normally serve in frontier areas.

It was generally believed that the staff work was good. The British

Military Attaché in Prague reported on September 3 that the Czechoslovak General Staff

> undoubtedly have a capacity for organization, and I do not expect any serious hitch in the process of rapid mobilization, concentration or subsequent dispositions, except in so far as these may be occasioned by enemy action. The whole process has been the subject of careful study, and such lessons as can be learnt from recent manoeuvres, the Sokols &c., give ground for confidence in this respect.[12]

Their equipment was generally first-rate. It was produced for the most part in three large factories which were among the biggest and most efficient in the world at that time. Besides weapons and vehicles, the Czechs produced very good aero engines. They were also equipped with a plant for the production of poison gas.

The essential military function of the Czech Army was to defend the national territory. In this task it was aided by the fact that the pre-Munich frontiers ran through difficult terrain, except in the south. To make the most of the natural advantages and to compensate where there were none, the Czechs had constructed a formidable chain of fortifications. It was an immense complex of underground blockhouses and casemates, forts, electric barriers, tank barriers, and underground aerodromes. By September 1938 all this was complete with the exception of the sector facing Austria. Even there, however, the frontier was very far from being easily passable.

The German Army at this time was by no means the large and self-confident force that cut through France and the Low Countries almost two years later. In April 1938 its effective strength was no more than twenty-seven divisions, only three of which were armored, cavalry, or mountain troops. It was then estimated that by dint of special call-ups another eighteen divisions of unequal value could be formed. (In the event, the Germans did better.) In September they planned to employ thirty-seven active divisions on the Czechoslovak frontier, leaving five on the western front. Four reserve divisions were to back up the five active ones in the west, together with fourteen Landwehr divisions.[13] The latter did not amount to much. The three remaining active divisions were left in East Prussia. Over and above this, the Germans were of course able to increase the size of the Army after the fighting had begun; the French estimated that they could do so at a rate of fifteen divisions per month,[14] but in September the thirty-seven divisions represented the maximum force available for the attack on Czechoslovakia, even on the assumption that no more than a covering force was needed in the west or on the Polish border. The decision to leave the western front practically bare was a most important element of the German plan.

The quality of the German formation commanders was almost certainly higher than that of their Czech opposite numbers, but that of the German troops was not. Many were still half-trained, and there were not enough junior commanders and NCO's. German equipment, too, was in many respects inferior to that of the Czechs, particularly the fighting vehicles and heavy artillery. Six months before, on the entry into Austria, the new German armored formations had disgraced themselves. Hitler later recounted how "In the spring of 1938 we entered Austria. On the stretch from Linz to Vienna we saw eighty tanks immobilized by the side of the road—and yet what an easy road it was! Our men hadn't enough experience." [15] On the other hand, a higher proportion of the German Army was mechanized, as indeed it had to be as it was the attacking force.

Thus in roughly measured terms of order of battle, quality of commanders and troops, morale, and equipment, neither side was obviously superior to the other. On the Czech side there were three strategic advantages, one of them immense. They were on the defensive, and there was no question of more than limited tactical surprise. They had the advantage of interior lines. And, above all, they had their fortifications.

The Germans took the Czech fortifications very seriously and considered them the major obstacle. At a fairly late stage in the operational planning, Hitler had altered the plan of battle lest, among other reasons, there be a "repetition of Verdun" and a "bleeding to death for a task which cannot be accomplished" by von Rundstedt's 2nd Army. But it soon emerged that there was no way of avoiding the major fortifications entirely, for where they were weakest, opposite Austria, a "thrust in the 14th Army area will fail because of [lack of] means of transport." Hitler therefore ruled that the motorized and armored divisions be assembled in the 10th Army, based on Schwandorf and roughly opposite Pilsen, and that the major thrust be made there. Only then would the 12th Army, based on Passau and coming up from the south, strike through to the heart of Bohemia.[16] At this time Keitel was denouncing those who doubted their ability to break through as planned. But at Nuremberg he admitted that

> We were extremely glad that it had not come to a military operation because throughout the time of preparation we had always been of the opinion that our means of attack against the frontier fortifications of Czechoslovakia were inadequate. From a purely military point of view we were not strong enough to stage an attack which would involve the piercing of the frontier fortifications; we lacked the material for such an attack.[17]

As against this, the Germans could, *in the long run*, bring up vast forces to augment their effort. Taking the rough French estimate that a month after the commencement of hostilities the Germans could increase their forces at the rate of fifteen divisions a month, the German force could have been more than doubled by the end of the year, *provided* there was no Western intervention.[18] Clearly, if the military balance of forces is considered in total isolation from the political scene, there can be little question that Germany had it in its power to defeat Czechoslovakia. Where two states are of comparable technological and social development and where one population outnumbers the other five to one (or seven to one if the minorities are left out of the Czech account, as perhaps they should be), there is no apparent reason why the greater nation should not defeat the smaller if it has the will to do so. And of this last factor, at any rate, there was no question. But only *in the long run,* whereas it was the clear purpose of the Germans to avoid an extended campaign at all costs. It was on this issue, whether in fact Czechoslovakia could be speedily beaten, that Hitler and his generals were divided.

Hitler saw from the first that the attack on Czechoslovakia had to be conducted with the speed of lightning—*blitzartig schnell.* This was foreseen at the now celebrated conference of November 5, 1937, and reiterated in all the operational directives. Thus, in the fully formulated "Directive for Operation Green" of May 30, 1938, it was clearly stated that

> If concrete successes are not achieved in the first few days by land operations, a European crisis will certainly arise. Realization of this ought to give commanders of all ranks an incentive to resolute and bold action.[19]

Precisely what a "European crisis" implied was not noted down; but it was clearly intended to point to a catastrophe of epic proportions which did not bear thinking about in detail. The reasoning behind this insistence on speed is plain enough. First, the western front had to be left practically bare for lack of troops. Determination and 2,000 anti-tank guns were expected to prevent disaster if the French moved, but clearly the Bohemian campaign had to be over and done with and the bulk of the troops back along the Siegfried Line before Berlin could breathe freely. Second, the prospect of being bogged down in a long campaign in Czechoslovakia, even if the French did not intervene, went against Hitler's political grain. It was not merely a matter of prestige. It could have a disastrous effect on morale at home and drastically alter the picture Germany now presented to the West and to the Russians. It would invite intervention. It would change the political and psychological climate in which the Germans were now operating. The time allowed for the completion of the task was, at first, "a few days"; later it was extended to eight. Whether from the political or military aspect, speed was an essential element of the plan.

The Czechoslovak Army was conceived by its commanders as a body that would act in strategic coordination with Allied forces. A war in which Czechoslovakia would have to fight alone was never envisaged. On the other hand, it was perfectly plain to all concerned that in terms of battle Czechoslovakia would indeed be alone, the difference being that *ultimately* the full weight of Western military pressure would be turned against the Germans and the day be saved. It was never for a moment in doubt at the Czech General Staff, or among competent professional observers, that initially the full weight of the German Army would be thrown against them and that they should and could withstand it.[20] Thus the immediate and crucial difference between what they had planned for and what they would be in for if their government decided for resistance was twofold: in military terms, the critical period would begin after a protracted resistance of, say, three months; in psychological terms they would be only too conscious of being alone in the ring with a powerful enemy and hostile bystanders.

The Czech generals' essential confidence in their ability to withstand a German attack was matched by the German generals' dislike of Operation Green. Their objections were technical and professional, not political. They did not believe the German Army was ready for war, they had no confidence in their ability to charge through the Czech fortifications, they were fearful of leaving the western front bare with a pitiful scattering of troops and a still incomplete Siegfried Line, and they did not believe that the feat could be performed in a week and the troops rushed back to the west. In their view, too, there was a distinct danger of the situation degenerating into a world war. They believed they had a good, professional case against Operation Green, and they were unanimous and not infrequently outspoken in their opposition to it, Keitel excepted.[21] Keitel and Jodl inveighed against them, but it was indeed a good case and no professional grounds for ignoring it could be adduced. Jodl complained about their *Miesmacherei* and noted in his diary that the General Staff did not really believe in Hitler's genius,[22] and this was very close to being the crux of the matter. Hitler had no military solution to the professional problem posed by his own requirements. Presumably he hoped that it could be entirely skirted by skillful political moves; if not, what was lacking in plain military potential and capability would have to be made up with dash, daring, and inspired leadership in the field.

Two final points should be mentioned. Not only was the morale of the Czech forces high, but the Germans were almost throughout convinced that the Czechs would put up heavy resistance. Not until September 21, i.e., upon the acceptance of the Anglo-French proposals, did the German assessment change. However, two days later they had changed their minds once again and had noted "the increase of the Czech will to fight." [23]

Second, there appeared to be the possibility that a rising among the Sudeten Germans could be instigated upon the outbreak of hostilities, or even before. A Freikorps was organized, and armed Nazi formations were included in the German order of battle. A rising of sorts did take place on September 12, but it was very firmly put down by the Czechs, thus showing what they could do when they had the will to do it.

It can thus be seen that it was the view of *both the Czech and the German military commanders* that the Czechoslovak Army, unaided, could put up stiff resistance and keep the Germans at bay, probably for several months, conceivably for many more.[24] Both the evidence available at the time and what has come to light since support this view. The defection of France did not materially alter this state of affairs. It was the political and psychological climate that changed.

It follows that had the Czechs determined to resist Anglo-French pressure and face the Germans alone it is—at the very least—unlikely that the Germans would have succeeded in destroying the Czechoslovak state, while it is very much more than likely that the "European crisis" that Hitler feared would have occurred. On the other hand, the final outcome of such resistance could not be certain. If certainty was sought it could be found only in surrender.

Precisely what occurred during the forty-eight hours or so of what must have been the heart-rending and humiliating debate during which the Czech authorities discussed the Anglo-French proposals has never been made public. Authoritative Czech spokesmen [25] have almost universally preferred to shift attention to the debate between the Czech authorities and the Western Powers. This reticence is perfectly comprehensible, but it means that any attempt to understand what transpired has to be highly conjectural.

It must be remembered that the Anglo-French proposals, severe and unpalatable though they were, did not specify a timetable for the transfer of territories to the Germans, nor did they go into the modalities of such a transfer. It meant a great loss of wealth, military installations, and skilled citizens. It meant too that there would be a loss of strategically advantageous borders. A weaker Czechoslovakia was implicit in the cession, but though it was offensive to national pride and extremely disturbing to those responsible for the defense of the country, it was nevertheless just conceivable that the re-fashioned state might be viable. General Syrovy was to say in his broadcast of September 30:

Our State will not be one of the smallest in the world. There are others which are much smaller, and yet they are sound and resistant. We shall have enough territory left to give us the possibility of further cultural and economic progress. It is true that we shall live within narrower boundaries, but we shall be entirely among ourselves. Many hindrances to the good and peaceful administration of our State will be removed. Agreement with our neighbours, too, will be easier. Our Army will continue to have its task and will protect the nation and the State and will continue to be on guard as formerly.[26]

If this was true after Munich, it was true a fortiori nine days before.

So far as national security was concerned, the loss of strategic frontiers could perhaps be offset by the fact that Britain would now formally join France in guaranteeing Czech independence. As against the implied cancellation of the Franco-Czech alliance there was an international Anglo-French guarantee: it was a new relationship with the West, suited to the new times, deriving much of its force from the fact that it was to be proclaimed at this difficult moment. It was madness to go to war over the differences between what had already been conceded and what was now demanded and lose the lifeline to the West in the bargain. A keen mind could have perceived how things would go even before the formal note was presented. All this could be argued. And, as we have seen, the minds of those in authority were already made up on the morning of September 19.

Benes, and presumably his close associates, believed this to be the wisest course. The soldiers had a much less certain and seemingly more cruel alternative to offer; in any case they "would obey." There does not seem to have been a real debate between the civilians and the military at this stage. But it was expected that many of the political leaders would oppose it and that the population at large would hate it.

There was another problem. It was clear to the President and to most of those who had actual dealings with the Western statesmen and diplomats that the Western Powers would not hesitate to use any available weapon in the political armory. They were intent on a Czechoslovak surrender; for them it was a matter of life or death and argument could not possibly sway them. But, at the same time, Czechoslovakia had not merely a moral but a formal and legal right to insist on Western support against Germany. It was therefore not enough that the *government* should sense or even know of the impending renunciation of their obligations by the West. The renunciation had to be clear and unmistakable and *public*. If the Western Powers—France in particular— balked at this and fought shy of actually certifying their refusal to honor their obligations, so much the better. A considerable diplomatic battle would have been won. Either way, the government could not be charged with failing to explore all available avenues of escape.

Thus on September 20, approximately twenty-four hours after his interview with Benes, Newton was telegraphing that he had had it from a very good source (Hodza?) that the official reply just handed to him that evening "should not be regarded as final."

A solution must however be imposed upon the Government as without such pressure many of its members are too committed to be able to accept what they realise to be necessary. If I can deliver a kind of ultimatum to President Benes, Wednesday, he and his Government will feel able to bow to *force majeure*. It might be to the effect that in the view of His Majesty's Government the Czechoslovak Government must accept the proposals without reserve and without further delay, failing which His Majesty's Government will take no further interest in the fate of the country. I understand that my French colleague is telegraphing to Paris in a similar sense.[27]

Lacroix, the French Minister, did indeed send a telegram, one which was later the subject of much dispute since part of it was exploited by the French Foreign Minister in the public debate that followed Munich.[28] After the war, Lacroix told the French Parliamentary Commission of Inquiry what had occurred:

M. Hodza, Président du Conseil, me convoqua par téléphone. J'interrompis aussitôt mon travail pour me rendre à son invitation. M. Hodza me demanda si j'étais certain que la France se déroberait en cas de conflit. Je lui répondis que je n'en savais rien et je lui proposai de télégraphier immédiatement à Paris pour avoir une réponse ferme. Il m'objecta que cette démarche serait trop longue et ajouta: "J'admets *a priori* que la France ne marchera pas et si vous pouvez cette nuit même obtenir de votre gouvernement un télégramme le confirmant, le Président de la République s'inclinera. C'est le seul moyen de sauver la paix." [29]

Lacroix received his telegram certifying the French decision to dissociate themselves from Czechoslovakia's fate and Newton got his ultimatum. The celebrated audience with Benes at just past two o'clock in the morning of September 21 ensued.

It was a long and painful interview. Benes pointed out his detailed objections to the plan and asked for clarification of a number of points, including the precise nature of the guarantee offered. Then he justified his country's foreign policy and stated that in pursuing it "he had not been driven by the Soviet Government which he had kept to one side."

He expected internal troubles and did not know whether the government could control them. Finally, toward the end,

> M. Benes said that he took our *démarche* to be a kind of ultimatum and indeed only such an ultimatum could justify him and his Government in accepting the Anglo-French proposals without obtaining beforehand the sanction of Parliament as was constitutionally required. We therefore told him that our *démarche* had the character of an ultimatum in the sense that it represented the final advice of our Governments and in their view the last possible moment for acceptance of their advice, if this country was to be saved.[30]

But of course it was not an ultimatum in any accepted sense. It was a threat to cut the Czechs loose on very stormy seas, wiping the slate clean of all that had been written on it since the French, twenty years before, had first recognized the Czechoslovak National Council "as the first basis" of the future Czechoslovak government.

As has been noted, Benes was careful to point out that he had not been guided by the Russians, and later it was often argued on his behalf that one of the main considerations underlying his policy was the fear that his country would find itself fighting with the Russians against the Germans, with the West on the sidelines or, worse, participating in a general crusade against communism. It is not clear how real this fear was. The Czechs were careful to maintain friendly contact with the Russians and explore the possibilities of assistance, should it be decided to call for their aid. When the crisis came, the Russians were duly informed. On September 19 Benes summoned the Soviet Minister, Alexandrovsky, and informed him of the Anglo-French proposals and what they implied. He also told the Minister that the government had rejected the proposals. Benes put two questions to the Russians: Would the Soviets fulfill their undertakings if France did? And, as Czechoslovakia would appeal to the League in the event of an attack, would the Soviet Union render assistance as a member of the League under Articles 16 and 17? A tougher Benes, more critical of the West, emerges from the Soviet diplomat's dispatch than is suggested by the reports of the Western envoys. The Soviet Minister also reported that Clement Gottwald, the communist leader, had seen Benes on September 19, but had not received a clear reply to his question whether the government had decided to accept the proposals. In any event, the Soviets lost no time in giving Benes an affirmative and unequivocal answer to both questions.[31] They also informed the French of the answer they were transmitting to the Czechs. This was on September 20, before the final confrontation with the Western representatives. On September 21 Litvinov told the Assembly of the League of Nations both of the Czech query and of the Soviet answer, and of a French query in the same vein that had preceded it. Having backed their privately transmitted replies with a public statement, the Soviet position was rendered formally impeccable. They appear to have wondered why the Czechs did not ask them outright whether they would offer *unconditional* aid if so requested, but did not insist. A request for, or an offer of, unilateral military aid, i.e., one which had neither the cover of a League of Nations resolution nor the cooperation of the Western Powers, would have implied a Russian invasion of Rumania or Poland under the worst possible circumstances. They were clearly reluctant to enter into a conflict with Germany with the strong possibility that much of Europe would be arrayed against them.[32] But to be set against the Soviet reluctance to enter into such a conflict was the Czechoslovak reluctance to invite them.

All this was, however, subsidiary to the main business of the relations with the Western Powers. Foreign Minister Krofta's circular telegram of September 21 to Czech missions abroad reviewing developments did not mention it and concluded, simply, with the following paragraph:

> In view of this [Anglo-French] ultimatum, and being completely isolated, the Czechoslovak Government will evidently have to yield to irresistible pressure. An answer will be handed to the British and French Ministers in the course of to-day.[33]

On the day after the Czech surrender to Anglo-French pressure the Sudeten German *Freikorps* entered Czech territory and occupied the border towns of Asch and Eger. "Reichgerman" SA and SS units joined them. Meanwhile the German Army proper continued to move toward the frontier in accordance with the Operation Green timetable, and a fully orchestrated and typically vicious propaganda campaign was loosed against Czechoslovakia. When, on the same day, Chamberlain met Hitler at Godesberg—with the Czech capitulation in his pocket—he was confronted with new demands. Briefly put, these were that the "German" territories of Czechoslovakia—to be delineated by the Germans themselves—were to be transferred to German authority within eight days. After the occupation by German troops a plebiscite could be held in those areas; a plebiscite would in any case be held in other areas not immediately occupied. This meant, in plain terms, that a panic flight of Czechs, Jews, German Social Democrats, and other potential victims of the Germans would ensue, that the Czech forces would not have time to remove their stores, destroy their installations, or organize new defenses before evacuation, and that, to crown it all, the entire procedure would be deliberately and unmistakably humiliating. As the Czechs rightly pointed out, the Godesberg Memorandum was "a *de facto* ultimatum of the sort usually presented to a vanquished nation and not a proposition to a sovereign state." Chamberlain was appalled and angered and, after concluding that Hitler could not be shaken, returned to London. But before leaving Germany he had reluctantly agreed with Halifax that in view of the German troop movements "the French and British Governments cannot continue to take responsibility of advising them not to mobilize." [34] The Czechs, who until then had obeyed the injunction not to mobilize, promptly and joyfully did so. The mobilization was an immense organizational success. It was more than a demonstration of the efficiency of the arrangements and the loyalty of the reservists. It was convincing proof of the high state of national morale and of the popular feeling against capitulation. "No one who was there to see," reported the special correspondent of *The Times* (September 26, 1938), "could ever forget the quietness and dignity with which the Czechoslovak nation took up their arms on Friday night." [35]

Thus by the time the Czech government met to consider the Godesberg terms on September 25 the situation seemed to have changed profoundly. At home, reconstituted under General Syrovy, they were riding on a new crest of popularity. Abroad, they could well believe that the Germans had finally and irrevocably revealed how brutal, unscrupulous, and insatiably ambitious they were, and that it was in the light of this recognition of the true state of affairs that the French and British ministers were meeting in London. The Czechs themselves had very properly been asked to send a delegation and make plain their views. The nightmare of isolation was surely over and the policy of acceding to Western wishes in order to retain Western friendship appeared to have justified itself. War was probably inevitable, but no blame could be attached to Czechoslovakia which had done all in its power to save the peace. It was urgently necessary to secure Polish neutrality in the event of war, but for the rest Prague could await developments. Thus fortified, the Czechs felt they could reject the German terms and face the prospect of war with all the necessary courage and with a determination eloquently expressed in Jan Masaryk's formal note to Halifax:

> My Government wish me to declare in all solemnity that Herr Hitler's demands in their present form are absolutely and unconditionally unacceptable to my Government. Against these new and cruel demands my Government feel bound to make their utmost resistance and we shall do so, God helping. The nation of St. Wenceslas, John Hus and Thomas Masaryk will not be a nation of slaves.
>
> We rely upon the two great Western democracies, whose wishes we have followed much against our own judgment, to stand by us in our hour of trial.[36]

The illusion, if illusion there was, that the Western Powers would now support them was of brief duration. The intense fear and detestation of war among the dominant members of the British and French governments was not diminished by the feeling that war might really be imminent. After a little while, when the immediate shock of Godesberg had worn off, the British pulled themselves together and dispatched Sir Horace Wilson to Hitler: ". . . So long as there remained even a slender chance of peace, we must not neglect any opportunity of securing it." [37] It is characteristic of the proceedings that this was done before the Anglo-French ministerial conference had ended or even arrived at any considered judgment on the policy to proceed with. Their purpose was clear and they were correspondingly swift and uncompromising in its pursuit. What Prague thought now mattered less and less, and they ceased to address themselves seriously to the Czech government. From this point on, Newton's instructions, in essence, were to calm their growing fears:

> You should explain to the Czechoslovak Government that the communication which is being made to the German Chancellor through Sir Horace Wilson in no way prejudices the position of the Czechoslovak Government.

This profound fear of war was one source of Czech weakness *vis-à-vis* the Western Powers. There was a second, less fundamental: the concessions they had already made continued to dog them. Looked at in cold blood, the difference between what they had already agreed to (i.e., the Anglo-French proposals), and did not even now denounce, and what the Germans required could be made to appear procedural. It concerned not the principle of cession, but "the way in which the territory is to be handed over." And this, in Chamberlain's view, could be settled by agreement. No doubt, as he knew and stated in his letter to Hitler (quoting Masaryk), the Germans were demanding a procedure that was harsh in the extreme, and probably endangered Czech national security. But it was nevertheless an incremental difference, a marginal addition to the great concession that had already been made. Thus in the battle for the minds of the Western leaders the Czechs were bound to lose and the Germans to win. The Czechs could only point to the injustice and the cruelty that would be done them. The Germans could (and did) argue that the Czechs were intent on precipitating a general war to avoid fulfilling their undertaking to hand over the Sudeten territories. All the Germans had to do was to stand firm. And this, despite their nervousness, the mutterings of the generals, and—in many cases—their own unwillingness to go to war at this time, they did. No doubt Hitler's iron nerve held them together. At any rate the debate was now conducted on this basis and it is hard to see how it could have had any other issue but a demand that the Czechs make one last, marginal concession.

At the Four Power Conference at Munich that followed on September 29, the question of Czech acceptance of the emerging *Diktat* hardly arose in a serious manner. When it did it was dismissed by Hitler on the grounds that if they rejected it, it proved they only respected force. Toward the end the conferees did ask themselves, What was to be done about the Czechs? But this was only a procedural question: namely, how the terms of the agreement were to be transmitted to Prague. The demand to accept them, when it came, was peremptory. "You will appreciate that there is no time for argument," Chamberlain telegraphed Newton from Munich; "it must be plain acceptance." [38]

The differences between the Munich terms and those of the Godesberg Memorandum—which the Czechs had firmly rejected—were extremely small, hardly amounting to technical or even cosmetic improvements. To Chamberlain they mattered because they implied the continued reign of international order, not anarchy. To the Czechs, the only significant comparison could be with the Anglo-French proposals. Ten days before, it could at least be argued that while the issue before them was one of a very severe loss of territory and wealth and defensive capacity, it was possible that the operation might be followed by renewed health. Now this could simply not be believed. At the very best, it could be hoped that somehow, some day, the nation would outlive its enemies.

The text of the agreement was received at a quarter past six in the morning. The Germans did not require an answer, but notified the Czechs that their representatives on the International Commission were expected at 5 P.M. the same day at the Berlin Foreign Ministry. The party leaders began a meeting with President Benes at 9.30 A.M. and the Cabinet met elsewhere at the same time. Shortly afterward both groups, joined by the members of Dr. Hodza's late government and two generals representing the Army, met together under the President's leadership. But if they believed they had until the afternoon to decide they were soon disillusioned. The British, French, and Italian envoys called and demanded a reply by noon that day. And in fact at noon, barely two and a half hours after the convening of the meeting, the decision to accept the terms was taken.

Just before this meeting Benes telephoned the Soviet Minister, Alexandrovsky. He informed him of the agreement and defined the Czech dilemma as between "beginning war with Germany, having against her Britain and France, at any rate in the sense of the attitude of their governments which are also working on the public mind, getting it to believe that Czechoslovakia is the cause of the war, or capitulating to the aggressor." Leaving open the question of the decision Czechoslovakia would take, the President wanted to know the attitude of the Soviet Union to these two possibilities: further struggle or capitulation.[39] An answer was requested by 6–7 P.M. However, at noon the Soviet envoy was informed that no answer was now required. Reporting this, in turn, Alexandrovsky added:

> From the words and behaviour of Smutny and General Husarek, whom I also met at the Castle, I have no doubt that Benes made no reference to the fact that he had received no answer from the USSR. Just the contrary. He and the Left group of the Government evidently acted on the assumption that the USSR would come to their assistance at the first opportunity. This is borne out by yesterday's broadcast by Minister Vavrecka and the former Minister . . . Derer who for the first time publicly announced that the USSR was the only one who remained a loyal ally of Czechoslovakia to the end. A similar statement, but not over the radio, was made by Beran, the leader of the Agrarians. All three took part in the said meeting of Ministers.[40]

Clearly, the question of invoking Soviet aid was never seriously discussed and the doctrine laying down that the Soviet alliance must be contingent upon an effective alliance with the West cannot have been seriously challenged. Nor was the military situation discussed, except insofar as the generals were asked questions, the answers to which could be used to support arguments advanced on other grounds.

The decisive confrontation between those who supported capitulation and those who opposed it took place after the official decision to capitulate had been made. A deputation of six senior generals called on President Benes (who was also Supreme Commander). It was composed of the Chief of the General Staff, General Krejci, three provincial commanders, the Inspector-General of the Forces, and the Prime Minister, General Syrovy.

The generals argued that the troops were already mobilized and deployed in the fortified areas and that, in consequence, this was the time to resist, if ever. They were convinced that the population would resist, even if the government did not. "We must go to war," they said, "regardless of consequences. The Western Powers will be forced to follow us. The population of the Republic is united, the Army is resolute, anxious to fight. And even if we were left alone we must not yield; the Army has the duty to defend the national territory, wants to go and will go to war." [41]

"They begged, entreated, threatened. Some of them wept." [42] President Benes admired them and sympathized, but refused to reconsider. He gave three reasons. The first related to the central fact of the French *de facto* denunciation of their Treaty of Alliance; the second to the Polish threat to occupy Teschen, with the military and political implications of fighting two enemies; the third, quite simply, to the foreseeable slaughter.

War will come quickly [the President told them]. Great Britain, France and the other nations will not help us fight now, but they will certainly have to fight later—perhaps under worse conditions. We would not be understood by Europe and the world if we provoked the war now. The nation must endure. Do not give way, whatever happens, and wait for the right moment. Then we shall enter the struggle again, as we did in 1914. And we shall win again.

Finally,

The generals left dissatisfied, embittered, and in a desperate mood. And as for me, I pondered seriously once more the question: Have I made the right decision in this terrible crisis? [43]

There could have been no greater demonstration of the President's vast authority. At five o'clock that afternoon General Syrovy himself broadcast the news of the capitulation to the Czechoslovak people.

As the President, in his farewell broadcast on October 5, expressly abstained from explaining what had occurred ("I will neither analyze these events in detail nor criticize them today"), General Syrovy's broadcast remains the authoritative public statement. The three key points were as follows:

We had the choice between a desperate and hopeless defence . . . and the acceptance of conditions . . . unparalleled in history for ruthlessness.

. . . we were deserted, and we stood alone.
All the States of Europe, including our neighbours to the North and South, are under arms. We are in a certain sense a fortress beleaguered by forces which are more powerful than ours.

Therefore the government

. . . came to the conclusion that if we had to choose between a reduction of our territory and the death of the nation, it was our sacred duty to preserve the life of our people, so that we might emerge from this time of terror unweakened.[44]

Thus it may be seen that the decision to accept the Munich terms was taken quickly and under the heaviest kind of pressure. There was none of the careful, if anguished, deliberation which characterized the lengthy discussions that preceded the full acceptance of the Anglo-French proposals. The only hint of a discussion of alternative policies is to be found in the confrontation between the President and the generals and it is characteristic that it took place on the generals' initiative, not the government's.

With one exception, the arguments that appear to have been advanced by Benes and those hinted at by Syrovy were based—at best—on half truths. The defense of Czechoslovakia was far from being a desperate undertaking. It was certainly not hopeless. And to say categorically, as General Syrovy did, that resistance "would have meant the sacrifice not only of an entire generation of our adult men, but also of women and children," was simply misleading. So far as the Poles were concerned, by September 30 the question had been settled in principle and the Poles informed that Teschen would be ceded. This had been done with the deliberate purpose of obtaining Polish neutrality.[45] The case of Teschen was neither so vital to the state nor so sound (from the formal point of view) that it could not be sacrificed in the interests of avoiding a greater sacrifice. Finally, the Czechs had not been entirely deserted. They had no strong reason to believe that the Soviets would not continue to support them. It was by their own decision that they denied themselves the opportunity to invoke Soviet aid. In the face of this, discussion as to whether the Rumanians would or would not have allowed Soviet forces through their territory or air space, or whether in fact transport facilities were or were not adequate, is rendered meaningless.

There remains the one—unanswerable—argument that resistance implied slaughter. No doubt the Czech leaders could not have foreseen what the German occupation of Bohemia and Moravia would be like. Perhaps they envisaged a new version, admittedly somewhat more brutal, of Habsburg rule. Even such a regime is really not comparable in terms of the physical pain it inflicts on the population with what is suffered in war. The dread of a great disaster and a national bloodletting was understandably very strong in Prague. Yet there can be no doubt that they would have gone to war without any reservation had the Western Powers been with them, even though for many months it would have been the same fighting against very nearly the same odds. "Nous n'attendons pas un nouvel Austerlitz, une armée française en Moravie. Nous tiendrons le coup nous-mêmes, le temps qu'il faudra, des semaines, des mois, quatre, six peut-être," Benes had told Henri Hauser only a few months before.[46]

Like all civilized men of his generation, Benes hated and feared war. But war in good company, in an honorable cause, was one thing. War conducted alone, with uncertain prospects, or war in the company of one barbarian state against another—that was different. For the Czechs, with their historic defeat in the seventeenth century in mind and their newly rewon and still fragile sovereign status, such a prospect was particularly terrible. The only way they themselves could act to preserve their national sovereignty—to be lost, in any case, at Munich—was by endangering it in a harsh and bloody departure from their political and moral norms.

The case of Czechoslovakia in 1938 is paradoxical. In certain respects it was an easily demonstrable model of what a small, enlightened nation could do to maximize its resources. Economically, the country was strong. Politically, it had been for many years the center of a system of alliances which was anchored to the French, to be sure, but which owed much of its strength and inspiration to the Czechs themselves. Militarily, it was capable of producing a machine that in the moment of crisis was the match of the adversary's. That Czechoslovakia's strength availed it nothing in the crisis is only natural: economic potential can be significant only as the basis of extended buildup of forces or as support in a lengthy conflict. But the Czech alliances melted the moment they were tested or were left uninvoked; and the military machine played no role in the defense of the state and only barely in the calculations of the political leaders.

How this situation arose and what alternatives faced the Czech leaders even as late as September 1938 have been described. Had they been less fixed in their minds as to the policy they should pursue and more unwilling from the start to pay the price and make the concessions demanded of them, it is possible that the situation facing them on September 30 would never have arisen. It would certainly have been different in its essentials. Had they decided on war when all other possibilities were exhausted there is no reason to believe that defeat was certain; on the contrary, they had every prospect of maintaining an effective and extended resistance and the European situation would most probably have been altered thereby, as Hitler understood from the first. Within the logic of what the Czechoslovak leaders had been trying to do for twenty years, the most that can be said is that, having recognized the failure of their policy, they accepted defeat and resolved to preserve their nation physically, until, "as in 1914 . . . we shall win again." In terms of humanity and private morality this argument is clearly unanswerable. In terms of the management of a sovereign state it borders on the absurd. For winning "as in 1914" meant total dependence on forces beyond their control and only marginally susceptible to their influence, if at all. It was the abnegation of statehood and the abdication of sovereignty.

It is difficult to escape the impression that these considerations were discussed and understood within an extremely rigid framework of ideas. Czechoslovakia must be linked to the West; must not fight alone; must not enter into an effective relationship with the Soviet Union unaccompanied by France; must preserve its reputation, even when the behavior of other powers belies theirs; and so on. All these principles had strong roots in history and in good sense. Employed together as a system of rules for political conduct it is not surprising that they led to disaster.

But another question arises. Was President Benes right after all in seeing or sensing that Czechoslovak sovereignty had too small a base to be more than intermittently effective, that in the long run it depended on the backing and approval of much larger, truly powerful, and sovereign states? How else can his own final, public judgment on his stewardship be understood?

> I only wish to make it clear that in the years 1936–38 Czechoslovak policy rightly diagnosed what was the matter with Europe. It did everything, really everything, to retrieve the situation of Czechoslovakia, of its friends and of all Europe in the face of Fascist gangsterism and pan-German Nazism and of war itself.
>
> In that period when the European and world crisis was approaching, there was no State in Europe which could have a clearer conscience of doing its duty towards its Nation and its friends than the Czechoslovak Republic under the presidency of Masaryk and myself.[47]

One answer would appear to be that effective sovereignty is less a direct function of size than of a complex relationship between the state, its purposes, and the external opposition to them. Granted unquestioned authority in the domestic sphere, full exercise of sovereignty would seem to depend principally on two factors: the will of its statesmen to exercise that independence and the ability of opposing states (if any) to impede them. The outcome of any conflict obviously depends, in the first instance, on the objective attributes of the opponents. But equally, where the will to employ those attributes is lacking, or where it is paralyzed by an apparent disproportion in relative strength or for any other reason, such as the private qualities and views of the leaders, physical strength and other objective attributes avail nothing. They are, in any case, only a *potential*.

The management of a state seems to require a special firmness of purpose and a blindness to all considerations extraneous to the overriding consideration of political survival. The leaders of "new nations"—as the Czechoslovaks were at the time—because they will have spent many years arguing their case in normative terms in other nations' chancelleries, are not always fully aware of this. When they are, their initial instinct is often to deny it. They remain in awe of the Great Powers even to the extent of privately disparaging their own formal equality with them. Given this frame of mind, the full range of possibilities available to the state is unlikely to be surveyed, still less exploited.

NOTES

1. President Benes was prepared to remind French listeners of this result *"dans l'hypothèse inconcevable de votre défaillance."* Interview with Prof. Henri Hauser on May 10, 1938, in *L'Année politique française et étrangère* (1939), p. 114.

2. *Documents on British Foreign Policy*, Third Series (henceforth *DBFP*), II, 395–396.

3. H. Beuve-Méry's testimony before the French Parliamentary Commission inquiring into the events leading up to World War II, in Assemblée Nationale, *Rapport fait au nom de la Commission chargée d'enquêter sur les événements survenus en France de 1933 à 1945* (henceforth *Les événements survenus en France*), Annexes (Dépositions), III, 818.

4. *DBFP*, II, 431–434.

5. *DBFP*, II, 333, 358, 364–365.

6. Daladier related this to the French Parliamentary Commission. He was testifying under oath, after the war. There is no apparent reason to disbelieve him. *Les événements survenus en France, Annexes* (Dépositions), I, 33–34.

7. *DBFP*, II, 389–390.

8. Halifax to Newton, *DBFP*, II, 406.

9. *DBFP*, II, 416, 417, 412.

10. Wickham Steed, "Edward Benes," in Jan Opocensky, ed., *Edward Benes* (London, 1945).

11. The figures that follow are all derived from published sources. Though the details cannot be entirely accurate, the figures do suggest the orders of magnitude involved. No unreasonable discrepancies were noted in the information supplied by the principal sources, which were: General Faucher, "La Défense nationale tchécoslovaque, 1918–1938," in *L'Année politique française et étrangère* (1939), pp. 85–102; H. Ripka, *Munich: Before and After* (London, 1939), pp. 134–135; S. Grant Duff, *Europe and the Czechs* (London, 1938), *passim;* Jiri Dolezal and Jan Kren, *La Tchécoslovaquie en lutte* (Prague, 1961), p. 131; *The Times* (London), September 27 and 28, 1938, and March 24, 1939; General Armengaud in *La Revue des Deux Mondes*, April 15, 1938, pp. 766–779; General Gamelin, *Servir* (Paris, 1946), II, 353–355; and *Czechoslovakia in Maps and Statistics* (London, 1944).

12. *DBFP*, II, 258. See also General Faucher's testimony, *Les événements survenus en France, Annexes* (Dépositions), V, 1191–1211.

13. Walter Goerlitz, *History of the German General Staff* (New York, 1953), p. 327; Telford Taylor, *Sword and Swastika* (New York, 1952), p. 210.

14. Gamelin, II, 347.

15. *Hitler's Secret Conversations* (New York, 1961), p. 207.

16. *Documents on German Foreign Policy*, Series D (henceforth *DGFP*), II, 686–687.

17. International Military Tribunal, *Proceedings*, IX, 2.

18. The British military attaché in Prague, commenting on a Czech General Staff estimate that 75 German divisions might be used against them, thought this two to one superiority "not excessive in view of the defence and the interior lines." Telegram dated September 27, *DBFP*, II, 567.

19. *DGFP*, II, 357.

20. See memorandum submitted to the Supreme Defense Council by the Chief of the General Staff on September 9, in J. Dolezal, *op. cit.*, pp. 17–19. General Krejci complained of the tendency to underestimate Czech strength and overestimate the opposition. Also: views of British military attaché, *DBFP*, II, 258, 412, 567, 581; of General Gamelin, *Servir*, II, 353–355; of General Faucher both in the article cited and in his testimony before the French Parliamentary Commission; and

almost all other authorities concerned. That it was also the considered view of the 2ème Bureau of the French General Staff may be gleaned from an article on the subject in *L'Europe nouvelle,* September 24, 1938. Those who thought differently were often plainly ignorant of the facts, though their influence on the formulation of policy was not impaired thereby. Thus Geoffrey Dawson, editor of *The Times:* "After all, with a great power like Germany surrounding your country on three sides, a row of fortresses in the hills cannot mean much more than the chance of holding up an invasion for a few days. It is a case of being killed on Friday instead of on Tuesday!" *History of The Times* (London, 1952), IV, 2, 935.

21. B. H. Liddell Hart, *The Other Side of the Hill* (London, 1948), pp. 39–40. Also, Goerlitz, *History of the German General Staff,* pp. 328–329; and Taylor, *Sword and Swastika,* pp. 200–201.

22. Jodl's diary, entry for August 10, 1938, in IMT *Documents,* No. 1780–PS.

23. Jodl's diary for September 22 and 23. See also E. M. Robertson, *Hitler's Pre-War Policy* (London, 1963), pp. 142–143.

24. There was a plan to retreat gradually to a redoubt in the eastern half of the country, and to that end arms factories had been established there. The French had encouraged the Czechs to do so.

25. Such as Hubert Ripka. Left-wing accounts (e.g., "Pierre Buk," *La Tragédie tchécoslovaque* [Paris, 1939], and more recent accounts published in Prague after the war) tend to lay great stress on Agrarian party machinations. In view of Benes' immense authority it would seem that the net effect of such pressure could not have been great, still less decisive.

26. RIIA, *Documents on International Affairs, 1938,* II, 328.

27. *DBFP,* II, 425.

28. See H. Beuve-Méry, "La vérité sur la pression franco-britannique," in *L'Europe nouvelle,* October 29, 1939; and J. W. Wheeler-Bennett, *Munich* (London, 1948), p. 122. Georges Bonnet, Hubert Beuve-Méry, and Lacroix himself were all closely questioned on the subject when they testified before the Commission. Lacroix's evidence is convincing.

29. *Les événements survenus en France,* Rapport, II, 268. The question has been raised whether Hodza had Benes' authority for his request or not. Lacroix, at any rate, did not doubt it at the time, although he told the Commission that Benes' capitulation surprised him. Even in retrospect he could not quite understand it and thought that internal difficulties, i.e., Agrarian party pressure, might have been a cause. For, said Lacroix, "à première vue . . . le Président Benes n'avait aucune raison de capituler puisque l'armée était prête à entrer en guerre et que le Parlement était en vacance. Je me suis toujours demandé si le courage ne lui a pas manqué au dernier moment."

30. *DBFP,* II, 450.

31. *New Documents on the History of Munich* (Prague, 1958) (henceforth *New Documents*), pp. 89, 90.

32. Cf. Fierlinger's dispatch of September 17 quoted in William V. Wallace, "New Documents on the History of Munich," *International Affairs,* October 1959, p. 453.

33. *New Documents,* p. 100.

34. *DBFP,* II, 519, 461.

35. Cf. Colonel Stronge's indignant comment on doubts cast by his colleague in Berlin on the morale of the Czech armed forces, *DBFP,* II, 581–582. There is abundant evidence to support his views in all the sources, Czech, French, British, and German.

36. *DBFP,* II, 519.

37. Chamberlain to the assembled ministers, September 26, in *DBFP,* II, 537.

38. *DBFP,* II, 630–635.

39. *New Documents,* pp. 126–127.

40. Telegram dated October 1, *New Documents,* pp. 130–131. Neither telegram reached Moscow until the late afternoon. However, the Czechs never denied their knowledge or belief that the Soviets were prepared to assist them. Thus, Dr. Hubert Ripka in "The Repudiation of Munich," *Czechoslovak Documents and Sources,* No. 6, 1943: "Soviet policy was prepared to implement its formal treaty pledges to us." At the time of writing, Ripka was Minister of State in the Czechoslovak Government in Exile.

41. Edvard Benes, *Mnichovske dny* (London, 1955), pp. 115–117, quoted in Otakar Odlozik, "Edvard Benes on Munich Days," *Journal of Central European Affairs,* January 1957.

42. Speech by President Benes at Chicago, May 27, 1943, quoted in B. Bilek, *Fifth Column at Work* (London, 1945), p. 75.

43. *Mnichovske dny.* What was said in detail, under these headings, is unknown; *Fifth Column at Work.*

44. RIIA, *Documents on International Affairs, 1938,* II, 327.

45. The notes exchanged between the Czechs and the Poles, as well as an important letter from Benes to Namier, are in L. B. Namier, *Europe in Decay.*

46. Henri Hauser interview, *L'Année politique française et étrangère.*

47. *Memoirs of Dr. Eduard Benes* (London, 1954), p. 33.

ALAN BULLOCK

Hitler and the Origins of the Second World War

More has been written on the years immediately preceding the outbreak of World War II than on any other period between the two wars. These are easily the most dramatic years; and while the outline of Hitler's "plot against peace" seemed pretty clear, there were always fresh details to be found among the voluminous captured German documents. As the documentation for the other countries, notably England, became more plentiful, however, the picture became more differentiated and some of the blame hitherto concentrated upon Hitler now was distributed among the other participants in the mounting prewar crisis. To judge the role of Hitler in the coming of the war and thus to apportion his share of responsibility, the historian must be thoroughly familiar with the man's character and aims.

No one knows more on this subject than Alan Bullock, Oxford historian and author of the leading biography, Hitler: A Study in Tyranny *(revised edition; New York, 1964). The evaluation of Hitler's foreign policy given below was originally presented as a Raleigh Lecture on History before the British Academy in 1967. It is reprinted from the* Proceedings of the British Academy, LIII (1967), *with permission of the author and the Academy.*

I

In the twenty years since the end of the war and the Nuremberg Trials, historical controversy has been largely concerned with the share of the other Powers in the responsibility for allowing war to break out in 1939. Thus, the British and French governments of the 1930's have been blamed for their policy of appeasement and for failing to secure an agreement with Russia; Mussolini for his alliance with Hitler; Stalin for the Nazi-Soviet Pact; the Poles for the illusions which encouraged them to believe that they could hold Russia as well as Germany at arm's length. Taking a wider sweep, historians have turned for an explanation of the origins of the Second World War to the mistakes made in the peace settlement that followed the First; to the inadequacies of British and French policy between the wars; the retreat of the United States into isolation; the exclusion of the Soviet Union; the social effects of the great depression; and so on.

All this is necessary work, in order to establish the historical situation in which the war began, but as the catalogue grows, I find myself asking what is left of the belief universally held outside Germany twenty years ago that the primary responsibility for the war rested on Hitler and the Nazis?

No one suggests that theirs was the sole responsibility. Hitler would never have got as near to success as he did if it had not been for the weakness, the divisions, the opportunism of the other governments, which allowed him to build up such power that he could not be prevented from conquering Europe without a major war. Still, there is a lot of difference between failing to stop aggression, even hoping to derive side profits from it—and aggression itself. Indeed, much of the criticism directed at the other Powers for their failure to stop Hitler in time would fall to the ground if there proved to have been nothing to stop.

Is the effect of filling in the historical picture to reduce this difference to the point where it no longer appears so important, where the responsibility for the war becomes dispersed, or is shifted onto the shortcomings of an anarchical system of international relations, or of militarism or of capitalism, as happened after the First World War? Is Mr. A. J. P. Taylor [1] the harbinger of a new generation of revisionist historians who will find it as anachronistic to hold Hitler—or anyone else—responsible for the outbreak of the Second World War as to hold the Kaiser responsible for the outbreak of the First?

The question is an important one, for to an extent which we only begin to realize when it is questioned, the accepted version of European history in the years between 1933 and 1945 has been built round a particular view of Hitler and of the character of German foreign policy, and if the centerpiece were removed, far more than our view of Hitler and German foreign policy would have to be revised—our view of the foreign policies of all the Powers and of the substantiality of the dangers which the other governments, and their critics, believed they confronted.

It occurred to me, therefore, that it would be interesting to take a fresh look at Hitler's foreign policy in the light of the new evidence that has become available in the twenty years since the Nuremberg Trials (and, no less important, of new ways of looking at familiar evidence) and then to go on and ask in what sense, if at all, it is still possible to speak of Hitler's and the Nazis' responsibility for what became a Second World War.

II

There are two contrasted versions of Hitler's foreign policy which for convenience's sake I will call the fanatic and the opportunist.

The first [2] fastens upon Hitler's racist views and his insistence that the future of the German people could be secured neither by economic development nor by overseas colonization, not even by the restoration of Germany's 1914 frontiers, but only by the conquest of living space (*Lebensraum*) in Eastern Europe. Here the scattered populations of Germans living outside the Reich could be concentrated, together with the surplus population of the homeland, and a Germanic empire established, racially homogeneous, economically self-sufficient, and militarily impregnable. Such *Lebensraum* could only be obtained at the expense of Russia and the states bordering on her and could only be won and cleared of its existing population by force, a view which coincided with Hitler's belief in struggle as the law of life, and war as the test of a people's racial superiority.

Hitler first set these views down in *Mein Kampf*, elaborated them in his so-called *Zweites Buch*,[3] and repeated them on almost every occasion when we have a record of him talking privately and not in public, down to the Table Talk of the 1940's[4] and his final conversations with Bormann in the early months of 1945[5] when his defeat could no longer be disguised. Not only did he consistently hold and express these views over twenty years, but in 1941 he set to work to put them into practice in the most literal way, by attacking Russia and by giving full rein to his plans, which the S.S. had already begun to carry out in Poland, for the resettlement of huge areas of Eastern Europe.

The alternative version [6] treats Hitler's talk of *Lebensraum* and racist empire in the East as an expression of the fantasy side of his personality and fastens on the opportunism of Hitler's actual conduct of foreign policy. In practice—so this version runs—Hitler was an astute and cynical politician who took advantage of the mistakes and illusions of others to extend German power along lines entirely familiar from the previous century of German history. So little did he take his own professions seriously that he actually concluded a pact with the Bolsheviks whom he had denounced, and when Hitler belatedly began to put his so-called program into practice, it marked the point at which he lost the capacity to distinguish between fantasy and reality and, with it, the opportunist's touch which had been responsible for his long run of successes. Thereafter he suffered nothing but one disaster after another.

These two versions of Hitler's foreign policy correspond to alternative versions of his personality. The first stresses his insistence on a fanatical will, force, and brutality of purpose, his conviction that he was a man of destiny, his reliance on intuition, his scorn for compromise, his declaration after the occupation of the Rhineland: "I go the way that Providence dictates with the assurance of a sleepwalker." [7]

The second takes this no more seriously than the rest of Nazi and fascist rhetoric and insists that in practice Hitler relied for his success upon calculation, total lack of scruple, and remarkable gifts as an actor. The suggestion that his opponents had to deal with a man who was fanatical in his purposes and would stop at nothing to accomplish them was part of the act, and a very successful part. His threats were carefully timed as part of a war of nerves, his ungovernable rages turned on or off as the occasion demanded, his hypnotic stare and loss of control part of a public *persona* skillfully and cynically manipulated. And when Hitler, carried away by his triumphs, himself began to believe in his own myth, and no longer to manipulate it, success deserted him.

It is a mistake, however, I believe, to treat these two contrasting views as alternatives, for if that is done, then whichever alternative is adopted, a great deal of evidence has to be ignored. The truth is, I submit, that they have to be combined and that Hitler can only be understood if it is realized that he was at once both fanatical *and* cynical; unyielding in his assertion of willpower *and* cunning in calculation; convinced of his role as a man of destiny *and* prepared to use all the actor's arts in playing it. To leave out either side, the irrational or the calculating, is to fail to grasp the combination which marks Hitler out from all his imitators.

The same argument, I believe, applies to Hitler's foreign policy, which combined consistency of aim with complete opportunism in method and tactics. This is, after all, a classical recipe for success in foreign affairs. It was precisely because he knew where he wanted to go that Hitler could afford to be opportunistic and saw how to take advantage of the mistakes and fears of others. Consistency of aim on Hitler's part has been confused with a timetable, blueprint, or plan of action fixed in advance, as if it were pinned up on the wall of the General Staff offices and ticked off as one item succeeded another. Nothing of the sort. Hitler frequently improvised, kept his options open to the last possible moment, and was never sure until he got there which of several courses of action he would choose. But this does not alter the fact that his moves followed a logical (though not a predetermined) course—in contrast to Mussolini, an opportunist who snatched eagerly at any chance that was going but never succeeded in combining even his successes into a coherent policy.

III

Hitler had established his power inside Germany by the late summer of 1934. By securing the succession to President Hindenburg, he became Head of State and Commander in Chief of the Armed Forces as well as leader of the only party in the country and head of a government in which no one dared to oppose him. From now on, apart from the one thing which he put before everything else, his own supremacy, Hitler took no great interest in internal affairs or administration. He turned his attention almost wholly to foreign policy and rearmament.

Shortly after he became Chancellor, on February 3, 1933, Hitler had met the leaders of the armed forces privately and told them that, once his political power was secure, his most important task would be to rearm Germany and then move from the revision of the Versailles Treaty to the conquest of *Lebensraum* in the East.[8]

Just over a year later, on February 28, 1934, Hitler repeated this at a conference of Army and S.A. leaders, declaring that here was a decisive reason for rejecting Roehm's plan for a national militia and for rebuilding the German Army. The Western Powers would never allow Germany to conquer *Lebensraum* in the East. "Therefore, short decisive blows to the West and then to the East could be necessary," tasks which could only be carried out by an army rigorously trained and equipped with the most modern weapons.[9]

Nonetheless, in the first two years, 1933 and 1934, Hitler's foreign policy was cautious. Politically, he had still to establish his own supremacy at home. Diplomatically, Germany was isolated and watched with suspicion by all her neighbors. Militarily, she was weak and unable to offer much resistance if the French or the Poles should take preventive action against the new régime.

These were all excellent reasons for Hitler to protest his love of peace, and innocence of aggressive intentions. As he told Rauschning, now that Germany had left Geneva, he would more than ever speak "the language of the League." [10] There is, in fact, a striking parallel between his conduct of foreign policy in this early period and the tactics of "legality" which he had pursued in his struggle for power inside Germany. By observing the forms of legality, staying within the framework of the constitution, and refusing to make a *Putsch*—which would have brought the Nazis into open conflict with the Army—Hitler was able to turn the weapons of democracy against democracy itself. His appeal to Wilsonian principles of national self-determination and equality of rights had precisely the same effect—and those who believed him were to be as sharply disillusioned as those who supposed Hitler would continue to observe the limits of legality in Germany once he had acquired the power to ignore them.

Although Nazi propaganda made the most of them, none of Hitler's foreign policy moves in his first two years did much to improve Germany's position. Leaving the Disarmament Conference and the League was a gesture; the pact with Poland clever but unconvincing, and more than counterbalanced by Russia's agreement to join the League and start negotiations for an alliance with France. The hurried repudiation of the Austrian Nazis in 1934 was humiliating, and the Saar plebiscite in January 1935 was largely a foregone conclusion. When Hitler announced the reintroduction of conscription in March 1935, Germany's action was condemned by the British, French, and Italian governments meeting at Stresa, as well as by the League Council, and was answered by the conclusion of pacts between Russia and France, and Russia and France's most reliable ally, Czechoslovakia.[11]

Between 1935 and 1937, however, the situation changed to Hitler's advantage, and he was able not only to remove the limitations of the Versailles Treaty on Germany's freedom of action but to break out of Germany's diplomatic isolation.

It is true that the opportunities for this were provided by the other Powers: for example, by Mussolini's Abyssinian adventure and the quarrel to which this led between Italy and the Western Powers. But Hitler showed skill in using the opportunities which others provided: for example, in Spain where he reduced the policy of nonintervention to a farce and exploited the civil war for his own purposes with only a minimum commitment to Franco. He also provided his own opportunities: for example, the offer of a naval treaty to Britain in 1935 and the military reoccupation of the Rhineland in 1936. This was a bold and risky stroke of bluff, taken against the advice of his generals, without anything like sufficient forces to resist the French if they had marched, and accompanied by a brilliantly contrived diversion in the form of the new peace pacts which he offered simultaneously to the other Locarno Powers.

Of course, there were failures—above all, Ribbentrop's failure to get an alliance with Britain. But between April 1935, when the Powers, meeting at Stresa, had unanimously condemned German rearmament, and Mussolini's state visit to Germany as a prospective ally in September 1937, Hitler could claim with some justification to have transformed Germany's diplomatic position and ended her isolation.

IV

The German Foreign Ministry and diplomatic service were well suited to the international equivalent of the policy of "legality," but Hitler soon began to develop instruments of his own for a new style of foreign policy.[12] One was the Nazi groups among the Volksdeutsche living abroad. The two most obvious examples are the Nazi party in Austria and Henlein's *Sudetendeutsche Partei* in Czechoslovakia. The former had to be hastily disavowed in the summer of 1934, when the *Putsch* against Dollfuss failed, but the subsidies to the Austrian Nazis continued, and so did the many links across the frontier from Munich and Berlin. Henlein's Sudeten party was also secretly in receipt of subsidies from Germany from early 1935,[13] and was to play a key role in the campaign against Czechoslovakia. These links were maintained outside the regular Foreign Ministry system and there were a number of Nazi agencies—Bohle's *Auslandsorganisation,* Rosenberg's *Außenpolitisches Amt,* VOMI (*Volksdeutsche Mittelstelle*) competing with each other, and with the Foreign Ministry, to organize the German-speaking groups living abroad.

At the same time Hitler began to make use of envoys from outside the foreign service for the most important diplomatic negotiations: Göring, for instance, who frequently undertook special missions to Italy, Poland, and the Balkans, and Ribbentrop whose Büro, originally set up to deal with disarmament questions in 1933, soon moved into direct competition with the *Auswärtiges Amt.* It was Ribbentrop who negotiated the naval treaty with London; Ribbentrop who was given the key post of ambassador in London in order to secure a British alliance; Ribbentrop who represented Germany on the Non-Intervention Committee, who negotiated and signed the Anti-Comintern Pact with Japan in 1936 and a year later brought in Italy as well.

It was not until the beginning of 1938 that Hitler appointed Ribbentrop as Foreign Minister; until then he left the German Foreign Ministry and diplomatic service as a respectable façade but increasingly took the discussion of policy and the decisions out of their hands and used other agents to carry them out. In Hitler's eyes the diplomats—like the generals, as he came to feel during the war—were too conservative, too preoccupied with the conventional rules of the game to see the advantages of scrapping rules altogether and taking opponents by surprise. Hitler's radicalism required a new style in the conduct of foreign affairs, as different from old style diplomacy as the Nazi party was from the old style political parties of the Weimar Republic.

This new style did not emerge clearly until 1938–1939, but there were unmistakable signs of it before then in the changed tone in which Hitler and German propaganda were speaking by 1937. Hitler receiving Mussolini and showing off the strength of the new Germany,[14] Hitler beginning to talk of Germany's "demands," was speaking a very different language from that of the man who only three or four years before had used all his gifts as an orator to convince the world of Germany's will to peace. German national pride and self-confidence had been restored, and, instead of trying to conceal, Nazi propaganda now boasted of her growing military strength.

V

The Nazis' claims about German rearmament were widely believed. Phrases like "Guns before butter," "total war," "a war economy in peacetime" made a deep impression. When Göring was appointed Plenipotentiary for the Four Year Plan in October 1936, this was taken to mean the speeding up of rearmament, and Hitler's secret memorandum to Göring found among Speer's papers after the war confirms this view.[15] Irritated by Schacht's opposition to his demands, he declared that the shortage of raw materials was "not an economic problem, but solely a question of will." A clash with Bolshevik Russia was unavoidable: "No State will be able to withdraw or even remain at a distance from this historical conflict. . . . We cannot escape this destiny."

Hitler concluded his memorandum to Göring with the words:

I thus set the following task:

1. The German Army must be operational (*einsatzfähig*) within 4 years.

2. The German economy must be fit for war (*kriegsfähig*) within 4 years.

Yet the evidence now available does not bear out the widespread belief in Germany's all-out rearmament before 1939.[16] The figures show that the rearmament program took a long time to get under way and did not really begin to produce the results Hitler wanted until 1939. Even then Germany's military superiority was not as great as both public opinion and the Allies' intelligence services assumed.

The really surprising fact, however, is the scale of German rearmament in relation to Germany's economic resources. At no time before September 1939 was anything like the full capacity of the German economy devoted to war production. The figures are well below what German industry could have achieved if fully mobilized, below what German industry had achieved in 1914–1918, and below what was achieved by the British when they set about rearmament in earnest.

The immediate conclusion which one might well draw from these facts is that they provide powerful support for the argument that Hitler was not deliberately preparing for war but was thinking in terms of an armed diplomacy in which he relied on bluff and the *threat* of war to blackmail or frighten the other Powers into giving way to his demands.

Before we accept this conclusion, however, it is worthwhile to carry the examination of the rearmament figures beyond the date of September 1, 1939. The attack on Poland may or may not have been due to mistaken calculation on Hitler's part (I shall come back to this later), but no one can doubt that the German attack on France and the Low Countries on May 10, 1940, was deliberate, not hastily improvised but prepared for over a six months' period. And this time it was an attack not on a second-class power like Poland but on two major Powers, France and Britain. Yet the interesting fact is that the proportion of Germany's economic resources devoted to the war hardly went up at all. Even more striking, the same is true of the attack on Russia in 1941. In preparation for Operation Barbarossa, the Army was built up to 180 divisions, but this was not accompanied by an all-out armaments drive and on the very eve of the invasion of Russia (June 20, 1941) Hitler actually ordered a reduction in the level of arms production. This was put into effect and by December 1941, when the German Army was halted before Moscow, the overall level of weapons production had fallen by 29 per cent from its peak in July of that year.[17]

In fact, it was not until 1942, the year in which Hitler lost the initiative and Germany was pushed on to the defensive, that Hitler was persuaded to commit the full resources of the German economy to an all-out effort.

This puts the facts I have mentioned in a different light. For if Hitler believed that he could defeat the Western Powers, subdue the Balkans, and conquer Russia without demanding more than a partial mobilization from the German people, then the fact that German rearmament before the war had limited rather than total objectives is no proof that his plans at that time did not include war.

The truth is that, both before and after September 1939, Hitler was thinking in terms of a very different sort of war from that which Germany had lost in 1914–1918 or was to lose again between 1942 and 1945. With a shrewder judgment than many of his military critics, Hitler realized that Germany, with limited resources of her own and subject to a blockade, was always going to be at a disadvantage in a long-drawn-out general war. The sort of war she could win was a series of short campaigns in which surprise and the overwhelming force of the initial blow would settle the issue before the victim had time to mobilize his full resources or the other Powers to intervene. This was the sort of war the German Army was trained as well as equipped to fight, and all the German campaigns between 1939 and 1941 conformed to this pattern—Poland, four weeks; Norway, two months; Holland, five days, Belgium, seventeen; France, six weeks; Yugoslavia, eleven days; Greece, three weeks. The most interesting case of all is that of Russia. The explanation of why the German Army was allowed to invade Russia without winter clothing or equipment is Hitler's belief that even Russia could be knocked out by a blitzkrieg in four to five months, before the winter set in. And so convinced was Hitler that he had actually achieved this that in his directive of July 14, 1941,[18] he spoke confidently of reducing the size of the Army, the Navy, and the armaments program in the near future.

This pattern of warfare, very well adapted both to Germany's economic position and the advantages of secrecy and surprise enjoyed by a dictatorship, fits perfectly the pattern of German rearmament. What was required was not armament in depth, the long-term conversion of the whole economy to a war footing which (as in Britain) would only begin to produce results in two to three years, but a war economy of a different sort geared (like German strategy) to the concept of the blitzkrieg. It was an economy which concentrated on a short-term superiority and the weapons which could give a quick victory, even when this meant neglecting the proper balance of a long-term armament program. What mattered, as Hitler said in his 1936 memorandum, was not stocks of raw materials or building up productive capacity, but armaments ready for use, plus the will to use them. How near the gamble came to success is shown by the history of the years 1939–1941 when Hitler's limited rearmament program produced an army capable of overrunning the greater part of Europe, and very nearly defeating the Russians as well as the French.

VI

But we must not run ahead of the argument. The fact that Germany was better prepared for war, and when it began proceeded to win a remarkable series of victories, does not prove that Hitler intended to start the war which actually broke out in September 1939. We have still to relate Hitler's long-term plans for expansion in the East and his rearmament program to the actual course of events in 1938 and 1939.

A starting-point is Colonel Hossbach's record of Hitler's conference with his three Commanders in Chief, War Minister, and Foreign Minister on November 5, 1937.[19] It was an unusual occasion, since Hitler rarely talked to more than one commander in chief or minister at a time, and he came nearer to laying down a program than he ever had before. Once again he named *Lebensraum* in the East and the need to provide for Germany's future by continental expansion as the objective, but instead of leaving it at that, he went on to discuss how this was to be achieved.

The obstacles in the way were Britain and France, Germany's two "hate-inspired antagonists." Neither was as strong as she seemed; still, "Germany's problems could only be solved by force and this was never without attendant risk."

The peak of German power would be reached in 1943–1945: after that their lead in armaments would be reduced. "It was while the rest of the world was preparing its defences that we were obliged to take the offensive." Whatever happened, he was resolved to solve Germany's problem of space by 1943–1945 at the latest. Hitler then discussed two possible cases in which action might be taken earlier—one was civil strife in France, disabling the French Army: the other, war in the Mediterranean which might allow Germany to act as early as 1938. The first objective in either case "must be to overthrow Czechoslovakia and Austria simultaneously in order to remove the threat to our flank in any possible operation against the West." Hitler added the comment that almost certainly Britain and probably France as well had already tacitly written off the Czechs.

To speak of this November meeting as a turning-point in Hitler's foreign policy at which Hitler made an irreversible decision in favor of war seems to me as wide of the target as talking about timetables and blueprints of aggression. Hitler was far too skillful a politician to make irreversible decisions in advance of events; no decisions were taken or called for.

But to brush the Hossbach meeting aside and say that this was just Hitler talking for effect and not to be taken seriously seems to me equally wide of the mark. The hypotheses Hitler outlined—civil strife in France, a Mediterranean war—did not materialize, but when Hitler spoke of his determination to overthrow Czechoslovakia and Austria, as early as 1938 if an opportunity offered, and when both countries *were* overthrown within less than eighteen months, it is stretching incredulity rather far to ignore the fact that he had stated this as his immediate program in November 1937.

The next stage was left open, but Hitler foresaw quite correctly that everything would depend upon the extent to which Britain and France were prepared to intervene by force to prevent Germany's continental expansion and he clearly contemplated war if they did. Only when the obstacle which they represented had been removed would it be possible for Germany to carry out her eastward expansion.

This was a better forecast of the direction of events in 1938–1941 than any other European leader including Stalin made at the end of 1937—for the very good reason that Hitler, however opportunist in his tactics, knew where he wanted to go, was almost alone among European leaders in knowing this, and so kept the initiative in his hands.

The importance of the Hossbach conference, I repeat, is not in recording a decision but in reflecting the change in Hitler's attitude. If the interpretation offered of his policy in 1933–1937 is correct, it was not a sudden but a gradual change, and a change not in the objectives of foreign policy but in Hitler's estimate of the risks he could afford to take in moving more rapidly and openly toward them. As he told the Nazi Old Guard at Augsburg a fortnight later: "I am convinced that the most difficult part of the preparatory work has already been achieved. . . . To-day we are faced with new tasks, for the *Lebensraum* of our people is too narrow." [20]

There is another point to be made about the Hossbach conference. Of the five men present besides Hitler and his adjutant Hossbach, Göring was certainly not surprised by what he heard and Raeder said nothing. But the other three, the two generals and Neurath, the Foreign Minister, showed some alarm and expressed doubts. It is surely another remarkable coincidence if this had nothing to do with the fact that within three months all three men had been turned out of office—the two generals, Blomberg and Fritsch, on barefaced pretexts. There is no need to suppose that Hitler himself took the initiative in framing Blomberg or Fritsch. The initiative seems more likely to have come from Göring and Himmler, but it was Hitler who turned both Blomberg's *mésalliance* and the allegations against Fritsch to his own political advantage. Blomberg, the Minister of War, was replaced by Hitler himself, who suppressed the office altogether, took over the OKW, the High Command of the armed forces, as his own staff and very soon made clear that neither the OKW nor the OKH, the High Command of the Army, would be allowed the independent position of the old General Staff. Fritsch, long regarded by Hitler as too stiff, conservative, and out of sympathy with Nazi ideas, was replaced by the much more pliable Brauchitsch as Commander-in-Chief of the Army, and Neurath, a survivor from the original coalition, by Ribbentrop, who made it as clear to the staff of the Foreign Ministry as Hitler did to the generals that they were there to carry out orders, not to discuss, still less question the Führer's policy.

VII

I find nothing at all inconsistent with what I have just said in the fact that the timing for the first of Hitler's moves, the annexation of Austria, should have been fortuitous and the preparations for it improvised on the spur of the moment in a matter of days, almost of hours. On the contrary, the *Anschluß* seems to me to provide, almost in caricature, a striking example of that extraordinary combination of consistency in aim, calculation, and patience in preparation with opportunism, impulse, and improvisation in execution which I regard as characteristic of Hitler's policy.

The aim in this case was never in doubt: the demand for the incorporation of Austria in the Reich appears on the first page of *Mein Kampf*. After the Austrian Nazis' unsuccessful *Putsch* of 1934, Hitler showed both patience and skill in his relations with Austria; he gradually disengaged

Mussolini from his commitment to maintain Austrian independence and at the same time steadily undermined that independence from within. By the beginning of 1938 he was ready to put on the pressure, but the invitation to Schuschnigg to come to Berchtesgaden was made on the spur of the moment as the result of a suggestion by an anxious Papen trying hard to find some pretext to defer his own recall from Vienna. When Schuschnigg appeared on February 12, Hitler put on an elaborate act to frighten him into maximum concessions with the threat of invasion, but there is no reason to believe that either Hitler or the generals he summoned to act as "stage extras" regarded these threats as anything other than bluff. Hitler was confident that he would secure Austria, without moving a man, simply by the appointment of his nominee Seyss-Inquart as Minister of the Interior and the legalization of the Austrian Nazis—to both of which Schuschnigg agreed.

When the Austrian Chancellor, in desperation, announced a plebiscite on March 9, Hitler was taken completely by surprise. Furious at being crossed, he decided at once to intervene before the plebiscite could be held. But no plans for action had been prepared: they had to be improvised in the course of a single day, and everything done in such a hurry and confusion that 70 per cent of the tanks and lorries, according to General Jodl, broke down on the road to Vienna. The confusion was even greater in the Reich Chancellery; when Schuschnigg called off the plebiscite, Hitler hesitated, then was persuaded by Göring to let the march-in continue, but without any clear idea of what was to follow. Only when he reached Linz did Hitler, by then in a state of self-intoxication, suddenly decide to annex Austria instead of making it a satellite state, and his effusive messages of relief to Mussolini show how unsure he was of the consequences of his action.

No doubt the *Anschluß* is an exceptional case. On later occasions the plans were ready: dates by which both the Czech and the Polish crises must be brought to a solution were fixed well in advance, and nothing like the same degree of improvisation was necessary. But in all the major crises of Hitler's career there is the same strong impression of confusion at the top, springing directly (as his generals and aides complained) from his own hesitations and indecision. It is to be found in his handling of domestic as well as foreign crises—as witness his long hesitation before the Roehm purge of 1934—and in war as well as peacetime.

The paradox is that out of all this confusion and hesitation there should emerge a series of remarkably bold decisions, just as, out of Hitler's opportunism in action, there emerges a pattern which conforms to objectives stated years before.

VIII

The next crisis, directed against Czechoslovakia, was more deliberately staged. This time Hitler gave preliminary instructions to his staff on April 21, 1938,[21] and issued a revised directive on May 30.[22] Its first sentence read: "It is my unalterable decision to smash Czechoslovakia by military action in the near future." It was essential, Hitler declared, to create a situation within the first two or three days which would make intervention by other Powers hopeless: the Army and the Air Force were to concentrate all their strength for a knock-out blow and leave only minimum forces to hold Germany's other frontiers.

It is perfectly true that for a long time in the summer Hitler kept out of the way and left the other Powers to make the running, but this was only part of the game. Through Henlein and the Sudeten party, who played the same role of fifth column as the Austrian Nazis, Hitler was able to manipulate the dispute between the Sudeten Germans and the Czech government, which was the ostensible cause of the crisis, from within. At a secret meeting with Hitler on March 28, Henlein sum-marized his policy in the words: "We must always demand so much that we can never be satisfied." The Führer, says the official minute, approved this view.[23]

At the same time through a variety of devices—full-scale press and radio campaigns, the manufacture of incidents, troop movements, care-fully circulated rumors, and diplomatic leaks—a steadily mounting pres-sure was built up, timed to culminate in Hitler's long-awaited speech at the Nuremberg Party Congress. Those who study only the diplo-matic documents get a very meager impression of the war of nerves which was maintained throughout the summer and which was skillfully directed to play on the fear of war in Britain and France and to heighten the Czechs' sense of isolation. It was under the pressure of this political warfare, something very different from diplomacy as it had been traditionally practiced, that the British and French governments felt themselves impelled to act.

What was Hitler's objective? The answer has been much confused by the ambiguous use of the word "war."

Western opinion made a clear-cut distinction between peace and war. Hitler did not, he blurred the distinction. Reversing Clausewitz, he treated politics as a continuation of war by other means, at one stage of which (formally still called peace) he employed methods of political warfare—subversion, propaganda, diplomatic and economic pressure, the war of nerves—at the next, the threat of war, and so on to localized war and up the scale to general war—a continuum of force in which the different stages ran into each other. Familiar enough now since the time of the Cold War, this strategy (which was all of a piece with Hitler's radical new style in foreign policy) was as confusing in its novelty as the tactics of the Trojan horse, the fifth column, and the "volunteers" to those who still thought in terms of a traditionally decisive break between a state of peace and a state of war.

So far as the events of 1938 go, there seem to be two possible answers to the question, What was in Hitler's mind?

The first is that his object was to destroy the Czech state by the sort of blitzkrieg for which he had rearmed Germany and which he was to carry out a year later against Poland. This was to come at the end of a six months' political, diplomatic, and propaganda campaign designed to isolate and undermine the Czechs, and to maneuver the Western Powers into abandoning them to their fate rather than risk a European war. The evidence for this view consists in the series of secret directives and the military preparations to which they led, plus Hitler's declaration on several occasions to the generals and his other collaborators that he meant to settle the matter by force, with October 1 as D-day. On this view, he was only prevented from carrying out his attack by the intervention of Chamberlain, which, however great the cost to the Czechs, prevented war or at least postponed it for a year.

The other view is that Hitler never intended to go to war, that his objective was from the beginning a political settlement such as was offered to him at Munich, that his military preparations were not intended seriously but were designed as threats to increase the pressure.

The choice between these two alternatives, however—*either* the one *or* the other—seems to me unreal. The obvious course for Hitler to pursue was to keep both possibilities open to the very last possible moment, the more so since they did not conflict. The more seriously the military preparations were carried out, the more effective was the pressure in favor of a political settlement if at the last moment he decided not to take the risks involved in a military operation. If we adopt this view, then we remove all the difficulties in interpreting the evidence which are created either by attempting to pin Hitler down on any particular declaration and say *now,* at this point, he had decided on war—or by the dogmatic assumption that Hitler *never* seriously contemplated the use of force, with the consequent need to dismiss his military directives as bluff.

Neither in 1938 nor in 1939 did Hitler deliberately plan to start a general European war. But this was a risk which could not be ignored, and in 1938 it was decisive. The generals were unanimous that Germany's rearmament had not yet reached the point where she could face a war with France and Britain. The Czech frontier defenses were formidable. Their army on mobilization was hardly inferior at all, either in numbers or training, to the thirty-seven divisions which the Germans could deploy, and it was backed by a first-class armaments industry.[24]

To overcome these would require a concentration of force which left the German commander in the West with totally inadequate strength to hold back the French Army. While the generals, however, added up divisions and struck an unfavorable balance in terms of material forces, Hitler was convinced that the decisive question was a matter of will, the balance between his determination to take the *risk* of a general war and the determination of the Western Powers, if pushed far enough, to take the *actual decision* of starting one. For, however much the responsibility for such a war might be Hitler's, by isolating the issue and limiting his demands to the Sudetenland, he placed the onus of actually starting a general war on the British and the French. How far was Hitler prepared to drive such an argument? The answer is, I believe, that while he had set a date by which he knew he must decide, until the very last moment he had not made up his mind and that it is this alternation between screwing up his demands, as he did at his second meeting with Chamberlain in Godesberg, and still evading an irrevocable decision, which accounts both for the zigzag course of German diplomacy and for the strain on Hitler.

In the end he decided, or was persuaded, to stop short of military operations against Czechoslovakia and "cash" his military preparations for the maximum of political concessions.

No sooner had he agreed to this, however, than Hitler started to regret that he had not held on, marched his army in, then and there, and broken up the Czechoslovak state, not just annexed the Sudetenland. His regret sprang from the belief, confirmed by his meeting with the Western leaders at Munich, that he could have got away with a localized war carried out in a matter of days, and then confronted the British and French with a *fait accompli* while they were still hesitating whether to attack in the West—exactly as happened a year later over Poland.

Almost immediately after Munich, therefore, Hitler began to think about ways in which he could complete his original purpose. Every sort of excuse, however transparent, was found for delaying the international guarantee which had been an essential part of the Munich agreement. At the same time, the ground was carefully prepared with the Hungarians, who were eager to recover Ruthenia and at least part of Slovakia, and with the Slovaks themselves who were cast for the same role the Sudeten Germans had played the year before. The actual moment at which the crisis broke was not determined by Hitler and took him by surprise, but that was all. The Slovaks were at once prodded into declaring their independence and putting themselves in Hitler's hands. The Czech government, after Hitler had threatened President Hacha in Berlin, did the same. The "legality" of German intervention was unimpeachable: Hitler had been invited to intervene by both the rebels and the government. War had been avoided, no shots exchanged, peace preserved—yet the independent state of Czechoslovakia had been wiped off the map.

IX

Within less than eighteen months, then, Hitler had successfully achieved both the immediate objectives, Austria and Czechoslovakia, which he had laid down in the Hossbach meeting. He had not foreseen the way in which this would happen, in fact he had been wrong about it, but this had not stopped him from getting both.

This had been true at every stage of Hitler's career. He had no fixed idea in 1930, even in 1932, about how he would become Chancellor, only that he would; no fixed idea in 1934–1935 how he would break out of Germany's diplomatic isolation, again only that he would. So the same now. Fixity of aim by itself, or opportunism by itself, would have produced nothing like the same results.

It is entirely in keeping with this view of Hitler that, after Czechoslovakia, he should not have made up his mind what to do next. Various possibilities were in the air. Another move was likely in 1939, if only because the rearmament program was now beginning to reach the period when it would give Germany a maximum advantage and Hitler had never believed that time was on his side. This advantage, he said in November 1937, would only last at the most until 1943–1945; then the other Powers with greater resources would begin to catch up. He had therefore to act quickly if he wanted to achieve his objectives.

Objectives, yes; a sense of urgency in carrying them out, and growing means to do so in German rearmament, but no timetable or precise plan of action for the next stage.

Ribbentrop had already raised with the Poles, immediately after Munich, the question of Danzig and the Corridor. But there is no evidence that Hitler had committed himself to war to obtain these, or to the dismemberment of Poland. If the Poles had been willing to give him what he wanted, Hitler might well have treated them, for a time at any rate, as a satellite—in much the same way as he treated Hungary—and there were strong hints from Ribbentrop that the Germans and the Poles could find a common objective in action against Russia. Another possibility, if Danzig and the Corridor could be settled by agreement, was to turn west and remove the principal obstacle to German expansion, the British and French claim to intervene in Eastern Europe.

After Prague, the German-Polish exchanges became a good deal sharper and, given the Poles' determination not to be put in the same position as the Czechs but to say "No" and refuse to compromise, it is likely that a breach between Warsaw and Berlin would have come soon in any case. But what precipitated it was the British offer, and

Polish acceptance, of a guarantee of Poland's independence. In this sense the British offer is a turning-point in the history of 1939. But here comes the crux of the matter. If Mr. Taylor is right in believing that Hitler was simply an opportunist who reacted to the initiative of others, then he is justified in calling the British offer to Poland a revolutionary event.[25] But if the view I have suggested is right, namely, that Hitler, although an opportunist in his tactics, was an opportunist who had from the beginning a clear objective in view, then it is very much less than that: an event which certainly helped—if you like, forced—Hitler to make up his mind between the various possibilities he had been revolving, but which certainly did not provoke him into an expansionist program he would not otherwise have entertained, or generate the force behind it which the Nazis had been building up ever since they came to power. On this view it was Hitler who still held the initiative, as he had since the *Anschluß,* and the British who were reacting to it, not the other way round; the most the British guarantee did was to give Hitler the answer to the question he had been asking since Munich, Where next?

The answer, then, was Poland, the most probable in any event, in view of the demands the Nazis had already tabled, and now a certainty. But this did not necessarily mean war—yet.

Hitler expressed his anger by denouncing Germany's Non-Aggression Pact with Poland and the Anglo-German Naval Treaty, and went on to sign a secret directive ordering the Army to be ready to attack Poland by September 1.[26] The military preparations were not bluff; they were designed to give Hitler the option of a military solution if he finally decided this way, or to strengthen the pressures for a political solution—either direct with Warsaw, or by the intervention of the other Powers in a Polish Munich. Just as in 1938 so in 1939, Hitler kept the options open literally to the last, and until the troops actually crossed the Polish frontier on September 1 none of his generals was certain that the orders might not be changed. Both options, however; there is no more reason to say dogmatically that Hitler was aiming all the time at a political solution than there is to say that he ruled it out and had made up his mind in favor of war.

Hitler's inclination, I believe, was always toward a solution by force, the sort of localized blitzkrieg with which in the end he did destroy Poland. What he had to weigh was the risk of a war which could not be localized. There were several reasons why he was more ready to take this risk than the year before.

The first was the progress of German rearmament—which was coming to a peak in the autumn of 1939. By then it represented an eighteen-fold expansion of the German armed forces since 1933.[27] In economists' terms this was not the maximum of which Germany was capable, at least in the long run, but in military terms it was more than adequate, as 1940 showed, not just to defeat the Poles but to deal with the Western Powers as well. The new German Army had been designed to achieve the maximum effect at the outset of a campaign and Hitler calculated—quite rightly—that, even if the British formally maintained their guarantee to Poland, the war would be over and Poland crushed before they could do anything about it.[28]

A second reason was Hitler's increased confidence, his conviction that his opponents were simply not his equal either in daring or in skill. The very fact that he had drawn back at Munich and then regretted it made it all the more likely that a man with his gambler's temperament would be powerfully drawn to stake all next time.

Finally, Hitler believed that he could remove the danger of Western intervention, or at least render the British guarantee meaningless, by outbidding the Western Powers in Moscow.

In moments of exaltation, e.g., in his talks to his generals after the signature of the Pact with Italy (May 23) and at the conference of August 22 which followed the news that Stalin would sign, Hitler spoke as if the matter were settled, war with Poland inevitable, and all possibility of a political settlement—on his terms—excluded. I believe that this was, as I have said, his real inclination, but I do not believe that he finally made up his mind until the last minute. Why should he? Just as in 1938, Hitler refused to make in advance the choice to which historians have tried to pin him down, the either/or of war or a settlement dictated under the threat of war. He fixed the date by which the choice would have to be made but pursued a course which would leave him with the maximum of maneuver to the last possible moment. And again one may well ask, Why not—since the preparations to be made for either eventuality—war or a political settlement under the threat of war—were the same?

Much has been made of the fact that for the greater part of the summer Hitler retired to Berchtesgaden and made no public pronouncement. But this is misleading. The initiative remained in Hitler's hands. The propaganda campaign went ahead exactly as planned, building up to a crisis by late August and hammering on the question, Is Danzig worth a war? So did the military preparations which were complete by the date fixed, August 26. German diplomacy was mobilized to isolate Poland and, if the pact with Italy proved to be of very little value in the event, and the Japanese failed to come up to scratch, the pact with Stalin was a major coup. For a summer of "inactivity" it was not a bad result.

Hitler's reaction when the Nazi-Soviet Pact was signed shows clearly enough where his first choice lay. Convinced that the Western Powers would now give up any idea of intervention in defense of Poland, he ordered the German Army to attack at dawn on August 26: i.e., a solution by force, but localized and without risk of a general European war, the sort of operation for which German rearmament had been designed from the beginning.

The unexpected British reaction, the confirmation instead of the abandonment of the guarantee to Poland—this, plus Mussolini's defection (and Mussolini at any rate had no doubt that Hitler was bent on a solution by force) upset Hitler's plans and forced him to think again. What was he to do? Keep up the pressure and hope that the Poles would crack and accept his terms? Keep up the pressure and hope that, if not the Poles, then the British would crack and either press the Poles to come to terms (another Munich) or abandon them? Or go ahead and take the risk of a general war, calculating that Western intervention, if it ever took place, would come too late to affect the outcome?

It is conceivable that if Hitler had been offered a Polish Munich, on terms that would by now have amounted to capitulation, he would still have accepted it. But I find it hard to believe that any of the moves he made, or sanctioned, between August 25 and September 1 were seriously directed to starting negotiations. A far more obvious and simple explanation is to say that, having failed to remove the threat of British intervention by the Nazi-Soviet Pact, as he had expected, Hitler postponed the order to march and allowed a few extra days to see, not if war could be avoided, but whether under the strain a split might not develop between the Western Powers and Poland and so leave the Poles isolated after all.

Now that the crisis had come, Hitler himself did little to resolve or control it. Characteristically, he left it to others to make proposals, seeing the situation not in terms of diplomacy and negotiation but as a contest of wills. If his opponents' will cracked first, then the way was open for him to do what he wanted and march into Poland without fear that the Western Powers would intervene. To achieve this he was prepared to hold on and bluff up to the very last minute, but if the bluff did not come off within the time he had set, then this time he steeled his will to go through with the attack on Poland even if it meant running the risk of war with Britain and France as well. All the accounts agree on the strain which Hitler showed and which found expression in his haggard appearance and temperamental outbursts. But his will held. This was no stumbling into war. It was neither misunderstanding nor miscalculation which sent the German Army over the frontier into Poland, but a calculated risk, the gambler's bid—the only bid, Hitler once told Göring, he ever made, *va banque,* the bid he made when he reoccupied the Rhineland in 1936 and when he marched into Austria, the bid he had failed to make when he agreed to the Munich conference, only to regret it immediately afterward.

X

Most accounts of the origins of the war stop in September 1939. Formally, this is correct: from September 3, 1939, Germany was in a state of war with Britain and France as well as Poland, and the Second World War had begun. But this formal statement is misleading. In fact, Hitler's gamble came off. The campaign in which the German Army defeated the Poles remained a localized war and no hostilities worth speaking of had taken place between Germany and the Western Powers by the time the Poles had been defeated and the state whose independence they had guaranteed had ceased to exist.

If Hitler had miscalculated at the beginning of September or stumbled into war without meaning to, here was the opportunity to avoid the worst consequences of what had happened. It is an interesting speculation what the Western Powers would have done if he had really made an effort to secure peace once the Poles were defeated. But it is a pointless speculation. For Hitler did nothing of the sort. The so-called peace offer in his speech of October 6 was hardly meant to be taken seriously. Instead of limiting his demands, Hitler proceeded to destroy the Polish state and to set in train (in 1939, not in 1941) the ruthless resettlement program which he had always declared he would carry out in Eastern Europe.

Even more to the point, it was Hitler who took the initiative in turning the formal state of war between Germany and the Western Powers into a real war. On October 9 he produced a memorandum in which he argued that, instead of waiting to see whether the Western Powers would back their formal declaration of war with effective force, Germany should seize the initiative and make an all-out attack on the French and the British, thereby removing once and for all the limitations on Germany's freedom of action.

The German generals saw clearly what this meant: far from being content with, and trying to exploit, the good luck which had enabled him to avoid a clash with the Western Powers so far, Hitler was deliberately setting out to turn the localized campaign he had won in Poland into a general war. Their doubts did not deter him for a moment and, although they managed on one pretext or another to delay operations, in May 1940 it was the German Army, without waiting for the French or the British, which launched the attack in the West and turned the *drôle de guerre* into a major war.

Even this is not the end of the story. Once again, Hitler proved to be a better judge than the experts. In the middle of events, his nerve faltered, he became hysterical, blamed everyone, behaved in short in exactly the opposite way to the copybook picture of the man of destiny, but when the battle was over he had inflicted a greater and swifter defeat upon France than any in history. And it is no good saying that it was "the machine" that did this, not Hitler. Hitler was never the prisoner of "the machine." If "the machine" had been left to decide things, it would never have taken the risk of attacking in the West, and, if it had, would never have adopted the Ardennes plan which was the key to victory. Pushing the argument further back, one can add that, if it had been left to "the machine," German rearmament would never have been carried out at the pace on which Hitler insisted, or on the blitzkrieg pattern which proved to be as applicable to war with the Western Powers as to the limited Polish campaign.

Once again, the obvious question presents itself: what would have happened if Hitler, now as much master of continental Europe as Napoleon had been, had halted at this point, turned to organizing a continental New Order in Europe, and left to the British the decision whether to accept the situation—if not in 1940, then perhaps in 1941— or to continue a war in which they had as yet neither American nor Russian allies, were highly vulnerable to attack, and could never hope by themselves to overcome the disparity between their own and Hitler's continental resources. Once again—this is my point—it was thanks to Hitler, and no one else, that this question was never posed. It was Hitler who decided that enough was not enough, that the war must go on— Hitler, not the German military leaders or the German people, many of whom would have been content to stop at this point, enjoy the fruits of victory, and risk nothing more.

If the war had to continue, then the obvious course was to concentrate all Germany's—and Europe's—resources on the one opponent left, Britain. If invasion was too difficult and dangerous an operation, there were other means—a Mediterranean campaign with something more than the limited forces reluctantly made available to Rommel, or intensification of the air and submarine war, as Raeder urged. The one thing no one thought of except Hitler was to attack Russia, a country whose government had shown itself painfully anxious to avoid conflict and give every economic assistance to Germany. There was nothing improvised about Hitler's attack on Russia. Of all his decisions it was the one taken furthest in advance and most carefully prepared for, the one over which he hesitated least and which he approached with so much confidence that he even risked a five-week delay in starting in order to punish the Yugoslavs and settle the Balkans.[29]

Nor was it conceived of solely as a military operation. The plans were ready to extend to the newly captured territory the monstrous program of uprooting whole populations which the S.S.—including Eichmann— had already put into effect in Poland.[30] Finally, of all Hitler's decisions it is the one which most clearly bears his own personal stamp, the culmination (as he saw it) of his whole career.

XI

It will now be evident why I have carried my account beyond the conventional date of September 1939. Between that date and June 1941, the scope of the war was steadily enlarged from the original limited Polish campaign to a conflict which, with the attack on Russia, was now on as great a scale as the war of 1914–1918. The initiative at each stage —except in the Balkans where he was reluctant to become involved— had been Hitler's. Of course he could not have done this without the military machine and skill in using it which the German armed forces put at his disposal, but the evidence leaves no doubt that the decision where and when to use that machine was in every case Hitler's, not his staff's, still less that all Hitler was doing was to react to the initiative of his opponents.

Now, it may be that the Hitler who took these increasingly bold decisions after September 1939 was a different person from the Hitler who conducted German foreign policy before that date, but this is surely implausible. It seems to me far more likely that the pattern which is unmistakable after September 1939, using each victory as the basis for raising the stakes in a still bolder gamble next time, is the correct interpretation of his conduct of foreign policy before that date. And this interpretation is reinforced by the fact that at the same time Hitler was carrying out the rearmament and expansion of the German armed forces on a pattern which exactly corresponds to the kind of war which he proceeded to wage after September 1939.

Let me repeat and underline what I said earlier: this has nothing to do with timetables and blueprints of aggression. Throughout his career Hitler was an opportunist, prepared to seize on and exploit any opportunity that was offered to him. There was nothing inevitable about the way or the order in which events developed, either before or after September 1939. The annexation of Austria and the attempt to eliminate Czechoslovakia, by one means or another, were predictable, but after the occupation of Prague there were other possibilities which might have produced a quite different sequence of events—as there were after the fall of France. Of what wars or other major events in history is this not true?

But Hitler's opportunism was doubly effective because it was allied with unusual consistency of purpose. This found expression in three things:

First, in his aims—to restore German military power, expand her frontiers, gather together the scattered populations of *Volksdeutsche,* and found a new German empire in Eastern Europe, the inhabitants of which would either be driven out, exterminated, or retained as slave-labor.

Second, in the firmness with which he grasped from the beginning what such aims entailed—the conquest of power in Germany on terms that would leave him with a free hand, the risk of preemptive intervention by other Powers, the need to shape German rearmament in such a way as to enable him to win a quick advantage within a limited time by surprise and concentration of force, the certainty that to carry out his program would mean war.

Third, in the strength of will which underlay all his hesitations, opportunism, and temperamental outbursts, and in his readiness to take risks and constantly to increase these by raising the stakes—from the reoccupation of the Rhineland to the invasion of Russia (with Britain still undefeated in his rear) within the space of no more than five years.

Given such an attitude on the part of a man who controlled one of the most powerful nations in the world, the majority of whose people were prepared to believe what he told them about their racial superiority and to greet his satisfaction of their nationalist ambitions with enthusiasm—given this, I cannot see how a clash between Germany and the other Powers could have been avoided. Except on the assumption that Britain and France were prepared to disinterest themselves in what happened east of the Rhine and accept the risk of seeing him create a German hegemony over the rest of Europe. There was nothing inevitable about either the date or the issue on which the clash actually came. It half came over Czechoslovakia in 1938; it might have come over another issue than Poland. But I cannot see how it could have been avoided sometime, somewhere, unless the other Powers were prepared to stand by and watch Hitler pursue his tactics of one-at-a-time to the point where they would no longer have the power to stop him.

If the Western Powers had recognized the threat earlier and shown greater resolution in resisting Hitler's (and Mussolini's) demands, it is possible that the clash might not have led to war, or at any rate not to a war on the scale on which it had finally to be fought. The longer they hesitated, the higher the price of resistance. This is their share of the responsibility for the war: that they were reluctant to recognize what was happening, reluctant to give a lead in opposing it, reluctant to act in time. Hitler understood their state of mind perfectly and played on it with skill. None of the Great Powers comes well out of the history of the 1930's, but this sort of responsibility—even when it runs to appeasement, as in the case of Britain and France, or complicity as in the case of Russia—is still recognizably different from that of a government which deliberately creates the threat of war and sets out to exploit it.

In the Europe of the 1930's there were several leaders—Mussolini, for instance—who would have liked to follow such a policy but lacked the toughness of will and the means to carry it through. Hitler alone possessed the will and had provided himself with the means. Not only did he create the threat of war and exploit it, but when it came to the point he was prepared to take the risk and go to war and then, when he had won the Polish campaign, to redouble the stakes and attack again, first in the West, then in the East. For this reason, despite all that we have learned since of the irresolution, shabbiness, and chicanery of other governments' policies, Hitler and the nation which followed him still bear, not the sole, but the primary responsibility for the war which began in 1939 and which, before Hitler was prepared to admit defeat, cost the lives of more than 25 million human beings in Europe alone.

NOTES

1. In *The Origins of the Second World War* (rev. ed., 1963). See also the article by T. W. Mason, "Some Origins of the Second World War," in *Past and Present*, No. 29, December 1964, and Mr. Taylor's reply in the same journal, No. 30, April 1965. For a German view of Mr. Taylor's book, see the review article by Gotthard Jasper in *Vierteljahrshefte für Zeitgeschichte*, July 1962, pp. 311–340.

2. This view is well stated by Professor H. R. Trevor-Roper in an article, "Hitlers Kriegsziele," *ibid.*, April 1960.

3. Written in 1928 but not published until 1961. An English translation, *Hitler's Secret Book*, has been published by Grove Press, New York. This book is almost entirely concerned with foreign policy.

4. An English version, *Hitler's Table Talk 1941–44*, was published in 1953, with an introduction by H. R. Trevor-Roper.

5. *The Testament of Adolf Hitler: The Hitler-Bormann Documents* (London, 1961).

6. For this view, see A. J. P. Taylor, *The Origins of the Second World War*.

7. March 14, 1936, in a speech at Munich. For the context, cf. Max Domarus, *Hitler, Reden und Proklamationen* (Würzburg, 1962), I, 606.

8. General Liebmann's note of Hitler's speech on this occasion is reprinted in *Vierteljahrshefte für Zeitgeschichte*, October 1954, pp. 434–435. Cf. K. D. Bracher, W. Sauer, and G. Schulz, *Die Nationalsozialistische Machtergreifung* (Köln, 1962), p. 748, and Robert J. O'Neill, *The German Army and the Nazi Party, 1933–1939* (London, 1966), pp. 125–126.

9. A report of Hitler's speech on this occasion, made by Field Marshal von Weichs, is printed by O'Neill, *ibid.*, pp. 39–42. For further discussion of the reliability of this report, see Bracher, Sauer, and Schulz, *Die Nationalsozialistische Machtergreifung*, p. 749, n. 14.

10. Hermann Rauschning, *Hitler Speaks* (London, 1939), p. 116.

11. A critical review of Hitler's foreign policy in these years is made by K. D. Bracher in *Vierteljahrshefte für Zeitgeschichte*, January 1957: "Das Anfangsstadium der Hitlerschen Aussenpolitik," pp. 63–76.

12. I am indebted in this section to Dr. H. A. Jacobsen who allowed me to see a forthcoming article: "Programm und Struktur der nationalsozialistischen Aussenpolitik 1919–1939."

13. *Documents on German Foreign Policy*, Series C, Vol. III, No. 509.

14. Mussolini's visit to Germany took place in the last ten days of September 1937 and left an indelible impression on the Italian dictator. A few weeks later, in November 1937, Mussolini agreed to sign the Anti-Comintern Pact, a further step in committing himself to an alliance with Hitler.

15. It is printed in *Documents on German Foreign Policy*, Series C, Vol. V, No.

490. Cf. Gerhard Meinck, *Hitler und die deutsche Aufrüstung* (Wiesbaden, 1959), p. 164. Meinck's book is a valuable guide to the problems connected with German rearmament. Reference should also be made to Georg Tessin, *Formationsgeschichte der Wehrmacht 1933–39,* Schriften des Bundesarchivs, Bd. 7 (Boppard/Rhein, 1959). A convenient summary is provided by O'Neill, *The German Army and the Nazi Party,* Chap. 6.

16. The evidence has been admirably summarized and reviewed by Alan S. Milward in *The German Economy at War* (London, 1965). Further details are to be found in Burton H. Klein, *Germany's Economic Preparations for War* (Cambridge, Mass., 1959).

17. Klein, *Germany's Economic Preparations for War,* pp. 191–195; Milward, *The German Economy at War,* pp. 43–45.

18. Reprinted in the English translation of Walter Hubatsch's *Hitlers Weisungen, Hitler's War Directives, 1939–45,* edited by H. R. Trevor-Roper (London, 1964), pp. 82–85.

19. Text in *Documents on German Foreign Policy,* Series D, Vol. I, No. 19. Cf. also Friedrich Hossbach, *Zwischen Wehrmacht und Hitler* (Hanover, 1949), pp. 207–220.

20. Speech at Augsburg, November 21, 1937. Domarus, *Hitler, Reden und Proklamationen,* pp. 759–760.

21. *Documents on German Foreign Policy,* Series D, Vol. II, No. 133. Cf. also Series D, Vol. VII, pp. 635–637.

22. *Ibid.,* Vol. II, No. 221.

23. *Ibid.,* Vol. II, No. 107.

24. For the strength of the Czech forces, see David Vital, "Czechoslovakia and the Powers," *Journal of Contemporary History,* Vol. I, No. 4, October 1966.

25. Taylor, *Origins of the Second World War,* Chap. 10.

26. International Military Tribunal Document C–120. Cf. also Walter Warlimont, *Inside Hitler's Headquarters* (London, 1964), p. 20.

27. O'Neill, *The German Army and the Nazi Party,* Chap. 6.

28. It is noticeable that there were far fewer doubts in the Army in 1939 than in 1938—and the major reason for this (apart from the fact that a war with Poland fitted in far better with the generals' traditionalist ideas than one with Czechoslovakia) was their belief that a war in 1939 involved fewer risks than in 1938.

29. See G. L. Weinberg, *Germany and the Soviet Union 1939–41* (The Hague, 1954).

30. See Robert L. Koehl, *RKFDV, German Resettlement and Population Policy 1939–45* (Cambridge, Mass., 1957), and Alexander Dallin, *German Rule in Russia, 1941–45* (London, 1957).

BIBLIOGRAPHICAL ESSAY

Diplomatic history should be written against the background, and set into the context, of a country's domestic affairs. A bibliographical essay on the subject should be equally inclusive. If our emphasis here is on specifically diplomatic sources and writings, the reason is lack of space. Readers looking for more varied bibliographical information will be best served by the Council on Foreign Relations' *Foreign Affairs Bibliography* (New York, 1933–1964), of which four volumes have appeared thus far. A fifth, the *Foreign Affairs 50-Year Bibliography,* will be published in 1972 and will have some 2,000 reviews of outstanding books on international relations published between 1920 and 1970. Another useful introduction to source material is Mario Toscano, *The History of Treaties and International Politics:* Part I, *The Documentary and Memoir Sources* (Baltimore, 1966), which covers the origins of both world wars.

DOCUMENTARY SOURCES

As was pointed out in the introduction, all the major powers are publishing selections from their diplomatic archives. The most useful of these are the collections published by Germany, Great Britain, and the United States. The German collection, *Akten zur deutschen auswärtigen Politik 1918–1945,* is being edited by a quadripartite board consisting of German, British, French, and American historians. Its Series B starts in late 1925, although an earlier Series A is contemplated. The documents for the Nazi period (Series C and D) are also available in English as *Documents on German Foreign Policy, 1918–1945.* In addition, most of the documents from which these collections have been prepared are available on microfilm in the National Archives in Washington and the Public Record Office in London. The rest may be examined at the Politisches Archiv of the German Foreign Ministry in Bonn. An invaluable guide to all these holdings is George O. Kent, ed., *A Catalog of Files and Microfilms of the German Foreign Ministry Archives, 1920–1945,* 3 vols. (Stanford, 1962–1966), with a fourth volume to come.

Additional material on German foreign policy under Hitler may be found in the collections compiled by the International Military Tribunal at Nuremberg in 1945–1946: *Trial of the Major War Criminals Before the International Military Tribunal, Proceedings and Documents,* 42 vols. (Nuremberg, 1947–1949); *Nazi Conspiracy and Aggression,* 10 vols. (Washington, 1946–1948); *The Trial of Major War Criminals,* 22 vols. (Washington, 1946–1950); and *Trials of the War Criminals Before the Nuremberg Military Tribunals Under Control Council Law No. 10,* 15 vols. (Washington, n.d.). Some German documents captured by the Russians have been published as *Documents secrets du Ministère des Affaires Etrangères d'Allemagne,* 3 vols. (Paris, 1946–1947); and *Documents and Materials Relating to the Eve of the Second World War,* 2 vols. (Moscow, 1948).

The British collection, *Documents on British Foreign Policy, 1919–1939,* is particularly useful for the early 1920's, where published documents are few. It is equally good on the later years. As with all document series still in progress, their exact state of publication must be ascertained by consulting the catalog of any major library. Under Britain's new thirty-year rule, most of the documents for our period are now open to research in London. The same applies to American documents which are available at the National Archives in Washington, and of which the most important have been published in the State Department's series, *Foreign Relations of the United States: Diplomatic Papers.*

As far as France and the Soviet Union are concerned, the situation is less satisfactory. A large part of France's archival holdings were destroyed or dispersed during World War II, and, as a result, coverage in the *Documents diplomatiques français 1932–1939* is quite uneven. Publication of documents for the 1920's has been postponed, although losses here have been smaller. A useful supplementary source is the records of a parliamentary investigating commission into the origins of World War II: *Les événements survenus en France de 1933 à 1945: Témoignages et documents recueillis par la Commission d'Enquête Parlementaire,* 10 vols. (Paris, 1947–1954). Further material may be found in the records of the various trials of public figures held after World War II. For references see Toscano, *History of Treaties and International Politics,* cited above.

The Soviet Union has been the most reluctant to reveal its diplomatic secrets. Its official series, begun in 1957, *Dokumenty vneshnei Politiki SSSR (Documents on the Foreign Policy of the USSR),* is judged reliable for what it contains, which is not very much. Jane Degras, ed., *Soviet Documents on Foreign Policy,* 3 vols. (London, 1951–1953), has only material published elsewhere, notably in the Soviet press.

The Italian collection, finally, *I Documenti Diplomatici Italiani,* which will ultimately cover the period from 1860 to 1943, is excellent. Its Series VI to VIII cover the years 1918–1939. Several of the smaller Powers also have published selections from their archives. Together with those of the major countries, these are carefully analyzed in Toscano, *op. cit.,* Chapter IV.

MEMOIR SOURCES

Toscano also provides a useful introduction to the most important personal sources—memoirs, letters, and other papers by leading diplomats—which are an essential supplement to government documents. Their number is vast, but their usefulness differs widely. The best coverage exists for Great Britain in the 1930's. Here the most rewarding are Winston S. Churchill, *The Gathering Storm* (London, 1948); Anthony Eden, *Facing the Dictators* (London, 1962); Alfred Duff Cooper, *Old Men Forget* (London, 1953); Lord Strang, *At Home and Abroad* (London, 1956); Hugh Dalton, *The Fateful Years: Memoirs, 1931–1945* (London, 1957); Lord Vansittart, *The Mist Procession* (London, 1958); R. J. Minney, *Private Papers of Hore-Belisha* (London, 1960); and, last but not least, Harold Nicolson, *Diaries and Letters 1930–1939* (London, 1966). Other public figures who could have told a lot but didn't are Samuel Hoare, Viscount Templewood, *Nine Troubled Years* (London, 1954); Sir John Simon, *Retrospect* (London, 1948); Nevile Henderson, *Failure of a Mission, Berlin 1937–1939* (London, 1940); and Earl of Halifax, *Fullness of Days* (London, 1957). The Earl of Birkenhead, *Halifax: The Life of Lord Halifax* (Boston, 1966), makes use of some family papers. None of the Prime Ministers after Lloyd George left any memoirs, but, except for MacDonald, they have found biographers who quote from their papers. The best book on Baldwin is Keith Middlemas and John Barnes, *Baldwin: A Biography* (London, 1969). Both Keith Feiling, *The Life of Neville Chamberlain* (London, 1946), and Ian Macleod, *Neville Chamberlain* (London, 1961), are very kind to their subject. Compared to the 1930's, British memoir sources for the 1920's are far fewer. The memoirs of Lord D'Abernon, *An Ambassador of Peace*, 3 vols. (London, 1929–1931), are important for Anglo-German relations; H. Nicolson, *Curzon: The Last Phase* (London, 1934), deals with the early postwar period; and Charles Petrie, *Austen Chamberlain*, 2 vols. (London, 1934–1940), has used the foreign minister's papers. Chamberlain's own account, *Down the Years* (London, 1935), is disappointing. It should be noted, finally, that the British are quite generous in granting access to unpublished papers, in private as well as public hands.

The same cannot be said for the French who, in general, are more secretive about their foreign policy. Yet because of the gaps in official documentation, France's memoir literature is of special significance. Among the most important works, some to be used with caution, are Georges Bonnet, *Défense de la paix*, 2 vols. (Geneva, 1946–1947); André François-Poncet, *The Fateful Years: Memoirs of a French Ambassador in Berlin, 1931–1939* (New York, 1949); Vicomte J. Davignon, *Berlin 1936-1940: Souvenirs d'une mission* (Paris, 1951); J. Paul-Boncour, *Entre deux guerres: souvenirs sur la IIIᵉ république*, 3 vols. (Paris, 1945–1946); Robert Coulondre, *De Staline à Hitler; souvenir de deux ambassades, 1936–1939* (Paris, 1950); Léon Noël, *Une ambassade à Varsovie, 1935–1939* (Paris, 1944); and Paul Reynaud, *In the Thick of the Fight, 1930–1945* (New York, 1955), and *Mémoires,* 2 vols. (Paris, 1960–1963). Pierre-Etienne Flandin, *Politique française, 1919–1940* (Paris, 1947), is evasive. Pierre Laval is the subject of an excellent study by G. Warner, *Pierre Laval and the Eclipse of France* (New York, 1968). Joel Colton, *Léon Blum: Humanist in Politics* (New York, 1966), is admirable. On the 1920's, Georges Suarez, *Briand: sa vie, son oeuvre, avec son journal et de nombreux documents inédits,* 6 vols. (Paris, 1938–1952), is a standard work. Briand's rival, Poincaré, has been treated in several biographies of which the best are Jacques Chastenet, *Raymond Poincaré* (Paris, 1948), and Pierre Miquel, *Poincaré* (Paris, 1961), the latter based on much fresh material. See also J. Laroche, *Au Quai d'Orsay avec Briand et Poincaré, 1913–1926* (Paris, 1957). Edouard Herriot, *Jadis: D'une guerre à l'autre, 1914–1936,* 2 vols. (Paris, 1948-52), is good as background.

German memoirs for the 1930's, for obvious reasons, are neither plentiful nor rewarding. There is ample material on Hitler—several editions of his autobiography, *Mein Kampf;* his "second book," *Hitler's Secret Book* (New York, 1961); various collections of his speeches; and, most interesting, the minutes of his after-dinner monologues, *Hitler's Secret Conversations, 1941–1944* (New York, 1953). None of these, however, permit any real insight into Hitler's thoughts and motivations. There are several biographies of Hitler, of which Alan Bullock, *Hitler: A Study in Tyranny,* rev. ed. (New York, 1964), is the best. The memoirs of the men who helped Hitler make foreign policy are too self-serving to be of much value. This is true especially for Ernst von Weizsäcker, *Memoirs* (London, 1951); Herbert von Dirksen, *Moskau, Tokyo, London: Erinnerungen und Betrachtungen zu 20 Jahren deutscher Aussenpolitik, 1919–1939* (Stuttgart, 1949), which differs from its English version; *The Ribbentrop Memoirs* (London, 1954); and Hjalmar Schacht, *Account Settled* (London, 1948). Schacht's later volume, *76 Jahre meines Lebens* (Munich, 1953), covers much the same ground but also has new material on the 1920's. Franz von Papen, *Memoirs* (London, 1952), is an informative apologia. Among minor figures, the reminiscences of the Wilhelmstrasse's star interpreter, Paul Schmidt, *Statist auf diplomatischer Bühne 1923–1945* (Bonn, 1950), are full of human interest; and Erich Kordt, *Nicht aus den Akten* (Stuttgart, 1950), tells of the workings of the *Auswärtiges Amt* during the Hitler years. As with most other countries, German memoir material for the 1920's is scarce. The most important single source is the unpublished papers of Gustav Stresemann, available on microfilm at the National Archives and at several university libraries. A partial collection, edited by Henry Bernhard *et al., Gustav Stresemann: Vermächtnis: Der Nachlass in drei Bänden* (Berlin, 1932–1933), while carefully edited to protect Stresemann's image, is still useful. This does not hold for the abbreviated English version. A major Stresemann biography remains to be written. (The sizable literature and the controversy surrounding Stresemann are discussed in Hans W. Gatzke, "Gustav Stresemann: A Bibliographical Article," *Journal of Modern History,* XXXVI [March

1964]). Stresemann's successor as foreign minister, Julius Curtius, has told his story in *Bemühungen um Österreich: Das Scheitern des Zollunionsplans von 1931* (Heidelberg, 1947). The long-awaited reminiscences of Heinrich Brüning, *Memoiren, 1918–1934* (Stuttgart, 1970), dwell more on domestic than foreign affairs and should be used with caution. The other foreign ministers, from Brockdorff-Rantzau to Neurath, still are awaiting biographers. The papers of the former, a key figure in Russo-German relations, also are available on microfilm at the National Archives. The German Federal Republic, finally, has made deliberate efforts to collect the papers of public figures, especially of the Weimar period, most of which may be seen at the Bundesarchiv in Koblenz. Wolfgang Mommsen, *Schriftliche Nachlässe in deutschen Archiven,* rev. ed. (Boppard, 1970), is an excellent bibliographical guide.

Among Italian memoir sources, the outstanding are the diaries of Count Ciano, *Ciano's Hidden Diary, 1937–1938* (New York, 1953), and *The Ciano Diaries, 1939–1943* (New York, 1946). They have a unique ring of authenticity and are an invaluable supplement to the official documents. Other significant diaries and memoirs are Baron Aloisi, *Journal: 25 juillet 1932–14 juin 1936* (Paris, 1957); Raffaele Guariglia, *Ricordi* (Naples, 1950), which covers the years 1922–1943; Massimo Magistrati, *L'Italia a Berlino, 1937–1939* (Milan, 1956); and, though not strictly in the memoir category, "Mario Donosti" (pseud. Mario Luciolli), *Mussolini e l'Europa: La politica estera fascista* (Rome, 1945). The Duce, like the Führer, did not live to write his memoirs. Ivone Kirkpatrick, *Mussolini: A Study in Power* (New York, 1964), is the best biography.

From the Russian side there are no memoirs worth reporting, with the possible exception of Ivan Maisky, *Who Helped Hitler?* (London, 1964), covering the author's ambassadorship to the United Kingdom from 1932 to 1939. Among American memoirs the following bear on European affairs and are of special interest: Cordell Hull, *The Memoirs of Cordell Hull* (New York, 1948); Sumner Welles, *The Time for Decision* (New York, 1944); Charles G. Dawes, *Journal as Ambassador to Great Britain* (New York, 1939); William C. Bullit, *The Great Globe Itself* (New York, 1946); Joseph E. Davies, *Mission to Moscow* (New York, 1941); Martha Dodd and William Dodd, Jr., eds., *Ambassador Dodd's Diary* (New York, 1941); Hugh R. Wilson, Jr., ed., *A Career Diplomat: The Third Chapter, The Third Reich* (New York, 1960); William Philipps, *Ventures in Diplomacy* (Boston, 1952); Nancy H. Hooker, ed., *The Moffat Papers: Selections from the Diplomatic Journals of Jay Pierrepont Moffat* (Cambridge, Mass., 1956); and George F. Kennan, *From Prague After Munich* (Princeton, 1968).

The reminiscences of politicians from the smaller powers are numerous, but only a few deserve mention. The story of Poland's foreign minister, Colonel Joseph Beck, *Final Report* (New York, 1957), is more interesting for the author's psychology than for the events he describes. More useful are the diaries of two of his subalterns: Count Jan Szembek, Polish Under Secretary for Foreign Affairs, *Journal, 1933–*

1939 (Paris, 1952), and *Papers and Memoirs of Jozef Lipski, Ambassa-
dor of Poland: Diplomat in Berlin, 1933–1939* (New York, 1968). *The
Memoirs of Dr. Edward Benes: From Munich to New War and New
Victory* (London, 1954), are disappointing. Austria's Chancellor Kurt
von Schuschnigg has given his version of the *Anschluss* in *Austrian
Requiem* (London, 1947); and Rumanian Foreign Minister Grigore
Gafencu's *The Last Days of Europe* (London, 1947) is a vivid eye-
witness account of Europe on the eve of World War II.

Before we turn to secondary works, we must mention two collections
that are not strictly primary sources but have much firsthand information.
The *Survey of International Affairs* and *Documents on International Affairs,* both published by the Royal Institute of International Affairs in
London and for many years edited by Arnold Toynbee, contain valuable
annual surveys and documents on world events. The volumes for 1938
and 1939 are among the best that has been written on those critical
years. Less important but often rewarding is a German publication,
Schulthess' Europäischer Geschichtskalender (Munich, 1861–1942), an
annual survey, including documents.

SECONDARY WORKS
1919–1939

There is no satisfactory general work in English on European diplomacy
between the wars. G. M. Gathorne-Hardy, *A Short History of International Affairs, 1920–1939* (London, 1950), goes beyond Europe and is
out of date. E. H. Carr, *International Relations Between the Two World
Wars, 1919–1939* (London, 1947), is an admirable summary. It should
be supplemented by Mr. Carr's perceptive *The Twenty Years' Crisis,
1919–1939* (London, 1946). There are several French works, most of
them written before many of the documents were available: Maurice
Baumont, *La faillité de la paix, 1918–1939,* rev. ed.; 2 vols. (Paris,
1961); J.-B. Duroselle, *Histoire diplomatique de 1919 à nos jours*
(Paris, 1953); and Jacques de Launay, *Histoire contemporaine de la
diplomatie secrète, 1914–1945* (Lausanne, 1965). The only volumes
translated into English—Pierre Renouvin's *War and Aftermath, 1914–
1929* (New York, 1968) and *World War II and Its Origins, 1929–
1945* (New York, 1969)—were originally published in 1957 and suffer from careless translation. Two other works that still merit attention
are W. M. Jordan, *Great Britain, France and the German Problem,
1918–1939* (London, 1943), and Arnold Wolfers, *Britain and France
Between Two Wars* (New York, 1940). Gordon A. Craig and Felix
Gilbert, eds., *The Diplomats, 1919–1939* (Princeton, 1953), is a collection of lively essays on the making and makers of inter-war diplomacy.

There are some good books on the diplomatic history of individual
Powers. For Great Britain, the best is W. N. Medlicott, *British Foreign
Policy Since Versailles,* rev. ed. (New York, 1968). F. S. Northedge,
The Troubled Giant: Britain Among the Great Powers, 1916–1939
(London, 1968), is more comprehensive but less readable. See also

P. A. Reynolds, *British Foreign Policy in the Inter-War Years* (New York, 1954); C. L. Mowat, *Britain Between the Wars, 1918–1940* (Chicago, 1955); and D. C. Watt, *Personalities and Politics: Studies in the Formation of British Foreign Policy in the Twentieth Century* (London, 1965). "John Connell" (pseud. John Henry Robertson), *The "Office": A Study of British Foreign Policy and Its Makers, 1919–1951* (London, 1958), is a useful analysis of the Foreign Office.

There are no comparable works for Germany or France, although for the latter the general French works cited above are relevant. Ludwig Zimmermann, *Deutsche Aussenpolitik in der Ära der Weimarer Republik* (Göttingen, 1958), goes only to 1933. For Italy, Ennio Di Nolfo, *Mussolini e la politica estera italiana, 1919–1933* (Padua, 1960), is excellent but also stops in 1933. Luigi Villari, *Italian Foreign Policy Under Mussolini* (New York, 1956), is pro-fascist. Adler Selig, *The Uncertain Giant, 1921–1941* (New York, 1966), is very good for the United States. On Russian foreign policy the best general work is Adam B. Ulam, *Expansion and Coexistence: The History of Soviet Foreign Policy, 1917–1967* (New York, 1968). George F. Kennan, *Russia and the West Under Lenin and Stalin* (Boston, 1961), is a perennial favorite; and Louis Fischer, *Russia's Road from Peace to War: Soviet Foreign Relations, 1917–1941* (New York, 1969), is well informed but confusing. See also Ivo Lederer, ed., *Russian Foreign Policy* (New Haven, 1962). Among general works on the diplomacy of the smaller powers of Eastern Europe the following stand out: Roman Debicki, *The Foreign Policy of Poland, 1919–1939* (New York, 1962); Stephan Horak, *Poland's International Affairs, 1919–1960* (Bloomington, 1964); and F. J. Vondracek, *The Foreign Policy of Czechoslovakia, 1918–1935* (New York, 1937). Good general introductions to the history of the "succession states" of Eastern Europe are Hugh Seton-Watson, *Eastern Europe Between the Wars 1918–1941*, rev. ed. (Cambridge, England, 1962); Stephen Borsody, *The Tragedy of Central Europe* (New York, 1962); and John A. Lukacs, *The Great Powers and Eastern Europe* (New York, 1953). The standard work on the League of Nations is F. P. Walters, *A History of the League of Nations*, 2 vols. (New York, 1952).

1919–1933

The literature on European diplomacy between 1919 and 1933 is voluminous but, with few exceptions, dated. On the Peace Conference of 1919, the best recent book is Arno J. Mayer, *Politics and Diplomacy of Peacemaking: Containment and Counterrevolution at Versailles, 1918–1919* (New York, 1967), where references to the vast literature on the peace settlements can be found. Among monographic reappraisals, the following are the best: S. P. Tillman, *Anglo-American Relations During the Paris Peace Conference of 1919* (Princeton, 1961); John M. Thompson, *Russia, Bolshevism, and the Versailles Peace* (Princeton, 1966); Jere Clemens King, *Foch Versus Clemenceau: France and German Dismemberment, 1918–1919* (Cambridge, Mass., 1960); and L. E.

Gelfand, *The Inquiry: American Preparations for Peace, 1917–1919* (New Haven, 1963). Among older works Paul Birdsall, *Versailles Twenty Years After* (New York, 1941), remains the best. On the early postwar period much work needs to be done. Heinrich Euler, *Die Aussenpolitik der Weimarer Republik, 1918–1923* (Aschaffenburg, 1957), is heavily factual. David Felix, *Walther Rathenau and the Politics of Reparations* (Baltimore, 1971), is a fresh start. The economic aftermath of the war and the reparations problem, including American involvement, are treated in Hans Ronde, *Von Versailles bis Lausanne: Der Verlauf der Reparationsverhandlungen nach dem Ersten Weltkrieg* (Stuttgart, 1950); Dieter Bruno Gescher, *Die Vereinigten Staaten von Nordamerika und die Reparationen, 1920–1924* (Bonn, 1956); W. Link, *Die Amerikanische Stabilisierungspolitik in Deutschland, 1921–32* (Düsseldorf, 1969); C. M. Frasure, *British Policy on War Debts and Reparations* (Philadelphia, 1940); and Etienne Weill-Reynal, *Les réparations allemandes et la France,* 3 vols. (Paris, 1947). See also Herbert Feis, *The Diplomacy of the Dollar, 1919–1932* (New York, 1966). On the later phase of the reparations problem see Stephen A. Schuker, "The French Financial Crisis and the Adoption of the Dawes Plan 1924" (unpublished dissertation, Harvard University, 1969); W. J. Helbich, *Die Reparationen in der Ära Brüning* (Berlin, 1962); and the collection of documents edited by Martin Vogt, *Reichsarchiv (1931–1933): Die Entstehung des Young-Plans* (Boppard, 1970).

The Ruhr crisis of 1923 still calls for a good book. Royal J. Schmidt, *Versailles and the Ruhr: Seedbed of World War II* (The Hague, 1968), has some useful material. Kenneth Paul Jones, "Stresemann and the Diplomacy of the Ruhr Crisis, 1923–1924" (unpublished dissertation, University of Wisconsin, 1970), is better. Jean-Claude Favez, *Le Reich devant l'occupation Franco-Belge de la Ruhr en 1923* (Geneva, 1969), is excellent. See also A. E. Cornebise, "Some Aspects of the German Response to the Ruhr Occupation" (unpublished dissertation, University of North Carolina, 1965). D. G. White, *Einige Kapitel aus der Grossen Politik zur Zeit der Ruhrbesetzung* (Berlin, 1939), remains important.

On Italian postwar diplomacy, Alan Cassels, *Mussolini's Early Diplomacy* (Princeton, 1970), is best. James Barros, *The Corfu Incident of 1923: Mussolini and the League of Nations* (Princeton, 1965), is an able monograph. Giampiero Carocci, *La politica estera dell 'italia fascista, 1925–1928* (Bari, 1969), is admirable for its broad documentation. The early years of the League are sympathetically discussed in Byron Dexter, *The Years of Opportunity: The League of Nations, 1920–1926* (New York, 1967).

Much has been written about the relations between the Weimar Republic and the Soviet Union. Gerald Freund, *Unholy Alliance: Russo-German Relations from the Treaty of Brest-Litovsk to the Treaty of Berlin* (New York, 1957), has been superseded by more recent studies using the German documents, notably Horst Günther Linke, *Deutsch-sowjetische Beziehungen bis Rapallo* (Cologne, 1970); Kurt Rosenbaum, *Community of Fate: German-Soviet Diplomatic Relations, 1922–*

1928 (Syracuse, 1965); and Harvey L. Dyck, *Weimar Germany and Soviet Russia, 1926–1933* (London, 1966). Günter Rosenfeld, *Sowjetrussland und Deutschland, 1917–1922* (Berlin/East, 1960), despite some bias, is a serious work. E. H. Carr, *German-Soviet Relations Between the Two World Wars, 1919–1939* (Baltimore, 1951), is out of date. Gustav Hilger, *Wir und der Kreml* (Berlin, 1955), is an important contribution by a former German diplomat. Herbert Helbig, *Die Träger der Rapallo-Politik* (Göttingen, 1958), and Theodor Schieder, *Die Probleme des Rapallo-Vertrags: Eine Studie über die deutsch-russischen Beziehungen, 1922–1926* (Cologne, 1956), are essential for an understanding of Brockdorff-Rantzau and his policy. The study of Allied relations with the Soviet Union has centered mainly on the early years. George F. Kennan, *Soviet-American Relations, 1917–1920*, 2 vols. (Princeton, 1956–1958), and R. H. Ullman, *Anglo-Soviet Relations, 1917–1921*, 2 vols. to date (Princeton, 1961–1968), are definitive works. See also John Bradley, *Allied Intervention in Russia: A Study of Allied Diplomatic and Military Plans in Russia, 1917–1920* (New York, 1968). Louis Fischer, *The Soviets in World Affairs, 1917–1929*, 2 vols. (London, 1930), remains unique because of the author's firsthand knowledge of Soviet affairs. The sections on foreign policy in E. H. Carr's multi-volumed *A History of Soviet Russia* (London, 1950–) are the best in English on the subject.

The foreign relations of the smaller powers of Eastern Europe during the 1920's have been the subject of some important books. Josef Korbel, *Poland Between East and West: Soviet and German Diplomacy Toward Poland, 1919–1933* (Princeton, 1963), and C. M. Kimmich, *Danzig and German Foreign Policy 1919–1934* (New Haven, 1968), are chiefly based on the German documents. Christian Höltje, *Die Weimarer Republik und das Ost-Locarno Problem* (Würzburg, 1958), is thorough but not without bias. On German-Czech relations see F. Gregory Campbell Jr., "Czechoslovak-German Relations During the Weimar Republic, 1918–1933" (unpublished dissertation, Yale University, 1967). Piotr S. Wandycz, *France and Her Eastern Allies, 1919–1925* (Minnesota, 1962), and the same author's *Soviet-Polish Relations, 1917–1921* (Cambridge, Mass., 1969), are models of scholarship. On relations among the small powers, both John Oliver Crane, *The Little Entente* (New York, 1931), and Robert Machray, *The Little Entente* (London, 1929), are dated. On the Balkans, see L. S. Stavrianos, *Balkan Federation: A History of the Movement Toward Balkan Unity in Modern Times* (Northampton, 1944).

There are fewer good books on the Western phases of European diplomacy before 1933. A major study of Locarno—its origins and aftermath—is still lacking. Jon Jacobsen, *Locarno Diplomacy*, to be published by the Princeton University Press, sounds promising. The articles and comments by various noted scholars in Hellmuth Rössler, ed., *Die Folgen von Versailles, 1919–1924*, and *Locarno und die Weltpolitik, 1924–1932* (Göttingen, 1969), are highly recommended. Raul B. Wehn, "Germany's Road to Locarno" (unpublished dissertation, Columbia University, 1968), and J. Spenz, *Die diplomatische Vorgeschichte des Beitritts Deutschlands zum Völkerbund, 1924–1926* (Göttingen, 1966), are helpful. Robert Gottwald, *Die Deutsch-Amerikanischen Beziehungen in der Ära Stresemann* (Berlin, 1965), is a competent monograph. On the later twenties and early thirties, Robert H. Ferrell, *Peace in Their Time: The Origins of the Kellogg-Briand Pact* (New Haven, 1952), and *American Diplomacy in the Great Depression* (New Haven, 1957), present the American side, while Edward W. Bennett, *The Diplomacy of the Financial Crisis 1931* (Cambridge, Mass., 1962), uses much fresh German material. The history of the futile disarmament efforts also needs rewriting. John Wheeler-Bennett's contemporary accounts, *Disarmament and Security, 1925–1931* (London, 1932), and *The Pipedream of Peace: The Story of the Collapse of Disarmament* (London, 1935), are still useful. Charles C. Bright, "Britain's Search for Security, 1930–1936" (unpublished dissertation, Yale University, 1970), deals with naval disarmament and is excellent. On Germany's attempts to evade the disarmament clauses of Versailles see Hans W. Gatzke, *Stresemann and the Rearmament of Germany* (Baltimore, 1954); Michael Salewski, *Entwaffnung und Militärkontrolle in Deutschland 1919–1927* (Munich, 1966); and Georges Castellan, *Le réarmement clandestin du Reich, 1930–1935* (Paris, 1954). Some recent monographs on British foreign policy include David Walder, *The Chanak Affair* (New York, 1969); David Carlton, *MacDonald Versus Henderson: The Foreign Policy of the Second Labour Government* (London, 1970); and on Locarno, Douglas Johnson, "Austen Chamberlain and the Locarno Agreements," *University of Birmingham Historical Journal,* VIII (1961–1962), and F. G. Stambrook, " 'Das Kind'—Lord D'Abernon and the Origins of the Locarno Pact," *Central European History,* I, 3 (1968). George A. Grün, "Locarno—Idea and Reality," *International Affairs,* XXXI (1955), is a thoughtful reappraisal.

1933–1939

The literature on European diplomacy between 1933 and the outbreak of World War II is far richer than for the preceding years, although here, too, there is no satisfactory general work. The revisionist book by A. J. P. Taylor, *The Origins of the Second World War* (London, 1961), has been much criticized and has caused heated controversy. But it has also led to some fruitful reappraisals; see the excellent bibliographical essay by D. C. Watt, "Appeasement: The Rise of a Revisionist School?", *Political Quarterly,* XXXVI (1965). The brief surveys of pre–World War II diplomacy by Keith Eubank, *The Origins of World War II* (New York, 1969), and Laurence Lafore, *The End of Glory: An Interpretation of the Origins of World War II* (Philadelphia, 1970), are useful. E. M. Robertson, ed., *The Origins of the Second World War* (New York, 1971), is a collection of essays by various authors. The books by L. B. Namier, *Europe in Decay: A Study in Disintegration,*

1936–1940 (New York, 1950), and *In the Nazi Era* (New York, 1952), consist mostly of reviews and are still worth reading.

The foreign policy of individual countries has been studied most thoroughly for Great Britain and Germany. Aside from the general works on Britain for the inter-war period cited above, a number of books concentrate on the years since 1933 in an effort to explain British appeasement. The best is Martin Gilbert, *The Roots of Appeasement* (London, 1966); see also Martin Gilbert and Richard Gott, *The Appeasers,* rev. ed. (Boston, 1963). Margaret George, *The Hollow Men: An Examination of British Foreign Policy Between the Years 1933 and 1939* (London, 1967), is an indictment of the Conservatives. See also Peter Lundgreen, *Die englische Appeasement-Politik bis zum Münchener Abkommen* (Berlin, 1968), and W. R. Rock, *Appeasement on Trial: British Foreign Policy and Its Critics* (Hamden, 1966). On the British press and appeasement see R. Kieser, *Englands Appeasement-Politik und der Aufstieg des Dritten Reiches im Spiegel der britischen Presse, 1933–1939* (Winterthur, 1964); and Gunter Holzweissig, *Das Deutschlandbild der britischen Presse im Jahre 1935* (Hamburg, 1967). Britain's military power and its effect on foreign policy is treated in D. Wood and D. Dempster, *The Narrow Margin* (New York, 1961).

Germany's foreign policy under Hitler has been the subject of two massive studies. Hans-Adolf Jacobsen, *Nationalsozialistische Aussenpolitik 1933–1938* (Frankfurt/Berlin, 1968), is excellent on the making of Nazi foreign policy and supersedes the earlier work by Paul Seabury, *The Wilhelmstrasse* (Berkeley, 1954). The best book on Hitler's early foreign policy is Gerhard Weinberg, *The Foreign Policy of Hitler's Germany: Diplomatic Revolution in Europe, 1933–1936* (Chicago, 1970). There will be a sequel dealing with the later period. See also Charles Bloch, *Hitler und die Europäischen Mächte 1933/34: Kontinuität oder Bruch* (Frankfurt, 1966), and Günter Schubert, *Anfänge nationalsozialistischer Aussenpolitik* (Cologne, 1962), which deals with Nazi plans before 1933. A good general analysis of Hitler's aims and ideas on foreign policy is Axel Kuhn, *Hitlers aussenpolitisches Programm: Entstehung und Entwicklung, 1919–1939* (Stuttgart, 1970). The relations between military planning and foreign policy are ably discussed in E. M. Robertson, *Hitler's Pre-war Policy and Military Plans 1933–1939* (London, 1963). On German rearmament, see Gerhard Meinck, *Hitler und die deutsche Aufrüstung* (Wiesbaden, 1959), and on Hitler's naval policy, Rolf Bensel, *Die deutsche Flottenpolitik von 1933–1939* (Frankfurt, 1958). Three partially overlapping books deal with Germany's economic preparations for war: Burton H. Klein, *Germany's Economic Preparations for War* (Cambridge, Mass., 1959); Alan S. Milward, *The German Economy at War* (London, 1965); and Berenice A. Carroll, *Design for Total War: Arms and Economics in the Third Reich* (The Hague, 1968).

There is as yet no study of French foreign policy during the thirties comparable to those by Jacobsen and Weinberg for Germany. Alexander

Werth, *The Twilight of France, 1938–1940* (New York, 1942), is still useful. Charles A. Micaud, *The French Right and Nazi Germany, 1933–1939: A Study of Public Opinion* (Durham, 1943), helps explain French appeasement. For Italy, Gaetano Salvemini, *Prelude to World War II* (New York, 1954); Mario Toscano, *The Origins of the Pact of Steel* (Baltimore, 1967); and Elizabeth Wiskemann, *The Rome-Berlin Axis*, rev. ed. (London, 1966), provide good introductions. Ferdinand Siebert, *Italiens Weg in den Zweiten Weltkrieg* (Frankfurt, 1962), is excellent. On Russian foreign policy in the 1930's, the best general work is still Max Beloff, *The Foreign Policy of Soviet Russia, 1929–1941*, 2 vols. (London, 1947–49). On American foreign policy see William L. Langer and S. Everett Gleason, *The Challenge to Isolation, 1937–1940* (New York, 1952); Arnold A. Offner, *American Appeasement: United States Foreign Policy and Germany* (Cambridge, Mass., 1969); and Manfred Jonas, *Isolationism in America 1935–1941* (Ithaca, 1966). Among general works on the foreign policy of some of the smaller powers of Eastern Europe in the 1930's, the following are recommended: Hans Roos, *Polen und Europa: Studien zur polnischen Aussenpolitik 1931–1939* (Tübingen, 1957); S. D. Kertesz, *Diplomacy in a Whirlpool: Hungary Between Nazi Germany and Soviet Russia* (Notre Dame, 1953); M. Adám *et al., Allianz Hitler-Horthy-Mussolini* (Budapest, 1966), a collection of documents; and J. B. Hoptner, *Yugoslavia in Crisis, 1934–1941* (New York, 1962). On the final years of the League of Nations, James Barros, *Betrayal from Within: Joseph Avenol, Secretary of the League of Nations, 1933–1940* (New Haven, 1969), is revealing.

Another category of works deals with relations among two or more powers during the years leading up to World War II. Dietrich Aigner, *Das Ringen um England: Das deutsch-britische Verhältnis: Die öffentliche Meinung, 1933–1939* (Munich, 1939), is a massive study with a separate volume of annotations. German-Soviet relations again have attracted much attention. O. Vehviläinen, *Nationalsozialistisches Deutschland und Sowjetunion: Die Geschichte ihrer diplomatischen Beziehungen, 1933–1939* (Wiesbaden, 1970), is a competent survey. Karlheinz Niclauss, *Die Sowjetunion und Hitlers Machtergreifung: Eine Studie über die deutsch-russischen Beziehungen der Jahre 1929 bis 1935* (Bonn, 1966), and Thomas Weingartner, *Stalin und der Aufstieg Hitlers* (Berlin, 1970), deal with the early years. James E. McSherry, *Stalin, Hitler, and Europe: The Origins of World War II* (Cleveland, 1968), is less detailed but broader. There are several books on German-American relations beside the one by Offner, cited above. James V. Compton, *The Swastika and the Eagle: Hitler, the United States, and the Origins of World War II* (Boston, 1967), is very good. Hans-Jürgen Schröder, *Deutschland und die Vereinigten Staaten, 1933–1939* (Wiesbaden, 1970), presents the German view. A. Frye, *Nazi Germany and the American Hemisphere, 1933–1941* (New Haven, 1967), ably covers a lot of ground. Ernest R. May, "Nazi Germany and the United States: A Review Essay," *Journal of Modern History*, XLI (June 1969), is an admirable bibliographical survey. Another area in which good work has been done is German-Japanese relations. F. W. Iklé, *German-Japanese Relations, 1936–1940* (New York, 1956), has been partly superseded by E. L. Presseisen, *Germany and Japan, 1933–1941* (The Hague, 1958), and by the more comprehensive work of Theodor Sommer, *Deutschland und Japan zwischen den Mächten, 1935–1940* (Tübingen, 1962). See also Karl Drechsler, *Deutschland-China-Japan, 1933–1939* (Berlin/East, 1964). On the diplomacy of Eastern Europe, the following are of special interest: R. Kiszling, *Die militärischen Vereinbarungen der Kleinen Entente, 1929–1937* (Munich, 1959); Bohdan B. Budurowycz, *Polish-Soviet Relations, 1932–1939* (New York, 1963); Johann Wuescht, *Jugoslawien und das Dritte Reich* (Stuttgart, 1969); and Bernd-Jürgen Wendt, *Appeasement 1938: Wirtschaftliche Rezession und Mitteleuropa* (Frankfurt, 1966). Germany's relations with the Vatican are discussed in Ernst Deuerlein, *Das Reichskonkordat* (Düsseldorf, 1956). Saul Friedländer, *Pius XII and the Third Reich,* rev. ed. (New York, 1966), deals mainly with the post-1939 period. Two important documentary collections on this controversial subject are Dieter Albrecht, ed., *Der Notenwechsel zwischen dem Heiligen Stuhl und der deutschen Reichsregierung,* 2 vols. (Mainz, 1965–1969), and *Actes et Documents du Saint-Siège relatifs à la Seconde Guerre Modiale:* Vol. I, *Le Saint-Siège et la Guerre en Europe, mars 1939–août 1940* (Rome, 1965), published by the Vatican. Hitler's colonial aims have been examined exhaustively in Klaus Hildebrand, *Vom Reich zum Weltreich* (Munich, 1969), which is better than the slight study by Wolfe W. Schmokel, *Dream of Empire: German Colonialism, 1919–1945* (New Haven, 1964). Finally, on relations between the Western Allies there is A. H. Furnia, *The Diplomacy of Appeasement: Anglo-French Relations and the Prelude to World War II, 1931–1938* (Washington, 1960), which was written before much of the documentation was available.

The books and articles on individual events and crises in pre–World War II diplomacy are quite uneven, and the number increases as the outbreak of war draws closer. K. H. Jarausch, *The Four Power Pact, 1933* (Madison, 1965), deals with early Western attempts to accommodate Hitler. On Germany's relations with Poland, see the articles by Zygmunt J. Gasiorowski, "Did Pilsudski Attempt to Initiate a Preventive War?", *Journal of Modern History,* XXVII (June 1955), and "The German-Polish Non-Aggression Pact of 1934," *Journal of Central European Affairs,* XV (April 1955). Poland's preventive-war plans are also dealt with in Hans Roos, "Die 'Präventivkriegspläne' Pilsudkis von 1933," *Vierteljahrshefte für Zeitgeschichte,* III (October 1955), and W. Jedrzejewicz, "The Polish Plan for a Preventive War Against Germany in 1933," *Polish Review,* XI (1966). On the background of the Saar plebiscite of 1935, see Helmut Hirsch, *Die Saar von Genf. Die Saarfrage während des Völkerbundregimes von 1920–1935* (Bonn, 1954). On the plebiscite itself, Sarah Wambaugh, *The Saar Plebiscite* (Cambridge, Mass., 1940), is the standard work. See also H. Shamir, "Le plebiscite de la Sarre et l'opinion publique en France," *Revue d'histoire moderne et contemporaine*, XVII (January/March 1970). The repercussions of the Anglo-German Naval Agreement of 1935 are discussed in the dissertation by Charles C. Bright (see above, p. 256). Of the negotiations themselves, D. C. Watt, "The Anglo-German Naval Agreement: An Interim Judgment," *Journal of Modern History*, XXVIII (June 1956), remains the best account. Robert Ingrim, *Hitlers glücklichster Tag: Am 18. Juli 1935* (Stuttgart, 1962), is pedestrian. The Rhineland crisis of 1936 has aroused understandable interest. Max Braubach, *Der Einmarsch deutscher Truppen in die entmilitarisierte Zone am Rhein im März 1936* (Cologne, 1956), was written before all the documents were available. The French side of the story is ably dealt with in Jean-Baptiste Duroselle, "France and the Crisis of March 1936," in E. M. Acomb and M. L. Brown, Jr., eds., *French Society and Culture Since the Old Regime* (New York, 1964). D. C. Watt, "German Plans for the Reoccupation of the Rhineland," *Journal of Contemporary History*, I (October 1966), provides an important military footnote. See also Roman Debicki, "The Remilitarization of the Rhineland and Its Impact on the Franco-Polish Alliance," *Polish Review*, XIV (Autumn 1969). William E. Scott, *Alliance Against Hitler: The Origins of the Franco-Soviet Pact* (Durham, 1962), deals with the event that gave Hitler the excuse to move into the Rhineland.

Two crises in the Mediterranean—the Ethiopian War and the Civil War in Spain—contributed much to the rising international tension that led to World War II. The best book on the origins of the Ethiopian War is George W. Baer, *The Coming of the Italian-Ethiopian War* (Cambridge, Mass., 1967). On the war itself, Angelo Del Boca, *The Ethiopian War, 1935–1941* (Chicago, 1969), is the most comprehensive treatment. A. J. Barker, *The Civilizing Mission: A History of the Italo-Ethiopian War of 1935–1936* (New York, 1968), and Manfred Funke, *Sanktionen und Kanonen: Hitler, Mussolini und der internationale Abessinienkonflikt, 1934–1936* (Düsseldorf, 1970), are narrower in scope. On the attitude of the Western Powers see Franklin D. Laurens, *France and the Italo-Ethiopian Crisis, 1935–1936* (The Hague, 1967); Brice Harris, *The United States and the Italo-Ethiopian Crisis* (Stanford, 1964); and Arthur Marder, "The Royal Navy and the Ethiopian Crisis of 1935–36," *American Historical Review*, LXXV (June 1970).

The literature on the Spanish Civil War is huge. The best general works are Gabriel Jackson, *The Spanish Republic and the Civil War, 1931–1939* (Princeton, 1965), and Hugh Thomas, *The Spanish Civil War* (New York, 1961). The international repercussions of the conflict are covered in D. A. Puzzo, *Spain and the Great Powers, 1936–1941* (New York, 1962). On Germany's involvement, see Manfred Merkes, *Die deutsche Politik gegenüber dem spanischen Bürgerkrieg, 1936–1939* (Bonn, 1961), and Glenn T. Harper, *German Economic Policy During the Spanish Civil War, 1936–1939* (The Hague, 1967). The British side is treated in W. L. Kleine-Ahlbrandt, *The Policy of Simmering: A Study of British Policy During the Spanish Civil War, 1936–1939* (The Hague, 1962). See also K. W. Watkins, *Britain Divided: The Effect of the Span-*

ish Civil War on British Political Opinion (London, 1963). On the United States, see Richard P. Traina, *American Diplomacy and the Spanish Civil War* (Bloomington, 1968). The role of the Soviet Union is discussed in David T. Cattell, *Soviet Diplomacy and the Spanish Civil War* (Berkeley, 1957).

The events of the last two years before the outbreak of World War II have been brilliantly summarized in Christopher Thorne, *The Approach of War, 1938–9* (New York, 1967). Walter Hofer, *War Premeditated* (London, 1955), is dated but still good. Leonard Mosley, *On Borrowed Time: How World War II Began* (New York, 1969), successfully re-creates the mood of the time. Leonidas Hill, "Three Crises, 1938–39," *Journal of Contemporary History*, III (January 1968), is excellent. The background of the Austrian *Anschluss* has most recently been studied by Dieter Ross, *Hitler und Dollfuss: Die deutsche Österreich-Politik 1933–1934* (Hamburg, 1966). The best general works on the Austrian crisis of 1938 are Ulrich Eichstädt, *Von Dollfuss zu Hitler: Geschichte des Anschlusses Österreichs, 1933–1938* (Wiesbaden, 1955), and Jürgen Gehl, *Austria, Germany, and the Anschluss* (London, 1963). Gordon Brook-Shepherd, *The Anschluss* (Philadelphia, 1963), is the most readable account. On the international aspects of the *Anschluss,* see Lajos Kerekes, *Anschluss 1938: Österreich und die internationale Diplomatie, 1933–1938* (Budapest, 1963). The Austrian side of the story is told by former Chancellor Kurt von Schuschnigg in *Austrian Requiem* (New York, 1946), and *Im Kampf gegen Hitler* (Vienna, 1969).

Much has been written about the Munich crisis and its aftermath. On its background, see J. W. Brügel, *Tschechen und Deutsche, 1918–1938* (Munich, 1967). The best book on the crisis itself is Boris Celovsky, *Das Münchener Abkommen von 1938* (Stuttgart, 1958). Among more recent treatments, Keith Eubank, *Munich* (Norman, 1963); Keith Robbins, *Munich* (London, 1968); and Laurence Thompson, *The Greatest Treason: The Untold Story of Munich* (New York, 1968), stand out. Henri Noguères, *Munich: "Peace for Our Time"* (London, 1965), is a French view. J. W. Wheeler-Bennett, *Munich: Prologue to Tragedy* (New York, 1948), though out of date, remains valuable. On Czechoslovakia's role there is the excellent article by David Vital, "Czechoslovakia and the Powers, September 1938," in *Journal of Contemporary History*, I (October 1966), as well as Fritz Berber, ed., *Europäische Politik, 1933–1938, im Spiegel der Prager Akten* (Essen, 1942), and Václav Král, *Das Abkommen von München 1938* (Prague, 1968), which contains additional Czech documents. The international side of the Czech crisis is covered in detail in Helmuth K. Rönnefarth, *Die Sudetenkrise in der internationalen Politik,* 2 vols. (Wiesbaden, 1961). See also D. N. Lammers, *Explaining Munich: The Search for Motive in British Policy* (Stanford, 1966), and Bernd-Jürgen Wendt, *München 1938: England Zwischen Hitler und Preussen* (Frankfurt, 1965).

The background of the Polish crisis of 1939 is given in Richard Breyer, *Das Deutsche Reich und Polen, 1932–1937* (Würzburg, 1955), and Ludwig Denne, *Das Danzig-Problem in der deutschen Aussenpolitik, 1934–1939* (Bonn, 1959). Anna M. Cienciala, *Poland and the Western Powers, 1938–1939* (Toronto, 1968), is an important reevaluation of Colonel Beck's foreign policy. See also Stanislaw Mackiewicz, *Colonel Beck and His Policy* (London, 1944). Hitler's last diplomatic *coup*, the Hitler-Stalin Pact, is the subject of Gerhard L. Weinberg, *Germany and the Soviet Union, 1939–1941* (Leiden, 1954), and Max Braubach, *Hitlers Weg zur Verständigung mit Russland im Jahre 1939* (Bonn, 1960). Philipp W. Fabry, *Der Hitler-Stalin-Pakt 1939–1941* (Darmstadt, 1962), has only limited value.

As has been said repeatedly, much of the history of European diplomacy between the wars remains to be written or rewritten. To keep abreast of new work, readers are advised to consult the following journals: *The Journal of Modern History, Central European History, Review of Politics, International Affairs* (London), *Journal of Contemporary History* (London), *Revue de l'histoire de la deuxième guerre mondiale, Revue d'histoire moderne et contemporaine,* and *Vierteljahrshefte für Zeitgeschichte. The American Historical Review* has excellent bibliographies on new publications, including periodical articles, and *Historical Abstracts* publishes brief synopses of important scholarly articles.

CHRONOLOGY OF IMPORTANT EVENTS
1919–1939

1919

June 28   Treaty of Versailles with Germany (ratified January 10, 1920)
U.S. and Britain guarantee French security vs. Germany (not ratified)

1920

April–
October   Russo-Polish war extends Polish territory

1921

February 19   Franco-Polish alliance
March 16   British trade agreement with Russia
November–
February   Washington conference on naval limitations and the Far East

1922

April 16   Treaty of Rapallo between Germany and Russia
October 30   Mussolini becomes Italian Prime Minister

1923

January 11   Occupation of Ruhr by French and Belgian troops; German passive resistance ends September 26; troops withdrawn July 31, 1925
August 12   Gustav Stresemann becomes German Chancellor and Foreign Minister

1924

February 1   Great Britain recognizes Soviet Union
August 16   Dawes Plan on German reparations adopted
October 28   France recognizes Soviet Union

1925

October 5–16 Locarno Conference and Agreements (signed December 1)

1926

January 31   First zone of occupied Rhineland evacuated by Allied troops
April 24   Russo-German treaty of friendship signed at Berlin
September 8   Germany admitted to League of Nations

1927

January 31   Withdrawal of Inter-Allied Military Control Commission on German disarmament
May 27   Great Britain severs diplomatic relations with Russia

1928

August 27   Kellogg-Briand Pact (Pact of Paris) outlawing war

1929

August 31   Approval of Young Plan on reparations by Hague Conference
October 3   Death of Stresemann

1930

January–April   London Naval Conference
June 30   End of Allied Rhineland occupation
September 14   German National Socialists score major election victory

1931

March–September   German-Austrian plan for customs union defeated by France
May 11   Failure of Austrian *Kreditanstalt* touches off European financial crisis
September 18   Japan opens military operations in Manchuria

1932

February 2   Disarmament Conference opens in Geneva
June–July   Lausanne Conference virtually ends German reparations

1933

January 30   Adolf Hitler becomes German Chancellor
May 5   Renewal of Russo-German Treaty of Berlin (1926)
October 14   Germany withdraws from Disarmament Conference and League of Nations

1934

January 26   German–Polish nonaggression pact
July 25   Abortive Nazi *Putsch* in Vienna
September 18   Russia admitted to League of Nations

1935

January 13	Saar plebiscite returns region to Germany
March 16	Hitler repudiates Versailles disarmament clauses
May 2	France and Russia sign mutual assistance pact (ratified February 27, 1936)
June 18	Anglo-German naval agreement
October 3	Italy invades Ethiopia

1936

March 7	Germany reoccupies Rhineland
May 9	Italy annexes Ethiopia
July 18	Beginning of Spanish Civil War
October 25	Rome-Berlin Axis formed

1937

July 7	Hostilities between Japan and China resumed

1938

March 13	Austria annexed by Germany
September 29	Munich Conference starts dismemberment of Czechoslovakia

1939

March 14–15	Germany occupies Bohemia and Moravia
March 21	German annexation of Memel
April 7	Italy occupies Albania
August 23	German-Soviet nonaggression pact
August 25	Anglo-Polish alliance
September 1	Germany invades Poland
September 3	Britain and France declare war on Germany

INDEX

Abrial, French Admiral, 180
Adenauer, Konrad, 74, 79
Adler, Friedrich, 22
Adowa, Battle of, 156
Air pact: and Anglo-German
Naval Treaty, 147–148; pro-
posals for, 136, 138
Air power; British, 135–136;
German, 126, 133–134
Albert, Heinrich Friedrich, 45
Alexander I, Tsar, 27–28
Alexandrovsky, Serge J. S., 208,
212–213
Allen, of Hurtwood, Lord, 129
Amery, L. S., 158
Amritsar massacre, 36
Anglo-German Naval Treaty,
126, 226; discussions on, 134,
137–140, 186; effects of, 147–
149, 186; and France, 140,
142, 156–157; Hitler's denun-
ciation of, 238; motives for,
146–147; reactions to, 141–
146
Anschluss, 94, 232–233, 238;
conditions conducive to, 99;
German demand for, 97, 98;
Mussolini's opposition to, 184
Anti-Comintern Pact, 227
Anti-communism, 6, 25, 147.
See also Bolshevism.
Appeasement policy, 12, 152,
222, 244

Armaments: air, in Germany,
129–130; limitations on, 132–
134, 186; production of, in
Russia, 42, 46, 47. See also Disarmament; Rearmament, German.
Attlee, Clement, 130
Austria, 18, 156, 157, 165; annexation of, 232–233, 243;
bolshevism in, 21; and customs union with Germany,
94–116; economic problems
of, 20, 99, 100–101, 104–
107, and France, 103, 105;
and Germany, 94–116, 133,
154–155, 231; government of,
22, 23; and Hitler, 202; and
Hungary, 105–107; independence of, 95, 100; and Italy,
104–107, 126, 154–155;
Nazism in, 125, 226, 227,
232–234, 237; plebiscite in,
233. See also Anschluss.
Aviation, 133–136, 138, 147–
148
Avon, Lord. See Eden, Anthony.

Badoglio, General Pietro, 161
Baker, Ray Stannard, 21, 28, 35
Baldwin, Stanley, 9, 76, 127;
and Anglo-German Naval
Treaty, 141; and British air

267

Hans W. Gatzke was born in Dülken, Germany, studied in America at Williams College, and came to live in the United States in 1937, later receiving M.A. and Ph.D. degrees from Harvard University. His articles have appeared in various scholarly journals, including the *American Historical Review,* the *Journal of Modern History,* and the *Vierteljahrshefte für Zeitgeschichte.* His books include *Germany's Drive to the West* (which won the Herbert Baxter Adams prize of the American Historical Association), *Stresemann and the Rearmament of Germany,* and *The Present in Perspective,* and he has edited and translated Clausewitz's *Principles of War.* Mr. Gatzke, who is a member of the editorial board of *Current History* and U.S. editor-in-chief of *Akten zur deutschen auswärtigen Politik,* is Professor of History at Yale University.